Not For Tourists Guide to
CHICAGO

Not For Tourists, Inc

Skyhorse Publishing

Designed by:
Not For Tourists, Inc
NFTₜₘ**—Not For Tourists**ₜₘ **Guide to Chicago**
www.notfortourists.com

Printed in China
Print ISBN: 978-1-5107-7159-8
eBook ISBN: 978-1-5107-7160-4
ISSN 2162-724X
Copyright © 2022 by Not For Tourists, Inc.
21st Edition

Every effort has been made to ensure that the information in this book is as up-to-date as possible at press time. However, many details are liable to change—as we have learned. Not For Tourists cannot accept responsibility for any consequences arising from the use of this book.

Not For Tourists does not solicit individuals, organizations, or businesses for listings inclusion in our guides, nor do we accept payment for inclusion into the editorial portion of our book; the advertising sections, however, are exempt from this policy. We always welcome communications from anyone regarding ANYTHING having to do with our books; please visit us on our website at www.notfortourists.com for appropriate contact information.

www.skyhorsepublishing.com

10 9 8 7 6 5 4 3 2 1

Dear NFT User,

There are certain things Chicagoans know: the best stories happen on the Red Line late at night; your out-of-town relatives are going to ask you about Al Capone; there's a 50/50 chance your alderman is going to be indicted this year; the winters make you stronger and the summers make you lazier; and every New Yorker you know will tell you how shocked they are that there aren't cows and corn filling up your downtown ("Wow, this actually is an amazing city!").

But you don't need us to tell you that Chicago is much more than this. As possessive and proud Chicagoans are of their city, they're even more so of their neighborhoods, each one offering its own unique experience. Travelling from one to the next is like a different vacation onto itself, and that's where we come in. Consider us your insider to the best of your own city. You're the ultimate urban adventurer and we can't wait to be your companion on the journey.

But print publishing has its shortcomings—it can only reflect what was happening in the city at the time of publication, and things are always changing. That's where the website (www.notfortourists.com) and mobile apps come in. And while you can't scribble notes on a computer screen or iPhone app, we think they nicely complement what you now hold in front of you.

Thank you for picking up the *Not For Tourists Guide to Chicago*. As the only guidebook of the city written by fellow Chicagoans that includes detailed map-by-map descriptions of every neighborhood in Chicago (as well as Evanston, Oak Park, and Skokie), we hope to worm our way into your heart as your indispensable right-hand tool for navigating this dynamic and energetic city that we love.

Table of Contents

45 46 33 34
35 36 37
38 39 40
47 48 41 42 43
44
27 28 29 30
21 22 31 32
1 2 3
49 50 23 24
4 5 6
25 26 7 8 9
10 11
51 52 12 13 14
15 16 17
18 19 20
53 54
57
58
55 56 59 60

INDIANA
ILLINOIS

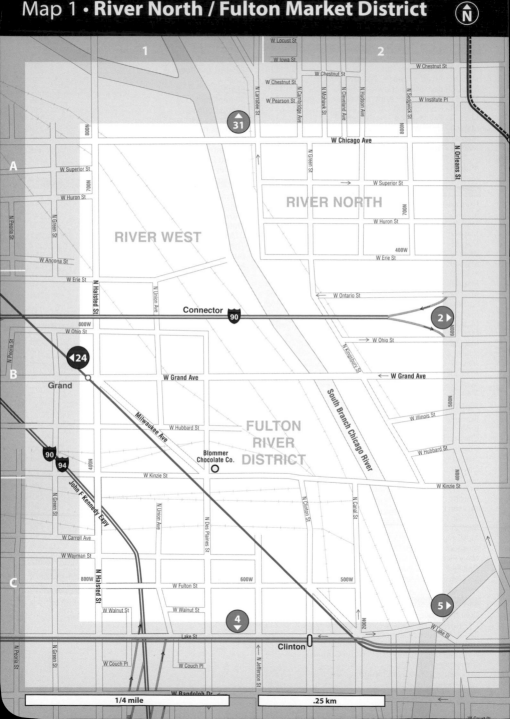

Map 1 • River North / Fulton Market District

Map 1

Crisscrossed by rail tracks, I-90/94 and the Chicago River, this section of the Windy City is quickly turning from industrial warehousing district to indie-hipster home.

Nightlife

- **Bub City** • 435 N Clark St
  312 610 4200
  Honky tonk for the River North scene.
- **Emmit's Irish Pub** • 495 N Milwaukee Ave
  312-563-9631
  An old-school Chicago establishment.
- **Richard's Bar** • 491 N Milwaukee Ave
  312-733-2251
  Old man bar good for starter drinks.

Restaurants

- **Carnivale** • 702 West Fulton Market St
  312-850-5005 • $$$
  Authentic, soulful Latin fusion cuisine.
- **Iguana Café** • 517 N Halsted St
  312-432-0663 • $
  Internet cafe with bagels and such.

- **La Scarola** • 721 W Grand Ave
  312-243-1740 • $$
  Authentic Italian in a super-close atmosphere.
- **Piccolo Sogno** • 464 N Halsted St
  312-421-0077 • $$$$
  You wish your mama in the old country cooked this good.
- **The Publican** • 837 W Fulton Market
  312-733-9555 • $$$
  Much buzzed Kahan joint is meat and beer lover's nirvana.
- **Ramen Takeya** • 819 W Fulton Market
  312-666-7710 • $$$
  First-class ramen plus small plates and cocktails.

Shopping

- **Doolin's** • 511 N Halsted St
  312-243-9424
  Party decorations galore, closed Sundays.

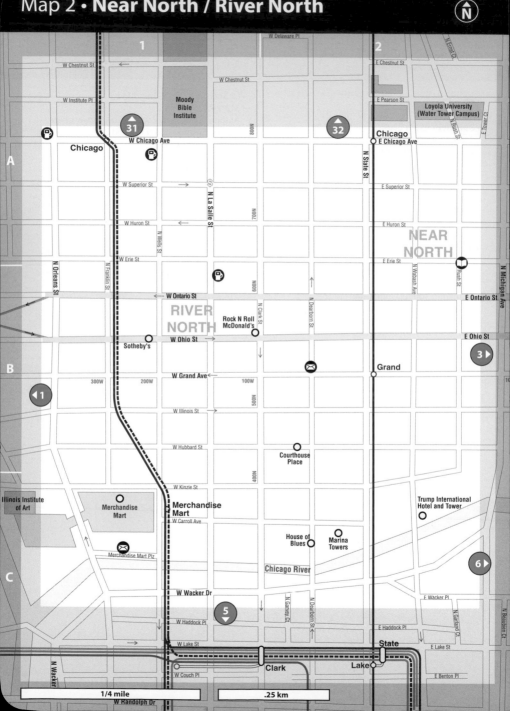

Map 2 • **Near North / River North**

Map 2

On the west side, monolithic **Merchandise Mart** (seriously—it has its own zip code) casts its shadow over River North, helping the area maintain its old industrial edge. On the east side, the **Trump International Hotel and Tower** rounds that edge into the pinnacle of luxury living.

○ Landmarks

- **Courthouse Place** • 54 W Hubbard St
  This Romanesque-style former courthouse has witnessed many legendary trials.
- **House of Blues** • 329 N Dearborn St
  312-923-2000
  Branch location of well-known chain o' blues clubs; music is far better than the crap-filled interior suggests…
- **Marina Towers** • 300 N State St
  Bertrand Goldberg's riverside masterwork. Love the parking.
- **Merchandise Mart** • 222 Merchandise Mart Plz
  800-677-6278
  Houses furniture showrooms and a small mall.
- **Sotheby's** • 980 N Michigan Ave
  312-475-7900
  Renowned auction house. We bid $5.
- **Trump International Hotel and Tower** •
  401 N Wabash Ave
  312-588-8000
  Shiny happy 92-story skyscraper.

Nightlife

- **Andy's Jazz Club** • 11 E Hubbard St
  312-642-6805
  Old-school jazz…a Chicago legend.
- **The Berkshire Room** • 15 E Ohio St
  312-256-2975
  Cocktail lounge at the hipster-swank Acme Hotel.
- **The Boss Bar** • 420 N Clark St
  312-527-1203
  Give tomorrow's hangover extra fuel at this 4 am dive.
- **Brehon Pub** • 731 N Wells St
  312-642-1071
  Irish pub, lots of TVs for Masterpiece Theater, er, sports.
- **Celeste** • 111 W Hubbard St
  312-828-9000
  Art deco-style cocktail bar.

- **Clark Street Ale House** • 742 N Clark St
312-642-9253
No pretense, just beer—and lots of it.
- **Gilt Bar** • 230 W Kinzie St
312-464-9544
Old-time cocktails meet the spirit of new-school alcohol artistry.
- **The Green Door Tavern** • 678 N Orleans St
312-664-5496
A Chicago landmark; old-school classic.
- **Havana Grill** • 412 N Clark St
312-644-1900
Cuban cocktail creations with a live Latin soundtrack.
- **Howl at the Moon** • 26 W Hubbard St
312-863-7427
Late-night dinner and pianists who encourage patrons to sing.
- **Pops for Champagne** • 601 N State St
312-266-7677
Jazz and champers.
- **The Redhead Piano Bar** • 16 W Ontario St
312-640-1000
Snug piano bar favorite of the area.
- **Rossi's Liquors** • 412 N State St
312-644-5775
A dive in the best sense of the word.

- **Snicker's** • 448 N State St
312-527-0437
Eastern European female bartenders imported for beauty at this dive.
- **Sound Bar** • 226 W Ontario St
312-787-4480
High-end bells and whistles dance club with tough door.
- **Spy Bar** • 646 N Franklin St
312-337-2191
Basement club, house music, fashionable crowd, pricey drinks.
- **Streeter's Tavern** • 50 E Chicago Ave
312-944-5206
Ritzy dive bar for students and tourists.
- **Three Dots and a Dash** • 435 N Clark St
312-610-4220
Downtown tiki bar.
- **Untitled** • 111 W Kinzie St
312-880-1511
Can't find this modern "speakeasy?" Just look for the CVS.
- **Watershed** • 601 N State St
312-266-7677
Drinking is easier without windows in this basement bar.

Whether you're hoping to enjoy craft beers with your dog (seriously, they're invited, too) at **Clark Street Ale House**. For can't-afford-to-miss Latin flavors that you probably can't afford, head to **Topolobampo** for gourmet Mexican cooking. Hint: go for lunch for less of a dent in your bank account.

Restaurants

- **Bavette's Bar and Boeuf** • 218 W Kinzie St
  312-624-8154 • $$$$
  Luscious steakhouse with a young creative bent.
- **Brett's Kitchen** • 233 W Superior St
  312-664-6354 • $
  Charming breakfast and sandwich stop.
- **Brindille** • 534 N Clark St
  312-595-1616 • $$$$$
  Luxe Parisian cuisine.
- **Chicago Chop House** • 60 W Ontario St
  312-787-7100 • $$$$$
  Old-school steaks meet old-school politicos and similar characters.
- **Chicago Cut** • 300 N Lasalle St
  312-329-1800 • $$$
  Dry aged cuts and panoramic river views.
- **Chick-fil-A** • 30 E Chicago Ave
  312-266-8888 • $
  Fast-food. 5-star service. For real.
- **Club Lago** • 331 W Superior St
  312-951-2849 • $$
  Generous servings of basic Italian.
- **Coco Pazzo** • 300 W Hubbard St
  312-836-0900 • $$$$$
  Hearty, high-end Italian.

- **Dough Bros. Pizzeria and Sub Shop** •
  400 N State St
  312-600-9078 • $$
  Italian subs and farm-to-table slices.
- **Eataly** • 43 E Ohio St
  312-521-8700 • $$
  High-end Italian foods at this new but already beloved emporium.
- **Firecakes Donuts** • 68 W Hubbard St
  312-329-6500 • $
  Old standbys (chocolate iced) and new favorites (lemon verbena meringue).
- **Frontera Grill** • 445 N Clark St
  312-661-1434 • $$
  Rick Bayless's famous cantina—expect to wait awhile.
- **Gene & Georgetti** • 500 N Franklin St
  312-527-3718 • $$$$$
  Big steaks.
- **Gilt Bar** • 230 W Kinzie St
  312-464-9544 • $$$
  Chandelier-lit dining room upstairs, speakeasy cellar lounge below.
- **GT Fish & Oyster** • 531 N Wells St
  312-929-3501 • $$$
  Proof that oysters are aphrodisiacs.
- **Havana Grill** • 412 N Clark St
  312-644-1900 • $$
  Soak up happy hour with a range of Southwestern flavors.
- **Iberico Express** • 737 N La Salle St
  312-573-1510 • $
  Shoulder-to-shoulder tapas joint.

- **The Kerryman** • 661 N Clark St
  312-335-8121 • $$
  Standard Irish pub, plus the bonus of an outdoor patio.
- **Kinzie Chophouse** • 400 N Wells St
  312-822-0191 • $$$
  Neighborhood steak house.
- **Lou Malnati's Pizzeria** • 439 N Wells St
  312-828-9800 • $
  Famous in a city famous for pizza.
- **Maggiano's Little Italy** • 516 N Clark St
  312-644-7700 • $$
  Gut-busting family-style Italian.
- **Meli Cafe & Juice Bar** • 540 N Wells St
  312-527-1850 • $$
  Fresh, inviting; favors healthy selections and early risers.
- **Mr. Beef** • 666 N Orleans St
  312-337-8500 • $
  Get your Italian beef fix at this tried-and-true Chicago classic.
- **Osteria Via Stato** • 620 N State St
  312-642-8450 • $$$$
  Menu-oriented Italian. Fancy, but reasonably priced.

- **Pizzeria Uno** • 29 E Ohio St
  312-321-1000 • $
  Legendary Chicago pizza.
- **Portillo's** • 100 W Ontario St
  312-587-8910 • $
  Classic Chicago-style dogs.
- **Quartino** • 626 N State St
  312-698-5000 • $$$
  Trendy Italian small plates and house-cured salami.
- **RL Restaurant** • 115 E Chicago Ave
  312-475-1100 • $$$$$
  Somehow they even got the Polo logo on the sole.
- **Rosebud on Rush** • 720 N Rush St
  312-266-6444 • $$
  A branch of Chicago's legendary, old-school Italian.
- **Ruth's Chris Steak House** • 431 N Dearborn St
  312-321-2725 • $$$$
  Consistent steak chain.
- **Shanghai Terrace** • 108 E Superior St
  312-573-6744 • $$$$
  The city's most extravagant Chinese restaurant.
- **Shaw's Crab House** • 21 E Hubbard St
  312-527-2722 • $$$$
  A seafood destination.
- **Siena Tavern** • 51 W Kinzie St
  312-595-1322 • $$$
  Housemade pastas made by "Top Chef" celeb Fabio Viviani.
- **Silver Spoon** • 710 N Rush St
  312-944-7100 • $$
  Solid Thai option; longtime local fave.
- **Smith & Wollensky** • 318 N State St
  312-670-9900 • $$$$
  Chicago branch of New York steak emporium.

Near North / River North

21	22	31	32
23	24	1	2	3
		4	5	6
25	26	7	8	9
		10	11

Map 2

Chicago is a pizza city and **Pizzeria Uno** and **Lou Malnati's** both serve deep dishes of it. For beef, try **Gene & Georgetti** or sleek chophouse **Chicago Cut**. Mammoth international emporium **Eataly** is sort of like what might happen if Dr. Frankenstein implanted the brain of a Trader Joe's with one of Mario Batali's shopping lists; it not only redefines "store-bought" but also offers the full gamut of dining—everything from a quick panini to a high-end five-course meal.

- **Soupbox** • 2943 N Broadway
  773-935-9800 • $
  12 fresh soups every day!
- **Sunda** • 110 W Illinois St
  312-644-0500 • $$$$
  Pretentious "New Asian" for folks with more attitude than taste.
- **Tanta** • 118 W Grand Ave
  312-222-9700 • $$$$
  Gaston Acurio's revelatory Peruvian cuisine.
- **Topolobampo** • 445 N Clark St
  312-661-1434 • $$$$
  Standard bearer for upscale Mexican.
- **Vermilion** • 10 W Hubbard St
  312-527-4060 • $$$
  Indian-Latin fusion—what next?
- **Wildfire** • 159 W Erie St
  312-787-9000 • $$
  Fun, trendy American.
- **XOCO** • 449 N Clark St
  312-723-2131 • $$
  Mexican food guru Rick Bayless's most affordable cantina.

🛍 Shopping

- **Doughnut Vault** • 401 N Franklin St
  312-285-2830
  Designer, oversized donuts worth the inevitable wait.
- **Firecakes Donuts** • 68 W Hubbard St
  312-329-6500
  Old standbys (chocolate iced) and new favorites (lemon verbena meringue).
- **Jonathan Adler** • 676 N Wabash Ave
  312-274-9920
  Hip and happy home furnishings.
- **Lightology** • 215 W Chicago Ave
  866-954-4489
  Lights, camera, chandeliers!
- **Orange Skin** • 419 W Superior St
  312-335-1033
  Contemporary Italian furniture.
- **P.O.S.H.** • 613 N State St
  312-280-1602
  An Aladdin's cave featuring old hotel silverware and other finds.
- **Paper Source** • 232 W Chicago Ave
  312-337-0798
  Great paper and invitations.

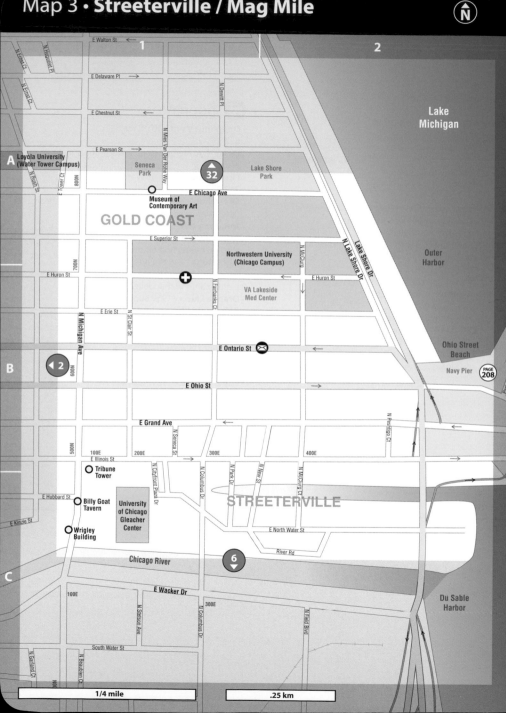

Map 3 · **Streeterville / Mag Mile**

PAGE 208

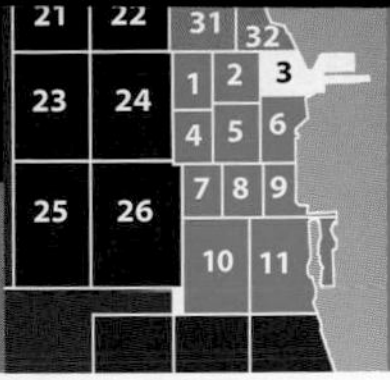

Map 3

As out-of-towners aiming to spend cash crash into each other, locals spend their time in lavish high-rises. Whether you're looking to rent a bike, take a Segway tour or see Lake Michigan via old-fashioned foot, the lakefront trail offers an escape from the epicenter of retail therapy.

o Landmarks

- **Billy Goat Tavern** • 430 N Michigan Ave
312-222-1525
Cheezborger! Cheezborger!
- **Museum of Contemporary Art** • 220 E Chicago Ave
312-280-2660
Party down on First Fridays.
- **Navy Pier** • 600 E Grand Ave
312-595-7437
Municipal wharf turned boffo tourist attraction.
- **Tribune Tower** • 435 N Michigan Ave
312-222-3994
Check out the stones from famous buildings around the world including a real-life rock from the moon!
- **Wrigley Building** • 401 N Michigan Ave
312-229-8941
Monument to chewing gum.

Nightlife

- **Timothy O'Toole's Pub** • 622 N Fairbanks Ct
312-642-0700
Irish sports bar with tons of TV space.

Restaurants

- **Bandera** • 535 N Michigan Ave
312-644-3524 • $$
Lunch above Mag Mile.
- **Billy Goat Tavern** • 430 N Michigan Ave
312-222-1525 • $
Cheezboiga; no fries, chips; pepsi, no coke.
- **The Capital Grille** • 633 N St Clair St
312-337-9400 • $$$$
Macho steak and zin.
- **D4 Irish Pub & Cafe** • 345 E Ohio St
312-624-8385 • $$$
Upscale Irish pub with a copy of the Book of Kells.
- **Gino's East** • 162 E Superior St
312-266-3337 • $$
Legendary deep dish pizza since 1966.
- **Grand Lux Cafe** • 600 N Michigan Ave
312-276-2500 • $$$
A Mag Mile vittle and view indulgence. Go ahead, be a tourist!
- **Indian Garden** • 247 E Ontario St
312-280-4910 • $$
Good veggie options.

- **Les Nomades** • 222 E Ontario St
312-649-9010 • $$$$$
Deluxe haute cuisine.
- **NoMI Kitchen** • 800 N Michigan Ave
312-239-4030 • $$$$$
Deluxe French fusion.
- **Sayat Nova** • 157 E Ohio St
312-644-9159 • $$
Armenian fare in a romantic setting.
- **Volare** • 201 E Grand Ave
312-410-9900 • $$$
Killer bolognese sauce; lick the plate clean.

Shopping

- **Apple Store** • 401 N Michigan Ave
312-529-9500
All of their newest, shiniest offerings plus classes and seminars.
- **Barbara's** • 201 E Huron St
312-926-2665
Branch of local book chain at Northwestern Memorial Hospital.
- **Bike and Roll Chicago–Navy Pier** • 700 E Grand Ave
312-729-1000
Bike Chicago: ride the amazing Lakefront Trail.
- **Bike and Roll Chicago–Ohio St Beach** •
400 N Lake Shore Dr
312-245-9300
Bike rentals and tours.
- **Garrett Popcorn** • 625 N Michigan Ave
884-476-7267
Chicago popcorn legend. Cheese caramel blend not-to-be-missed.
- **Neiman Marcus** • 737 N Michigan Ave
312-642-5900
Affectionately known as "Needless Mark-up" by those who can afford it anyway.
- **Niketown** • 669 N Michigan Ave
312-642-6363
Nike label sports clothing.
- **Ralph Lauren** • 750 N Michigan Ave
312-280-1655
If you love those little polo horses…
- **Tiffany & Co.** • 730 N Michigan Ave
312-944-7500
Lacks appropriate breakfast options.

Map 4 • **West Loop Gate / Greek Town**

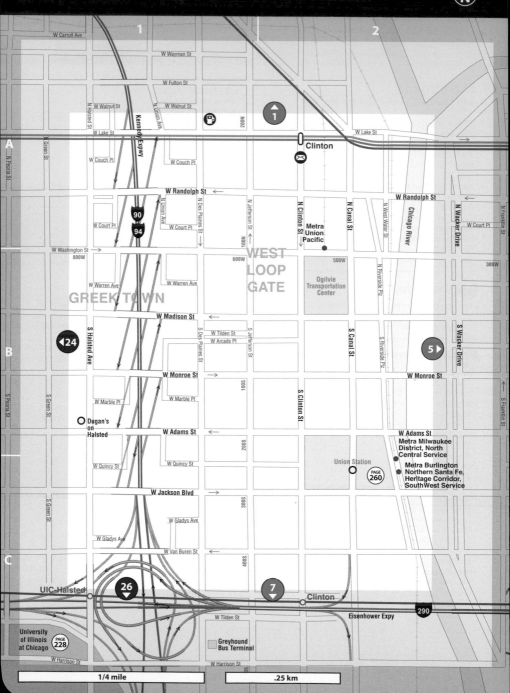

Map 4 • West Loop Gate / Greek Town

1   2

W Carroll Ave
W Wayman St
W Fulton St
W Walnut St   W Walnut St
W Lake St   Clinton   W Lake St
W Couch Pl   W Couch Pl
W Randolph St   W Randolph St
W Court Pl   Metra Union Pacific   W Court Pl
W Washington St 800W
WEST LOOP GATE
W Warren Ave   W Warren Ave
GREEK TOWN   Ogilvie Transportation Center
W Madison St
24   W Tilden St W Arcade Pl
W Monroe St   W Monroe St
W Marble Pl   W Marble Pl   5
Dugan's on Halsted
W Adams St   W Adams St
Metra Milwaukee District, North Central Service
W Quincy St   W Quincy St   Union Station   PAGE 260   Metra Burlington Northern Santa Fe, Heritage Corridor, SouthWest Service
W Jackson Blvd
W Gladys Ave
W Gladys Ave   W Van Buren St
26   7   Clinton
UIC-Halsted   Eisenhower Expy   290
University of Illinois at Chicago   PAGE 228   Greyhound Bus Terminal
W Harrison St   W Harrison St

1/4 mile   .25 km

21	22	31	32
23	24	1	2	3
		4	5	6
25	26	7	8	9
		10	11

Map 4

Trains, buses and gyros define this 'hood. From suburban 9 to 5-ers arriving on the Metra at **Union Station** to Megabus passengers traveling on a mega-budget, this is commuter central. While plenty of lofts have risen to jump start residential growth, there are an equal number of gritty pockets here, too. Not surprising when you consider that some passengers buy their bus tickets for $1, is it?

○ Landmarks

- **Dugan's on Halsted** • 128 S Halsted St
  312-421-7191
  Sports bar in Greektown. Fantastic beer garden and favorite cop hangout.
- **Union Station** • 225 S Canal St
  312-322-4269
  Built in 1925, the architecture is not to be missed!

🍸 Nightlife

- **Dugan's on Halsted** • 128 S Halsted St
  312-421-7191
  Lively Irish pub. Free popcorn to help soak up the booze.
- **Haymarket Pub and Brewery** •
  737 W Randolph St
  312-638-0700
  Lesser-known member of Chicago's beer scene with late-night eats.
- **Lone Wolf** • 806 W Randolph St
  312-600-9391
  Thematic drink suggestions match your dinner reservations down the street.
- **Spectrum Bar & Grill** • 233 S Halsted St
  312-715-0770
  Sports bar with Mediterranean flair.

Map 4

West Loop Gate / Greek Town

🍴 Restaurants

- **Athena** • 212 S Halsted St
  312-655-0000 • $$$
  Goddess Athena-inspired outdoor and indoor.
- **Au Cheval** • 800 W Randolph St
  312-929-4580 • $$
  5-star flavor pairings in a more affordable diner vibe.
- **Avec** • 615 W Randolph St
  312-377-2002 • $$
  Small plates, big flavors, chefs' hangout. 'Nuff said.
- **Chicken & Farm Shop** • 113 N Green St
  312-521-8000 • $$$
  UK poultry professionals on restaurant row.
- **Greek Islands** • 200 S Halsted St
  312-782-9855 • $$$
  Noisy, fun, crowd-pleasing spectacle.
- **Green Street Smoked Meats** • 112 N Green St
  312-754-0431 • $$$
  Smoked meat, curated cocktails, and crafted beer.

- **Jubilee Juice** • 140 N Halsted St
  312-491-8500 • $$
  A Better Smoothie.
- **Little Goat** • 820 W Randolph St
  312-888-3455 • $$
  Comfy little sib to famed Girl and the Goat.
- **Lou Mitchell's** • 565 W Jackson Blvd
  312-939-3111 • $
  Rub shoulders with local pols at this legendary grill.
- **Meli Cafe & Juice Bar** • 301 S Halsted St
  312-454-0748 • $
  Brunch spot makes us wanna challah.
- **Momotaro** • 820 W Lake St
  312-733-4818 • $$$$
  Stylish, comprehensive Japanese.
- **Mr. Greek Gyros** • 234 S Halsted St
  312-906-8731 • $
  The best late night gyro spot in the city, hands down.
- **Nando's** • 953 W Randolph St
  312-488-3062 • $$
  South African chicken specialists.
- **Nine Muses** • 315 S Halsted St
  312-902-9922 • $$$
  Brick bars and backgammon.

West Loop Gate / Greek Town

Map 4

This marks the beginning of foodie central in Chicago. Randolph Street includes some of the best upscale eats, from Girl and the Goat-related **Little Goat** to the date-friendly **Avec**. On a budget? Head to **Mr. Greek Gyros**. Wash it all down with a craft beer at **Haymarket Brewing**.

- **Robinson's No. 1 Ribs** • 225 S Canal St
  312-579-0423 • $
  Dress down and dig in.
- **Sepia** • 123 N Jefferson St
  312-441-1920 • $$$$
  Contemp. American with flare.
- **Takumi** • 555 W Madison St
  312-669-1999 • $$
  Tiny sushi spot with excellent lunch specials.

🛍 Shopping

- **Athenian Candle Co.** • 300 S Halsted St
  312-332-6988
  Candles, curse-breakers, Greek trinkets, and much more.
- **Northwestern Cutlery** • 7138 W Higgins Ave
  312-421-3666
  The self-described "candy store for cooks."

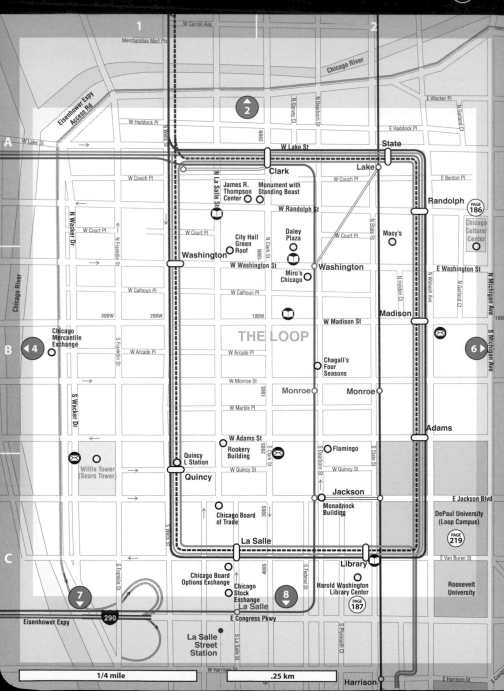

Map 5 • The Loop

N

W Carroll Ave
Merchandise Mart Plz

Chicago River

1
2

Eisenhower Expy Access Rd

W Haddock Pl
E Haddock Pl

2

A W Lake St
W Lake St
State
E Wacker Pl

N Garland Ct

Clark
Lake

W Couch Pl
N La Salle St
James R. Thompson Center
Monument with Standing Beast
W Couch Pl
E Benton Pl

Randolph
PAGE 186

N Wacker Dr
W Court Pl
N Franklin St
W Court Pl
W Randolph St
N State St
W Court Pl

Chicago Cultural Center

City Hall Green Roof
Daley Plaza
Macy's

Washington
N Clark St
N Dearborn St
Washington
E Washington St

Chicago River
W Calhoun Pl
W Washington St
N Holden Ct
N Wabash Ave
N Garland Ct
N Michigan Ave

Miro's Chicago

W Calhoun Pl
Madison
100E

300W
200W
100W

THE LOOP
W Madison St

B 4
Chicago Mercantile Exchange
S Franklin St
W Arcade Pl
W Arcade Pl
Chagall's Four Seasons
6

S Michigan Ave

W Monroe St
S Wacker Dr
Monroe
Monroe

W Marble Pl

W Adams St
Adams

Willis Tower (Sears Tower)
Quincy L Station
Rookery Building
S Clark St
Flamingo
S State St

Quincy
W Quincy St
W Quincy St

Chicago Board of Trade
Monadnock Building
Jackson
E Jackson Blvd

S Wells St
La Salle
S Dearborn St
S Federal St
DePaul University (Loop Campus)
PAGE 219

C
Library
E Van Buren St

S Franklin St
Chicago Board Options Exchange
Chicago Stock Exchange
Harold Washington Library Center
Roosevelt University

7
8
La Salle
PAGE 187

Eisenhower Expy
290
E Congress Pkwy
S Plymouth Ct

La Salle Street Station
S La Salle St

1/4 mile
.25 km
W Harrison St
Harrison
E Harrison St

Map 5

The Loop derives its moniker from the L tracks that lasso the city's heart. This here is the bustling financial and business district, where banks are plentiful and parking is pricey. The intersection of State and Madison is literally ground zero (0 east, 0 west, 0 north, 0 south) for Chicago's easy-to-follow street numbering grid. Watching over it all is the Sears Tower—no wait, the **Willis Tower**, but don't ever call it that in public.

○ Landmarks

- **Chagall's Four Seasons** • 10 S Dearborn St
Mosaic by Marc Chagall—you know, the one who did all those flying people.
- **Chicago Board of Trade** • 141 W Jackson Blvd
312-435-7180
The goddess Ceres tops this deco monolith.
- **Chicago Board Options Exchange** •
400 S LaSalle St
312-786-5600
The world's largest options market.
- **Chicago Cultural Center** • 78 E Washington St
312-744-6630
The spot for free lectures, exhibits, concerts, and movies.
- **Chicago Mercantile Exchange** • 20 S Wacker Dr
312-930-1000
Economics at work in polyester jackets.
- **Chicago Stock Exchange** • 440 S La Salle St
312-663-2222
The second-largest stock exchange in the country.
- **City Hall Green Roof** • 121 N La Salle St
First green roof on a municipal building. Cool.
- **Daley Plaza** • 50 W Washington St
Home of a Picasso sculpture, a Christmas tree ceremony, and many alfresco lunches.
- **Flamingo** • 230 S Dearborn St
Alexander Calder's fabulous red flamingo.

- **Harold Washington Library Center** •
400 S State St
312-747-4300
The world's largest public library building; nearly 100 works of art on every floor.
- **James R. Thompson Center** • 100 W Randolph St
312-814-6676
Lots of glass combined with the colors red, silver, and blue. Ghastly!
- **Macy's** • 111 N State St
312-781-1000
Folks are still mourning the passing of Marshall Fields. Luckily the clock and Tiffany dome remain.
- **Miro's Chicago** • 77 W Washington St
Part of the Loop's outdoor public artwork program.
- **Monadnock Building** • 53 W Jackson Blvd
312-922-1890
Claim to fame: world's largest office building when completed in 1893.
- **Monument with Standing Beast** •
100 W Randolph St
Jean DuBuffet sculpture. Looks like melted snow.
- **Quincy L Station** • 220 S Wells St
Restored to its original glory.
- **The Rookery** • 209 S La Salle St
312-553-6100
Take a peek inside at Frank Lloyd Wright's spectacular remodelled interior.
- **Willis Tower (Sears Tower)** • 233 S Wacker Dr
312-875-0066
Until recently the tallest building in the US, with a cool skydeck.

Map 5

21	22	31	32	
23	24	1 2 3		
		4 5 6		
25	26	7 8 9		
		10 11		

The Loop

♈ Nightlife

- **Brando's Speakeasy** • 343 S Dearborn St
773-216-3213
Karaoke to "Free Bird" drunk on fancy martinis or cheap beer.
- **Ceres Cafe** • 141 W Jackson Blvd
312-427-3443
The epitome of a stiff drink.
- **Exchequer** • 226 S Wabash Ave
312-939-5633
Loop location for the working class.
- **Miller's Pub** • 134 S Wabash Ave
312-263-4988
A Loop tradition.
- **Monk's Pub** • 205 W Lake St
312-357-6665
Wall of books. And beer.
- **Petterino's** • 150 N Dearborn St
312-422-0150
Go to church on Sunday, then cabaret here on Monday.
- **Potter's Lounge** • 17 E Monroe St
312-917-4933
Posh cocktails in the Palmer House Hilton.
- **Roof on The Wit** • 201 N State St
312-239-9502
A rooftop playground for those who want to be seen.
- **South Branch Tavern & Grille** • 100 S Wacker Dr
312-546-6177
Sip martinis on the patio.
- **Stocks and Blondes** • 40 N Wells St
312-372-3725
Happy hour dive stocked with blond (and brunette) waitresses.

🍴 Restaurants

- **Atwood Café** • 1 W Washington St
312-368-1900 • $$$
High tea with contemporary flair.
- **Hannah's Bretzel** • 180 W Washington St
312-621-1111 • $
Homemade pretzels and organic lunch fare.
- **Heaven on Seven** • 111 N Wabash Ave
312-263-6443 • $$
Cajun Chicago classic. Closed for dinner.
- **La Cantina Enoteca** • 71 W Monroe St
312-332-7005 • $$
Casual Italian with seafood specialty.
- **La Cocina** • 45 N Wells St
312-346-1638 • $
Cinco de Mayo. All year long.
- **Oasis Café** • 21 N Wabash Ave
312-443-9534 • $$
Middle Eastern hideout inside of a jewelry store.

The post-work crowd hangs here just long enough to forget that they have to return to the office the next morning. From stomping on a floor covered in peanut shells at **Monk's Pub** to sipping martinis at **South Branch**, drinking environments range from dive to high-dollar. If you're here past happy hour, head to "Broadway in Chicago" for proof that, yes, you are cultured. Make your mom proud and your wallet happy with a free history lesson at the **Chicago Cultural Center**.

• **Plymouth Restaurant** • 327 S Plymouth Ct
312-362-1212 • $
24-hour diner with bar and grill.
• **Protein Bar** • 235 S Franklin St
312-346-7300 • $
On-the-go meals for eaters avoiding grease.
• **Russian Tea Time** • 77 E Adams St
312-360-0000 • $$$
Rich food. Richer interior. Copious amounts of vodka.
• **The Village** • 71 W Monroe St
312-332-7005 • $$
Quaint, casual Italian looks; like a village.
• **Vivere** • 71 W Monroe St
312-332-4040 • $$$
Dated Italian luxury.

🛍 Shopping

• **After School Matters Retail Store** • 66 E Randolph St
312-742-4182
Specialty gifts & art made by local teens.

• **Barbara's** • 111 N State St
312-781-3033
Branch of local book chain in Macy's.
• **Blick Art Materials** • 42 S State St
312-920-0300
Get creative here.
• **Block 37** • 108 N State St
312-261-4700
All the mall's greatest hits right here in the Loop.
• **Central Camera Company** • 230 S Wabash Ave
312-427-5580
Family-owned camera shop.
• **Florodora** • 330 S Dearborn St
312-212-8860
Vintage-inspired, wildly-priced.
• **Macy's** • 111 N State St
312-781-1000
The former home of Chicago establishment Marshall Field's.
• **Reckless Records** • 26 E Madison St
312-795-0878
Instant satisfaction for the vinyl-hungry masses.

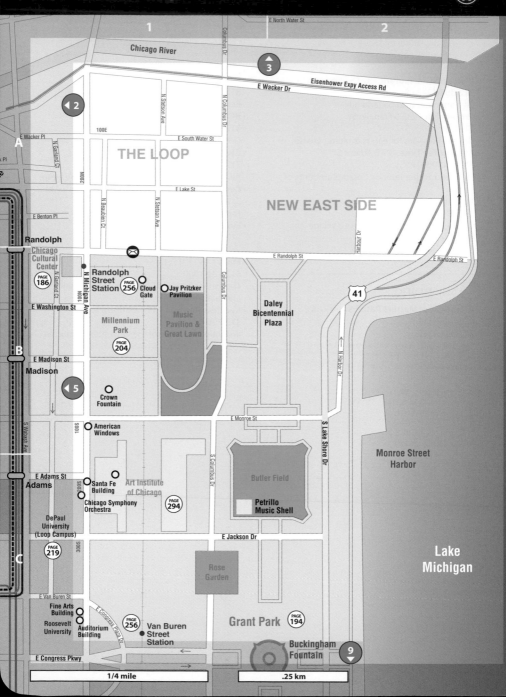

Map 6 • **The Loop / Grant Park**

N

1

2

E North Water St

Chicago River

3

E Wacker Dr

Eisenhower Expy Access Rd

2

E Wacker Pl

100E

E South Water St

THE LOOP

200N

E Lake St

NEW EAST SIDE

Harbor Dr

E Benton Pl

Randolph

Chicago Cultural Center

PAGE 186

E Randolph St

E Randolph St

41

Randolph Street Station

PAGE 256

Cloud Gate

Jay Pritzker Pavilion

Daley Bicentennial Plaza

E Washington St

Millennium Park

Music Pavilion & Great Lawn

Columbus Dr

PAGE 204

E Madison St

Madison

5

Crown Fountain

E Monroe St

N Harbor Dr

American Windows

S Columbus Dr

Monroe Street Harbor

E Adams St

Adams

Santa Fe Building

Art Institute of Chicago

Butler Field

S Lake Shore Dr

Chicago Symphony Orchestra

PAGE 294

Petrillo Music Shell

DePaul University (Loop Campus)

PAGE 219

300S

E Jackson Dr

Lake Michigan

Rose Garden

E Van Buren St

Fine Arts Building

Roosevelt University

Auditorium Building

PAGE 256

Van Buren Street Station

Grant Park

PAGE 194

Buckingham Fountain

9

E Congress Pkwy

1/4 mile

.25 km

N Stetson Ave

N Columbus Dr

Columbus Dr

N Garland Ct

N Beaubien Ct

N Michigan Ave

N Stetson Ave

S Wabash Ave

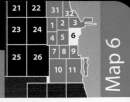

Map 6

A giant silver bean and 50-foot-tall animated faces…yes, really! **Millennium Park** is definitely the Chicago show-stopper, with its unique blend of artwork and landscaping. Farther down Michigan Avenue, the more traditional **Grant Park** brings highbrow and lowbrow culture side by side. Tasteful music or Taste of Chicago, there's something for everyone.

○ Landmarks

- **America Windows** • 111 S Michigan Ave
  312-443-3600
  Spectacular stained glass by Marc Chagall.
- **Art Institute of Chicago** • 111 S Michigan Ave
  312-443-3600
  World-class art museum.
- **Auditorium Building** • 430 S Michigan Ave
  Designed by Louis Sullivan; on National Register of Historic Places.
- **Chicago Symphony Orchestra** • 220 S Michigan Ave
  312-294-3000
  Classical music headquarters.
- **Cloud Gate** • 201 E Randolph St
  312-742-5000
  Much-photographed sculpture, affectionately known as "the bean."
- **Crown Fountain** • 201 E Randolph St
  Captivating modern take on traditional fountain, swarming with kids.
- **Fine Arts Building** • 410 S Michigan Ave
  312-566-9800
  The country's first artists' colony, converted from a Studebaker carriage plant in 1898.
- **Grant Park** • 337 E Randolph St
  312-742-3918
  Where Marathon, Music, and Taste all begin and end.
- **Jay Pritzker Pavilion** • 201 E Randolph St
  Frank Gehry signature steel structure, offering free outdoor concerts.
- **Millennium Park** • 201 E Randolph St
  312-742-1168
  One of the best public spaces on the planet.
- **One Prudential Plaza** • 130 E Randolph St
  Classic '50s skyscraper.
- **Santa Fe Building** • 224 S Michigan Ave
  312-427-5772
  Home to the world-renowned Chicago Architecture Foundation.

🍴 Restaurants

- **American Craft Kitchen & Bar** •
  151 E Upper Wacker Dr
  312-565-1234 • $$
  Lunch with your wi-fi.
- **Eggy's Diner** • 333 E Benton Pl
  773-234-3449 • $
  Varied menu at this airy diner.
- **The Gage** • 24 S Michigan Ave
  312-372-4243 • $$
  Classy brews, burgers, and meat.

🛍 Shopping

- **Bike and Roll Chicago-Millennium Park** •
  34 South Michigan Ave
  312-729-1000
  Rentals.
- **Chicago Architecture Foundation** •
  224 S Michigan Ave
  312-922-3432
  Great architecture book selection.
- **Mariano's** • 333 E Benton Pl
  312-228-1349
  Full-service gourmet grocery, butcher, and deli.
- **Museum Shop of the Art Institute** •
  111 S Michigan Ave
  312-443-3600
  Art Institute gift shop.
- **Precious Possessions** • 28 N Michigan Ave
  312-726-8118
  Mineral shop.

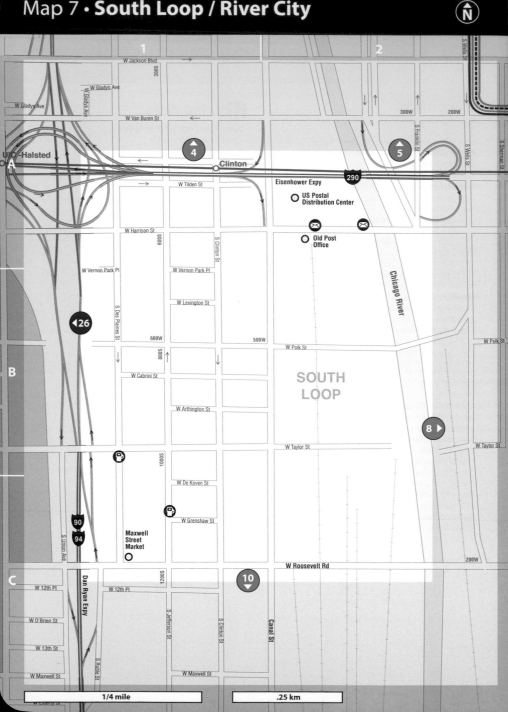

Map 7 · **South Loop / River City**

N

1   2

W Jackson Blvd

W Gladys Ave

W Gladys Ave

W Gladys Ave

300W   200W

W Van Buren St

S Franklin St

S Wells St

S Sherman St

4

5

UIC-Halsted
A

Clinton

Eisenhower Expy   290

W Tilden St

US Postal
Distribution Center

Old Post
Office

W Harrison St

S Clinton St

Chicago River

W Vernon Park Pl

W Vernon Park Pl

W Lexington St

◄26

S Des Plaines St

600W   500W

W Polk St   W Polk St

B

W Cabrini St

SOUTH
LOOP

W Arthington St

W Taylor St   W Taylor St

8 ►

W De Koven St

90
94

S Union Ave

W Grenshaw St

200W

Maxwell
Street
Market

W Roosevelt Rd

C

W 12th Pl

Dan Ryan Expy

W 12th Pl

1200S

10

W O'Brien St

S Jefferson St

S Clinton St

Canal St

W 13th St

W Maxwell St

S Ruble St

W Maxwell St

| 1/4 mile | .25 km |

		21	22	31	32
		23	24	1	2	3
				4	5	6
		25	26	7	8	9
				10	11

Map 7

This longtime industrial deadzone is emerging as a bustling business district—including a swanky new **Whole Foods**—to serve the rampant residential growth in all of the adjacent 'hoods. River City residents have never had it so good. Seriously, they haven't.

○ Landmarks
- **Maxwell Street Market** •
  W Roosevelt Rd & S Des Plaines St
  Outdoor bazaar where you can shop for dish soap or bicycle parts while grazing at authentic taco stands.
- **Old Post Office** • 404 S Canal St
  This massive, vacant edifice straddling I-90/94 and I-290 is a benchmark for traffic reports.
- **US Postal Distribution Center** • 433 W Harrison St
  800-275-8777
  The city's main mail routing center, employing over 6,000 people and operating 24 hours a day.

🍴 Restaurants
- **Manny's** • 1141 S Jefferson St
  312-939-2855 • $
  Famous deli popular with politicians.
- **White Palace Grill** • 1159 S Canal St
  312-939-7167 • $
  An ode to grease, and some fine omelettes to boot.

🛍 Shopping
- **Fishman's Fabrics** • 1101 S Des Plaines St
  312-922-7250
  Huge fabric wholesaler.
- **Lee's Foreign Car Service** • 727 S Jefferson St
  312-633-0823
  Import parts and service.
- **Maxwell Street Market** •
  W Roosevelt Rd & S Des Plaines St
  Hagglers welcome.
- **Morris & Sons** • 557 W Polk St
  312-243-5635
  Mostly men, off-price Italian designers.
- **Whole Foods Market** • 1101 S Canal St
  312-435-4600
  Perhaps not quite Bertrand Goldberg's vision, but works for us.

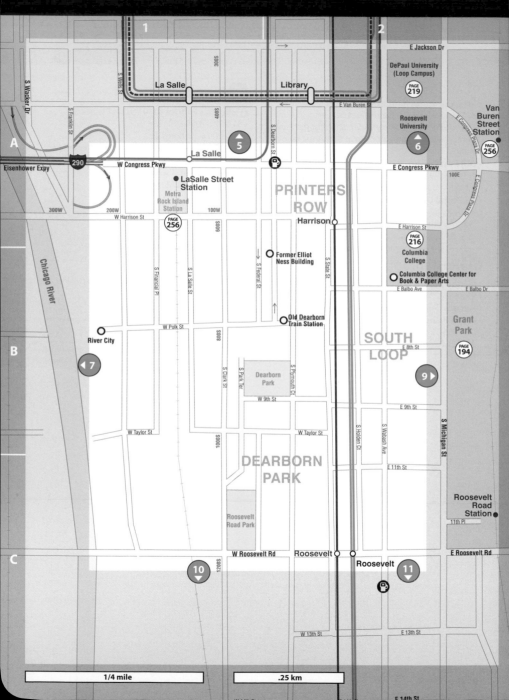

Map 8 · **South Loop / Printers Row / Dearborn Park**

Map 8

With all the student-friendly dining near the Columbia College campus, the upscale **Mercat a la Planxa** is a welcome addition, offering elegant tapas and lovely wines. Meanwhile, **Epic Burger** offers trendy organic burgers for about double the price of Micky D's but exactly none of whatever else goes into a Big Mac. As to be expected in a 'hood with such a dense student population, undergrads, grads, and profs alike frequent local watering holes **George's**, **Kasey's**, and the **South Loop Club**.

○ Landmarks

- **Former Elliot Ness Building** • 600 S Dearborn St
  If he sends one of yours to the hospital, you send one of his to the morgue…
- **Old Dearborn Train Station** • 47 W Polk St
  312-554-8100
  Turn-of-the-century train station with a lighted clocktower visible for several blocks. Al Capone took a train to prison from here.
- **River City** • 800 S Wells St
  A fluid cement design experiment built by architect Bertrand Goldberg in the '80s; considered a flop, but actually brilliant.

🍴 Nightlife

- **Buddy Guy's Legends** • 700 S Wabash Ave
  312-427-1190
  One of the oldest blues clubs in Chicago, and the hardest to get a drink in.
- **Jazz Showcase** • 806 S Plymouth Ct
  312-360-0234
  Intimate jazz venue since 1947.
- **Kasey's Tavern** • 701 S Dearborn St
  312-427-7992
  108-year-old neighborhood oasis.
- **South Loop Club** • 701 S State St
  312-427-2787
  There's something creepy about this place.
- **Tantrum** • 1023 S State St
  312-939-9160
  Tucked-away, nicely appointed bar that attracts a lively South Loop following.

🍽 Restaurants

- **Amarit** • 600 S Dearborn St
  312-939-1179 • $$
  Pretty good Thai.
- **Devil Dawgs** • 767 S State St
  312-583-9100 • $
  Chicago-style hot dogs with requisite crazy toppings.
- **Eleven City Diner** • 1112 S Wabash Ave
  312-212-1112 • $$
  Traditional Jewish deli.
- **Epic Burger** • 517 S State St
  312-913-1373 • $$
  Organic fast food burger joint featuring grass-fed beef. Eye roll.
- **Mercat a La Planxa** • 638 S Michigan Ave
  312-765-0524 • $$$
  Precious Catalan tapas or a whole suckling pig (with 48-hour notice).
- **South Loop Club** • 701 S State St
  312-427-2787 • $
  Very casual bar/restaurant with surprisingly good kitchen.

🛍 Shopping

- **Sandmeyer's Bookstore** • 714 S Dearborn St
  312-922-2104
  Dream come true if you love books and atmosphere.
- **Yarnify!** • 633 S Plymouth Ct
  312-583-9276
  For all your knitting needs. Classes, too.

Map 9 · **South Loop / South Michigan Ave.**

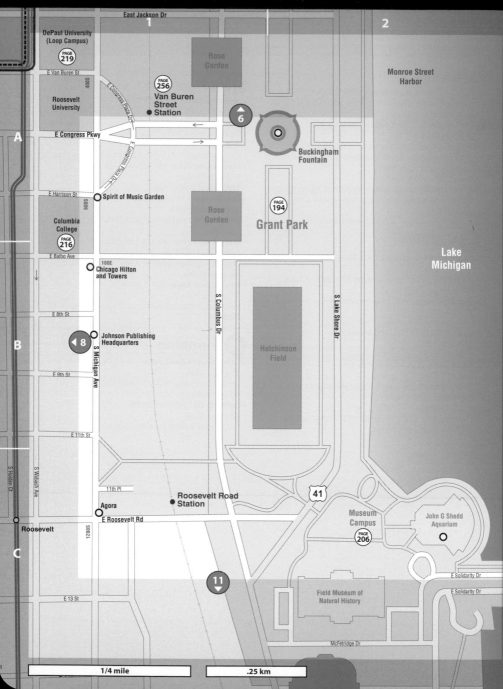

East Jackson Dr

Rose Garden

DePaul University
(Loop Campus)
PAGE 219

E Van Buren St

PAGE 256
Van Buren
Street
Station

Monroe Street
Harbor

6

Roosevelt
University

A

E Congress Pkwy

Buckingham
Fountain

E Harrison St   ○ Spirit of Music Garden

Rose
Garden

PAGE 194

Columbia
College
PAGE 216

Grant Park

Lake
Michigan

E Balbo Ave

100E
Chicago Hilton
and Towers

E 8th St

B

S Columbus Dr

S Lake Shore Dr

◄ 8   ○ Johnson Publishing
Headquarters

S Michigan Ave

E 9th St

Hutchinson
Field

E 11th St

S Holden Ct

S Wabash Ave

11th Pl

Roosevelt Road
● Station

E Roosevelt Rd

41

Agora

1200S

Museum
Campus
PAGE 206

John G Shedd
Aquarium
○

Roosevelt

C

E Solidarity Dr

E Solidarity Dr

11

E 13 St

Field Museum of
Natural History

McFetridge Dr

| 1/4 mile | .25 km |

Map 9

Built atop the rubble of the Great Chicago Fire of 1871, **Grant Park** is now affectionately known as Chicago's front yard. Ring the doorbell for a spectacular view, no matter where you turn: the skyline to the north, Lake Michigan to the east, Museum Campus to the south, or the gardens of the park itself.

○ Landmarks

- **Agora** • S Michigan Ave & E Roosevelt Rd
  If you've ever wanted to see 106 headless metal people, here's where you can.
- **Buckingham Fountain** • 301 S Columbus Dr
  312-742-7529
  Built of pink marble; inspired by Versailles.
- **Columbia College** • 600 S Michigan Ave
  312-369-1000
  Private arts school known for film, TV, and fiction programs.
- **Hilton Chicago** • 720 S Michigan Ave
  312-922-4400
  Check out the frescoes in the lobby; sneak a kiss in the palatial ballroom.
- **Johnson Publishing Headquarters** •
  200 S Michigan Ave
  312-322-9444
  Largest African American-owned publishing company, home of Ebony and Jet magazines.
- **Shedd Aquarium** • 1200 S Lake Shore Dr
  312-939-2438
  Marine and freshwater creatures from around the world are on view in this 1929 Classical Greek-inspired Beaux Arts structure.
- **Spirit of Music Garden** • 601 S Michigan Ave
  Where the city struts during Chicago SummerDance.

Restaurants

- **Yolk** • 1120 S Michigan Ave
  312-789-9655 • $$
  Bright, clean brunch spot with eggs o' plenty.

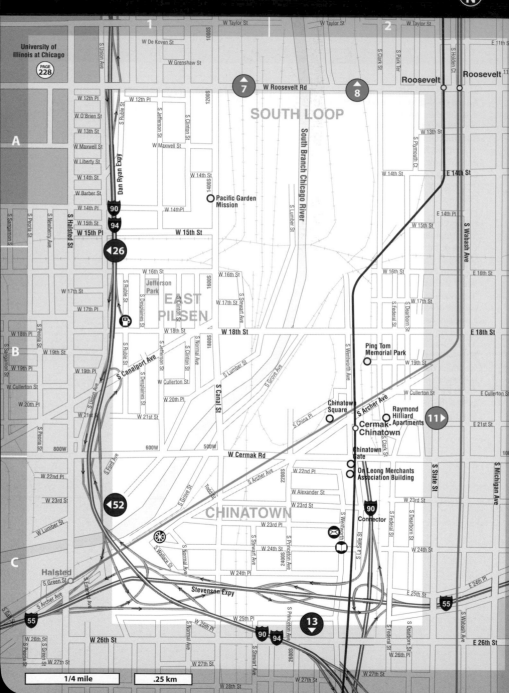

Map 10 · **East Pilsen / Chinatown**

Map 10

Nestled between the University of Illinois at Chicago campus and the official South Side, East Pilsen gives artists, families and hipsters all a place to call home. The neighborhood's up and coming qualities haven't quite up and came, making rent more affordable than most of its northern counterparts. Celebrate the Chinese New Year just across the river with street sales reminiscent of Shanghai.

○ Landmarks

- **Chinatown Gate** •
S Wentworth Ave & W Cermak Rd
Built in 1976. The characters on the gate read "The world belongs to the people."
- **Hilliard Apartments** • 2111 S Clark St
312-225-3715
Another Bertrand Golberg gem going from subsidized senior housing to mixed-income residential.
- **On Leong Merchants Association Building** •
2216 S Wentworth Ave
312-328-1188
1926 building inspired by architecture of the Kwangtung district of China. Now the home of the Pui Tak Center.
- **Pacific Garden Mission** • 1458 S Canal St
312-492-9410
America's oldest continuously-operating rescue mission with free showings of long -unning radio drama "Unshackled!"

🍴 Restaurants

- **Ahjoomah's Apron** • 218 W Cermak Rd
312-326-2800 • $$
Lone taste of Korea amidst dim sum and duck sauce.
- **Chi Cafe** • 2160 S Archer Ave
312-842-9993 • $
Crowd-pleasing Pan-Asian.
- **Emperor's Choice** • 2238 S Wentworth Ave
312-225-8800 • $
Start with seafood; finish with tea.
- **Evergreen** • 2411 S Wentworth Ave
312-225-8898 • $$
More upscale than most Chinatown grub.

- **Joy Yee's Noodles** • 2139 S China Pl
312-328-0001 • $$
Huge portions of Korean and Chinese, plus bubble tea.
- **Lao Sze Chuan** • 2172 S Archer Ave
312-326-5040 • $
Authentic Chinese dishes plus great evening karaoke.
- **MingHin Cuisine** • 2168 S Archer Ave
312 808 1999 • $$
Encyclopedic menu and, of course, the dim sum.
- **Phoenix** • 2131 S Archer Ave
312-328-0848 • $
The best Chinese breakfast in town.
- **Saint's Alp Teahouse** • 2157 S China Pl
312-842-8882 • $
Teahouse chain that bears bubble tea.
- **Three Happiness** • 209 W Cermak Rd
312-842-1964 • $
Long waits for dim sum.

🛍 Shopping

- **Chinatown Bazaar** • 2221 S Wentworth Ave
312 225 1088
Part clothing store, part knick-knack shop.
- **Feida Bakery** • 2228 S Wentworth Ave
312-808-1113
Tasty Chinese baked goods.
- **Giftland** • 2212 S Wentworth Ave
312-225-0088
With a premium on Hello Kitty and other sorts of "Asian adorableness."
- **Pacific Furniture** • 2200 S Wentworth Ave
312-808-0456
Mostly home furnishings.
- **Sun Sun Tong Co.** • 2260 S Wentworth Ave
312-842-6398
Stock up on Chinese herbs and teas.

Map 11 · **South Loop / McCormick Place**

N

1   2

W Taylor St

E 11th St

Roosevelt Road Station

PAGE 194

Grant Park

Lake Michigan

Roosevelt   **Roosevelt**

8

9

E Roosevelt Rd   E Roosevelt Dr

E 13th St

41

Museum Campus

Shedd Aquarium

America's Courtyard

S Columbus Dr

A

Field Museum

PAGE 206

Adler Planetarium

W 14th St

E 14th St

E Solidarity Dr

America's Courtyard

McFetridge Dr

S Wabash Ave

E 14th Pl

Indiana Ave

CENTRAL STATION

Soldier Field

PAGE 240

Burnham Park Yacht Harbor

Lynne White Dr

W 15th St

S State St

S Dearborn St

PRAIRIE DISTRICT

E 16th St

E Waldron Dr

Northerly Island Park

W 16th St

W 17th St

S Prairie Ave

S Lake Shore Dr

10

National Vietnam Veterans Art Museum

E 18th St

18th St Station

E 18th Dr

Clarke House

S Calumet Ave

Merrill C Meigs Field

W 19th St

B

Second Presbyterian Church

Hillary Rodham Clinton Women's Park and Gardens of Chicago

S Archer Ave

W Cullerton St

E Cullerton St

The Wheeler Mansion

W 21st St

E 21st St

S Clark St

Willie Dixon's Blues Heaven Foundation

100E

200E   300E

S Calumet Ave

S Dr Martin L King Jr Dr

100W

S Michigan Ave

E Cermak Rd

Hyatt Regency McCormick Place

Arie Crown Theater

W 23rd St

S Cottage Grove Ave

E 23rd St

400E

23rd St McCormick Place Station

E 23rd Dr

S Calumet Ave

Burnham Park

S Dearborn St

S Federal St

Quinn Chapel

E 24th St

McCormick Place

PAGE 202

W 24th St

S La Salle St

E 24th Pl

C

55

E 24th Pl

Stevenson Expy

S Prairie Ave

S Calumet Ave

W 25th St

E 25th St

14

S Federal St

E 26th St

S Wabash Ave

S Dr Martin L King Jr Dr

S Dr Martin L King Jr Dr

E 26th St

W 26th St

Mercy Hospital & Medical Center

E 27th St

27th St Station

S Ellis Ave

W 27th St

1/4 mile   .25 km

E 28th St

Map 11

In the summer, joggers and bicyclists crowd the lakefront trail and soak in the sun in Burnham Park. Once temperatures reach a friendly sub-zero reading in December, Bears fans turn parking lots into 6:30 a.m. Sunday Funday spots. Throughout the year, **McCormick Place** looms over the neighborhood to welcome meetings, trade shows, and business gatherings of all kinds.

○ Landmarks

- **Adler Planetarium** • 1300 S Lake Shore Dr
  312-922-7827
  Depression-era wonder that thrilled millions at 1933 Century of Progress Exposition.
- **America's Courtyard** • 1300 S Lake Shore Dr
  A spiral of stones that echoes both the Milky Way and ancient structures. Designed by Denise Milan and Ary R. Perez.
- **Chicago Women's Park and Gardens** • 1801 S Indiana Ave
  312-328-0821
  A garden from a former first lady.
- **Clarke House Museum** • 1827 S Indiana Ave
  312-744-3316
  Built in 1836 by an unknown architect, this Greek Revival-style home has been relocated twice and is now an official Chicago landmark.
- **The Field Museum** • 1400 S Lake Shore Dr
  312-922-9410
  Go to see Sue, world's largest known T. rex; stay for the jam-packed halls of vaguely macabre taxidermy.
- **McCormick Place** • 2301 S Lake Shore Dr
  312-791-7000
  Hard to miss.
- **Museum Campus** • S Lake Shore Dr
  The ultimate destination for educational field trips.
- **Northerly Island Park** • 1521 S Linn White Dr
  312-745-2910
  Greenspace now encompassing former site of Meigs Field airport.
- **Quinn Chapel African Methodist Episcopal Church** • 2401 S Wabash Ave
  312-791-1846
  Built in 1892, this Victorian Gothic-style church houses Chicago's oldest African American congregation.
- **Second Presbyterian Church** • 1936 S Michigan Ave
  312-225-4951
  Reconstructed in 1900 by Howard Van Doren Shaw, this ponderous Gothic Revival-style church has stained glass by Tiffany.
- **Soldier Field** • 1410 Museum Campus Dr
  312-235-7000
  Once on the National Register of Historic Places, this renovated monster is home to Da Bears.
- **The Wheeler Mansion** • 2020 S Calumet Ave
  312-945-2020
  This Second Empire-style mansion now houses a boutique hotel for high-end travelers.
- **Willie Dixon's Blues Heaven Foundation** • 2120 S Michigan Ave
  312-808-1286
  Former Chess Records studio. Tours, exhibits, workshops, and performances.

🍸 Nightlife

- **M Lounge** • 1520 S Wabash Ave
  312-447-0201
  Chic lounge with live jazz.
- **Reggie's** • 2105 S State St
  312-949-0120
  Record store, all-age live music venue, and sports bar & grill all in one place.
- **Square 1** • 1400 S Michigan Ave
  312-786-1750
  Craft brews, cocktails and…wait for it…self-service wine dispensers.

🍴 Restaurants

- **Kroll's** • 1736 S Michigan Ave
  312-235-1400 • $$
  Chicago outpost of Green Bay grill. Packers backers better watch their backs.
- **La Cantina Grill** • 1911 S Michigan Ave
  312-842-1911 • $$
  Comfy Mexican with no surprises.
- **Nepal House** • 1301 S Michigan Ave
  312-922-0601 • $$
  Nepalese and Himalayan cuisine.
- **Tapas Valencia** • 1530 S State St
  312-842-4444 • $$
  Par for the course tapas for the South Loop.
- **Waffles** • 1400 S Michigan Ave
  312-854-8572 • $$
  Your morning made better with syrup.

🛍 Shopping

- **Cycle Bike Shop** • 1465 S Michigan Ave
  312-987-1080
  Bike shop, obviously.
- **Waterware** • 1829 S State St
  312-225-4549
  Designer plumbing fixtures.

Map 12 • Bridgeport (West)

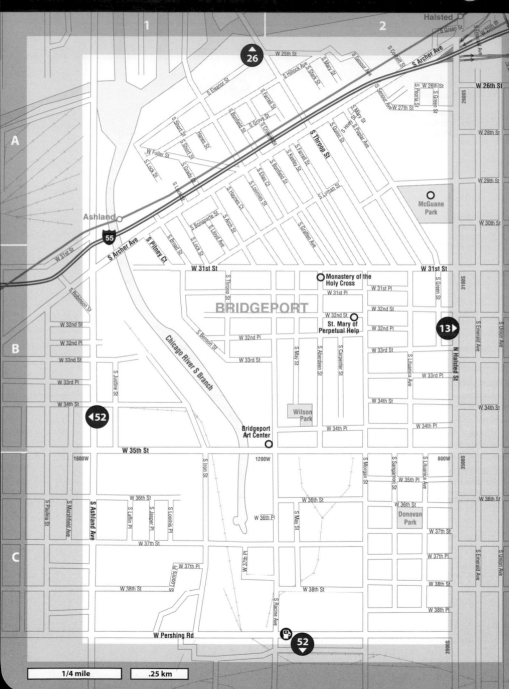

Nestled just north of the old stockyards, this working-class neighborhood's plentiful land and warehouses ripe for conversions have spurred a recent wave of development and given rise to a bustling arts district. Most notable is tony Bridgeport Village, set smack-dab on a stretch of the Chicago River known as Bubbly Creek, so-named for its gaseous stew made from the animal carcasses dumped in it by the former stockyards. Its banks now boast pricey homes, but the bubbles still linger.

○ Landmarks

- **Bridgeport Art Center** • 1200 W 35th St
  773-247-3000
  Huge gallery/event/studio warehouse space, catalyst for Bridgeport's burgeoning art scene.
- **McGuane Park** • 2901 S Poplar Ave
  312-747-6497
  A park for playing.
- **Monastery of the Holy Cross** •
  3111 S Aberdeen St
  773-927-7424
  Have your breakfast served by monks in this bed and breakfast monastery.
- **St. Mary of Perpetual Help Parish** •
  1039 W 32nd St
  773-927-6646
  Built in the 1880s, this was the first Polish Roman Catholic Church in the US to be consecrated.

⚇ Nightlife

- **Maria's Packaged Goods & Community Bar** •
  960 W 31st St
  773-890-0588
  Liquor store and bar with artisanal beers and craft cocktails.

🍴 Restaurants

- **The Duck Inn** • 2701 S Eleanor St
  312-724-8811 • $$$
  Trendy gastropub hits Bridgeport.
- **Pleasant House Bakery** • 2119 S Halsted St
  773-523-7437 • $$
  Handmade meat/vegetables pies, pasties, and other British classics.
- **Polo Cafe and Catering** • 3322 S Morgan St
  773-927-7656 • $$$
  Frequented by Bridgeport locals, and famous for their "Bloody Mary Brunch."
- **Pot Sticker House** • 3139 S Halsted St
  312-326-6898 • $$
  Authentic Northern Chinese cuisine in the heart of Bridgeport.

🛍 Shopping

- **Unique Thrift Store** • 3000 S Halsted St
  312-842-0942
  Half-off Mondays and Early-Bird Thursdays!

Map 13 · **Bridgeport (East)**

Map 13

Bridgeport exemplifies how the "City That Works" actually works. The stomping grounds of the Daley family and de facto political center of the city, Bridgeport is also the quintessential Chicago neighborhood with its close-knit residents, legions of patronage workers, and distinctive "dese, dem, and dose" vernacular.

○ Landmarks

- **Guaranteed Rate Field** • 333 W 35th St
  312-674-1000
  Beats paying through the nose to watch ivy grow.
- **Illinois Institute of Technology** •
  10 W 35th St
  312-567-3000
  Mies van der Rohe-designed campus. Jewel in the crown? Crown Hall, of course.
- **Old Neighborhood Italian American Club** •
  3031 S Shields Ave
  312-326-6420
  Founded by Angelo LaPietra, a former high-ranking Chicago mobster, after his release from Leavenworth.
- **Richard J. Daley House** • 3536 S Lowe Ave
  Childhood home of Mayor Richard J. Daley.
- **Richard J. Daley Library Fountain** •
  3400 S Halsted St
  Pretty water.

Y Nightlife

- **Bernice's Tavern** • 3238 S Halsted St
  312-961-5516
  60+ year-old dive bar with live music and open mics.

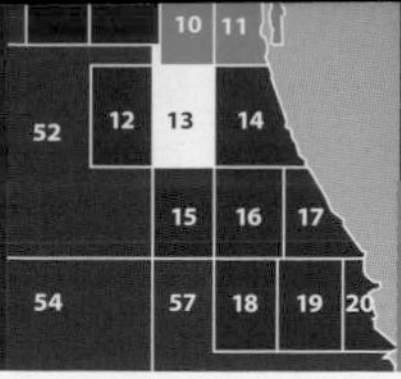

Map 13

Bridgeport (East)

Restaurants

- **All Star Stand** • 333 W 35th St
  312-674-1000 • $
  Multifarious food offerings between innings.
- **Carbon** • 300 W 26th St
  312-225-3200 • $
  So what if they use gas? The food is still delicious.
- **Franco's Ristorante** • 300 W 31st St
  312-225-9566 • $$
  Family-style Italian near Sox park.
- **Freddie's** • 701 W 31st St
  312-808-0147 • $
  Italian ice, beef sandwiches, and appropriate attitude.
- **Gio's** • 2724 S Lowe Ave
  312-225-6368 • $
  BYOB Italian deli with groceries.
- **Grand Palace** • 225 W 26th St
  312-225-3888 • $
  Cheap eats and authentic homestyle Chinese food at this hole-in-the-wall.
- **Han 202** • 605 W 31st St
  312-949-1314 • $$$
  Trendy BYOB featuring an eclectic Asian/Fusion menu.

- **Kevin's Hamburger Heaven** • 554 W Pershing Rd
  773-924-5771 • $
  Hamburgers and milkshakes.
- **Maxwell Street Depot** • 411 W 31st St
  312-326-3514 • $
  Counter-service only joint serving signature pork chop sandwiches 24 hours a day.
- **Nana** • 752 W 33rd St
  312-929-2486 • $$$
  Organic, sustainable, locally sourced restaurant famous for their brunches.
- **New Furama** • 2828 S Wentworth Ave
  312-225-6888 • $
  Great dim sum; far easier to find parking than in Chinatown.
- **Pancho Pistolas** • 700 W 31st St
  312-225-8808 • $$
  Two words: Eggs and beans.
- **Phil's Pizza** • 1102 W 35th St
  773-523-0947 • $
  Pizza-rific.
- **Scoops** • 608 W 31st St
  312-842-3300 • $
  Family-owned ice cream parlor serving up old-fashioned shakes and other desserts.

The South Side proves that you don't have to be glitzy to get the job done. Ditto for the much-maligned Guaranteed Rate Field, where pure baseball and terrific sight lines trump drunken revelry at crosstown Wrigley.

52	10	11		
	12	13	14	
	15	16	17	
54	57	18	19	20

🛍 Shopping

• **Ace Bakery** • 3241 S Halsted St
312-225-4973
Excellent breads and pastries.
• **Augustine's Eternal Gifts & Spiritual Goods** •
3327 S Halsted St
773-843-1933
Mystical and religious knick-knacks.

• **Blue City Cycles** • 3201 S Halsted St
312-225-3780
Welcome addition for Bridgeport peddlers.
• **Health King Enterprise & Balanceuticals Group** •
238 W 31st St
312-567-9978
Natural remedies.
• **Henry's Sports & Bait Shop** • 3130 S Canal St
312-225-8538
Fishing mecca.
• **Let's Boogie Records & Tapes** • 3321 S Halsted St
773-254-0139
Pick up some vintage vinyl here.

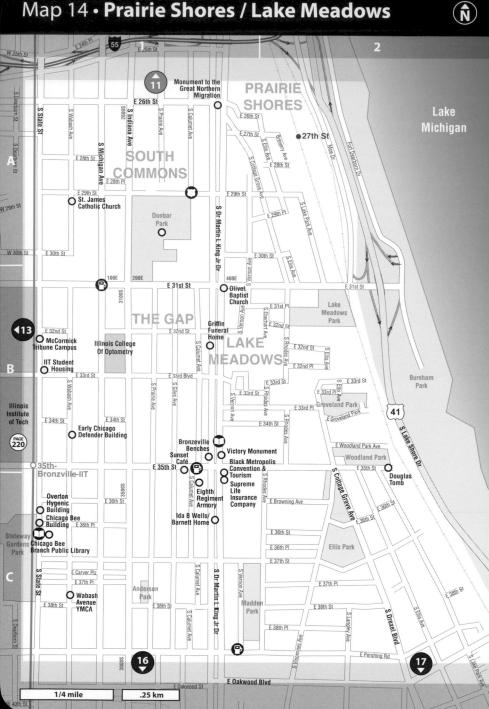

Map 14 • **Prairie Shores / Lake Meadows**

N

W 25th St

55

E 24th Pl

E 25th St

W 26th St

S Dearborn St
S State St
S Wabash Ave
S Michigan Ave
S Indiana Ave
S Prairie Ave
S Calumet Ave

11

Monument to the
Great Northern
Migration

**PRAIRIE
SHORES**

E 26th St

E 27th St

●27th St

Brewery Ave

S Ellis Ave

S Cottage Grove Ave

Fort Dearborn Dr

Moe Dr.

**Lake
Michigan**

E 28th St

E 28th Pl

**SOUTH
COMMONS**

E 29th St

St. James
Catholic Church

E 29th St

W 29th St
S Dearborn St

S Lake Park Ave

E 29th Pl

E 30th St

S Vernon Ave

W 30th St

E 30th St

E 31st St

S Ellis Ave

E 31st St

100E

200E

Dunbar
Park

S Dr. Martin L King Jr Dr.

400E

Olivet
Baptist
Church

E 31st St

Lake
Meadows
Park

A

13

3100S

THE GAP

E 31st Pl
E 32nd St

E 32nd St

S Champlain Ave
S Eberhart Ave

S Rhodes Ave

E 32nd St
E 32nd Pl

S Ellis Ave

Burnham
Park

McCormick
Tribune Campus

Illinois College
Of Optometry

Griffin
Funeral
Home

**LAKE
MEADOWS**

IIT Student
Housing

S Wabash Ave

E 33rd St

S Calumet Ave

S Prairie Ave

S Giles Ave

E 33rd Blvd

E 33rd St

S Vernon Ave

E 33rd St

S Rhodes Ave

E 33rd St

Groveland Park

B

Illinois
Institute
of Tech

E 34th St

E 34th St

Early Chicago
Defender Building

E 34th St

E 34th St

Groveland Park

E Woodland Park Ave

Woodland Park

41

S Lake Shore Dr

PAGE
220

Bronzeville
Benches

Victory Monument

E 35th St

Douglas
Tomb

35th-
Bronzville-IIT

Sunset
Café

E 35th St

Black Metropolis
Convention &
Tourism

E 35th St

S Cottage Grove Ave

Overton
Hygenic
Building

3500S

E 36th St

Eighth
Regiment
Armory

Supreme
Life
Insurance
Company

E Browning Ave

E 36th St

Chicago Bee
Building

E 36th Pl

Ida B Wells/
Barnett Home

S Rhodes Ave

E 36th St

S Calumet Ave

Stateway
Gardens
Park

Chicago Bee
Branch Public Library

E 36th St

E 36th Pl

E 37th St

Ellis Park

C

S State St

E Carver Plz

E 37th St

S Calumet Ave

S Vernon Ave

E 37th Pl

E 38th St

Wabash
Avenue
YMCA

Anderson
Park

E 38th St

Madden
Park

E 38th St

E 38th Pl

S Drexel Blvd

S Ellis Ave

S Langley Ave

S Dearborn St

E 38th St

S Dr. Martin L King Jr Dr.

E 38th Pl

16

S Vincennes Ave

E Pershing Rd

17

S Lake Park Ave

S Cottage Grove Ave

E Oakwood St

E Oakwood Blvd

W 40th St

E 40th St

1/4 mile

.25 km

Map 14

Named after two rather imposing urban apartment complexes, this area has experienced a recent rebirth with the expansion of the nearby Illinois Institute of Technology campus. An influx of student residents, plenty of green space, and its proximity to the Loop and lakefront have made this area one of the fastest growing new residential communities in Chicago.

○ Landmarks

- **Bronzeville Benches** •
  S Dr Martin Luther King Jr Dr b/n E 25th & E 35th St
  13 artists created these 24 unique bench sculptures. Sit on them.
- **Chicago Bee Building** • 3647 S State St
  Formerly the HQ of the *Chicago Bee* newspaper; now offices.
- **Chicago Bee Public Library** • 3647 S State St
  312-747-6872
  Originally home of black newspaper, *Chicago Bee*.
- **Douglas Tomb** • 636 E 35th St
  312-225-2620
  Resting place of Lincoln's nemesis, overlooking tracks of Illinois Central railroad and the subdivision he founded. The entrance is on the east side of the Lake.
- **Dunbar Park** • 300 E 31st St
  312-590-5993
  Dunbar High's girls' softball team plays here.
- **Early Chicago Defender Building** •
  3435 S Indiana Ave
  Originally an 1899 synagogue, was home of *Chicago Defender* from 1920-1940.
- **Eighth Regiment Armory** • 3533 S Giles Ave
  First armory built in US for black regiment, 1914-1918, now a Chicago public high school.
- **Ida B. Wells-Barnett Home** • 3624 S King Dr
  Former home of the journalism and civil rights pioneer.
- **McCormick Tribune Campus Center** • 3201 S State St
  Student center wrapped around the L. Wow!
- **Monument to the Great Northern Migration** •
  345 E Eastgate Pl
  Statue by Alison Sarr depicts a man with a briefcase atop a pile of old shoes. Represents the journey of African Americans from the South.

- **Olivet Baptist Church** • 3101 S King Dr
  312-528-0124
  Church with a longstanding tradition of civil rights organizing ranging from abolitionist and feminist mass meetings to Black Panther Party programs.
- **Overton Hygienic Building** • 3619 S State St
  Former headquarters of foremost producer of black cosmestics.
- **St. James Catholic Church** • 2907 Wabash Ave
  312-842-1919
  Traditional community caretaking that included caring for Confederate POWs at Camp Douglas.
- **State Street Village (IIT Student Housing)** •
  3303 S State St
  312-808-9771
  Supercool housing for this iconic institute.
- **Sunset Café** • 315 E 35th St
  One of Chicago's earliest and most legendary jazz venues.
- **Supreme Life Insurance Company Head Office** •
  3501 S King Dr
  Built in 1921 and remodeled in 1950, this former major black insurance company enjoys new life as a mixed commercial structure.
- **Victory Monument** • S King Dr & E 35th St
  Early postwar tribute to WWI's black Eighth Regiment of the Illinois National Guard that served as part of the US 370th Infantry in France.

🍴 Restaurants

- **Pearl's Place** • 3901 S Michigan Ave
  773-285-1700 • $
  Mama's soul food at a snail's pace.

Map 15 • **Canaryville / Fuller Park**

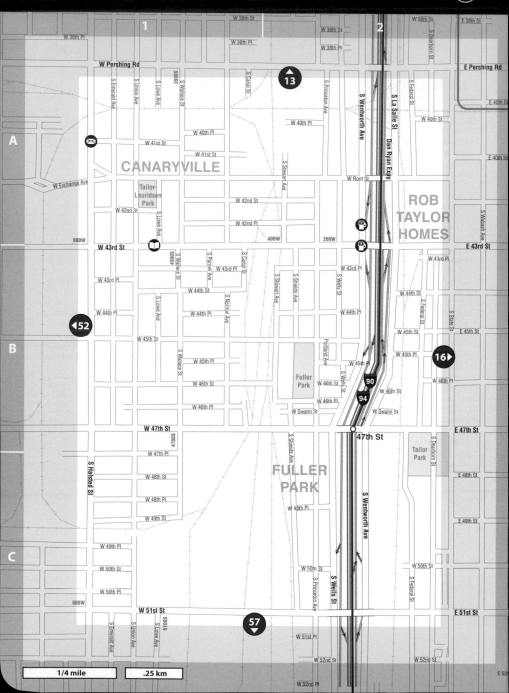

Map 15

Christmas 1865 was a bad day for livestock, as the sprawling Union Stock Yards opened, all beasts on the lookout. All that's left now is the imposing limestone gate (moment of silence). While cattle around the country breathed a collective sigh when the Yards closed, this area headed south afterward and is still in recovery.

 Nightlife

• **Kelly's Tavern** • 4403 S Wallace St
  773-924-0796
  A neighborhood place.

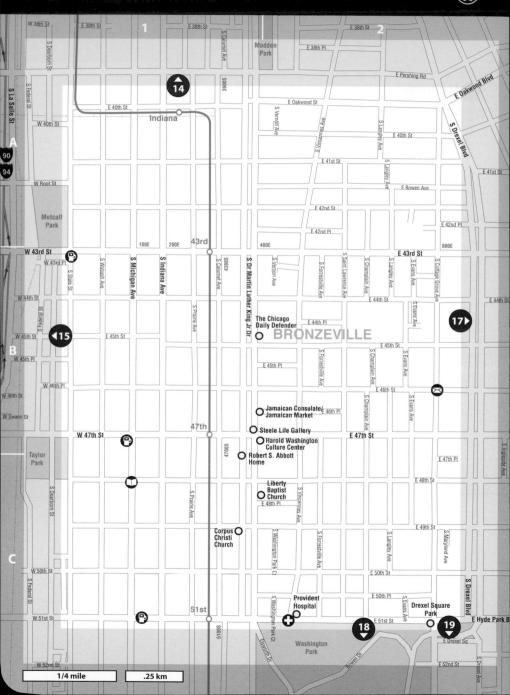

Map 16 • Bronzeville

Once the glorious heart of Chicago's African American community, Bronzeville is in the midst of an impressive 21st century urban renewal. Decades of poverty, crime, empty lots, and dilapidated housing projects have given way to yuppie transplants, restored greystones, and glitzy condos.

○ Landmarks

- **Chicago Defender** • 4445 S King Dr
312-225-2400
Founded in 1905, it was the country's most influential black newspaper through the '50s. Still in operation, but much-diminished.
- **Drexel Square Park** • 5101 S Cottage Grove Ave
Victorian gem boasting city's oldest surviving fountain donated by prominent banking family.
- **Harold Washington Cultural Center** • 4701 S King Dr
773-373-1900
Beautiful homage to the late mayor; it's a jaw-dropping technology & arts center.
- **Jamaican Consulate** • 4655 S King Dr
773-373-8988
A bit of Kingston on the Old South Side.
- **Liberty Baptist Church** • 4849 S King Dr
773-268-6757
An afrocentric 1958 go-go styled temple considered King's original Chicago workshop.
- **Provident Hospital** • 500 E 51st St
312-527-2000
First to train black medical professionals and site of first successful open-heart surgery.
- **Robert S. Abbott Home** • 4742 S King Dr
Former home of *Chicago Defender* founder.
- **Steelelife Gallery** • 4655 S King Dr
773-538-4773
House of art that inspires the people.

Restaurants

- **Abundance Bakery** • 105 E 47th St
773-373-1971 • $$
Neighborhood bakery famous for cobblers and caramel upside-down cakes.
- **Ain't She Sweet** • 526 E 43rd St
773-373-3530 • $
Fresh, hearty sandwiches, yummy treats, and uncompromised service.
- **Chicago's Home of Chicken & Waffles** •
3947 S King Dr
773-536-3300 • $$$
Authentic Southern classics, including their famous fried chicken and waffles.

Shopping

- **Ibiza Couture** • 233 E 47th St
773-924-5199
High-fashion hip-hop rock star gear & denim.

Map 17 • Kenwood

Map 17

Many a 19th-century suburb prided itself on wide lawns and tranquil settings, and Kenwood was no exception. Though it was annexed to Chicago over a century ago, the suburban feeling lingers. These days, the architecturally-enriched neighborhood contains everything from the residence of Louis Farrakhan to the oldest Jewish congregation in the city, KAM Isaiah Israel.

○ Landmarks

- **Barack Obama's Chicago Residence** • 5046 S Greenwood Ave
- **George Blossom House** • 4858 S Kenwood Ave
  Frank Lloyd Wright's early work—note the Roman influences.
- **Hyde Park Art Center** • 5020 S Cornell Ave
  773-324-5520
  Has plenty of visual arts activities for the shorties and grown folk. Check out the Cocktails & Clay night!
- **KAM Isaiah Israel** • 1100 E Hyde Park Blvd
  773-924-1234
  Oldest Jewish congregation in the city.
- **Little Black Pearl Art & Design Center** •
  1060 E 47th St
  773-285-1211
  One of the most beautiful & spacious visual arts centers on the South Side.
- **Louis Farrakhan Home** • 4855 S Woodlawn Ave
  Well-guarded home of the leader of the Nation of Islam.
- **Rainbow/PUSH Coalition Headquarters** •
  930 E 50th St
  773-373-3366
  Originally the 1924 home of KAM Isaiah Israel, Chicago's oldest Jewish congregation, with late 1940s addition.
- **Warren McArthur House** • 4852 S Kenwood Ave
  More work by Frank Lloyd Wright, still tethered to Louis Sullivan.

Restaurants

- **Fung's Chop Suey** • 1400 E 47th St
  773-924-2328 • $
  When you're thinking delivery.
- **Lake Shore Café** • 4900 S Lake Shore Dr
  773-288-5815 • $$
  Basic hotel food.

Shopping

- **Fort Smith** • 1007 E 43rd St
  773-268-8200
  Stylish boutique featuring apparel, jewelry, and accessories designed in-house.
- **Goree Shop** • 1122 E 47th St
  773-285-1895
  Fabric and crafts boutique featuring Senegalese and other imported items.
- **Max & Co. Hair Designs** • 1453 E Hyde Park Blvd
  773-288-2255
  The place to go if you need to straighten every kink on your nappy little head.

Map 18 • Washington Park

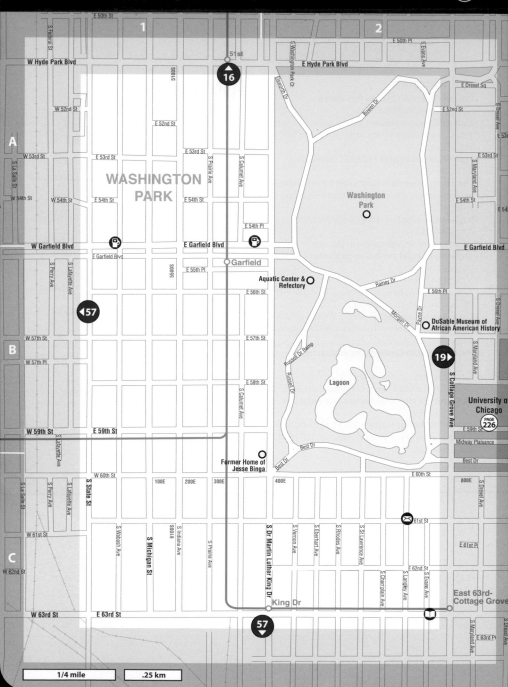

N

1 **2**

E 50th St

W Hyde Park Blvd · 51st · E Hyde Park Blvd

E 50th Pl

16

E Drexel Sq

W 52nd St · E 52nd St

E 52nd St

A

W 53rd St · E 53rd St · E 53rd St · E 53rd St

WASHINGTON PARK

W 54th St · E 54th St · E 54th St

Washington Park · E 54th St

E 54th Pl

W Garfield Blvd · E Garfield Blvd · E Garfield Blvd

E Garfield Blvd

Garfield · E 55th Pl

Aquatic Center & Refectory · E 56th St · Rainey Dr · E 56th Pl

57 · DuSable Museum of African American History

W 57th St · E 57th St · Morgan Dr

B

W 57th Pl

E 58th St · **19**

Lagoon · S Cottage Grove Ave

University of Chicago

PAGE 226

W 59th St · E 59th St · E 59th St · Best Dr · Midway Plaisance

Best Dr

Former Home of Jesse Binga

W 60th St · 100E · 200E · 300E · 400E · E 60th St · 800E

61st St

W 61st St · E 61st Pl

C

W 62nd St · E 62nd St

East 63rd-Cottage Grove

W 63rd St · E 63rd St · King Dr · E 63rd St

57

S Federal St · S La Salle St · S Perry Ave · S Lafayette Ave · S State St · S 500W · S Wabash Ave · S Michigan St · S Indiana Ave · S 100W · S Prairie Ave · S Calumet Ave · S Dr Martin Luther King Dr · S Vernon Ave · S Eberhart Ave · S Rhodes Ave · S St Lawrence Ave · S Champlain Ave · S Langley Ave · S Evans Ave · S Maryland Ave · S Drexel Ave

S Washington Park Ct · Ellsworth Dr · Bowen Dr · Russell Dr Ramp · Russell Dr · Best Dr

---

| 1/4 mile | .25 km |

Map 18

Anchored by its namesake park and the **DuSable Museum**, one of the nation's most important institutions dedicated to African American history and culture, this area has seen a bit of urban renewal lately. **Washington Park** itself is a registered historic district and features Lorado Taft's 127-foot-long concrete sculpture, Fountain of Time, at its eastern gate, as well as a pond, track, and swimming pool.

○ Landmarks

• **DuSable Museum of African American History** •
740 E 56th Pl
773-947-0600
Founded in 1961 and dedicated to preserving and honoring African American culture. The oldest non-profit institution of its kind.

• **Jesse Binga House** • 5922 S King Dr
Home of nation's first African American banker.

• **Washington Park** •
5531 S Dr Martin Luther King Jr Dr
773-256-1248
A sprawling 367-acre park with beautiful lagoons and fields. Check out the "Fountain of Time" sculpture in the southeast corner of the park.

• **Washington Park Refectory** •
5531 S Martin Luther King Dr
Designed by Daniel Burnham's firm, the Refectory now holds locker rooms for the Aquatic Center and its 36-foot waterslide.

Nightlife

• **Odyssey II** • 211 E Garfield Blvd
773-947-0956
So laid back, they don't even have set hours.

Shopping

• **Bike and Roll Chicago- DuSable Museum** •
740 E 56th Pl
773-947-0600
Bike rentals and tours.

• **The Cat's Meow** • 6107 S Martin Luther King Dr
773-684-3220
Sexy lingerie, games, toys, and other classy smut to keep his/her attention.

Map 19 · Hyde Park

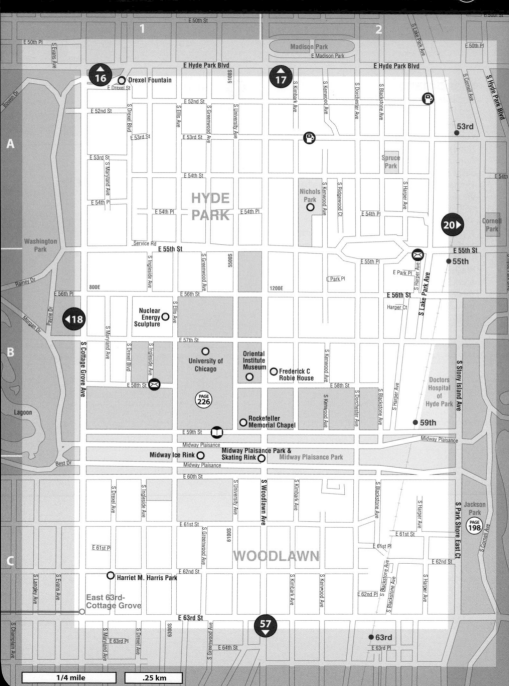

Map 19

A university's best attempt to summon up images of Oxford collides with its misguided efforts toward urban renewal in this neighborhood, where the student and middle classes drink in the same bars as the academics and politicians governing their lives. In one of Chicago's most racially integrated neighborhoods, ethnic dining abounds, as does artistic graffiti. Don't miss the bookstores along 57th Street; replicas of Borges's libraries?

o Landmarks

- **Drexel Fountain** • 5100 S Drexel Ave
  The city's oldest remaining fountain.
- **Frederick C. Robie House** • 5757 S Woodlawn Ave
  Designed by Frank Lloyd Wright; renovations
  proceeding, stay tuned.
- **Harriet M. Harris Park** • 6200 S Drexel Ave
  312-747-2706
  Historic Park building with Mural of Woodlawn
  Heroes, swimming, and arts.
- **Midway Plaisance Ice Rink** •
  1130 Midway Plaisance
  312-745-2470
  Professors' kids collide while the speakers blare
  Motown and the Beatles.
- **Midway Plaisance Park** • 1130 Midway Plaisance
  312-745-2470
  Olympic-sized outdoor skating rink.
- **Nichols Park** • 1355 E 53rd St
  312-747-2703
  Home of the Parrots of Hyde Park.
- **Nuclear Energy Sculpture** • 5625 S Ellis Ave
  Birthplace of the Atomic Age.
- **The Oriental Institute** • 1155 E 58th St
  773-702-9514
  Educate yourself.
- **Rockefeller Memorial Chapel** •
  5850 S Woodlawn Ave
  773-702-2667
  Built in 1928, this English Gothic-styled cathedral
  contains one of the world's largest carillons.
- **University of Chicago** • 5801 S Ellis Ave
  773-702-1234
  A pretty spot for wandering on the south side.

Nightlife

- **Falcon Inn** • 1601 E 53rd St
  Cheap dive of regulars where you can hide out.
- **The Pub** • 1212 E 59th St
  773-702-9737
  A basement student bar redeemed by the people-
  watching and wood panels.
- **Woodlawn Tap** • 1172 E 55th St
  773-643-5516
  U of Chicago legend.

Map 19

10 11
52 12 13 14
15 16 17
54 57 18 19 20

Hyde Park

Restaurants

- **Bonjour Café Bakery** • 1550 E 55th St
773-241-5300 • $
Have a pastry and be seen.
- **Boston Market** • 1424 E 53rd St
773-288-2600 • $
Hyde Park outpost of the ubiquitous rotisserie chicken chain.
- **Cedars Mediterranean Kitchen** • 1206 E 53rd St
773-324-6227 • $$
Great food, horrible service.
- **Chant** • 1509 E 53rd St
773-324-1999 • $$$
Upscale Asian for Hyde Parkers.
- **Harold's Chicken Shack** • 1208 E 53rd St
773-752-9270 • $
Buckets and buckets of crispy, crumbling chicken. Best in the 'hood.
- **Kikuya** • 1601 E 55th St
773-667-3727 • $$
Best sushi in the neighborhood.

- **La Petite Folie** • 1504 E 55th St
773-493-1394 • $$$$
The only haute cuisine in the neighborhood. Expensive and worth it.
- **Maravillas Restaurant** • 5506 S Lake Park Ave
773-643-3155 • $
Cheap, good Mexican. Stinging salsa. Open real late.
- **Medici on 57th** • 1327 E 57th St
773-667-7394 • $
The essence of life at U of C.
- **Mellow Yellow** • 1508 E 53rd St
773-667-2000 • $
Comfort food for morning and night.
- **Nathan's Chicago Style** • 1372 E 53rd St
773-288-5353 • $
A taste of Jamaica.
- **Rajun Cajun** • 1459 E 53rd St
773-955-1145 • $
Neon lights oversee the marriage of chicken tikka masala and cornbread.
- **Salonica** • 1440 E 57th St
773-752-3899 • $
Where to go the morning after.
- **The Sit Down Cafe & Sushi Bar** • 1312 E 53rd St
773-324-3700 • $$
Sake with your caprese salad? Must be fusion.
- **Valois** • 1518 E 53rd St
773-667-0647 • $
See Your Food.

Hyde Park boasts plentiful entertainment and dining options, including many of President Obama's favorites, such as **Valois** and **57th Street Books**. For more upscale dining, savor the cuisine at **La Petite Folie**. The University of Chicago's Logan Arts Center built on a vibrant arts and entertainment scene.

Shopping

- **57th Street Books** • 1301 E 57th St
  773-684-1300
  Brainy, independent bookstore.
- **Blackstone Bicycle Works** • 6100 S Blackstone Ave
  773-241-5458
  Super friendly and welcoming Woodlawn bike shop.
- **Futons N More** • 919 W Irving Park Rd
  773-324-7083
  Futons 'n' more.
- **House of Africa** • 1510 E 63rd St
  773-324-6858
  Afrocentric everything.
- **Hyde Park Produce Market** • 1226 E 53rd St
  773-324-7100
  A grocery store full of cheap produce and ethnic ingredients.
- **Hyde Park Records** • 1377 E 53rd St
  773-288-6588
  Buy/sell vintage LPs.

- **Powell's Bookstore** • 1501 E 57th St
  773-955-7780
  Famous bookstore.
- **Seminary Co-op Bookstore** •
  5751 S Woodlawn Ave
  773-752-4381
  Underground trove of scholarly books for all.
- **Toys Et Cetera** • 1502 E 55th St
  773-324-6039
  Just for fun.
- **Wesley's Shoe Corral** • 1506 E 55th St
  773-667-7463
  Quality shoes from around the world.

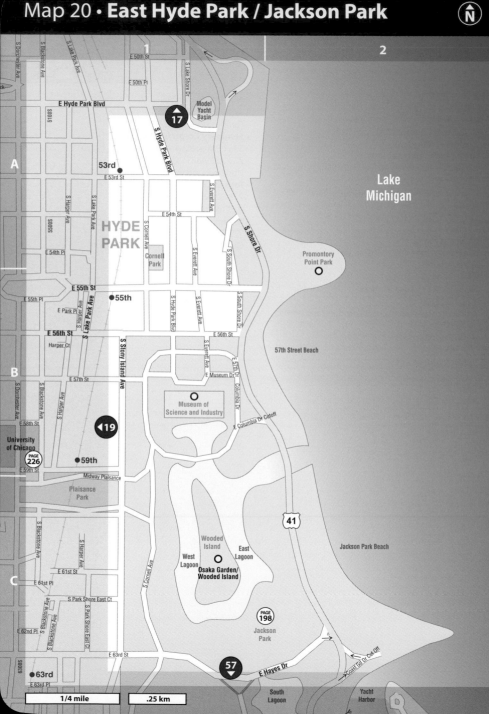

Map 20 · **East Hyde Park / Jackson Park**

Welcome to the ritzier side of Hyde Park. Here, Victorian houses span Kenwood to the north down to the **Museum of Science and Industry**, housed in a building from the 1893 World's Columbian Exposition. Check out the modern interpretations of this architectural theme on Harper and Dorchester Avenues, climb the model tractor at the Museum, and don't forget the Japanese garden in Jackson Park.

○ Landmarks

- **Jackson Park** • 6401 S Stony Island Ave
  773-256-0903
  543-acre park, site of the 1893 Columbian Exposition.
- **Museum of Science and Industry** •
  5700 S Lake Shore Dr
  773-684-1414
  Get your geek on.
- **Osaka Garden/Wooded Island** •
  6401 S Stony Island Ave
  312-742-7529
  A Japanese garden in the middle of Jackson Park— why not?
- **Promontory Point** • 5491 S Shore Dr
  312-742-5369
  Picnic with a view.

▼ Nightlife

- **The Cove Lounge** • 1750 E 55th St
  773-684-1013
  Down-and-outers meet life-of-the-minders.

Restaurants

- **Morry's Deli** • 5500 S Cornell Ave
  773-363-3800 • $
  Good on the go.
- **The Nile** • 1162 E 55th St
  773-324-9499 • $
  Varied Middle Eastern.
- **Piccolo Mondo** • 1642 E 56th St
  773-643-1106 • $$
  Best Italian in the area.
- **Siam Restaurant** • 1639 E 55th St
  773-324-9296 • $
  More Thai in Hyde Park.
- **The Snail Thai Cuisine** • 1649 E 55th St
  773-667-5423 • $
  Great Hyde Park Thai.
- **Thai 55 Restaurant** • 1607 E 55th St
  773-363-7119 • $
  Good Americanized Thai.

Map 21 • **Wicker Park / Ukrainian Village**

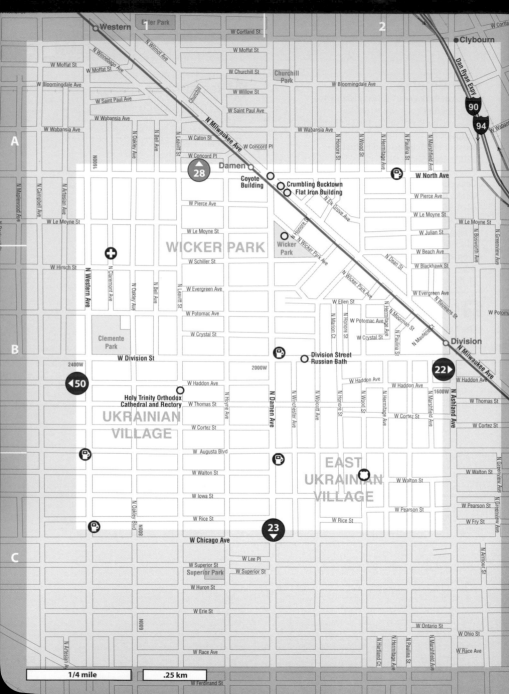

Map 21

Wicker Park/Ukrainian Village play host to a brewing battle between shiny gentrified district and gritty arts enclave. Mammoth Victorian homes and angular new constructions line the leafy and historic streets. Stroller-wielders and tattooed-cyclists share Milwaukee Avenue: each equally comfortable sipping Metropolis Coffee next to the full-size replica of a Delorean time machine at **Wormhole**. Who will ultimately claim the territory as their own? Just ask Bucktown.

○ Landmarks

- **Coyote Building** • 1600 N Milwaukee Ave
  This 12-story Art Deco building was constructed in 1929 and is currently a shrine to actor Peter Coyote.
- **Flat Iron Arts Building** • 1579 N Milwaukee Ave
  This distinct triangular-shaped building is a part of the Chicago Coalition of Community Cultural Centers and houses artist studios.

- **Holy Trinity Orthodox Cathedral and Rectory** •
  1121 N Leavitt St
  773-486-6064
  Designed by Louis Sullivan to look like a Russian cathedral.
- **Wicker Park** • W Schiller St & N Damen Ave
  The homes in this district reflect the style of Old Chicago.

Map 21

Wicker Park / Ukrainian Village

🍸 Nightlife

• **Davenport's Piano Bar** • 1383 N Milwaukee Ave
773-278-1830
Once legendary skanker bar, now yuppy fern bar.
Whattya gonna do?

• **Debonair Social Club** • 1575 N Milwaukee Ave
773-227-7990
Friendly and glam go hand in hand in this hipster
club.

• **Emporium Arcade Bar** • 1366 N Milwaukee Ave
773-697-7922
Number of retro arcade games and an extensive
beer list.

• **Empty Bottle** • 1035 N Western Ave
773-276-3600
Avant-garde jazz and indie rock. Smells like cat.

• **Estelle's Café & Lounge** • 2013 W North Ave
773-782-0450
Last time we were here a girl puked on my shoes
and no one cared.

• **Gold Star Bar** • 1755 W Division St
773-227-8700
Hear the Cars and Cash in under an hour.

• **Inner Town Pub** • 1935 W Thomas St
773-235-9795
Wicker Park art dorks.

• **Innjoy** • 2051 W Division St
773-394-2066
WP scene-ster place for drinking and local acts.

• **The Lincoln Lodge** • 2040 N Milwaukee Ave
773-251-1539
A funny night on the town.

• **Ola's Liquor** • 947 N Damen Ave
773-384-7250
Polish-Ukrainian liquor store-bar (Old Style, literally
and figuratively).

• **Phyllis' Musical Inn** • 1800 W Division St
773-486-9862
Divey hot-spot for local music acts.

• **Piece** • 1927 W North Ave
773-772-4422
Beer. Pizza.

• **Rainbo Club** • 1150 N Damen Ave
773-489-5999
Cool-kid mecca and favorite hang of local celeb
John Cusack. Enough said.

• **Revel Room** • 1566 N Milwaukee Ave
773-278-1600
Craft cocktails.

• **Standard Bar and Grill** • 1332 N Milwaukee Ave
773-904-8615
The name says it all at this newbie sports bar.

• **Subterranean** • 2011 W North Ave
773-278-6600
Semi-cool music spot.

• **The Violet Hour** • 1520 N Damen Ave
773-252-1500
Speakeasy that makes perfect drinks. Get there
early.

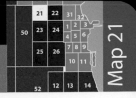
🍴 Restaurants

- **Antique Taco** • 1360 N Milwaukee Ave
  773-687-8697 • $$
  Shabby-chic taqueria.
- **Bangers & Lace** • 1670 W Division St
  773-252-6499 • $$
  Brit pub meets Wisconsin lodge.
- **Big Star** • 1531 N Damen Ave
  773-235-4039 • $$
  Pretty long wait, pretty good tacos, pretty pretty people.
- **Black Dog Gelato** • 859 N Damen Ave
  773-235-3116 • $
  Beloved local spot for the frozen Italian delicacy.
- **Blue Line Lounge & Grill** • 1548 N Damen Ave
  773-395-3700 • $$
  Mix a diner with a Martini club and here you go.
- **Cumin** • 1414 N Milwaukee Ave
  773-342-1414 • $$
  Modern take on Nepalese and Indian cuisines.
- **Dove's Luncheonette** • 1545 N Damen Ave
  773-645-4060 • $$
  Throwback diner serving up Southern/Mexican cuisine.

- **The Fifty/50** • 2047 W Division St
  773-489-5050 • $
  Great inexpensive food.
- **Flash Taco** • 1570 N Damen Ave
  773-772-1997 • $
  Cheap late-night tacos.
- **Handlebar** • 2311 W North Ave
  773-384-9546 • $$
  Bicycle-themed (largely) vegetarian restaurants decorated with off-duty messengers.
- **Hash** • 1357 N Western Ave
  773-661-2964 • $
  Beyond traditional corned beef at this 70s-inspired brunch spot.
- **Letizia's Natural Bakery** • 2144 W Division St
  773-342-1011 • $
  Addictive sweets and savory fare that holds its own
- **Lillie's Q** • 417 N Ashland Ave
  773-295-1270 • $$$
  Well-appointed, beer-friendly ecumenical barbecue joint.

Map 21

Wicker Park / Ukrainian Village

- **Milk & Honey** • 1920 W Division St
773-395-9434 • $
Heaven for breakfast.
- **Mirai** • 2020 W Division St
773-862-8500 • $$
Chic dining and good sushi.
- **Native Foods Cafe** • 1484 N Milwaukee Ave
773-489-8480 • $$
Vegan selections made daily with a West Coast vibe.
- **Oiistar** • 1385 N Milwaukee Ave
773-360-8791 • $$
Pan-Asian ramen that meanders through France and Italy.
- **Piece** • 1927 W North Ave
773-772-4422 • $$
Beer. Pizza.
- **Red Square** • 1914 W Division St
773-227-2284 • $$
Russian café and spa within the historic bathhouse.

- **Silli Kori Restaurant** • 2053 W Division St
773-384-5352 • $
Cheap, tasty, and great outdoor seating.
- **Smoke Daddy** • 1804 W Division St
773-772-6656 • $
Barbecue and blues.
- **Sultan's Market** • 2057 W North Ave
773-235-3072 • $
Cheap Middle Eastern, groceries.
- **Takito** • 2013 W Division St
773-687-9620 • $
Contemporary taqueria.
- **Tamale Spaceship** • 2296 S Blue Island Ave
312-622-4460 • $$
Where the Tamale Spaceship docks; scrumptious namesake dishes and tacos.
- **Taxim** • 1558 N Milwaukee Ave
773-252-1558 • $$
Fancy, contemporary greek. Duck gyros, anyone?
- **Thai Lagoon** • 2322 W North Ave
773-489-5747 • $$
Great Thai, funky atmosphere.

Piece serves up New Haven-style pizza with a selection of microbrews crafted in-house. **Carriage House** is trendy but good.

Shopping

- **Akira** • 1814 W North Ave
  312-438-4762
  High fashion for wannabe Eurotrash.
- **Art + Science Salon** • 1554 N Milwaukee Ave
  773-227-4247
  Beakers bring you back to science class. Student discounts available.
- **Artemio's Bakery** • 1443 N Milwaukee Ave
  773-342-0757
  Mexican sweetstuffs.
- **Asrai Garden** • 1935 W North Ave
  773-782-0680
  Unique home accents and garden doodads.
- **Beadniks** • 1937 W Division St
  773-276-2323
  DIY activity of the 00s.
- **Brobagel** • 1931 W North Ave
  773-276-2243
  Good bagels, inventive spreads, and sandwiches; they're actually brothers.
- **Cattails** • 1434 W Fullerton Ave
  773-486-1621
  A unique flower market.
- **City Soles** • 1630 N Milwaukee Ave
  773-489-2001
  You could wear your paycheck, one on each foot. But beautifully handcrafted European soles.
- **DeciBel Audio** • 1429 N Milwaukee Ave
  773-862-6700
  New and used stereo equipment.
- **Dr. Martens** • 1561 N Milwaukee Ave
  773-489-5499
  Yep, they're back.
- **John Fluevog** • 1539 N Milwaukee Ave
  773-772-1983
  Funky, eco-friendly shoes.

- **Moon Voyage** • 2010 W Pierce Ave
  773-423-8853
  Luxe boho clothing, accessories, and home goods.
- **Myopic Books** • 1564 N Milwaukee Ave
  773-862-4882
  A Wicker Park brainy-hipster institution.
- **Penelope's** • 1913 W Division St
  773-395-2351
  Pad your wardrobe with adorable at remarkably reasonable prices.
- **Personal Privilege** • 1442 N Milwaukee Ave
  773-235-6090
  Amazing vintage.
- **Quimby's** • 1854 W North Ave
  773-342-0910
  Books and music.
- **Ragstock** • 1459 N Milwaukee Ave
  773-252-4880
  Funky vintage clothes and trendy irregulars.
- **Ruby Room** • 1743 W Division St
  773-235-2323
  A "spa for the spirit" of the chic.
- **Saint Alfred** • 1531 N Milwaukee Ave
  773-486-7159
  Who knew Alfred was the patron saint of super cool sneakers?
- **The Silver Room** • 1506 E 53rd St
  773-947-0024
  Clothing and accessories.
- **Una Mae's** • 1528 N Milwaukee Ave
  773-276-7002
  A Wicker Park staple—vintage and new clothing.

Map 22 • **Noble Square / Goose Island**

GOOSE ISLAND

NOBLE SQUARE

North/Clybourn

Weed Street District

North Branch Chicago River

Turning Basin

W North Ave
North Avenue Bridge

Arandas Tire Repair & Rims

Pulaski Park/ Pulaski Fieldhouse

Pulaski Park

St Stanislaus Kostka Church

Morton Salt Elston Facility

Nelson Algren Fountain

Division

Polish Museum of America

Eckhart Park

W Division St

Chicago River

Chicago

Connector

Grand

29

21

31

24

90

94

90

1600W

800W

800W

1200W

1200W

1000N

800N

1600W

1/4 mile   .25 km

Map 22

Gritty Goose Island industry crosses paths with arty fringes of East Ukrainian Village. Lovely historical churches exist, often buried under scaffolding. Expressway access abounds, and there's a cab stand by the **Nelson Algren Fountain** on Milwaukee. Elston is a popular route to crisscross the city. Wave to the **Morton Salt Girl** as you pass by.

○ Landmarks

- **Arandas Tires & Rims** • 1511 N Ashland Ave
773-252-6292
Glowing, plastic palm trees, metal flames on the gate, and rows of tricked-out hubcaps in the second-floor, neon-lit windows above the tire bays.
- **Nelson Algren Fountain** •
Ashland Ave & Division St
Has a recent controversial addition.
- **North Avenue Bridge** • 1200 W North Ave
Wretched traffic jams; river view.
- **Polish Museum of America** •
984 N Milwaukee Ave
773-384-3352
Right-to-life painting on the side.
- **Pulaski Park Fieldhouse** • 1419 W Blackhawk St
312-742-7559
Has an outdoor swimming pool.
- **St. Stanislaus Kostka Parish** •
1351 W Evergreen Ave
773-278-2470
One of the oldest in Chicago.
- **Weed Street District** • W Weed St
Several bars and clubs in one area. Party on.

▼ Nightlife

- **The Chipp Inn** • 832 N Greenview Ave
312-421-9052
Swig a Schlitz with hipsters at this vintage storefront tavern.
- **Exit** • 1315 W North Ave
312-248-0087
Ooohhh. Dark and scary. Eighties punk/goth throwback.
- **Joe's Bar** • 940 W Weed St
312-337-3486
Huge sports bar and music venue for national bands and drunk people.

Map 22

Noble Square / Goose Island

🍴Restaurants

- **Alegrias Seafood** • 1024 N Ashland Ave
  773-252-7200 • $
  Escape grimy Ashland for this tiny Mexican playa-style seafood shack.
- **El Barco** • 1035 N Ashland Blvd
  773-486-6850 • $$
  Outdoor seating, terrific ceviche.
- **Hollywood Grill** • 1601 W North Ave
  773-395-1818 • $
  1950s style dining 24/7.
- **Jieyi Sushi** • 1178 N Milwaukee Ave
  773-292-5885 • $$
  Affordable sushi.

- **Mott Street** • 1401 N Ashland Ave
  773-687-9977 • $$$
  Family-style Asian street food.
- **NYC Bagel Deli** • 1001 W North Ave
  312-274-1278 • $
  NY-style deli, best egg salad in the city.
- **Podhalanka** • 1549 W Division St
  773-486-6655 • $
  Authentic Polish hole-in-the-wall with potato pancakes, buttery pierogies, and more.
- **Schwa** • 1466 N Ashland Ave
  773-252-1466 • $$$$
  Innovative fine dining with a hipster vibe.

Funky shops and studios cluster around Milwaukee, Division, and Ashland. Savor ceviche with humorously monikered margaritas at **El Barco**, or have your mind blown at the molecular level at **Schwa**. The clubby **Weed Street District** is a breeding laboratory, while at **Exit**, the pierced and leather-clad pretend there still is a punk scene in Chicago.

🛍 Shopping

- **Blick Art Materials** • 1574 N Kingsbury St
312 573 0110
Get creative here.
- **Circa Modern** • 1114 N Ashland Ave
773-697-9239
Thoughtfully edited collection of refurbished mid-century modern furniture pieces.
- **Dusty Groove Records** • 1120 N Ashland Ave
773-342-5800
Vinyl and CDs. Specializes in funk, soul, rare groove, now sound, and world music.
- **Figaro Antiques** • 904 W Blackhawk St
312-943-9303
Custom-made furniture from the English and French countryside.

- **Nina** • 1256 W Chicago Ave
773-486-8996
Yarn shop includes delicate, frayed thread from old saris.
- **Quick Release Bike Shop** • 1527 N Ashland Ave
773-871-3110
Savvy bike mechanics.
- **Roots & Culture** • 1034 N Milwaukee Ave
773-580-0102
Find contemporary art and a community-minded spirit at this non-profit art center.
- **Shuga Records** • 1272 N Milwaukee Ave
773-278-4085
Vinyl haven.

Map 23 • **West Town / Near West Side**

1　**2**

W Walton St

W Iowa St

W Rice St

W Rice St

21

N 800 W

Ukrainian
Cultural Center

W Chicago Ave

W Lee Pl

W Superior St

Ukrainian
National Museum

Superior
Park

W Superior St

W Huron St

A

N Western Ave

N Oakley Blvd

N Leavitt St

N Hoyne Ave

N Damen Ave

N Wolcott Ave

N Wood St

N Paulina St

N Ashland Ave

N Armour St

Smith
Park

N 600 W

W Erie St

W Ontario St

WEST TOWN

W Ohio St

N Artesian Ave

W Race Ave

N Hartland Ct

N Hermitage Ave

N Marshfield Ave

W Race Ave

W Ferdinand St

W Grand Ave

W Hubbard St
W Anson Pl

N Winchester Ave

N Seeley Ave

N Hart St

N Hermitage Ave

N Oswego St

N Marshfield Ave

W Kinzie St.

Western Ave

N Claremont Ave

N Bell Ave

W Carroll Ave

W Arbor

W Carroll

◀50

N Artesian Ave

W Fulton St

W Justine St

W Fult

W Walnut St

B

200 N

2000 W

1600 W

Ashland

W Lake St

W Rand

2400 W

N Hermitage Ave

24▶

W Maypole Ave

100 N

Union
Park

Metropolitan Missionary
Baptist Church

W Washington Blvd

NEAR WEST SIDE

W Warren Blvd

W Madison St

S Western Ave

S Oakley Blvd

S Bell Ave

S Hoyne Ave

S Seeley Ave

S Winchester Ave

United Center

N Paulina St

S Honore St

S Wood St

W Monroe St

**PAGE
242**

W Arcade Pl

W Monroe St

N Ogden Ave

S Laflin St

Rockwell
Park

S Oakley Blvd

S Bell Ave

S Hamilton Ave

S 100 S

Touhy
Park

S Wolcott Ave

S Ashland Ave

W Adams St

W Quincy St

C

W Jackson Blvd

S Hermitage Ave

W Monroe St

W Gladys Ave

S Claremont Ave

S Leavitt St

W Gladys Ave

S 300 S

W Gladys Ave

**Medical
Center**

Western

N Damen Ave

W Van Buren St

W Van B

25

Eisenhower Expy

290

S Hoyne Ave

S Marshfield Ave

S Ashland Ave

W Congress Pkwy

W Congress Pkwy

W Congress Pkwy

W Congress Pkwy

S Claremont Ave

S Bell Ave

S 600 S

W Harrison St

W Flournoy St

W Flourn

Claremont

St Lukes
Medical Center

W Flourn

1/4 mile　　.25 km

W Campbell Park Dr

W Flournoy St

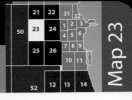

Map 23

This neighborhood was once the heart of the city's produce and meat markets. **United Center**, a.k.a. The House That Mike Built, infused energy into the area. A few food supplier warehouses still exist, mixing in with new loft conversions. Today it's a great place to spend your money, lots of your money, on locally made and grown necessaries.

○ Landmarks

- **Metropolitan Missionary Baptist Church** •
  2151 W Washington Blvd
  312-738-0053
  An attempt to find an appropriate design for
  the then-new Christian Science religion. Sold to
  Baptists in 1947.
- **Ukrainian Cultural Center** • 2247 W Chicago Ave
  773-384-6400
  A gathering place to share and celebrate Ukrainian
  culture. Yeah!
- **Ukrainian National Museum** • 2249 W Superior St
  312-421-8020
  Museum, library, and archives detail the heritage,
  culture, and people of Ukraine.
- **United Center** • 1901 W Madison St
  312-455-4500
  Statue of His Airness still draws tourists.

Nightlife

- **Cleo's** • 1935 W Chicago Ave
  312-243-5600
  Hooray for Wing Night Mondays.
- **Tuman's Tap & Grill** • 2159 W Chicago Ave
  773-782-1400
  Ukranian Village cozy bar. Respectable weekend
  dance floor.

Map 23

West Town / Near West Side

🍴Restaurants

• **A Tavola** • 2148 W Chicago Ave
773-276-7567 • $$$
Upscale Italian charm in an intimate setting.

• **Fatso's Last Stand** • 2258 W Chicago Ave
773-245-3287 • $$
Highly regarded char dogs and shrimps.

• **Old Lviv** • 2228 W Chicago Ave
773-772-7250 • $
Eastern European buffet.

• **Sunrise Café** • 2012 W Chicago Ave
773-276-8290 • $
Good coffee, good breakfast puts a smile on the face.

• **Takie Outit** • 2132 W Chicago Ave
773-252-1880 • $
Dim sum in the tum tum.

• **Tecalitlan Restaurant** • 3220 W Grand Ave
773-384-4285 • $
Popular family-style Mexican restaurant.

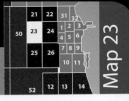
Between the architectural haven **Salvage One**, cowboy costumer **Alcala**'s, retro fashion treasure trove **Very Best Vintage**, and gardening boutique **Sprout Home**, the shopping is anything but ordinary in this neck of the woods. If you've got the leggings for it, head over to **Tuman**'s for cheap drinks and priceless people-watching.

🛍 Shopping

- **Alcala's Western Wear** • 1733 W Chicago Ave
312-226-0152
Western-wear emporium sells boots, jeans, and cowboy hats.
- **Modern Times** • 2100 W Grand Ave
312-243-5706
Vintage mid-century modern funishings.
- **Rotofugi** • 2780 N Lincoln Ave
773-868-3308
Really cool toy store with urban vinyl figures.
- **Salvage One** • 1840 W Hubbard St
312-733-0098
Warehouse of antique, vintage, and salvaged architectural pieces for home/loft restoration.

- **Sprout Home** • 745 N Damen Ave
312-226-5950
Plants and gardening supplies meet modernism.
- **Very Best Vintage** • 1346 W 28th St
312-929-2441
Huge selection of vintage threads, shoes, and accessories.

Map 24

Food distribution centers and wholesalers, warehouses, and loading docks rub shoulders with an alternative gallery scene, trendy restaurants, and hot clubs in the transitional 'hood. Once a transit abyss, a shiny new el station just opened up smack dab in the middle of both scenes. Loft-style warehouses-turned event spaces (read: weddings $$$) abound.

o Landmarks

- **First Baptist Congregational Church** •
  1613 W Washington Blvd
  312 243 8047
  Can seat 2,000 people and houses one of the largest totally enclosed organs in the country. There's a joke here somewhere.
- **Ida Crown Natatorium** • 1330 W Chicago Ave
  312-746-5490
  One of two swimming pools in the area.
- **Jackson Boulevard Historic District** •
  W Jackson Blvd & S Laflin St
  Amazingly, this cluster of preserved late-nineteenth century mansions survives in this declining area.

Nightlife

- **The Aviary** • 955 W Fulton Market
  312-226-0868
  Reservations by email only at this upscale cocktail creation destination.
- **City Winery** • 1200 W Randolph St
  312-733-9463
  Red, white, and everything in between made in-house.
- **Cobra Lounge** • 235 N Ashland Ave
  312-226-6300
  Live bands, DJ, and no TVs.
- **Five Star Bar** • 1424 W Chicago Ave
  312-850-2555
  Thirty bourbons, upscale bar menu, pool, and a stripper pole.
- **The Matchbox** • 770 N Milwaukee Ave
  312-666-9292
  Chicago's smallest bar…bar none.
- **Park Tavern** • 1645 W Jackson Blvd
  312-243-4276
  Pre-Bulls/Hawks game stop for craft beers.
- **Twisted Spoke** • 501 N Ogden Ave
  312-666-1500
  $2 Jim Beams served by Suicide Girls and free porn on Saturday nights.

Map 24

21	22	31	32
50	23	24	1	2	3
			4	5	6
25	26	7	8	9
		10	11
52	12	13	14

River West / West Town

🍴 Restaurants

- **Bella Notte** • 1374 W Grand Ave
  312-733-5136 • $$$$
  Romantic, Italian, and schmoozy.
- **Billy Goat Tavern** • 1535 W Madison St
  312-733-9132 • $
  Cheezeboiga chain.
- **The Breakfast Club & Grill** • 1381 W Hubbard St
  312-666-2372 • $$
  Brunch and then some.
- **Burger Baron** • 1381 W Grand Ave
  312-733-3285 • $
  Burgers and beer for the Everyman.
- **Butterfly Sushi Bar and Thai Cuisine** •
  1139 W Grand Ave
  312-563-5555 • $$
  Cute BYOB sushi storefront in the East Village.
- **Café Central** • 1437 W Chicago Ave
  312-243-6776 • $$
  Tasty Puerto Rican cuisine, diner décor, and
  vintage neighborhood photos.
- **Coalfire** • 1321 W Grand Ave
  312-226-2625 • $$
  Chicago's first coal-fired pizza.
- **Corned Beef Factory** • 1016 W Lake St
  312-666-2535 • $$
  Skeletal menu; everything has already been carved
  and corned.
- **Flo** • 1434 W Chicago Ave
  312-243-0477 • $$
  Mexican-influenced breakfast in a relaxed
  atmosphere.

- **Girl and the Goat** • 809 W Randolph St
  312-492-6262 • $$$
  Ultra popular gastropub from "Top Chef" favorite
  Stephanie Izard.
- **Next** • 953 W Fulton Market
  312-226-0858 • $$$$
  Advance tix required for this trendy tour of world
  cuisine.
- **Nonna's** • 925 W Randolph St
  312-690-7323 • $$
  Striving to serve exceptional Italian sandwiches.
- **Oggi Trattoria** • 1118 W Grand Ave
  312-733-0442 • $$
  One of the godfathers of the neighborhood.
- **Palace Grill** • 1408 W Madison St
  312-226-9529 • $
  Stop in for classic diner fare pre-Hawks game.
- **Salerno's Pizza and Pasta** • 1201 W Grand Ave
  312-666-3444 • $
  Tony Soprano would be proud, and full.

River West restaurants continue to build celebrity status. Foodies fight for coveted tickets to **NEXT**, recent winner of the prestigious James Beard award for Best New Restaurant. Meanwhile, Top Chef fans ogle as **Girl and the Goat** owner Stephanie Izard expedites food. Down the road, Union Park annually hosts Lolla's more chill, indie counterpart, Pitchfork Music Festival.

- **Sushi X** • 1136 W Chicago Ave
  312-491-9232 • $$
  Speakeasy sushi bar with fish so fresh they swim to your plate. BYOB.
- **Twisted Spoke** • 501 N Ogden Ave
  312-666-1500 • $
  Famous for serving smut movies and eggs simultaneously.
- **Vinnie's Sub Shop** • 1204 W Grand Ave
  312-738-2985 • $
  No frills, handy for construction workers.
- **Windy City Café** • 1062 W Chicago Ave
  312-492-8010 • $
  Small town diner feel and menu, grab a booth.

🛍 Shopping

- **65Grand** • 3252 W North Ave
  312-719-4325
  Contemporary art comes at an affordable price by local and national artists.
- **Casati Gallery** • 1500 S Western Ave
  312-421-9905
  Mid-century Italian furniture and accessories.
- **Chicago Antique Market** • 1341 W Randolph St
  312-666-1200
  Leases space to a variety of vendors.
- **Dovetail** • 1452 W Chicago Ave
  312-508-3398
  Accessories, clothing, and cabinetry. Vintage.
- **Green Grocer** • 1402 W Grand Ave
  312-624-9508
  Give the planet a high-five. Local, organic, awesome groceries.

- **Hoosier Mama Pie Company** •
  1618 W Chicago Ave
  312-243-4846
  "Keep your fork, there's pie!"
- **J.P. Graziano Grocery Co.** • 901 W Randolph St
  312-666-4587
  Spices, pasta, and dried beans in bulk.
- **Lush Wine and Spirits** • 1412 W Chicago Ave
  312-666-6900
  Wine, microbrews, and booze!
- **Marshall Erb Design** • 1847 W Grand Ave
  312-563-0000
  Architecturally centered home design.
- **Pet Care Plus** • 350 N Laflin St
  312-397-9077
  For the pet-obsessed.
- **Roots Hair Salon** • 1140 W Grand Ave
  312-666-6466
  Trendy hair salon.
- **RR #1 Chicago** • 814 N Ashland Ave
  312-421-9079
  Idiosyncratic gift shop in a 1930s pharmacy.
- **Seek Vintage** • 1433 W Chicago Ave
  312-526-3164
  Retro clothing and housewares from the "Mad Men" era.
- **Terry's Toffee** • 1009 W Armitage Ave
  312-733-2700
  Gourmet, house-made toffee, ice creams, and biscotti.

75

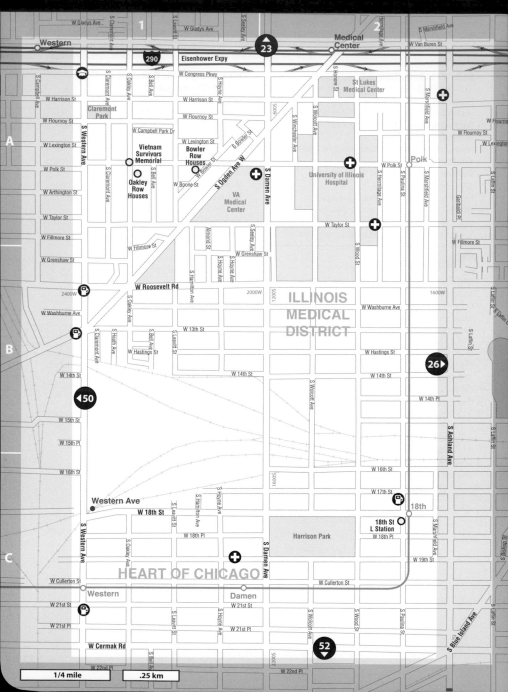

Map 25 • **Illinois Medical District**

Ⓝ

1   2

W Gladys Ave   W Gladys Ave   S Marshfield Ave

Western   Medical Center   W Van Buren St
Eisenhower Expy   23
290   W Congress Pkwy

St Lukes Medical Center

W Harrison St   W Harrison St

Claremont Park   W Flournoy St

W Campbell Park Dr   W Lexington St   Polk

A   Vietnam Survivors Memorial   Bowler Row Houses

W Polk St   Oakley Row Houses   W Boone St   University of Illinois Hospital

W Arthington St   VA Medical Center   W Taylor St

W Taylor St

W Fillmore St   W Fillmore St

W Grenshaw St   W Grenshaw St

W Roosevelt Rd

2400W   2000W   **ILLINOIS**   1600W

W Washburne Ave   **MEDICAL**   W Washburne Ave

W 13th St   **DISTRICT**

B   W Hastings St   W Hastings St

◀50   W 14th St   W 14th St   26▶

W 15th St   W 14th Pl

W 15th Pl

W 16th St   W 16th St

W 17th St

Western Ave   18th

W 18th St   18th St L Station
W 18th Pl   W 18th Pl   W 18th Pl

Harrison Park   W 19th St

C   **HEART OF CHICAGO**

W Cullerton St   W Cullerton St

Western   Damen

W 21st St   W 21st St   W 19th St

W 21st Pl   W 21st Pl

W Cermak Rd   52

W 22nd Pl   W 22nd Pl

| 1/4 mile | .25 km |

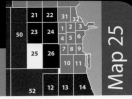

The conglomerated facilities making up the Illinois Medical District comprise the second largest such quarter in the nation. Rush University recently opened the doors to its architecturally complex but simply named Tower building, a butterfly-shaped, hard-to-miss facility at the eastern end of the medical campus. A townhouse colony of new constructions in the area house green MDs.

○ Landmarks

- **18th St L Station** • W 18th St & S Paulina St
  Gateway to Pilsen features colorful murals celebrating Mexican culture.
- **Bowler Row Houses** • 2148 W Bowler St
  Historical row houses that have survived the wrecking ball.
- **Oakley Row Houses** • 801 S Oakley Ave
  Italianate row houses that date back to 1870s.
- **Vietnam Survivors Memorial** • 815 S Oakley Ave
  Privately funded memorial was erected by vets.

Nightlife

- **Water Hole Lounge** • 1400 S Western Ave
  312-243-7988
  Neighborhood hangout hosting occasional live blues shows.

Restaurants

- **Carnitas Uruapan** • 1725 W 18th St
  312-226-2654 • $
  Carnitas muy necesitas.
- **Damenzo's** • 2324 W Taylor St
  312-421-1142 • $
  Pizza, pizza puffs, small bar.
- **Lulu's Hot Dogs** • 1000 S Leavitt St
  312-243-3444 • $
  Dog's popular with local med students.
- **Original Ferrara Bakery** • 2210 W Taylor St
  312-666-2200 • $
  Serving Italian pastries since 1908.
- **Taqueria Los Alamos** • 2157 S Damen Ave
  773-254-8095 • $
  Great taqueria.
- **TJ's Family Restaurant** • 1928 W Cermak Rd
  773-927-3349 • $
  Neighborhood diner.

Shopping

- **Textile Discount Outlet** • 2121 W 21st St
  773-847-0572
  City block-wide fabric mecca.

77

Map 26 · University Village/Little Italy/Pilsen

Map 26

Jane Addams wouldn't recognize her old 'hood today, but it retains her feisty spirit. From the nearby **National Museum of Mexican Art** (just across the border in Map 25) to the **National Italian American Sports Hall of Fame**, institutions pay homage to diverse native groups. UIC definitely holds sway around here; the area bustles with the textbook-toting set from sunup to sundown. Farther south, a proud Mexican community rubs shoulders with working creatives around the 18th and Halsted artistic epicenter of Pilsen.

o Landmarks

• **National Italian American Sports Hall of Fame** •
3417 N Harlem Ave
312 226 5566
How many Italian American sports stars do you know? DiMaggio is right out front.
• **University of Illinois at Chicago** •
1200 W Harrison St
312-996-7000
The largest university in the city.

Nightlife

• **Hawkeye's Bar & Grill** • 1458 W Taylor St
312-226-3951
Quality bar food (on the healthy side).
• **Simone's** • 960 W 18th St
312-666-8601
Hipster bar made from funky recycled materials.
• **Skylark** • 2149 S Halsted St
312-948-5275
Hip hangout for Pilsen arty crowd.
• **Thalia Hall** • 1807 S Allport St
312-526-3851
Live music and cocktails at the restored Pilsen landmark.

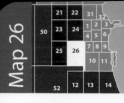

Map 26

University Village / Little Italy / Pilsen

🍴 Restaurants

- **Al's Beef** • 1079 W Taylor St
  312-226-4017 • $
  Where's the beef? Right here.
- **Birreria Reyes de Ocotlan** • 1322 W 18th St
  312-733-2613 • $$
  Local no-frills Mexican favored by Rick Bayless.
- **Carm's Beef and Italian Ice** • 1057 W Polk St
  312-738-1046 • $
  Italian subs and sausages.
- **Chez Joel** • 1119 W Taylor St
  312-226-6479 • $$$
  Delicious French cuisine in Little Italy.
- **China Dragon Restaurant** • 1737 W 18th St
  312-666-3766 • $$
  Dependably fantastic Chinese.
- **Couscous** • 1445 W Taylor St
  312-226-2408 • $$
  Middle Eastern and Maghrebin Cuisine. Unique falafel.
- **De Pasada** • 1517 W Taylor St
  312-243-6441 • $
  Inexpensive, good quality Mexican—friendly staff.
- **Decolores** • 1626 S Halsted St
  312-226-9886 • $$
  Pilsen's burgeoning arts scene and Latino culinary traditions unite.
- **Demitasse Coffee** • 1066 W Taylor St
  312-226-7666 • $
  Delightful breakfast spot.
- **Don Pedro Carnitas** • 1113 W 18th St
  312-829-4757 • $
  Mexican fast food muy authentico.
- **Dusek's** • 1227 W 18th St
  312-526-3851 • $$$
  Beer-centric dining in Thalia Hall trifecta.
- **Express Grill** • 1260 S Union Ave
  312-738-2112 • $
  A 24/7 greasy spoon with noteworthy hot dogs.

- **Golden Thai** • 1509 W Taylor St
  312-733-0760 • $
  Always busy, but there's better Thai out there.
- **Hashbrowns** • 731 W Maxwell St
  312-226-8000 • $$
  Sweet potato hashbrowns—enough said.
- **Joy Yee's Noodles** • 1335 S Halsted St
  312-997-2128 • $$
  Good Asian food, better bubble tea.
- **Kohan** • 730 W Maxwell St
  312-421-6254 • $$
  Sushi for UIC students.
- **May Street Café** • 1146 W Cermak Rd
  312-421-4442 • $
  Inexpensive, super casual pan-Latin.
- **The Rosebud** • 1500 W Taylor St
  312-942-1117 • $
  Popular with the United Center crowd.
- **Steak 'n Egger** • 1174 W Cermak Rd
  312-226-5444 • $
  24-hour comfort food.
- **Sweet Maple Cafe** • 1339 W Taylor St
  312-243-8908 • $
  Super-homey breakfast, homemade biscuits.
- **Taqueria el Milagro** • 1923 S Blue Island Ave
  312-433-7620 • $
  Good, cheap Mexican standbys from the tortilla giant.
- **Taqueria Los Comales** • 1544 W 18th St
  312-666-2251 • $
  Mexican fast food in cheerful environment.
- **Tuscany** • 1014 W Taylor St
  312-829-1990 • $$
  Elegant Taylor Street Italian.

Map 26

Sprawling over the city's Near West Side is the University of Illinois at Chicago. On your next trip to Little Italy, skip the marked up vino with your pasta. In Pilsen, local artists frequent the **Skylark**, and people travel from far and wide for the authentic Mexican food on 18th Street.

🛍Shopping

• **Conte Di Savoia** • 1438 W Taylor St
312-666-3471
European and Italian specialties.
• **Knee Deep Vintage** • 1219 W 18th St
312-850-2510
Beautiful vintage. Kindhearted proprietors.

• **Mario's Italian Lemonade** • 1068 W Taylor St
312-829-0672
The best summer treat in the city. Prepare to wait.

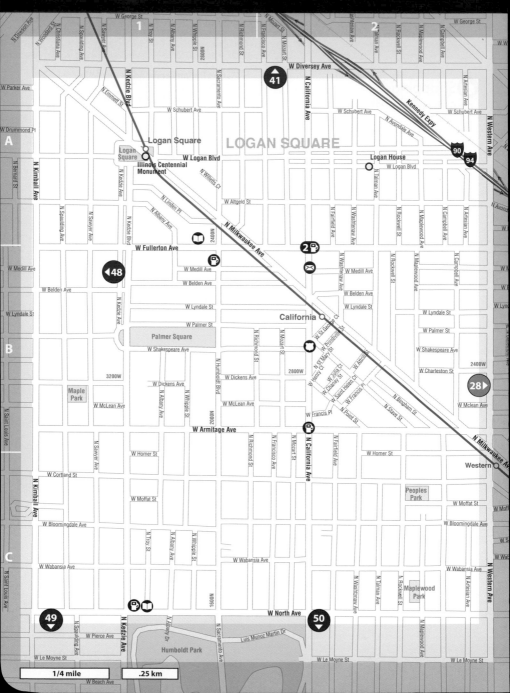

Map 27 · **Logan Square**

The natural redoubt for creative professionals fleeing higher rent and stroller gridlock in Wicker Park, Logan Square's leafy boulevards seem to sprout new bars and restaurants every month. Milwaukee forms the spread-out strip of commercial activity, where artsy bars mingle with auto shops and tasty 24-hour taquerias.

o Landmarks

- **Illinois Centennial Monument** •
  3100 W Logan Blvd
  Every city needs an obelisk or two…
- **Logan House** • 2656 W Logan Blvd
  Renowned for over-the-top holiday décor.

☿ Nightlife

- **Billy Sunday** • 3143 W Logan Blvd
  773-661-2485
  Cocktail-focused bar named after the infamous 1920s prohibitionist.
- **Boiler Room** • 2210 N California Ave
  773-276-5625
  Great beer, cocktails, pizza, and, of course, Jameson on draft (!).
- **Chicago Distilling Company** •
  2359 N Milwaukee Ave
  872-206-2774
  Vodka and whisky production (and sampling) in action.
- **Cole's** • 2338 N Milwaukee Ave
  773-276-5802
  For music buffs, free live music nightly.
- **Fireside Bowl** • 2646 W Fullerton Ave
  773-486-2700
  No longer a punk rock venue, it's just bowling now.
- **Longman & Eagle** • 2657 N Kedzie Ave
  773-276-7110
  Bourbon like nobody's business; also a restaurant and six-room inn.
- **Scofflaw** • 3201 W Armitage Ave
  773-252-9700
  Neighborhood spot with meticulously crafted gin cocktails.
- **Whirlaway Lounge** • 3224 W Fullerton Ave
  773-276-6809
  Old Style, old couches, and a truly eclectic jukebox.
- **The Whistler** • 2421 N Milwaukee Ave
  773-227-3530
  Classic cocktails, live music, and art gallery all in one!

Logan Square

🍴Restaurants

- **Azucar** • 2647 N Kedzie Ave
773-486-6464 • $$
Clubby tapas spot.
- **Bang Bang Pie Shop** • 2051 N California Ave
773-276-8888 • $
Pie, pie, and more homemade pie.
- **Buona Terra Ristorante** • 2535 N California Ave
773-289-3800 • $$
Logan Square schmoozy Italian.
- **Choi's Chinese Restaurant** •
2638 N Milwaukee Ave
773-486-8496 • $$
Good, fresh Chinese food.
- **Cozy Corner Diner & Pancake House** •
2294 N Milwaukee Ave
773-276-2215 • $
Perfect if your brunch doesn't need salmon or capers.
- **Dante's Pizzeria** • 3028 W Armitage Ave
773-342-0002 • $
NY-style crust and diverse, fun toppings.
- **El Cid II** • 2645 N Kedzie Blvd
773-395-0505 • $$
Sip a margarita on the summer patio.
- **El Nandu** • 2731 N Fullerton Ave
773-278-0900 • $$
Argentinian delicacies mixed with music.

- **Fat Rice** • 2957 W Diversey Pkwy
773-661-9170 • $$$
Fans line up early at this Portuguese-Macanese fusion spot.
- **Gaslight Coffee Roasters** • 2385 N Milwaukee Ave
$
Coffee fluent in the neighborhood dialect: house roasted, locally sourced.
- **Longman & Eagle** • 2657 N Kedzie Ave
773-276-7110 • $$
Bourbon like nobody's business; also a restaurant and six-room inn.
- **Lula** • 2537 N Kedzie Blvd
773-489-9554 • $$
Pan-ethnic nouveau for hipsters.
- **Parson's Chicken & Fish** • 2952 W Armitage Ave
773-384-3333 • $$
Comfort-y unassailable fried stuff.
- **Reno** • 2607 N Milwaukee Ave
773-697-4234 • $$
Wood-fired bagels by day, artisanal pizzas by night
- **Taqueria Moran** • 2226 N California Ave
773-235-2663 • $
Stand apart marinated pork tacos.
- **Webster's Wine Bar** • 2601 N Milwaukee Ave
773-292-9463 • $$$
Wine bar with a flair of gastropub.

Map 27

Even with a (mostly ignored) Starbucks lurking nearby, the businesses clustered around the actual square preserve the 'hood's indie status. Pick up Chicago-designed duds at **Wolfbait & B-Girls**, brave the lines at **Lula** for innovative, seasonally focused brunch, or secure a bottomless coffee and a controller for the original Nintendo at **New Wave Coffee**.

Shopping

- **Boulevard Bikes** • 2679 N Milwaukee Ave
773-235-9109
Friendly neighborhood bike shop.
- **Dill Pickle Food Co-op** • 2746 N Milwaukee Ave
773-252-2667
Tiny as an organic kumquat, but with a dense food selection.
- **Disco City Records No. 6** • 2630 N Milwaukee Ave
773-486-1495
Latin music emporium.
- **Fleur** • 2651 N Milwaukee Ave
773-395-2770
Not your mother's floral arrangements, plus handmade goods from locals.

- **Smart Bike Parts** • 3031 W Armitage Ave
773-384-3010
Unpretentious Logan Square bike shop.
- **Tusk** • 3205 W Armitage Ave
423-903-7093
Hipster-chic shop mixing vintage and new pieces.
- **Village Discount Outlet** • 2032 N Milwaukee Ave
708-388-4772
Tons of clothes and weekly specials.
- **Wolfbait & B-Girls** • 3131 W Logan Blvd
312-698-8685
Two young designers showcase funky wares by dozens of locals.

Map 28 · **Bucktown**

41	42	43	44
27	28	29	30
21	22	31	32
50	23	24	1	2	3
			4	5	6
25	26		7	8	9

Map 28

Separated from Lincoln Park by the freeway, Bucktown is not quite as well-situated, but its (slightly) more affordable real estate has brought in the young professionals in droves. Gentrification is gaining pace, with an ongoing influx of polished boutiques and hip baby stores. Meanwhile, the thriving art scene that once characterized Bucktown is all but a memory.

○ Landmarks

• **Margie's Candies** • 1960 N Western Ave
773-384-1035
The Beatles ate here.

ⓨ Nightlife

• **The Charleston** • 2076 N Hoyne Ave
773-489-4757
Yuppie dive.
• **Cortland's Garage** • 1645 W Cortland St
773-862-7877
Garage-themed bar for wannabe grease monkeys.
• **Ed and Jean's** • 2032 W Armitage Ave
773-851-8054
Your dive bar home away from home.
• **Gallery Cabaret** • 2020 N Oakley Ave
773-489-5471
Hip dive bar with local acts, attracts plenty of wannabe barflies.
• **Green Eye Lounge** • 2403 W Homer St
773-227-8851
Microbrews within crawling distance of the Blue Line Western stop.

• **Lemming's** • 1850 N Damen Ave
773-862-1688
Lite Brite works of art.
• **Liar's Club** • 1665 W Fullerton Ave
773-665-1110
Only sometimes overly hipster, otherwise rad music and good times.
• **Map Room** • 1949 N Hoyne Ave
773-252-7636
Global theme mixed with the occasional free buffet.
• **WhirlyBall** • 1825 W Webster Ave
773-486-7777
Drinking while driving bumper cars. Safety is nothing to me.

Map 28

41 | 42 | 43 | 44
27 | 28 | 29 | 30
21 | 22 | 31 | 32
50 | 23 | 24 | 1 | 2 | 3
4 | 5 | 6
25 | 26 | 7 | 8 | 9

Bucktown

🍴 Restaurants

• **Arturo's Tacos** • 2001 N Western Ave
773-772-6785 • $
24-hour taqueria boasts cheap eats and a
boisterous crowd.

• **The Bento Box** • 2246 W Armitage Ave
773-278-3932 • $$
Asian BYOB no bigger than an actual bento box.

• **The Bristol** • 2152 N Damen Ave
773-862-5555 • $$$
Charcuterie lover's dream with Mediterranean
roots.

• **Club Lucky** • 1824 W Wabansia Ave
773-227-2300 • $$
Italian retro-styled joint.

• **Coast Sushi Bar** • 2045 N Damen Ave
773-235-5775 • $$
BYOB sushi.

• **En Hakkore** • 1840 N Damen Ave
773-772-9880 • $$
Korean fusion tacos and traditional dishes.

• **Honey 1 BBQ** • 746 E 43rd St
773-285-9455 • $$
BBQ cooked in a big ole smoker. Yum.

• **Irazu** • 1865 N Milwaukee Ave
773-252-5687 • $
Hipsters and bikers gather 'round for Central
American staples.

• **Le Bouchon** • 1958 N Damen Ave
773-862-6600 • $$
Affordable, crowded French.

• **Margie's Candies** • 1960 N Western Ave
773-384-1035 • $
Immense ice cream concoctions.

• **Mindy's Hot Chocolate** • 1747 N Damen Ave
773-489-1747 • $$
Much more than just hot chocolate.

• **Owen and Engine** • 2700 N Western Ave
773-235-2930 • $$
Rustic British meals served with artisan crafted
ales.

• **Quesadilla La Reina del Sur** • 2235 N Western Ave
773-235-8807 • $
Vegan taqueria.

• **Red Hot Ranch** • 2449 W Armitage Ave
773-772-6020 • $$
All-over-the-map hot dogs open late.

• **Rio's D'Sudamerica** • 2010 W Armitage Ave
773-276-0170 • $$$$
Swanky South American for date nights.

• **Small Cheval** • 1732 N Milwaukee Ave
312-243-9712 • $$
Do one thing and do it well: burgers.

You need never be hungry, thirsty, or poorly clothed in Bucktown—or have to walk more than a block or two. Budget and upscale still co-exist; take **Margie's Candies** and **Goddess and the Grocer**. Meanwhile, **Mindy's Hot Chocolate** is stroller heaven by day, chic eatery by night. Find your niche, or better yet, do it all.

🛍 Shopping

- **Alan Design Studio** • 2134 N Damen Ave
  773-278-2345
  House and home goodies.
- **BFF Bikes** • 2056 N Damen Ave
  773-666-5153
  Female-centric bike shop.
- **Bluemercury** • 1633 N Damen Ave
  773-278-9770
  The NYC shopper's mecca.
- **Cynthia Rowley** • 1648 N Damen Ave
  773-276-9209
  Cute feminine designs that flatter the body.
- **Fjällräven** • 1708 N Damen Ave
  773-661-0277
  Swedish high-end outdoor gear.
- **The Goddess and Grocer** • 1649 N Damen Ave
  773-342-3200
  Gourmet groceries and take-out.
- **ID Chicago** • 2130 N Damen Ave
  773-755-4343
  A treasure trove of ribbons, buttons, and trim.
- **Lululemon** • 1627 N Damen Ave
  773-227-1869
  Canadian-based yoga wear brand brings soft-as-cashmere soy clothes and sleek attire.
- **p.45** • 1643 N Damen Ave
  773-862-4523
  Edgy women's boutique.
- **Pavilion** • 2055 N Damen Ave
  773-645-0924
  Antique furniture.
- **Prery** • 1714 N Damen Ave
  312-529-8162
  Fine Asian antiques.
- **Psycho Baby** • 3139 N Lincoln Ave Suite II
  773-772-2815
  Hip gear for the urban baby.
- **The Red Balloon** • 1940 N Damen Ave
  773-489-9800
  A unique store for children—toys, clothes, and furniture.
- **Robin Richman** • 2108 N Damen Ave
  773-278-6150
  Arty, indie boutique.
- **Sideshow Gallery** • 2219 N Western Ave
  773-276-1300
  Step right up at this art, antiques, and oddities boutique.
- **T-Shirt Deli** • 1739 N Damen Ave
  773-276-6266
  Pricey—but quality—custom-made T-shirts.

Map 29 · **DePaul / Wrightwood / Sheffield**

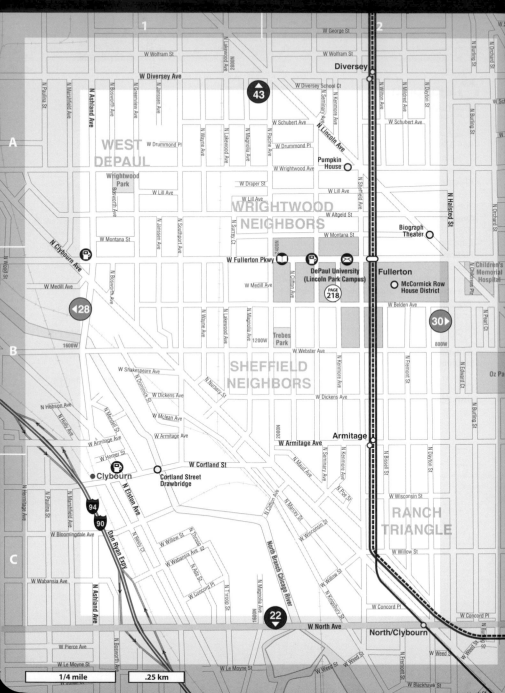

41 42 43 44
27 28 29 30
21 22 31 32
23 24 1 2 3
50 4 5 6
25 26 7 8 9
10 11

Map 29

College students rule the scene with DePaul University's central location, filling the neighborhood with fun-filled late nights and early morning walks-of-shame, while still maintaining a vibrant academic environment for both students and residents (consider the free **DePaul Art Museum**). Less raucous areas have an upscale collection of restaurants and boutiques for those who can afford to live on the charming tree-lined residential streets.

○ Landmarks

- **Cortland Street Drawbridge** •
1440 W Cortland St
Built in 1902 by John Ernst Erickson, this innovative leaf-lift bridge changed the way the world built bridges, and vice versa.
- **DePaul University** • 2400 N Sheffield Ave
312-362-8300
The country's largest Catholic university.
- **McCormick Row House District** •
800 W Chalmers Pl
Quaint example of late 19th-century urban planning and architecture.
- **Pumpkin House** • 1052 W Wrightwood Ave
A Halloween spectacle of lighted pumpkins.
- **Victory Gardens Biograph Theater** •
2433 N Lincoln Ave
773-871-3000
Site of gangster John Dillinger's infamous death in 1934.

🍸 Nightlife

- **Bird's Nest** • 2500 N Southport Ave
773-472-1502
Cheap wings, live music, and plenty of bros.
- **Delilah's** • 2771 N Lincoln Ave
773-472-2771
Punk rock dive specializing in whisky.
- **The Hideout** • 1354 W Wabansia Ave
773-227-4433
Haven for alt-country and other quirky live tune-age.
- **Irish Eyes** • 2519 N Lincoln Ave
773-348-9548
…are often crying.
- **Kincade's** • 950 W Armitage Ave
773-348-0010
Happy-hour sports bar.
- **Lincoln Hall** • 2424 N Lincoln Ave
773-525-2501
Rock concert venue serving food and drink.
- **Local Option** • 1102 W Webster Ave
773-348-2008
Neighborhood hole-in-the-wall and proud of it.
- **Rose's Lounge** • 2656 N Lincoln Ave
773-327-4000
DePaul dive chock full of tchotchkes and cheap beer.
- **Tapster** • 1059 W Wrightwood Ave
773-549-4949
Neighborhood feel-good spot.
- **Tripoli Tap** • 1147 W Armitage Ave
773-477-4400
Quality bar food.

Map 29

DePaul / Wrightwood / Sheffield

🍴 Restaurants

• **Ada Street** • 1664 N Ada St
773-234-1753 • $$$
Small plates and backyard dining tucked into an industrial corridor.

• **Ambrosia Café** • 1963 N Sheffield Ave
773-404-4450 • $
Smoothies and hookahs? Huh.

• **Butcher & the Burger** • 1021 W Armitage Ave
773-697-3735 • $$
DIY gourmet burger joint.

• **Goose Island** • 1800 N Clybourn Ave
312-915-0071 • $
Pub grub at its best.

• **Homeslice** • 938 W Webster Ave
312-789-4600 • $$
Pizza from the Pacific Northwest? Yep, it's a thing.

• **Jam 'n Honey** • 958 W Webster Ave
773-327-5266 • $$
Creative, classic breakfast restaurant also serving lunch and dinner.

• **Juno Sushi** • 2638 N Lincoln Ave
773-935-2000 • $$$$
Splurge-worthy sushi tasting menus.

• **Pequod's Pizzeria** • 2207 N Clybourn Ave
773-327-1512 • $$
Signature deep dish with a caramelized crust.

• **Sai Café** • 2010 N Sheffield Ave
773-472-8080 • $$$
Traditional sushi place.

• **Sweet Mandy B's** • 1208 W Webster Ave
773-244-1174 • $
Picture-perfect sweet shoppe.

• **Taco & Burrito House** • 1548 W Fullerton Ave
773-665-8389 • $
Super-cheap burrito shack, open very late.

Facets runs a slate of obscure art-house films and rents DVDs as well. For music, **The Hideout** draws Bloodshot Records fans with its basement rec-room ambience and **Lincoln Hall** brings musical acts into the heart of the neighborhood. Aging punk rockers tipple a vast array of spirits at **Delilah's**. Armitage Avenue boasts a variety of boutiques.

🛍 Shopping

- **Art Effect** • 934 W Armitage Ave
773-929-3600
"A modern day general store" for everything fabulous.
- **Balance Health + Wellness** •
1901 N Clybourn Ave
773-472-0560
Striving to help clients return to a state of balance.
- **Dirk's Fish** • 2070 N Clybourn Ave
773-404-3475
Carry-out fresh fish and seafood spot.
- **Jayson Home** • 1885 N Clybourn Ave
773-248-8180
Dedicated to making sure you live beautifully.
- **Lush Cosmetics** • 859 W Armitage Ave
773-281-5874
Handmade soaps and natural cosmetics— too bad they aren't edible!
- **Roy's Furniture** • 2455 N Sheffield Ave
773-248-7878
For the IKEA grad.
- **Wine Discount Center** • 1826 N Elston Ave
773-489-3454
Wine warehouse—free tastings every Saturday.

27	28	29	30
21	22	31	32
50	23	24	1 2 3
			4 5 6
25	26	7 8 9
		10 11

Map 30

Lincoln Park's yuppie vibe may strike fear into the heart of the city's hipsters, but with the famed **Steppenwolf Theatre** and cultural institutions like the **Chicago History Museum**, the **Peggy Notebaert Nature Museum**, and **Lincoln Park Zoo**'s Nature Boardwalk just for starters, the neighborhood is one of the tops in popularity for a reason. High rent and real estate prices make most want to just pay a visit.

○ Landmarks

• **Kaufmann Store and Flats** • 2312 N Lincoln Ave
One of the oldest existing buildings designed by Adler and Sullivan. It's amazing that its characteristic features have survived.

• **Lincoln Park** • N Lake Shore Dr
312-742-7726
1200-acre park along the lakefront between Streeterville and Edgewater.

• **Lincoln Park Boat Club** • 2341 N Cannon Dr
312-715-7220
Paddling, rowing, and sculling since 1910.

• **Lincoln Park Conservatory** • 2391 N Stockton Dr
312-742-7736
The place to warm up in those brutal Chicago winters.

• **Lincoln Park Cultural Center** •
2045 N Lincoln Park W
312-742-7726
Programming in visual arts for all ages.

• **Lincoln Park Zoo** • 2001 N Clark St
312-742-2000
Oldest free zoo in the U.S.

• **Midwest Buddhist Temple** • 435 W Menomonee St
312-943-7801
Enter their annual haiku contest.

• **Oz Park** • 2021 N Burling St
312-742-7898
You're not in Kansas anymore.

• **The Peggy Notebaert Nature Museum** •
2430 N Cannon Dr
773-755-5100
An oasis for adults and kids to reconnect with nature by playing with wildflowers and butterflies.

• **The Point at Diversey** •
Lakefront at Diversey Harbor
One of the best views of the skyline. Ever.

• **Steppenwolf Theatre Company** •
1650 N Halsted St
312-335-1650
The one John Malkovich, Gary Sinise, and co. started.

• **Theurer-Wrigley House** • 2466 N Lakeview Ave
Early Richard E. Schmidt (and maybe Hugh H.G. Garden) based on late-Italian Renaissance architecture.

• **Waterlily Pond** • W Fullerton Pkwy & N Cannon Dr
You might forget you're in a city.

Map 30

27	28	29	30
21	22	31	32
50	23	24	1	2	3
			4	5	6
25	26	7	8	9
		10	11

Lincoln Park

Nightlife

- **B.L.U.E.S.** • 2519 N Halsted St
773-528-1012
Smaller but notorious blues bar with an older
African American crowd.
- **The Burwood Tap** • 724 W Wrightwood Ave
773-525-2593
Chug-a-lug.
- **Glascott's** • 2158 N Halsted St
773-281-1205
Wannabe Irish joint with frat-boy written all over it.
- **Kingston Mines** • 2548 N Halsted St
773-477-4646
Chicago blues bar in a neighborhood safe for
tourists.

- **Lincoln Station** • 2432 N Lincoln Ave
773-472-8100
Back room is good for events.
- **Lion Head Pub** • 2251 N Lincoln Ave
773-348-5100
DePaul nightspot.
- **Park West** • 322 W Armitage Ave
773-929-1322
Costs extra to reserve a table.
- **The Second City** • 1616 N Wells St
312-337-3992
Drama and food in front of you.

While **Alinea** may get the most attention as the nation's most renowned restaurant, less expensive fare at spots like **Frances' Deli** (Lincoln Park's oldest) keep people coming to eat. Halsted Street's designer boutiques might be too much for some, but the bricks-and-mortar location of online consigner **eDrop-Off** saves the day for today's recessionista fashionistas.

Restaurants

- **Alinea** • 1723 N Halsted St
  312-867-0110 • $$$$$
  Conceptual experiments in fine dining.
- **Aloha Eats** • 2534 N Clark St
  773-935-6828 • $
  Tropical treats made with aloha (and Spam).
- **Boka** • 1729 N Halsted St
  312-337-6070 • $$$
  Ambitious menu, swank décor.
- **Café Ba-Ba-Reeba!** • 2024 N Halsted St
  773-935-5000 • $$$
  Noisy, bustling tapas joint.
- **Del Seoul** • 2568 N Clark St
  773-248-4227 • $$
  Cali-Korean cuisine, including Korean tacos and takes on street foods.

- **Frances' Deli** • 2552 N Clark St
  773-248-4580 • $
  Inventive deli.
- **Geja's Café** • 340 W Armitage Ave
  773-281-9101 • $$$
  Romantic fondue with live flamenco.
- **Lito's Empanadas** • 2460 N Clark St
  773-857-1337 • $
  He don't make no burritos.
- **Mon Ami Gabi** • 2300 N Lincoln Park W
  773-348-8886 • $$$
  French bistro.
- **Nookies** • 1746 N Wells St
  312-337-2454 • $
  Inventive omelettes with some strong coffee.

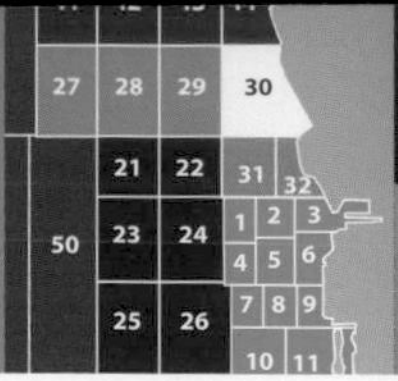

Map 30

Lincoln Park

- **Nookies Too** • 2114 N Halsted St
773-327-1400 • $
Inventive omelettes with some strong coffee.
- **North Pond** • 2610 N Cannon Dr
773-477-5845 • $$$$
Earthy contemporary American.
- **The Pasta Bowl** • 2434 N Clark St
773-525-2695 • $$
Mangia huge portions of pasta in an intimate
neighborhood joint.
- **R.J. Grunts** • 2056 N Lincoln Park W
773-929-5363 • $$
Comfy, psychedelic salad bar and burger joint.
- **Riccardo Trattoria** • 2119 N Clark St
773-549-0038 • $$$
Authentic Italian cuisine.
- **Salvatore's Ristorante** • 525 W Arlington Pl
773-528-1200 • $$$
Cute neighborhood Italian.
- **Sultan's Market** • 2521 N Clark St
312-638-9151 • $
Same great falafel in Northside digs.
- **Sushi O Sushi** • 346 W Armitage Ave
773-871-4777 • $$
Newly remodeled fresh seafood.
- **Sushi Para II** • 2258 N Clark St
773-477-3219 • $$
A.Y.C.E. sushi that's good. No, really.

- **Tandoor Char House** • 2652 N Halsted St
773-327-2652 • $$
Traditional Indian and Pakistani faire.
- **Toro Sushi** • 2546 N Clark St
773-348-7255 • $$
Worth the wait for raw fish lovers
- **Twin Anchors** • 1655 N Sedgwick St
312-266-1616 • $$
Sinatra came for the ribs and stayed for the drinks
and atmosphere.
- **Vinci** • 1732 N Halsted St
312-266-1199 • $$$
Homemade pasta raises the bar.
- **Wiener's Circle** • 2622 N Clark St
773-477-7444 • $
Classic dogs served with a generous helping of
sass.

Wiener's Circle are a Lincoln Park rite-of-passage, where the servers are infamous for their saucy attitudes. Elsewhere on the food chain, raw foodies flock to **Karyn's**. Meanwhile, **Nookies** is your greasy spoon option. Visit **Hema's Kitchen** for Indian fare and **Robinson's** for barbecue.

🛍 Shopping

- **Cocoa + Co.** • 1651 N Wells St
  312-624-8540
  Global chocolate and pastry selection.
- **Crossroads Trading Co.** • 2711 N Clark St
  773-296-2438
  Hip styles, thrift store prices.
- **Cycle Smithy** • 2468 N Clark St
  773-281-0444
  Cute Lincoln Park bike parts & repair option.
- **Dave's Records** • 2604 N Clark St
  773-929-6325
  All LPs, from Janacek to Jay-Z.
- **Graham Crackers Comics** • 3162 N Broadway
  773-665-2010
  Where good and evil meet.
- **Lori's—The Sole of Chicago** • 824 W Armitage Ave
  773-281-5655
  Designer shoes.
- **McShane's** • 815 W Armitage Ave
  773-525-0282
  Designer resale. Head on upstairs for some serious markdowns.
- **Molly's Cupcakes** • 2536 N Clark St
  773-883-7220
  Featuring "build-your-own-cupcakes."
- **Old Town Triangle** • 1763 N North Park Ave
  312-337-1938
  Don't miss their openings.
- **Urban Outfitters** • 2352 N Clark St
  773-549-1711
  Retro fun clothing, nifty gifts, and silly T-shirts.

Map 31 • **Old Town / Near North**

South Pond

Lincoln Park

PAGE 200

W Wisconsin St

W Menomonee St

W Willow St

W Saint Paul Ave

W Eugenie St

W Concord Pl
Steppenwolf Theatre

W North Ave

A

North/ Clybourn

Sedgwick

30

OLD TOWN

W Weed St

W Blackhawk St

W Schiller St

W Evergreen Ave

W Fair Pl

W Goethe St

Stanton Schiller Park

W Scott St

22

32

Clark/ Division

B

W Division St

CABRINI GREEN

Seward Park

NEAR NORTH

Washington Square Park

W Walton St

W Delaware Pl

Moody Bible Institute

1

2

W Chicago Ave

Chicago

Chicago

Loyola Univ. (Water Tower Cam)

C

Connector

90

90

Grand

Grand

1/4 mile

.25 km

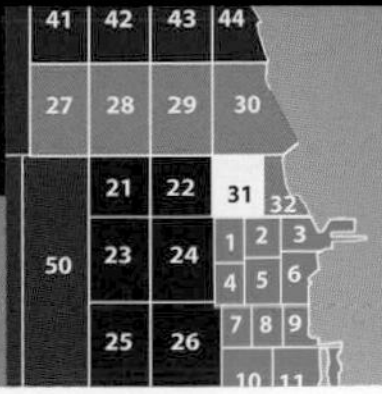

Map 31

With its narrow, cobblestoned streets lined with Queen Anne-style homes and rehabbed cottages, Old Town's appropriate moniker perfectly encapsulates its nineteenth century charms. Only a few blocks to the south, the vast land where the Cabrini Green housing project stood waits for development.

Nightlife

- **Burton Place** • 1447 N Wells St
312 664 4699
Great late night; good bar food.
- **Old Town Ale House** • 219 W North Ave
312-944-7020
Crusty old-timers meet performing arts crowd.
- **UP Comedy Club** • 230 W North Ave
312-662-4562
Stand-up and improv seven nights a week.
- **Weeds** • 1555 N Dayton St
312-943-7815
Pinball, bras, shoes, poetry, and tequila.
- **Zanies Comedy Club** • 1548 N Wells St
312-337-4027
After a few drinks, everything is funny. Well, almost.

Map 31

Old Town / Near North

🍴 Restaurants

- **Big & Little's** • 860 N Orleans St
  312-943-0000 • $
  Fish-and-chips shack run by Hell's Kitchen contestant.
- **Dining Room at Kendall College** •
  900 N North Branch St
  312-261-3660 • $$
  When students cook: Gourmet food, layman price!
- **The Fireplace Inn** • 1448 N Wells St
  312-664-5264 • $$$
  Popular spot to watch sports.
- **The Goddess and Grocer** • 901 N Larrabee St
  312-988-9870 • $
  Newest installment of the gourmet to-go food shop.
- **Kamehachi** • 1531 N Wells St
  312-664-3663 • $$$
  Sushi favorite with upstairs lounge.
- **Old Jerusalem** • 1411 N Wells St
  312-944-0459 • $$
  Cheap, good food.
- **Old Town Pour House** • 1419 N Wells St
  312-477-2800 • $$
  A beer lover's dream come true.
- **Topo Gigio** • 1516 N Wells St
  312-266-9355 • $$$
  Crowded, reliable Italian. Big outdoor area.

Map 31

Wells Street provides the neighborhood's main drag with an array of new and old restaurants, shops, and stores. **The Spice House**, **The Fudge Pot** and **Up Down Cigar** have been providing Old Town with their specialty items for over half a century. Second City's **UP Comedy Club** breathes new life into the city's historic comedy scene.

🛍 Shopping

• **Bike and Roll Chicago- Oak St Beach** •
N Lake Shore Dr & E Oak St
312-729-1000
Bike rentals.

• **Design Within Reach** • 755 W North Ave
312-585-9600
North side outpost for the hip modern design studio.

• **The Fudge Pot** • 1532 N Wells St
312-943-1777
A chocolate institution.

• **Judy Maxwell Home** • 1349 N Wells St
312-787-9999
Joan Cusack's funhouse of hyperbolic gifts, art, and, ahem, more.

• **La Fournette** • 1547 N Wells St
312-624-9430
Pitch-perfect French bakery.

• **Old Town Gardens** • 1555 N Wells St
312-266-6300
Beautiful plants and flowers.

• **REI** • 905 W Eastman St
312-951-6020
This co-op gets Chicago outdoors.

• **The Spice House** • 1512 N Wells St
312-274-0378
Spice up your cooking.

• **Up Down Cigar** • 1550 N Wells St
800-587-3696
One stop shopping for the cigar enthusiast.

• **Village Cycle Center** • 1337 N Wells St
312-751-2488
Good urban cycling store.

Map 32 · **Gold Coast / Mag Mile**

Map 32

	41	42	43	44
	27	28	29	30
	21	22	31 32
50	23	24	1 2 3 / 4 5 6
	25	26	7 8 9 / 10 11

Between the sticky bars on Division Street and the Viagra Triangle pick-up joints on Rush, it's easy for locals to find fun. But the Gold Coast/Mag Mile (actually only eight-tenths of a mile, but who's counting?) is also home to some of Chicago's most impressive architecture, libraries (including **The Newberry**), and beautiful beaches. The **Museum of Contemporary Art** and the **Lookingglass Theatre** add to the cultural cache.

○ Landmarks

• **Charnley-Persky House** • 1365 N Astor St
312-573-1365
Louis Sullivan and Frank Lloyd Wright designed this national historic landmark. Go look before it becomes a CVS.

• **John Hancock Observatory** • 875 N Michigan Ave
888-875-8439
Zone out the tourists, and focus in on the prettiest view of the city.

• **Lake Shore Drive Apartments** •
860 Lake Shore Dr
Less is more—by Mies van der Rohe.

• **The Newberry** • 60 W Walton St
312-943-9090
There's plenty to offer at this humanities library.

• **Old Playboy Mansion** • 1340 N State Pkwy
You have no idea what happened here.

• **Water Tower Place** • 835 N Michigan Ave
312-440-3580
Huge shopping—6 floors—Marshall Field's, er, Macy's.

Nightlife

- **Butch McGuire's** • 20 W Division St
  312-787-4318
  Wet T-shirt contests anyone?
- **Coq d'Or** • 140 E Walton St
  312-787-2200
  A sophisticate's lodge: red leather, dark wood, torch singers, and pub food.
- **Dublin's** • 1050 N State St
  312-266-6340
  Gold Coast pub.

- **The Hangge Uppe** • 14 W Elm St
  312-337-0561
  No-frills, all fun, dancing. Hip hop upstairs, '80s classics downstairs.
- **Shenannigan's** • 16 W Division St
  312-642-2344
  Another Rush vicinity hellhole.
- **The Signature Room** • 875 N Michigan Ave
  312-787-9596
  It's the view, not the food. Proposal hot spot.
- **Zebra Lounge** • 1220 N State Pkwy
  312-642-5140
  Garish, cramped piano bar—in other words, it's a hit.

Gucci, Chanel, Barney's, Prada; they don't call it the Gold Coast for nothing. But with Urban Outfitters and H&M, there's plenty for us regular folk as well. On Rush Street, Ikram is a favorite of FLOTUS Michelle Obama. Speaking of whom, the Obamas' favorite Chicago date place happens to be Spiaggia.

🍴 Restaurants

- **Cafe des Architectes** • 20 E Chestnut St
312-324-4063 • $$$
French Mediterranean with late kitchen.
- **Carmine's** • 1043 N Rush St
312-988-7676 • $$$
Crowded and pricey Italian.
- **Fornetto Mei** • 107 E Delaware Pl
312-573-6301 • $$$
Authentic pizza. Deep dish lovers stay away.
- **Freshii** • 835 N Michigan Ave
312-202-9009 • $
Tasty wraps, hold the guilt.
- **Gaylord** • 100 E Walton St
312-664-1700 • $
Improbably named Indian spot.
- **Gibson's Steakhouse** • 1028 N Rush St
312-266-8999 • $$$$$
If you love steak, get a reservation.
- **Hugo's Frog Bar & Fish House** • 1024 N Rush St
312-640-0999 • $$$
Hearty seafood.
- **Le Petit Paris** • 260 E Chestnut St
312-787-8260 • $$$$
Shhh! Don't tell anyone about this Gallic hideaway!

- **Mario's Table** • 21 W Goethe St
312-944-0199 • $$$
Classic Italian neighborhood gem.
- **Mr. J's Dawg & Burger** • 822 N State St
312-943-4679 • $
Mom-and-pop burger joint.
- **Nico Osteria** • 1015 N Rush St
312-994-7100 • $$$
Seafood-focused Italian hot spot.
- **Original Pancake House** • 22 E Bellevue Pl
312-642-7917 • $$
The apple waffle/pancake is right!
- **Spiaggia** • 980 N Michigan Ave
312-280-2750 • $$$$$
One of Chicago's best—gorgeous lake view and Italian cuisine.
- **Sprinkles Cupcakes** • 50 E Walton St
312-573-1600 • $
Gourmet cupcakes for the Gold Coast crowd.
- **Tavern on Rush** • 1031 N Rush St
312-664-9600 • $$$$
Summer mainstay, American menu.
- **Tempo Cafe** • 6 E Chestnut St
312-943-4373 • $$
24/7 patio seating and huge menu.

Map 32

Gold Coast / Mag Mile

🛍 Shopping

- **900 North Michigan Shops** • 900 N Michigan Ave
312-915-3916
High-end mall stores.
- **Bravco** • 43 E Oak St
312-943-4305
For those who like to be pampered.
- **Chanel** • 65 E Oak St
312-787-5500
Classic, expensive clothing, accessories, and fragrances.

- **Club Monaco** • 900 N Michigan Ave
312-787-8757
Fashion-forward clothing that doesn't try too hard.
- **Gucci** • 900 N Michigan Ave
312-664-5504
Tom Ford's alluring and provocative clothes and accessories.
- **H&M** • 840 N Michigan Ave
855-466-7467
European department store taking Chicago by storm.
- **Hendrickx Belgian Bread Crafter** •
100 E Walton St
312-649-6717
Artisanal breads, croissants, and coffee with a European flair.
- **Hermes** • 25 E Oak St
312-787-8175
Fancy scarves and more.

Map 32

Nico Osteria specializes in seafood. If you want something to take home, head over to **Goddess and the Grocer**. Speaking of being thrifty, dodge admission to the **Hancock Observatory** by getting a martini at **The Signature Room** at the 96th two floors above.

- **Ikram** • 15 E Huron St
  312-587-1000
  The First Lady's favorite boutique.
- **Independence** • 171 N Sangamon St
  312-675-2105
  Menswear and shoes made in the Land of Liberty.
- **Intermix** • 40 E Delaware Pl
  312-640-2922
  The NYC shoppers' mecca.
- **Lululemon** • 930 N Rush St
  312-915-0627
  Canadian-based yoga wear brand brings soft-as-cashmere soy clothes and sleek attire.
- **More Cupcakes** • 1 E Delaware Pl
  312-951-0001
  The BLT cupcake is exactly what it sounds like.
- **Prada** • 30 E Oak St
  312-951-1113
  Expensive, but delightful, clothing and accessories.

- **Tod's** • 121 E Oak St
  312-943-0070
  Italian luxury leather goods.
- **Ultimate Bride** • 106 E Oak St
  312-337-6300
  Bridal gear.
- **Water Tower Place** • 835 N Michigan Ave
  312-440-3580
  Marshall Fields, er, Macy's.

Map 33 • **Rogers Park / West Ridge**

Dobson St

W Howard St

W Jerome St

W Birchwood Ave

N Francisco Ave

N California Ave

N Fairfield Ave

N Talman Ave

N Maplewood Ave

N Artesian Ave

N Oakley Ave

N Bell Ave

N Ridge Blvd

N Birchwo

W Fargo Ave

W Fargo A

W Jarvis Ave

W Jarvis

A

N Kedzie Ave

W Sherwin Ave

N Albany Ave

N Sacramento Ave

W Chase Ave

Rogers Park

N Campbell Ave

N Claremont Ave

N Bell Ave

N Hamilton Ave

W Chas

W Jarlath St

7200N

High Ridge
YMCA

Bernard
Horwich JCC

W Touhy Ave

W Touhy Ave

ROGERS PARK AND WEST RIDGE

W Fitch Ave

W Estes Ave

◀**46**

B

W Estes Ave

W Greenleaf Ave

W Greenleaf Ave

N Washtenaw Ave

Indian Boundary
Park

W Lunt Ave

2800W

N Rockwell St

2400W

34▶

Lerner
Park

W Coyle Ave

W Morse Ave

N Oakley Ave

N Bell Ave

N Hamilton Ave

W Farwell Ave

6000N

W Pratt Ave

W Pratt Ave

N Kedzie Ave

Chippewa
Park

N Richmond St

N Francisco Ave

N Mozart St

N Maplewood Ave

N Western Ave

W North Shore Ave

Warren Park

W Albion Ave

C

N Troy Ave

N Albany Ave

N Whipple St

N Sacramento Ave

N California Ave

N Fairfield Ave

N Washtenaw Ave

N Claremont Ave

N Oakley Ave

N Bell Ave

N Leavitt St

N Hamilton Ave

N Hoyne

W Arthur Ave

Thillen's
Stadium

N Kedzie Ave

W Devon Ave

6000N

W Devon Ave

Croatian
Cultural Center

India
Town

N Talman Ave

N Rockwell St

N Maplewood Ave

N Campbell Ave

N Artesian Ave

35
▼

36
▼

W Highland Ave

W Rosemont Ave

| 1/4 mile | .25 km |

W Thorne A

Map 33

As far north as you can go and still be in Chicago, Rogers Park and West Ridge have an intimate, residential feel drawing many families and retirees. Edged by Evanston, the neighborhoods are dotted with gardens, parks, sledding hills, baseball diamonds, tennis courts, and jogging paths. Thanks in part to the spill-over population from East Rogers Park and Loyola University, Rogers Park has a tendency to attract academics and students.

○ Landmarks

- **Bernard Horwich JCC** • 3003 W Touhy Ave
773-761-9100
Community center with programming for kids/adults, pool/fitness center, senior center, and sports leagues.
- **Croatian Cultural Center** • 2845 W Devon Ave
773-338-3839
A place where families can relax, socialize, and congregate. Intended to benefit the Croatian community in Chicago (duh).
- **India Town** • W Devon Ave & N Washtenaw Ave
Features Indian and Pakistani shops, grocery stores, restaurants, and more.
- **Indian Boundary Park** • 2500 W Lunt Ave
773-764-0338
Petting zoo, tennis courts, chess tables, ice rink, skate park, batting cages, spray pool, with seasonal community center classes.
- **Thillens Stadium** • 6404 N Kedzie Ave
312-742-4870
Chicago landmark. 16 softball fields. Features little league baseball and various other games and benefits.
- **Warren Park** • 6790 N Damen Ave
773-262-6314
Seasonal free entertainment, pony rides, ethnic food festivals, amusement park rides, arts and crafts, winter sledding hill, baseball diamond, picnic pavilions, and dog play areas.

Nightlife

- **Cary's Lounge** • 2251 W Devon Ave
773-743-5737
Locals' place to go for a nightcap.
- **McKellin's** • 2800 W Touhy Ave
773-973-2428
Cozy neighborhood Irish bar.
- **Mullen's** • 7301 N Western Ave
773-465-2113
Food until 1 am (10 pm on Sundays).

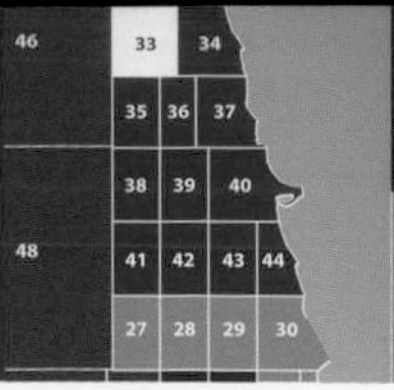

Map 33
Rogers Park / West Ridge

🍴 Restaurants

- **Arya Bhavan** • 2508 W Devon Ave
  773-274-5800 • $$
  Northern Indian all-vegetarian.
- **Candlelite** • 7452 N Western Ave
  773-465-0087 • $
  Rogers Park pizza institution, with cocktails.
- **Hema's Kitchen** • 2439 W Devon Ave
  773-338-1627 • $$
  Like naan other.
- **Sabri Nihari** • 2502 W Devon Ave
  773-465-3272 • $$
  No booze here but super way delicious Pakistani food. Let's go!
- **Siam Pasta** • 7416 N Western Ave
  773-274-0579 • $
  Bangkok home cookin'.
- **Sukhadia Sweets and Snacks** •
  2559 W Devon Ave
  773-338-5400 • $
  Indian sweet maker and caterer.

- **Tiffin** • 2536 W Devon Ave
  773-338-2143 • $$
  Most upscale Indian restaurant on Devon, yet moderately priced.
- **Uru-Swati** • 2629 W Devon Ave
  773-381-1010 • $
  Vegetarian fast food and snacks.

Most of the action in West Rogers Park occurs on Devon Avenue. Thanks to the culture clash of its residents, the international marketplace is supported by dozens of inexpensive Indian and Pakistani restaurants, Bollywood video rentals, the best saris you'll find in the States, and a slew of Islamic, Russian, and Jewish bookstores and bakeries.

Shopping

- **AutoZone** • 2555 W Touhy Ave
  773-764-5277
  Stuff for your car.
- **JR Dessert Bakery** • 2841 W Howard St
  773-465-6733
  Over 20 flavors of cheesecakes.
- **Levinson's Bakery** • 2856 W Devon Ave
  773-761-3174
  Always fresh!

- **Resham's** • 2540 W Devon Ave
  773-764-9692
  Saris and fabric fill the store.
- **Taj Sari Palace** • 2658 W Devon Ave
  773-338-0177
  Beautiful Indian clothing and accessories.
- **Tel-Aviv Kosher Bakery** • 2944 W Devon Ave
  773-764-8877
  Under the supervision of Rabbi Chaim Goldzweig!

Map 34 · **East Rogers Park**

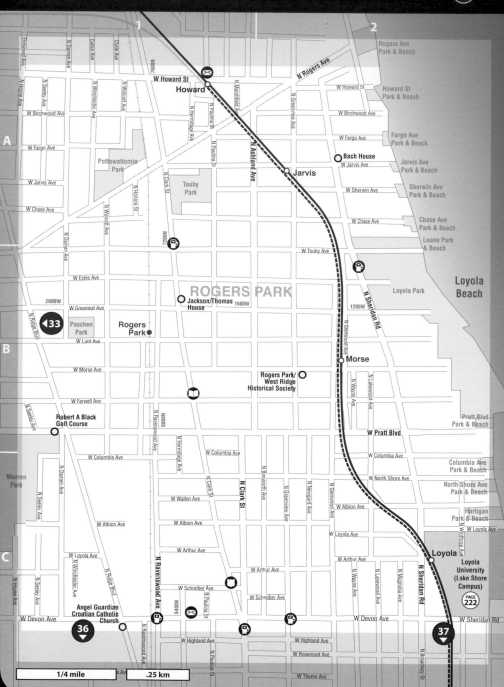

Elmwood Ave
N Horne Ave
N Damen Ave
N Seeley Ave
Callan Ave
N Winchester Ave
Clyde Ave
N Wolcott Ave
N Marshfield Ave
N Hermitage Ave
N Paulina St
N Paulina St
7400W

W Howard St
Howard ✉

N Ashland Ave
N Greenview Ave
N Rogers Ave
Rogers Ave
Park & Beach

W Birchwood Ave
W Howard St
Howard St
Park & Beach

W Birchwood Ave

A

W Fargo Ave
W Fargo Ave
Fargo Ave
Park & Beach

Pottawattomie
Park

N Clark St
N Honore St

Touhy
Park

Bach House
W Jarvis Ave
Jarvis Ave
Park & Beach

● **Jarvis**

W Jarvis Ave
W Sherwin Ave
Sherwin Ave
Park & Beach

W Chase Ave
N Wolcott Ave
W Chase Ave
Chase Ave
Park & Beach

Leone Park
& Beach

7200N
Ⓟ

N Damen Ave
W Estes Ave
W Touhy Ave
Ⓟ

Loyola Park
N Sheridan Rd
**Loyola
Beach**

2000W
ROGERS PARK
W Greenleaf Ave

◀**33**
Paschen
Park

N Ridge Blvd
● Jackson/Thomas
House
1600W
1200W

**Rogers
Park**●

W Lunt Ave
N Glenwood Ave
B

W Morse Ave
● **Morse**

W Farwell Ave
N Bosworth Ave
N Greenview Ave
N Newgard Ave
N Wayne Ave
N Lakewood Ave
▢
● Rogers Park/
West Ridge
Historical Society

**Robert A Black
Golf Course**
N Seeley Ave
N Ravenswood Ave
N Hermitage Ave
Pratt Blvd
Park & Beach

○
W Pratt Blvd
W Pratt Blvd

Warren
Park
N Damen Ave
W Columbia Ave
W Columbia Ave
W Columbia Ave
Columbia Ave
Park & Beach

N Seeley Ave
N Clark St
W Wallen Ave
W North Shore Ave
North Shore Ave
Park & Beach

W Albion Ave
N Glenwood Ave
W Albion Ave
Hartigan
Park & Beach

W Albion Ave
N Ridge Blvd
W Arthur Ave
W Loyola Ave
N Winthrop Ave
W Loyola Ave

N Ravenswood Ave
W Loyola Ave
W Arthur Ave
● **Loyola**
C

N Winchester Ave
W Arthur Ave
W Schreiber Ave
N Wayne Ave
N Lakewood Ave
N Magnolia Ave
N Sheridan Rd
**Loyola
University
(Lake Shore
Campus)**

N Hoyne Ave
N Seeley Ave
N Ridge Blvd
▢
W Schreiber Ave
W Schreiber Ave
PAGE
222

**Angel Guardian
Croatian Catholic
Church**
Ⓟ
✉
N Paulina St
W Devon Ave
N Sheridan Rd

36
▼
Ⓟ
W Highland Ave
W Highland Ave
37
▼

N Ravenswood Ave
W Rosemont Ave
N Broadway St
W Sheridan Rd

1/4 mile · .25 km
W Thome Ave

Map 34

East Rogers Park is stitched together with Loyola students, civic-minded young professionals, new immigrants, old hippies, and blue-collared middle-class denizens. While densely populated and lively, the neighborhood's seams sometimes show as crime and gang activity continues to be a problem. The draw of easy access to public transportation, lakefront accessibility, cultural diversity, and Loyola's campus makes East Rogers Park an inexpensive, colorful neighborhood to reside in.

o Landmarks

- **Angel Guardian Croatian Catholic Church** •
  6346 N Ridge Ave
  773-262-0535
  1905 red-brick Romanesque church. Turn-of-the-century German stained glass windows by Franz Mayer and F. X. Zettler.
- **Bach House** • 7415 N Sheridan Rd
  One of Frank Lloyd Wright's final "small" houses, c. 1915.
- **Jackson/Thomas House** • 7053 N Ridge Ave
  Lovely Italianate home dates back to 1874.
- **Loyola University of Chicago** •
  1032 W Sheridan Rd
  773-274-3000
  One of the largest Jesuit universities in the US.
- **Robert A. Black Golf Course** • 2045 W Pratt Blvd
  773-596-2581
  The newest Chicago Park District course. 2,300-yard, par 33 layout for all skill levels.
- **Rogers Park/West Ridge Historical Society** •
  7363 N Greenview Ave
  773-764-4078
  Photos/memorabilia/historical documents of the community's history detailing its ethnic diversity.

Nightlife

- **Jackhammer** • 6406 N Clark St
  773-743-5772
  Gay bar with a welcoming neighborhood vibe.
- **Touche** • 6412 N Clark St
  773-465-7400
  Drunken gay leather bar.

Map 34

East Rogers Park

🍴 Restaurants

- **Buffalo Joe's** • 1841 W Howard St
773-764-7300 • $
Wings and fast food carryout spot, with a soul food flava.
- **Capt'n Nemos** • 7367 N Clark St
773-973-0570 • $
Free soup sample while you wait at this always jovial local sandwich chain.
- **Caribbean American Bakery** • 1539 W Howard St
773-761-0700 • $
Jamaican bakery featuring meat pies, pastries, and jerk chicken for carryout.
- **El Famous Burrito** • 7047 N Clark St
773-465-0377 • $
Best greasy burrito in Chicago.
- **Ghareeb Nawaz** • 2032 W Devon Ave
773-761-5300 • $
Indo-Pakistani lunch counter on the east side of the strip.
- **Good to Go Jamaican Jerk and Juice Bar** •
711 W Howard St
847-868-8226 • $$
Jamaican cuisine.

- **Insomnia Cookies** • 6470 N Sheridan Rd
773-839-4662 • $
Late night cookie delivery service hits Loyola.
- **Jamaica Jerk** • 3357 Dempster St
847-933-3304 • $
Jamaican comfort food best for carry-out.
- **Noon Hour Grill** • 6930 N Glenwood Ave
773-338-9494 • $
Korean diner and grill is neighborhood favorite.
- **Pho's Spicier Thai Cuisine** • 1320 W Devon Ave
773-973-0504 • $
Look beyond the grim exterior for freshly prepared Thai.
- **Sauce and Bread Kitchen** • 6338 N Clark St
773-942-6384 • $
Sandwiches starring the café's housemade hot sauces and baked goods.
- **Tamales Lo Mejor de Guerrero** • 7024 N Clark St
773-338-6450 • $
Carry-out tamales so good, they may ruin "the tamale guy" for you.
- **Taste of Peru** • 6545 N Clark St
773-381-4540 • $
Barebones spot for cheap, authentic Peruvian food.

Cheap eats abound if you know where to look in East Rogers Park (hint: follow the students). Health-nuts will feel at home in the **Heartland Café** which features a gift shop, open mic nights, and live music. Head to Clark Street where Mexican eateries offering authentic food at low prices dot the area, while Howard Street's **Caribbean American Bakery** gives you a sweet taste of Afro-Caribbean culture. The **Jackhammer** complex of gay bars offers something for everyone—a sports bar, a fern bar, and a leather bar, all in one.

Shopping

- **The Armadillo's Pillow** • 6753 N Sheridan Rd
773-761-2558
Score some paperbacks for cheap.
- **Flatts & Sharpe Music Company** •
6749 N Sheridan Rd
773-465-5233
Cheap guitars ($150), offering lessons and music accessories.

- **Marjen Furniture** • 1536 W Devon Ave
773-338-6636
Cheap futons, dorm furniture.
- **Romanian Kosher Sausage Co.** • 7200 N Clark St
773-761-4141
Kosher meat and poultry.

Map 35 • **Arcadia Terrace / Peterson Park**

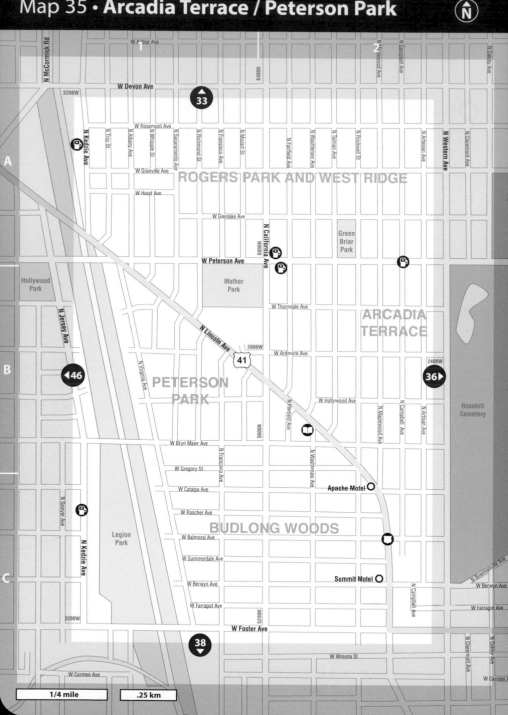

Map 35

This quiet enclave snuggled between the Chicago River and Rosehill Cemetery is home to many Koreans, Middle Easterners, and Eastern Europeans. Real estate agents tout this hood as an up-and-comer, as the seedy motels on Lincoln Avenue, once reputable, are being torn down one-by-one due to their decrepit conditions and increasingly bad reputations, and new condos dot the skyline. Arcadian Terrace and Peterson Park are becoming increasingly desirable for young families priced out of Ravenswood and Andersonville.

○ Landmarks

- **Apache Motel** • 5535 N Lincoln Ave
773-728-9400
Another sleazy motel on Lincoln with cool vintage signs.

🍸 Nightlife

- **Hidden Cove** • 5336 N Lincoln Ave
773-275-6711
Sports bar with trivia, darts, and karaoke.
- **Lincoln Karaoke** • 5526 N Lincoln Ave
773-895-2299
Korean karaoke parlor with bar and private party rooms.
- **Yeowoosai** • 6248 N California Ave
773-465-7660
Korean food and private karaoke rooms.

🍴 Restaurants

- **The Angry Crab** • 5665 N Lincoln Ave
773-784-6848 • $$$
Crowds pack in for spicy Cajun seafood.
- **Charcoal Delights** • 3139 W Foster Ave
773-583-0056 • $
Great gyros to go.
- **Fondue Stube** • 2717 W Peterson Ave
773-784-2200 • $$
Fun fondue!
- **IHOP** • 5929 N Lincoln Ave
773-769-1550 • $
It's an IHOP for Pete's sake. What else do you need to know?
- **Pueblito Viejo** • 5429 N Lincoln Ave
773-784-9135 • $$
Adorable Columbian village-theme with live music on weekends.
- **Wolfy's Hot Dogs** • 2734 W Peterson Ave
773-743-0207 • $
Dine-in and carry-out dogs, burgers, and such.
- **Woo Chon** • 5744 N California Ave
773-728-8001 • $
Authentic Korean BBQ. Brusque but oddly fun service.

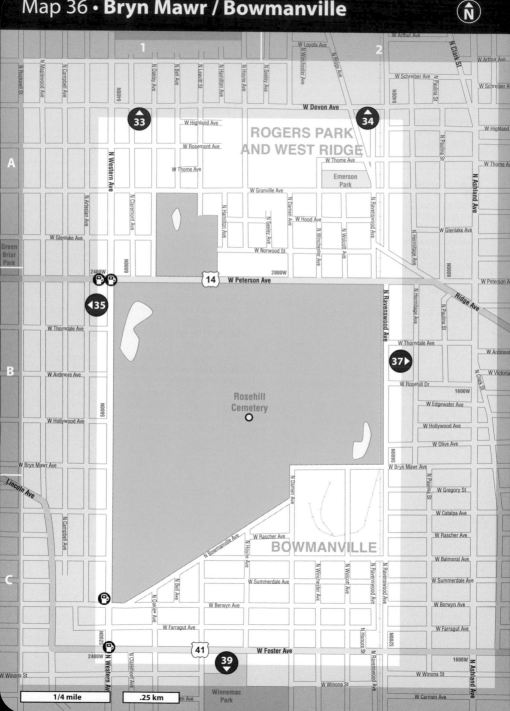

Map 36 · **Bryn Mawr / Bowmanville**

N

1

2

W Arthur Ave

W Loyola Ave

N Clark St

W Arthur Ave

W Schreiber Ave

N Paulina St

W Schreiber Ave

N Rockwell St

N Maplewood Ave

N Campbell Ave

N 1600N

N Oakley Ave

N Bell Ave

N Leavitt St

N Hamilton Ave

N Hoyne Ave

N Seeley Ave

W Winchester Ave

N Ridge Ave

N 1600N

W Devon Ave

33

34

N Ashland Ave

W Highland Ave

W Highland Ave

ROGERS PARK

W Rosemont Ave

AND WEST RIDGE

N Paulina St

A

N Artesan Ave

W Thorne Ave

N Western Ave

W Thome Ave

W Thome Ave

N Claremont Ave

Emerson
Park

W Granville Ave

N Hamilton Ave

N Damen Ave

W Hood Ave

N Wolcott Ave

N Ravenswood Ave

N Hermitage Ave

W Glenlake Ave

Green
Briar
Park

W Glenlake Ave

N 1600N

N Seeley Ave

N Winchester Ave

W Norwood St

N 1600N

2400W

2000W

N 1600N

W Peterson Ave

14

W Peterson Ave

Ridge Ave

W Peterson A

35

N Ravenswood Ave

N Hermitage Ave

N Paulina St

N Clark St

W Thorndale Ave

W Thorndale Ave

W Ardmore

B

W Ardmore Ave

W Thorndale Ave

37

W Victoria

N 5600N

W Rosehill Dr

1600W

W Hollywood Ave

W Edgewater Ave

Rosehill
Cemetery

W Hollywood Ave

N 5600N

W Olive Ave

W Bryn Mawr Ave

W Bryn Mawr Ave

N Paulina St

W Gregory St

Lincoln Ave

N Damen Ave

W Catalpa Ave

N Campbell Ave

W Rascher Ave

W Rascher Ave

N Bowmanville Ave

N Hoyne Ave

N Winchester Ave

N Wolcott Ave

N Ravenswood Ave

W Balmoral Ave

BOWMANVILLE

C

N Bell Ave

N Oakley Ave

W Summerdale Ave

W Summerdale Ave

W Berwyn Ave

N Ravenswood Ave

N Honore St

W Berwyn Ave

W Farragut Ave

N 2400N

W Farragut Ave

N Claremont Ave

41

W Foster Ave

39

N Western Ave

2400W

1600W

W Winona St

W Winona St

N Carmen Ave

1/4 mile

.25 km

Winnemac
Park

W Carmen Ave

Map 36

Old fashioned iron lamp posts line Bryn Mawr's charming historic district while young families push strollers, walk dogs, and have brunch. Bryn Mawr/Bowmanville also boasts **Rosehill Cemetery**, a 350-acre Chicago landmark that is the final resting place for luminaries like Montgomery Ward, Richard Sears, Oscar Mayer, several Chicago mayors, and one Vice President (Charles Gates Dawes).

○ Landmarks

- **Rosehill Cemetery** • 5800 N Ravenswood Ave
773-561-5940
Chicago's historical glitterati entombed among unsurpassed sculpture and architecture.

Nightlife

- **Big Joe's** • 1818 W Foster Ave
773-784-8755
Corner bar endorsed by the Windy City Darters.
- **Bobbie's Runaway** • 5305 N Damen Ave
773-271-6488
Mr. Winkie holds court here.
- **Fireside Restaurant & Lounge** •
5739 N Ravenswood Ave
773-561-7433
Good late-night bar with above average grub.
- **K's Dugout** • 1930 W Foster Ave
773-561-2227
Drink and watch sports, drink and watch sports, drink and…

Restaurants

- **Fireside Restaurant & Lounge** •
5739 N Ravenswood Ave
773-561-7433 • $$
Cajun-tinged barfood and late kitchen.
- **Greenhouse Inn** • 6300 N Ridge Ave
773-273-4182 • $
Church and bridge groups meet for homemade soups.
- **Pauline's** • 1754 W Balmoral Ave
773-561-8573 • $
Weekend breakfast hotspot; try the famous five-egg omelet, if you must.
- **San Soo Gab San** • 5247 N Western Ave
773-334-1589 • $$
Do-it-yourself Korean barbeque at 4 am.
- **Yes Thai** • 5211 N Damen Ave
773-878-3487 • $
Noodles and curries in a cozy atmosphere.

Shopping

- **Target** • 2112 W Peterson Ave
773-761-3001
All you need, under one roof.

Map 37 · **Edgewater / Andersonville**

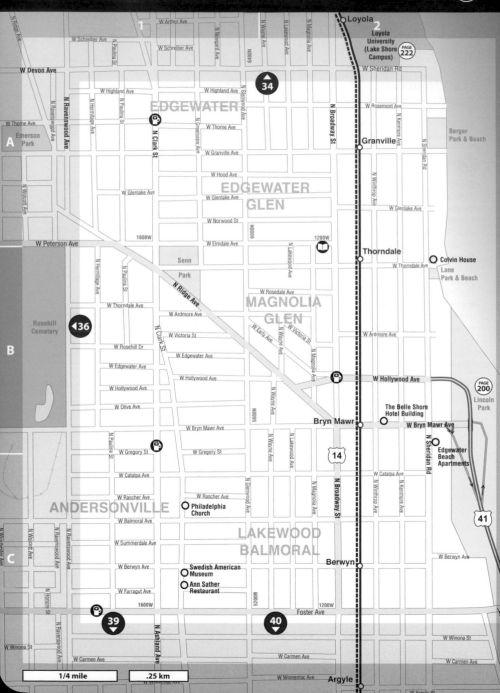

Map 37

A century ago, Chicago had a robust Swedish population whose epicenter was Andersonville. The Swedish influence remains, dotting the stroll-friendly commercial areas with Swedish businesses and restaurants, but gentrification is slowly creeping in with swelling property taxes and encroaching big chains. Lakefront community Edgewater is a liberal, pretty paradise and features Chicago's gay beach at Hollywood.

○ Landmarks

- **Belle Shore Apartment Hotel** •
  1062 W Bryn Mawr Ave
  Former homes of roaring 1920s nightlife, now historic landmarks restored to their former glory as apartments.
- **Colvin House** • 5940 N Sheridan Rd
  Designed by George Maher and built in 1909.
- **Edgewater Beach Apartments** •
  5555 N Sheridan Rd
  The big pink building symbolizing the end of the lakeshore bike path.
- **Philadelphia Church** • 5437 N Clark St
  Complete with can't-miss neon sign.
- **Swedish American Museum** • 5211 N Clark St
  773-728-8111
  Everything you want to know about Swedish culture, which is more than you thought.

ⓨ Nightlife

- **@tmosphere** • 5355 N Clark St
  773-784-1100
  Trendy gay bar with dance floor and DJs.
- **Farraguts** • 5240 N Clark St
  773-728-4903
  Neighborhood dive, less yuppie than Simon's.
- **Granville Anvil** • 1137 W Granville Ave
  773-973-0006
  Gay old-timers drink here.
- **Marty's Martini Bar** • 1511 W Balmoral Ave
  773-944-0082
  Compact and classy.
- **Moody's Pub** • 5910 N Broadway St
  773-329-5694
  Best beer garden in the city. Long wait times.
- **Simon's Tavern** • 5210 N Clark St
  773-878-0894
  Thrift-store-attired hipsters and Swedish nautical theme.
- **Sovereign Liquors** • 6202 N Broadway St
  773-274-0057
  Cheap, laidback neighborhood joint frozen in time.

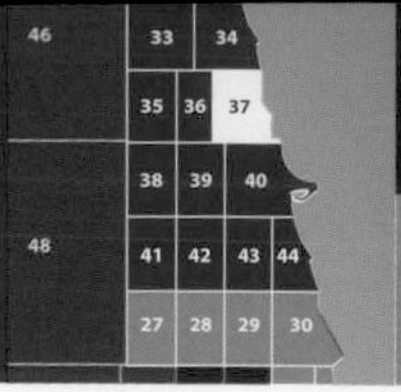

Map 37

Edgewater / Andersonville

🍴 Restaurants

- **Andies** • 5253 N Clark St
  773-784-8616 • $$
  Fresh Middle Eastern in airy atmosphere.
- **Ann Sather** • 1147 W Granville Ave
  773-274-0557 • $
  Swedish breakfast classic.
- **Anteprima** • 5316 N Clark St
  773-506-9990 • $$$
  This cozy A-Ville Italian just feels right.
- **Big Jones** • 5347 N Clark St
  773-275-5725 • $$$
  High falutin' Southern chow.
- **Edgewater Beach Cafe** • 5545 N Sheridan Rd
  773-275-4141 • $$$
  Neighborhood Frenchie in the pink building.
- **Ethiopian Diamond** • 6120 N Broadway St
  773-338-6100 • $$$
  Visit for jazz on Fridays.
- **George's Ice Cream and Sweets** • 5306 N Clark St
  773-271-7600 • $
  Ice cream of every flavor. Fat Elvis tastes the best.

- **Indie Café** • 5951 N Broadway St
  773-561-5111 • $$
  Thai and sushi. Yummy and cheap.
- **Jin Ju** • 5203 N Clark St
  773-334-6377 • $$$
  Upscale Korean.
- **M. Henry** • 5707 N Clark St
  773-561-1600 • $$
  Stylish brunch option in Andersonville.
- **Moody's Pub** • 5910 N Broadway St
  773-329-5694 • $
  Burgers only, but the best.
- **Ras Dashen** • 5844 N Broadway
  773-506-9601 • $$
  Traditional Ethiopian comfort food; vegan-friendly.
- **Reza's** • 5255 N Clark St
  773-561-1898 • $$
  Many Persian options, leftovers for lunch the next day.
- **Svea** • 5236 N Clark St
  773-275-7738 • $
  Adorable, tiny Swedish diner.
- **Tanoshii** • 5547 N Clark St
  773-878-6886 • $$
  Order from the chef for innovative sushi.
- **Taste of Lebanon** • 1509 W Foster Ave
  773-334-1600 • $
  Dingy room, rock-bottom prices, above-average Middle Eastern fare.

No other neighborhood rewards a weekend afternoon ramble like Andersonville. **Big Jones** serves up high falutin' Southern chow and **Ann Sather** is a Swedish breakfast classic. Follow an indulgent meal with a stroll down Clark Street, populated with independently owned shops with international wares including the **Swedish Bakery**.

Shopping

- **Alamo Shoes** • 5321 N Clark St
  773-784-8936
  Large selection for the soles from local retailer.
- **Andersonville Galleria** • 5247 N Clark St
  773-878-8570
  Indie mall with over 90 vendors.
- **Broadway Antique Market** • 6130 N Broadway St
  773-743-5444
  BAM! Calling all mall rats and antique freaks—one of America's most reviewed antique stores.
- **The Brown Elephant** • 5404 N Clark St
  773-271-9382
  Resale shop benefits local HIV clinic.
- **Brownstone Antiques** • 5234 N Clark St
  773-878-9800
  Cluttered estate sale finds.
- **Cassona** • 5241 N Clark St
  773-506-7882
  Gorgeous home furnishings.
- **Early to Bed** • 5044 N Clark St
  773-271-1219
  Woman-oriented grown-up toys. Boy friendly.

- **Gary's Cycle Shop** • 6317 N Clark St
  773-743-4201
  Crunchy Edgewater bike repair & parts.
- **Gethsemane Garden Center** • 5739 N Clark St
  773-878-5915
  Like mini-trip to a botanical garden; but you can take it home.
- **The Hutch** • 1550 W Olive St
  773-506-0406
  Recreate your grandmother's kitchen (delicious baked goods not included).
- **Middle East Bakery & Grocery** •
  1512 W Foster Ave
  773-561-2224
  So good, so cheap.
- **Roost** • 5634 N Clark St
  773-506-0406
  Cute furniture for your cute home.
- **Scout** • 5221 N Clark St
  773-275-5700
  Beautiful urban antiques.
- **Women & Children First** • 5233 N Clark St
  773-769-9299
  World's biggest feminist bookstore.

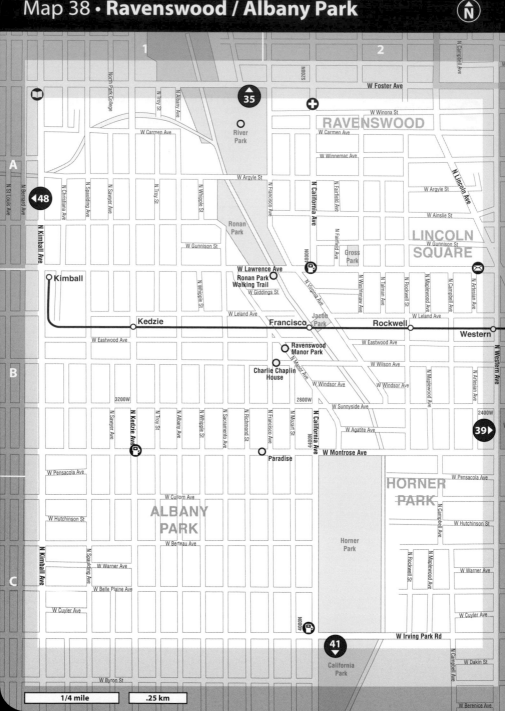

Map 38 • **Ravenswood / Albany Park**

N

1   2

N Campbell Ave

W Foster Ave

RAVENSWOOD

W Winona St

N 3025

W Carmen Ave

W Carmen Ave

River Park

W Winnemac Ave

A

N St Louis Ave

N Bernard Ave

N Kimball Ave

W Argyle St

N Christiana Ave

N Spaulding Ave

N Sawyer Ave

N Troy St

N Whipple St

N Francisco Ave

N California Ave

N Fairfield Ave

N Fairfield Ave

W Argyle St

N Lincoln Ave

◄ 48

Ronan Park

W Ainslie St

LINCOLN SQUARE

W Gunnison St

W Gunnison St

Gross Park

N Washtenaw Ave

N Talman Ave

N Rockwell St

N Maplewood Ave

N Campbell Ave

N Artesian Ave

Kimball

W Lawrence Ave

Ronan Park Walking Trail

N 3000

N Virginia Ave

W Giddings St

W Leland Ave

W Leland Ave

Kedzie

W Whipple St

Francisco   Jacob Park

Rockwell

Western

N Western Ave

W Eastwood Ave

W Eastwood Ave

Ravenswood Manor Park

W Wilson Ave

B

3200W

Charlie Chaplin House

N Manor Ave

W Windsor Ave

W Windsor Ave

N Maplewood Ave

N Artesian Ave

2800W

W Sunnyside Ave

2400W

N Sawyer Ave

N Kedzie Ave

N Troy St

N Albany Ave

N Whipple St

N Sacramento Ave

N Richmond St

N Francisco Ave

N Mozart St

N California Ave

W Agatite Ave

39 ►

N 4700

W Montrose Ave

Paradise

W Pensacola Ave

HORNER PARK

W Pensacola Ave

N Campbell Ave

W Cullom Ave

W Hutchinson St

ALBANY PARK

W Hutchinson St

W Berteau Ave

Horner Park

N Rockwell St

N Maplewood Ave

C

N Kimball Ave

N Spaulding Ave

W Warner Ave

W Warner Ave

W Belle Plaine Ave

W Cuyler Ave

W Cuyler Ave

N 4000

W Irving Park Rd

41 ▼

California Park

W Byron St

W Dakin St

N Campbell Ave

1/4 mile   .25 km

W Berenice Ave

35	36	37
38	39	40
48	41	42	43	44
27	28	29	30
21	22	31	32

Map 38

Once home to Charlie Chaplin, and hallowed jogging ground of infamously incarcerated Governor Rod "Blago" Blagojevich, a Ravenswood local, the quarter-mile section of Ravenswood known as The Manor has been a charming riverside haven for generations of Chicago's elite. Farther west, Albany Park boasts the distinction of being one of the nation's most culturally diverse 'hoods, a diversity reflected in local shops where you'll find the kim chee shelved between taramasalata and queso quesadillas.

○ Landmarks

- **Charlie Chaplin House** • 4637 N Manor Ave
  Charlie Chaplin's home during his Essanay studio stint.
- **Ravenswood Manor Park** • 4626 N Manor Ave
  It's just a tiny triangle wedged between the non-elevated L and several streets, but it's ground zero for garden sales, neighborhood associations, dogs, kids, and community activity.
- **River Park** • 5100 N Francisco Ave
  312-742-7516
  More than 30 acres of park, including one of the few city canoe launches.
- **Ronan Park Nature Trail** • 3000 W Argyle St
  These boots are made for…walking!

○ Nightlife

- **Montrose Saloon** • 2933 W Montrose Ave
  773-463-7663
  Classic Chicago "Old Style." No cell phones, please.
- **The Peek Inn** • 2825 W Irving Park Rd
  773-267-5197
  Cool little dive worth a peek.

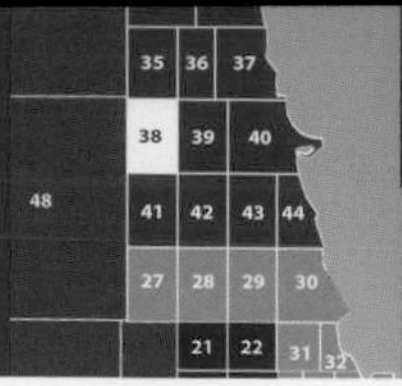

Map 38

Ravenswood / Albany Park

🍴Restaurants

- **Arun's** • 4156 N Kedzie Ave
  773-539-1909 • $$$$$
  Worldwide rep for four-star prix fixe Thai.
- **Brasa Roja** • 3120 W Montrose Ave
  773-866-2252 • $$
  Friendly Columbian place specializing in flame-roasted chicken.
- **Golden Crust Pizzeria** • 4620 N Kedzie Ave
  773-539-5385 • $
  Honkin' portions of the Italian-American comfort food of yore.
- **Goosefoot** • 2656 W Lawrence Ave
  773-942-7547 • $$$$$
  Upscale Contemporary American cuisine nestled in Chicago's North Side.
- **Lutz Café & Pastry Shop** • 2458 W Montrose Ave
  773-478-7785 • $$
  If Grandma was German, she would serve these pastries.

- **Nhu Lan's Bakery** • 2612 W Lawrence Ave
  773-878-9898 • $
  Vietnamese sandwich shop.
- **Noon O Kabab** • 4701 N Kedzie Ave
  773-279-8899 • $
  Bring a doggie bag for day-after lunch.
- **Rockwell's Neighborhood Grill** •
  4632 N Rockwell St
  773-509-1871 • $
  Familiar bar food and brunchtime favorites in a friendly atmosphere.
- **Salam** • 4636 N Kedzie Ave
  773-583-0776 • $
  Home of the 19-cent falafel.
- **Thai Valley** • 4600 N Kedzie Ave
  773-588-2020 • $
  BYOB Thai restaurant with lunch specials.

If you're in the mood for halal meat or in the market to purchase a hookah, North Kedzie around Lawrence Avenue is a magnificent Middle Eastern mélange of grocery stores and restaurants. If, on the other hand, you're in the mood for a wild night, be prepared to hail a cab. There isn't much of a nightlife in this charming but sleepy neighborhood.

Shopping

- **Lincoln Antique Mall** • 3115 W Irving Park Rd
  773-604-4700
  Mid-sized antique mall.
- **Village Discount Outlet** • 4027 N Kedzie Ave
  866-545-3836
  Tons of clothes and weekly specials.

Map 39 • Ravenswood / North Center

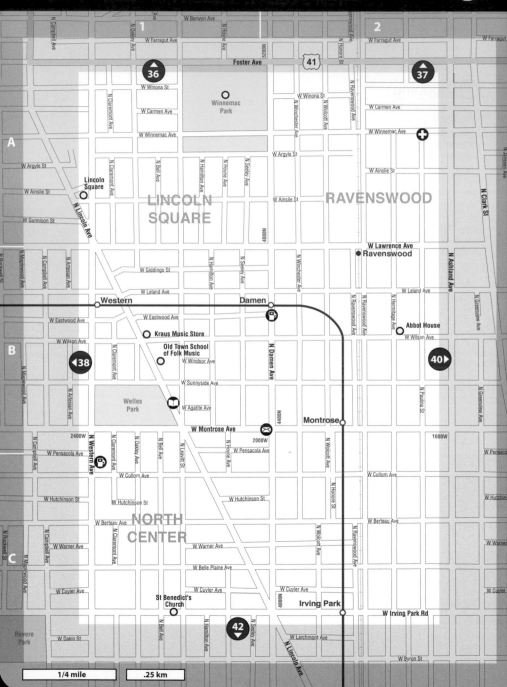

Map 39

Ravenswood and North Center are by and large the hip place to be seen pushing an expensive stroller. Lincoln Square is its epicenter, featuring plenty of wine stores and bars with stroller parking. It's not all yuppie, though.

○ Landmarks

- **Krause Music Store** • 4611 N Lincoln Ave
  It's easy to overlook this Louis Sullivan beauty on a bustling commercial strip.
- **Lincoln Square** • 4800 N Lincoln Ave
  773-728-3890
  A virtual tour through a European-style neighborhood.

- **Old Town School of Folk Music** •
  4544 N Lincoln Ave
  773-728-6000
  Northern expansion of beloved Chicago institution. Classes and concert venue.
- **St. Benedict Parish & School** •
  2215 W Irving Park Rd
  773-588-6484
  The namesake of the St. Ben's neighborhood.
- **Winnemac Park** • 5001 N Leavitt St
  312-742-5101
  Cute neighborhood park, replete with families and children playing.

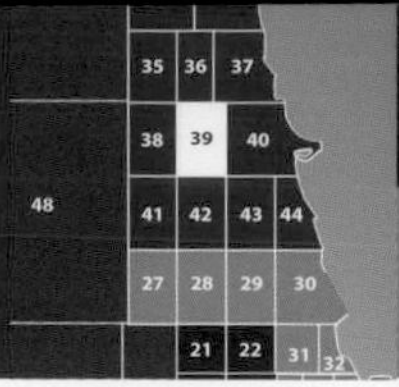

Map 39

Ravenswood / North Center

35	36	37	
38	39	40	
41	42	43	44
27	28	29	30
21	22	31	

48

⍾ Nightlife

- **Celtic Crown Public House** • 4301 N Western Ave
  773-588-1110
  Great specials without over-Irishing it!
- **Daily Bar & Grill** • 4560 N Lincoln Ave
  773-561-6198
  Bar food in retro ambiance.
- **The Globe Pub** • 1934 W Irving Park Rd
  773-871-3757
  Great music venue gone sports bar.
- **The Grafton** • 4530 N Lincoln Ave
  773-271-9000
  Outstanding bar food and friendly atmosphere.
- **Half Acre Beer Company** • 4257 N Lincoln Ave
  773-754-8488
  Where cans met craft beer.

- **Koval Distillery** • 4241 N Ravenswood Ave
  312-878-7988
  Tour, sip, and mix in the whisky wonderland.
- **Laschet's Inn** • 2119 W Irving Park Rd
  773-478-7915
  Pull on the Lederhosen!
- **O'Donovan's** • 2100 W Irving Park Rd
  773-478-2101
  It's a neighborhood bar. You can watch sports.
- **Oakwood 83** • 1959 W Montrose Ave
  773-327-2785
  Glorified version of your uncle Frank's basement.
- **Ravenswood Station** • 4709 N Damen Ave
  773-878-9400
  One-time dive, the rail rocks in Ravenswood.
- **Resi's Bierstube** • 2034 W Irving Park Rd
  773-472-1749
  Wear your lederhosen.
- **Wild Goose** • 4265 N Lincoln Ave
  773-281-7112
  Guy's bar. Cheap eats, TVs, and games.

By day, local yuppies shop at places like the **Book Cellar**, a cute bookshop cum wine café, and browse-friendly **Merz Apothecary**. By night, a stretch of Lincoln Avenue becomes restaurant row featuring mouth-watering international fare including **Opart Thai** and **Spacca Napoli**. The **Davis Theater** sates cinephiles with their no-frills, low-priced flicks.

🍴Restaurants

- **Bistro Campagne** • 4518 N Lincoln Ave
  773-271-6100 • $$
  Organic French fare in a cozy room.
- **Budacki's Drive-In** • 4739 N Damen Ave
  773-561-1322 • $
  Artery clogging late-night eats.
- **Café Selmarie** • 4729 N Lincoln Ave
  773-989-5595 • $$
  Bright, clean, bakery/cafe with wine and beer.
- **Diner Grill** • 1635 W Irving Pk Rd
  773-248-2030 • $
  Home to the infamous "Slinger." Motto: Eat it here, leave it somewhere else.
- **Elizabeth** • 4835 N Western Ave
  773-681-0651 • $$$$$
  Communal dining at its finest.
- **Essence of India** • 4601 N Lincoln Ave
  773-506-0002 • $$
  Traditional northern Indian food, fancier than Devon St.

- **Glenn's Diner** • 1820 W Montrose Ave
  773-506-1720 • $$
  Fish-focused American fare.
- **House of Wah Sun** • 4319 N Lincoln Ave
  773-477-0800 • $
  Chinese/Cantonese/Mandarin eatery.
- **La Amistad** • 1914 W Montrose Ave
  773-878-5800 • $
  No fusion here, just reliable Mexican.
- **Margie's Candies** • 1813 W Montrose Ave
  773-348-0400 • $
  Ridiculously decadent sundaes and homemade confections.
- **Orange Garden** • 1942 W Irving Park Rd
  773-525-7479 • $$
  Over seventy years of Cantonese cooking.
- **Snappy's Shrimp House** • 1901 W Irving Park Rd
  773-244-1008 • $
  Frozen or friend shrimp to go.
- **Spacca Napoli** • 1769 W Sunnyside Ave
  773-878-2420 • $$
  Neapolitan-style pizza in Ravenswood.
- **Sticky Rice** • 4018 N Western Ave
  773-588-0133 • $
  No frills storefront, serves amazing Thai for cheap!

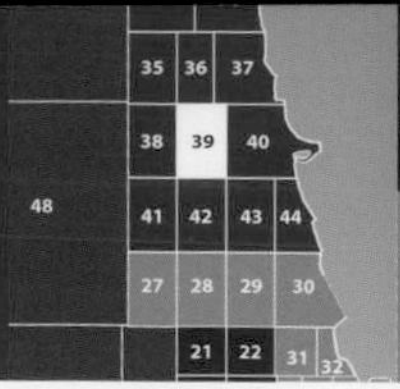

Map 39

35 36 37
38 39 40
48 41 42 43 44
27 28 29 30
21 22 31 32

Ravenswood / North Center

🛍 Shopping

- **Augusta Food and Wine** • 2312 W Leland Ave
  773-784-2314
  Select offerings of wine, cheese, olives, and other gourmet fare.
- **Book Cellar** • 4736 N Lincoln Ave
  773-293-2665
  Book store/coffee shop/wine bar. Also has sandwiches.
- **Chicago Soccer** • 4839 N Western Ave
  773-271-2255
  All things soccer store.
- **The Chopping Block** • 4747 N Lincoln Ave
  773-472-6700
  Gourmet cooking utensils and cooking classes.

- **Dark Tower Comics & Collectibles** •
  4835 N Western Ave
  773-654-1490
  Comics with extra awesome service.
- **Fleet Feet Sports** • 4762 N Lincoln Ave
  773-271-3338
  Runner's mecca.
- **Gallimaufry Gallery** • 4712 N Lincoln Ave
  773-728-3600
  Artisan crafts including instruments, incense, stone fountains.

Katerina's, on an unassuming stretch of Irving Park, features regular live gypsy music along with local acts. **Koval Distillery** offers classes, tours, and plenty of bottled varieties of whiskey to take home. For beer, **Half Acre** fills growlers at their tap room. **The Globe Pub** is just a great Irish bar.

- **Hazel** • 1835 W Montrose Ave
773-769-2227
Stylish gifts and jewelry, plus an extensive stationery section.
- **Laurie's Planet of Sound** • 4639 N Lincoln Ave
773-271-3569
Funky CD shop with unpretentious service.
- **Margie's Candies** • 1813 W Montrose Ave
773-348-0400
Second generation of a Chicago classic.
- **Merz Apothecary** • 4716 N Lincoln Ave
773-989-0900
German and other imported toiletries, herbal supplements, etc. The original.
- **Mineralogy Jewelry** • 1944 W Montrose Ave
773-780-0811
Terrariums and other home goods.
- **Nadeau** • 4433 N Ravenswood Ave
773-728-3497
This furniture warehouse may change your life.
- **Neighborly** • 1909 W Division St
773-840-2456
Your friendly print, design, and gift shop.

- **Old Town School Music Store** •
4544 N Lincoln Ave
773-751-3398
Guitars and such.
- **Quake Collectibles** • 4628 N Lincoln Ave
773-878-4288
Vintage toys and fun!
- **Ravenswood Used Books** • 2005 W Montrose Ave
773-593-9166
General used, classic literature.
- **Rock N Roll Vintage** • 4727 N Damen Ave
773-878-8616
Guitars galore.
- **Timeless Toys** • 4749 N Lincoln Ave
773-334-4445
Old-fashioned toys.

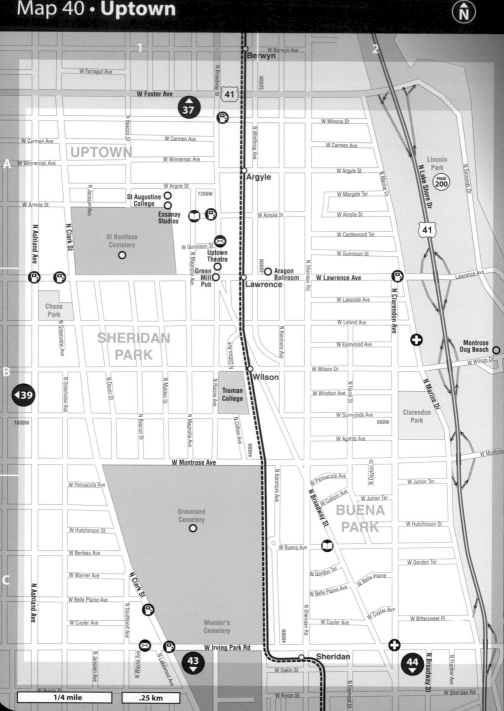

Map 40 · **Uptown**

N

1
2

W Berwyn Ave
Berwyn

W Farragut Ave

W Foster Ave

37

41

W Winona St

W Carmen Ave

UPTOWN

W Carmen Ave

W Carmen Ave

W Winnemac Ave

W Winnemac Ave

W Argyle St

Lincoln
Park
PAGE
200

A

W Winnemac Ave

W Argyle St

Argyle

N Broadway St

N Winthrop Ave

N Beacon St

N Janssen Ave

N Clark St

W Ainslie St

St Augustine
College

1200W

Essanay
Studios

St Boniface
Cemetery

N Magnolia Ave

W Margate Ter

W Ainslie St

W Ainslie St

W Castlewood Ter

N Marine Dr

N Lake Shore Dr

N Simonds Dr

41

W Gunnison St

Uptown
Theatre

Green
Mill
Pub

Lawrence

N Clifton Ave

W Gunnison St

N Sheridan Rd

Aragon
Ballroom

W Lawrence Ave

W Lakeside Ave

Lawrence Ave

N Clarendon Ave

N Ashland Ave

N Greenview Ave

Chase
Park

SHERIDAN
PARK

W Leland Ave

W Eastwood Ave

Montrose
Dog Beach

B

39

1600W

N Greenview Ave

N Dover St

N Maiden St

N Beacon St

N Magnolia Ave

N Racine Ave

N Clifton Ave

Truman
College

Wilson

W Wilson Dr

N Kenmore Ave

W Wilson Dr

W Windsor Ave

N Hazel St

W Sunnyside Ave

W Agatite Ave

N Marine Dr

800W

Clarendon
Park

W Wilson Dr

W Montrose Ave

W Pensacola Ave

W Hutchinson St

W Berteau Ave

W Warner Ave

W Belle Plaine Ave

N Ashland Ave

N Clark St

N Southport Ave

Graceland
Cemetery

N Kenmore Ave

W Pensacola Ave

W Cullom Ave

N Broadway St

N Dayton St

W Junior Ter

W Junior Ter

BUENA
PARK

W Buena Ave

N Sheridan Rd

W Gordon Ter

W Belle Plaine

W Belle Plaine Ave

W Hutchinson St

W Gordon Ter

C

W Cuyler Ave

W Cuyler Ave

W Cuyler Ave

W Bittersweet Pl

N Janssen Ave

N Marine Ave N

N Lakewood Ave

Wunder's
Cemetery

W Irving Park Rd

43

W Dakin St

Sheridan

N Sheridan Rd

N Fremont St

N Broadway St

N Frontier Ave

44

W Byron St

W Sheridan Rd

1/4 mile
.25 km

Map 40

An uneasy truce exists in Uptown amongst Starbucks-hopping yuppies and the perpetually displaced poor. Gentrification is slowly creeping into Uptown as condos and super chains like Target pop up, but be wary of where you are, block to block. Uptown boasts several milestones of Chicago history including still operational **Green Mill** and the **Uptown Theatre**, currently in renovation. **Graceland Cemetery** is a pretty walk for those who don't mind the morbid. The landmark is full of elaborate mausoleums, the final resting place of the men and women who built the Second City.

○ Landmarks

- **Aragon Ballroom** • 1106 W Lawrence Ave
  773-561-9500
  One of the better smaller music venues in the city.
- **Essanay Studios** • 1346 N North Branch St
  312-664-4400
  Former movie studio. Charlie Chaplin and Gloria
  Swanson made movies here.
- **Graceland Cemetery** • 4001 N Clark St
  773-525-1105
  Chicago's famous buried in a masterpiece of
  landscape architecture.
- **Green Mill** • 4802 N Broadway St
  773-878-5552
  Live jazz seven nights a week. Capone drank here.
- **Montrose Dog Beach** •
  W Wilson Ave & N Simonds Dr
  Fun and frolic with your pup.
- **St. Augustine College** • 1345 W Argyle St
  773-878-8756
  Episcopalian bilingual training school occupying
  original headquarters of Essanay Studios, where
  Chaplin, Broco Billy, and Swanson made films
  before moving to Southern CA.
- **St. Boniface Cemetery** • 4901 N Clark St
  847-864-3050
  Historic gravestones in a scenic cemetery.
- **Uptown Theatre** • 4816 N Broadway
  An acre of seats in a magic city.

🍸 Nightlife

- **The Bar on Buena** • 910 W Buena Ave
  773-525 8665
  Microbrews and tasty burgers in this plush
  neighborhood café.
- **Big Chicks** • 5024 N Sheridan Rd
  773-728-5511
  Friendly gay bar with fabulous art collection.
- **Carol's Pub** • 4659 N Clark St
  773-754-8000
  Hillbillies gone yuppie…thanks to a little press.
- **Drink and Ink** • 4443 N Broadway St
  773-989-4077
  Watch live feed video of in-house tattooing from
  your bar stool.
- **Green Mill** • 4802 N Broadway St
  773-878-5552
  Chicago legend…and birthplace of the poetry
  slam.
- **Hopleaf** • 5148 N Clark St
  773-334-9851
  Tons of imports if you can get a seat.
- **Konak** • 5150 N Clark St
  773-271-6688
  Overflow option for when Hopleaf is too packed,
  which means always.
- **The Long Room** • 1612 W Irving Park Rd
  773-665-4500
  Yes, it's long, but not as long as you might think.
- **Max's Place** • 4621 N Clark St
  773-784-3864
  At $1.25 per draft, who wouldn't pass out?
- **The Sofo Tap** • 4923 N Clark St
  773-784-7636
  Friendly boy's bar by owner of T's.
- **Uptown Lounge** • 1136 W Lawrence Ave
  773-878-1136
  Former dump becomes trendy lounge in up-and-
  coming neighborhood.

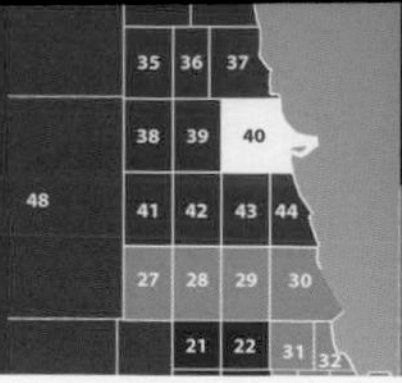

Map 40

Uptown

35	36	37	
38	39	40	
41	42	43	44
27	28	29	30
21	22	31	32

48

🍴Restaurants

- **Agami** • 4712 N Broadway St
773-506-1845 • $$$
Swanky sushi.
- **Anna Maria Pasteria** • 4400 N Clark St
773-506-2662 • $$
Cute, neighborhood Italian, casual date spot.
- **Bongo Room** • 5022 N Clark St
773-728-7900 • $$
Brunch worth the wait. Really.
- **Carmela's Taqueria** • 1206 W Lawrence Ave
773-275-5321 • $
Above average al pastor (for the northside).
- **Demera** • 4801 N Broadway St
773-334-8787 • $$
Neighborhood Ethiopian.
- **Furama** • 4936 N Broadway St
773-271-1161 • $$
Dim sum with karaoke.
- **Hai Yen** • 1055 W Argyle St
773-561-4077 • $$
Chinese and veggie pho.
- **Iyanze** • 4623 N Broadway St
773-944-1417 • $$
Spacious pan-African from folks who brought us
Lakeview's Bolat.

- **Palace Gate** • 4548 N Magnolia Ave
773-769-1793 • $$
True blue Ghanaian grub.
- **Pho 777** • 1065 W Argyle St
773-561-9909 • $
Try the tripe.
- **Siam Noodle & Rice** • 4142 N Broadway
773-769-6694 • $
Damn fine Thai food.
- **Silver Seafood** • 4829 N Broadway St
773-784-0668 • $
Asian delights from the sea.
- **Sun Wah BBQ** • 5039 N Broadway St
773-769-1254 • $$
Notable for the barbequed ducks hanging in the
window.
- **Tac Quick** • 1011 W Irving Park Rd
773-327-5253 • $$
Cheap and delicious. Thai-language menu
available for the adventurous.
- **Thai Pastry** • 4925 N Broadway St
773-784-5399 • $
Free pastry with every order!
- **Tiztal Cafe** • 4631 N Clark St
773-271-4631 • $
Chilaquiles and oatmeal shakes.
- **Tweet** • 5020 N Sheridan Rd
773-728-5576 • $$
Gourmet food without pretension.

Uptown's nightlife is lively, chock full of shiny new bars as well as reliable old standbys. **Green Mill** (famous for live jazz, Big Band Thursdays, and Sunday night poetry slams) and **Big Chicks** (a favored, gay neighborhood bar with great art) have long drawn folks to Uptown. **Bar on Buena** is justifiably renowned for their beer menus and flights, and **Bongo Room**'s brunch is worth the wait.

Shopping

- **Foursided** • 5061 N Clark St
  773-506-8300
  Framing and more at this funky shop.
- **La Patisserie P** • 1052 W Argyle St
  773-878-3226
  The Euro-Asian bakery of your dreams.
- **Milk Handmade** • 5137 N Clark St
  773-234-7053
  Fashion forward, handmade, AND affordable? A first time for everything.
- **Tai Nam Market** • 4925 N Broadway St
  773-275-5666
  Vietnamese. Very good.
- **Tattoo Factory** • 4441 N Broadway St
  773-989-4077
  High-profile place to get inked.

- **Uptown Bikes** • 4653 N Broadway St
  773-728-5212
  Cool, grungy bike shop.
- **Village Discount Outlet** • 4898 N Clark St
  708-388-4772
  Tons of clothes and weekly specials.
- **The Wooden Spoon** • 5047 N Clark St
  773-293-3190
  Heaven for foodies.

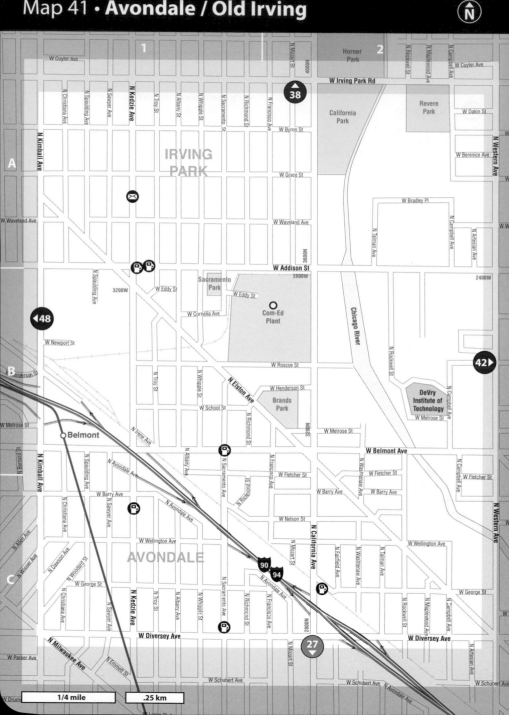

Map 41

That screeching sound you hear is Avondale development, which, like much of Chicago's westward expansion, has been riding the breaks since the recession-fueled decline. Even real estate speculators are hard-pressed to gild the dandelion of frame two-flats in foreclosure in this "park poor," mostly concrete area. The results: bleary-eyed hipsters wandering around in confusion, wondering how the hell they ended up here.

○ Landmarks

- **ComEd Plant** • N California Ave & W Roscoe St
  What's that humming sound in Avondale? Must be this ginormous electrical plant.

🍸 Nightlife

- **Barra Ñ** • 2977 N Elston Ave
  773-866-9898
  Argentine flair with electro grooves.
- **Chief O'Neill's** • 3471 N Elston Ave
  773-583-3066
  Celtic music and top-of-the-line pub food.
- **Kuma's Corner** • 2900 W Belmont Ave
  773-604-8769
  Heavy metal bar with great microbrew selection and kobe beef sliders.
- **Revolution Brewery** • 3340 N Kedzie Ave
  773-588-2267
  Grab a pint and glimpse behind-the-scenes of the local brewer.
- **Small Bar** • 2956 N Albany Ave
  773-509-9888
  This Logan Square watering hole offers great domestic and imported booze and a chill vibe.

🍴 Restaurants

- **Burrito House** • 3145 W Addison St
  773-279-9111 • $
  At least they're open late.
- **Chief O'Neill's** • 3471 N Elston Ave
  773-583-3066 • $
  Excellent traditional pub fare.
- **Honey Butter Fried Chicken** • 3361 N Elston Ave
  773-478-4000 • $$
  Wholesome. Sustainable. Fried chicken.
- **Kuma's Corner** • 2900 W Belmont Ave
  773-604-8769 • $$
  Heavy metal bar and grill with famous burgers and lots of ink.
- **Mr. Pollo** • 3026 W Belmont Ave
  773-509-1208 • $
  South American chicken joint. Get a guanabana shake.
- **Parachute** • 3500 N Elston Ave
  773-654-1460 • $$$
  Destination Korean spot sending foodies northwest.
- **Taqueria Traspasada** • 3144 N California Ave
  773-539-4533 • $
  Tasty, cheap tacos and salsas—no atmosphere.

🛍 Shopping

- **Andy's Music** • 3139 N Elston Ave
  773-868-1234
  Knock yourself out browsing all the exotic musical instruments sold here.

Map 42 · **North Center / Roscoe Village / West Lakeview**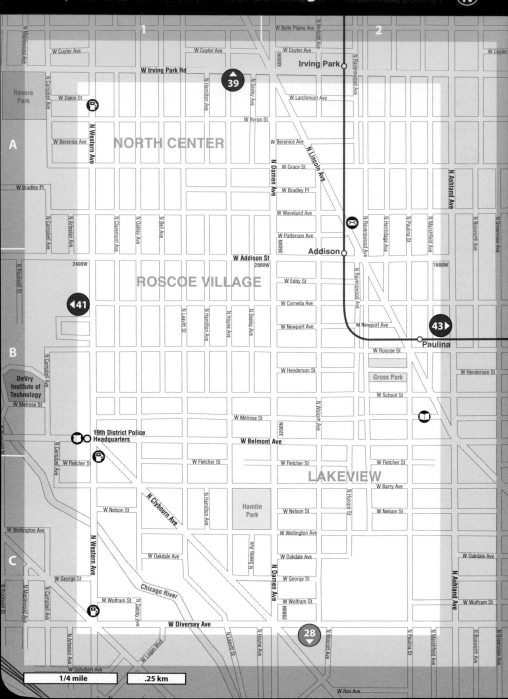

35	36	37	
38	39	40	
48	41	42	43	44
	27	28	29	30
		21	22	31	32

Map 42

The tan, fit, stroller-pushing set rule in Roscoe Village and West Lakeview. The north side jewel is populated with greystones and brownstones, lush, tiny green lawns, funky boutiques, expensive grocery stores, and cozy neighborhood restaurants. The nightlife here is mostly subdued with Saturday nights consisting of dive bar crawls.

○ Landmarks

• **19th District** • 2452 W Belmont Ave
312-744-5983
Going to "Western & Belmont" is synonymous for being in deep sh#*.

Nightlife

• **Beat Kitchen** • 2100 W Belmont Ave
773-281-4444
Hip music spot in a not so hip hood.
• **Brownstone Tavern and Grill** •
3937 N Lincoln Ave
773-528-3700
Charming sports bar with a lovely summer patio.
• **Constellation** • 3111 N Western Ave
Links Hall-Mike Reed partnership in former Viaduct Theatre.
• **Four Moon Tavern** • 1847 W Roscoe St
773-929-6666
Neighborhood tavern. Cozy back room. Thespian crowd.

• **The Four Treys** • 3333 N Damen Ave
773-549-8845
One of 5,000 drinking options in this area.
• **Goldie's Bar** • 3839 N Lincoln Ave
773-404-5322
Cozy dive with daily $1 PBR and battered board games.
• **Grace & Leavitt Tavern** • 2157 W Grace St
773-472-1138
Attention ladies! It's a fireman's hangout!
• **Martyrs'** • 3855 N Lincoln Ave
773-404-9494
Great stage for live acts.
• **Roscoe Village Pub** • 2159 W Addison St
773-472-6160
Karaoke in a dive bar…doesn't get much better than that.
• **Village Tap** • 2055 W Roscoe St
773-883-0817
Neighborhood icon with a touch of class.
• **Waterhouse** • 3407 N Paulina Ave
773-871-1200
Local lounge aiming for a classy feel.

35 36 37
38 39 40
48 41 42 43 44
27 28 29 30
21 22 31 32

🍴 Restaurants

- **90 Miles Cuban Cafe** • 3101 N Clybourn Ave
773-248-2822 • $
Casual Cuban, counter-seating only.
- **Brownstone Tavern and Grill** •
3937 N Lincoln Ave
773-528-3700 • $
Charming sports bar with a lovely summer patio.
- **Café Orchid** • 1746 W Addison St
773-327-3808 • $$
Authentic Turkish food served in a romantic hideaway.
- **C'est Bien Thai** • 3900 N Lincoln Ave
773-327-8818 • $$
Traditional Thai in a slick, big city setting.
- **Frasca** • 3358 N Paulina St
773-248-5222 • $$
European-style pizza with a cozy wine bar and outdoor seating.
- **Hot Woks Cool Sushi** • 2032 W Roscoe St
773-880-9800 • $$$
Try the crispy egg rolls.
- **Kitsch'n on Roscoe** • 2005 W Roscoe St
773-248-7372 • $$
Clever retro food and tiki bar. Friendly staff.

- **Murphy & Sons Irish Bistro** • 3905 N Lincoln Ave
773-248-3905 • $$$
Fancy Irish food: An oxymoron, or reality? Decide for yourself here.
- **Piazza Bella Trattoria & Osteria** •
2114 W Roscoe St
773-477-7330 • $$$
Neighborhood Italian.
- **Scooter's Frozen Custard** • 1658 W Belmont Ave
773-477-7330 • $
The tastiest custard this side of St. Louis.
- **Turquoise Restaurant** • 2147 W Roscoe St
773-549-3523 • $$
Fresh and creative Middle-Eastern fare.
- **Volo Restaurant Wine Bar** • 2008 W Roscoe St
773-348-4600 • $$$
New American small plates with swirl.

Catch a show at **Beat Kitchen**, try the crispy egg rolls at **Hot Woks Cool Sushi** and enjoy the generous portions at **Piazza Bella Trattoria**. Unwind with a late night pint at local favorites **The Village Tap** and rugby bar **Black Rock**.

🛍 Shopping

- **Andy's Music** • 3139 N Elston Ave
  773-868-1234
  Knock yourself out browsing all the exotic musical instruments sold here.
- **Antique Resources** • 1741 W Belmont Ave
  773-871-4242
  Large inventory of antique furniture.
- **Dinkel's Bakery** • 3329 N Lincoln Ave
  773-281-7300
  Old-school German bakery since 1922.
- **Father Time Antiques** • 2108 W Belmont Ave
  773-880-5599
  A plethora of timepieces.
- **Good Old Days** • 2138 W Belmont Ave
  773-472-8837
  Antiques and treasures.
- **Hubba Hubba** • 1105 Central Ave
  847-728-0272
  Boutique clothing and jewelry at moderate prices.

- **Lush Wine and Spirits** • 2232 W Roscoe St
  773-281-8888
  Wine, microbrews, and booze.
- **MegMade** • 2728 N Elston Ave
  312-636-3583
  Refurbished vintage furniture.
- **The Pleasure Chest** • 1448 N Milwaukee Ave
  773-525-7151
  Sextastic adult store.
- **Roscoe Books** • 2142 W Roscoe St
  773-857-2676
  Indie bookstore with an extensive children's section.
- **Roscoe Village Bikes** • 2016 W Roscoe St
  773-477-7550
  Friendly Village shop for bike repair and parts.
- **Shangri-La Vintage** • 1952 W Roscoe St
  773-348-5090
  Funky pleather jackets, plenty o' accessories, nylon shirts galore.
- **Skyscraper Heels** • 2202 W Belmont Ave
  773-477-8495
  Sky-high heels up to size 17.

Map 43 · **Wrigleyville / East Lakeview**

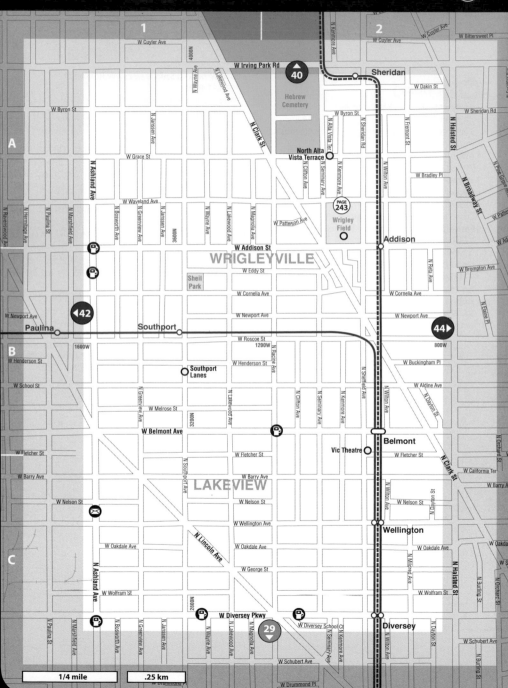

Map 43

The population of Wrigleyville/East Lakeview swells during beautiful summer afternoons and evenings while the Cubs are at home (making the parking impossible and towing imminent). To avoid the crowds, walk the pleasant, pretty streets during away games. Try Clark Street for rows and rows of sports bars and airy patio dining, and Southport Avenue for quieter date-and-family-friendly establishments.

○ Landmarks

• **North Alta Vista Terrace** •
3809 W Alta Vista Terrace
London-style row houses with Edwardian elegance.

• **The Vic** • 3145 N Sheffield Ave
773-472-0449
Drink, watch films, and take in an occasional band at this old theatre.

• **Wrigley Field** • 1060 W Addison St
773-404-2827
Charm-filled ballpark that remains indifferent to wins or losses.

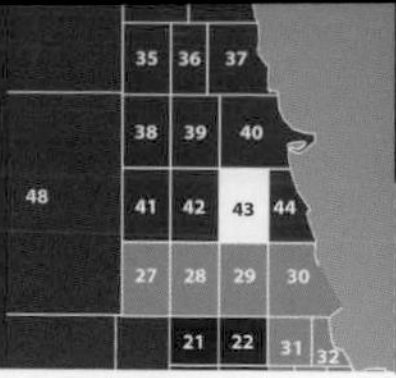

Map 43

Wrigleyville / East Lakeview

🍸 Nightlife

- **Berlin** • 954 W Belmont Ave
773-348-4975
Tiny classic "pansexual" dance club.
- **Bernie's** • 3664 N Clark St
773-525-1898
Favored Wrigleyville spot.
- **The Cubby Bear** • 1059 W Addison St
773-327-1662
Drunk Cubs fans and bar bands.
- **Elbo Room** • 2871 N Lincoln Ave
773-549-5549
Didn't RATT play here?
- **The Full Shilling** • 3724 N Clark St
773-248-3330
Best Wrigleyville bar.
- **The Gingerman Tavern** • 3740 N Clark St
773-549-2050
Plays classical music to ward off Cubs fans.

- **Houndstooth Saloon** • 3369 N Clark St
773-244-1166
Southern hospitality and Crimson Tide alumni and fans.
- **The Irish Oak** • 3511 N Clark St
773-935-6669
Seriously authentic Irish pub.
- **Kirkwood** • 2934 N Sheffield Ave
773-770-0700
Drink like a fish or out of a fish bowl.
- **L&L Tavern** • 3207 N Clark St
773-528-1303
Overfriendly dive bar with decent jukebox.
- **Lange's Lounge** • 3500 N Southport Ave
773-472-6030
Total dive, but not disgusting.
- **Lincoln Tap Room** • 3010 N Lincoln Ave
773-868-0060
Great mix of people, comfortable couches.
- **Lowcountry Lakeview** • 3343 N Clark St
888-883-8375

Since the Friendly Confines dominate the neighborhood, it's no surprise that most local bars and restaurants cater to sports fans. Jocks will feel at home in the 3-floor sports bar mecca, **Slugger's**, featuring dueling pianos, batting cages, and, during the winter, the basketball/trampoline hybrid, Hi-Ball. Non-sports fans have plenty to do on the weekends too: head to the **Metro** for live rock or the gorgeous, historic **Music Box Theatre** for art films and trashy/fun midnight movies.

- **Merkle's Bar & Grill** • 3516 N Clark St
  773-244-1025
  Cubs + Iowa Hawkeyes = sports year-round.
- **Metro** • 3730 N Clark St
  773 549 4140
  Internationally renowned venue for top local and touring rock music.
- **Murphy's Bleachers** • 3655 N Sheffield Ave
  773-281-5356
  Outdoor Cubbie haven with drunks galore.
- **Old Crow Smokehouse** • 3506 N Clark St
  773-537-4452
  A little bit country. A little bit…Wrigleyville.
- **Schubas** • 3159 N Southport Ave
  773-525-2508
  Top live music staple with attached restaurant.
- **Sheffield's** • 3258 N Sheffield Ave
  773-281-4989
  Outdoor area attracts afternoon revelers. Great beer selection.
- **Slugger's** • 3540 N Clark St
  773-248-0055
  Batting cages—some people's heaven, others' hell.
- **Smart Bar** • 3730 N Clark St
  773-549-4140
  Club kids unite!
- **Stretch Bar & Grill** • 3485 N Clark St
  773-755-3980
  Wrigleyville's upscale choice for watching sports and eating good grub.

- **Tai's Til 4** • 3611 N Ashland Ave
  773-655-6176
  Well, they're open till 4 am, so you can probably guess what it's like. Hookup central.
- **Ten Cat Tavern** • 3931 N Ashland Ave
  773-935-5377
  Artsy-type relaxing spot.
- **Toons Bar & Grill** • 3857 N Southport Ave
  773-935-1919
  Buncha characters in that joint (groan).
- **Uncommon Ground** • 3800 N Clark St
  773-929-3680
  Local acts play while sipping a latte.
- **Underground Lounge** • 952 W Newport Ave
  773-871-4343
  Cool music spot tucked away below the street.
- **Yak-Zies Wrigleyville** • 3710 N Clark St
  773-525-9200
  Loud post-Cubs hangout.

Map 43

35	36	37
38	39	40
48	41	42	43	44
27	28	29	30
21	22	31	32

Wrigleyville / East Lakeview

🍴 Restaurants

- **Ann Sather** • 909 W Belmont Ave
773-348-2378 • $
Warm, family-friendly ambience, Swedish comfort food.
- **Cozy Noodles n' Rice** • 3456 N Sheffield Ave
773-327-0100 • $$
Yep, it's cozy.
- **Dimo's Pizza** • 3463 N Clark St
773-525-4580 • $
Late night pizza (sometimes topped with mac and cheese).
- **Fish Bar** • 2956 N Sheffield Ave
773-360-8686 • $$
DMK Burger Bar's cousin serves seafood and refreshing "sea sippers."
- **Golden Apple** • 2971 N Lincoln Ave
773-528-1413 • $
24-hour greasy hangover food. Once featured on This American Life.

- **Lucky's Sandwich Company** • 3472 N Clark St
773-549-0665 • $
They put fries IN the sandwich. Genius.
- **Mia Francesca** • 3311 N Clark St
773-281-3310 • $$
Contemporary Italian date place.
- **P.S. Bangkok** • 3345 N Clark St
773-871-7777 • $
Popular neighborhood Thai that delivers.
- **Panes** • 3002 N Sheffield Ave
773-665-0972 • $
Homemade sandwiches, muffins, cookies, and brownies.
- **S&G** • 3000 N Lincoln Ave
773-935-4025 • $
Cop hangout with chintzy decorating and fake plants. In other words, we love it.
- **Tango Sur** • 3763 N Southport Ave
773-477-5466 • $$
Vegetarian's vision of hell: big juicy Argentine steaks.
- **Wrigleyville Dogs** • 3737 N Clark St
773-296-1500 • $
Post Metro stop for chili-cheese fries.

Hit **Sheffield's** for its beer selection or **The Irish Oak** if you're looking for an authentic Irish pub. **Art of Pizza** wins awards for its pies. If you're looking to savor South American flavors while sipping your own bottle of red, head to **Tango Sur** for massive cuts of Argentine steak.

Shopping

- **Bittersweet Pastry Shop and Cafe** •
  1114 W Belmont Ave
  773-929-1100
  Cookies as big as your head.
- **Chicago Comics** • 3244 N Clark St
  773-528-1983
  Fun! Not geeky, really…
- **Heritage Bicycles** • 2959 N Lincoln Ave
  773-245-3005
  Gourmet coffee and treats with your handcrafted bike.
- **Krista K** • 3458 N Southport Ave
  773-248-1967
  Snobby clothes for snobby women but good selection of jeans.

- **Play It Again Sports** • 3939 N Ashland Ave
  773-305-9900
  Sporting goods.
- **Saturday Audio Exchange** • 1021 W Belmont Ave
  773-935-4434
  Great bargains on name brand audio.

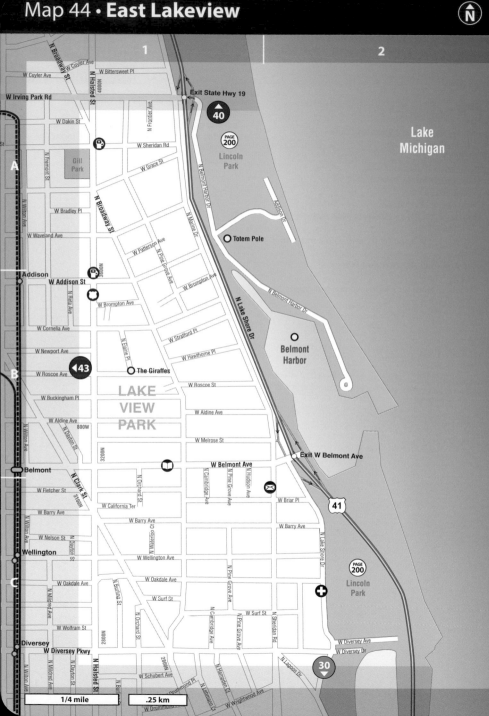

Map 44 · **East Lakeview**

N

1

2

W Cuyler Ave

N Broadway St

W Bittersweet Pl

W Cuyler Ave

N Halsted St

W Irving Park Rd

Exit State Hwy 19

4000N

40

W Dakin St

N Frontier Ave

PAGE 200

W Sheridan Rd

Lincoln Park

Lake Michigan

A

N Fremont St

Gill Park

W Grace St

N Broadway St

W Bradley Pl

N Marine Dr

N Belmont Harbor Dr

W Waveland Ave

Addison Dr

W Patterson Ave

Totem Pole

N Pine Grove Ave

N Wilton Ave

Addison

W Addison St

3600N

N Lake Shore Dr

N Reta Ave

W Brompton Ave

W Brompton Ave

N Belmont Harbor Dr

W Cornelia Ave

W Stratford Pl

W Newport Ave

N Eldine Pl

W Hawthorne Pl

Belmont Harbor

B

43

W Roscoe Ave

The Giraffes

W Roscoe St

W Buckingham Pl

LAKE VIEW PARK

N Wilton Ave

N Clarion St

W Aldine Ave

W Aldine Ave

800W

3200N

W Melrose St

Belmont

N Clark St

3100N

Exit W Belmont Ave

W Fletcher St

W Belmont Ave

41

N Cambridge Ave

N Pine Grove Ave

N Hudson Ave

N Orchard St

W California Ter

W Briar Pl

W Barry Ave

N Wilton Ave

W Barry Ave

N Dayton St

W Barry Ave

N Waterloo Ct

N Lake Shore Dr

Wellington

W Nelson St

W Wellington Ave

N Pine Grove Ave

W Oakdale Ave

N Mildred Ave

W Oakdale Ave

C

N Burling St

W Surf St

2800N

N Orchard St

W Surf St

N Cambridge Ave

N Pine Grove Ave

N Sheridan Rd

PAGE 200

Lincoln Park

W Wolfram St

Diversey

W Diversey Pkwy

N Halsted St

W Diversey Ave

W Diversey Dr

N Mildred Ave

N Dayton St

2600N

N Burling St

W Schubert Ave

N Hampden Ct

N Lehmann Ct

30

N Wilton Ave

N Lagoon Dr

W Wrightwood Ave

W Drummond Pl

| 1/4 mile | .25 km |

Map 44

A.K.A. Boystown thanks to its highly visible gay community, East Lakview is brimming with great shopping and dining. The Chicago summer festival season piques in Boystown with the annual Pride Parade and the equally flamboyant Halsted Street Market Days. The neighborhood quiets down a bit in the beautiful gray- and brownstone-lined blocks south of Belmont.

○ Landmarks

• **Belmont Harbor** • 3600 Recreation Dr
312-742-7673
Home to the Chicago Yacht Club sailing school.
• **Totem Pole** • 3600 N Lake Shore Dr
Where did it come from? Why is it there? Nobody knows.

🍸 Nightlife

• **Charlie's Chicago** • 3726 N Broadway St
773-871-8887
Gay country and western bar. That's right.
• **The Closet** • 3325 N Broadway St
773-477-8533
Boy-friendly lesbian bar, 4 am license.
• **DryHop Brewers** • 3155 N Broadway St
773-857-3155
In-house brews, local collaborations, and elevated bar food.
• **Duke of Perth** • 2913 N Clark St
773-477-1741
Shades of Edinburgh, along with requisite whiskies and haddock.
• **F. O'Mahony's** • 3701 N Broadway St
773-549-0226
Food when you need it (late!) and a seasonal menu.

• **Friar Tuck** • 3010 N Broadway St
773-327-5101
Enter through a barrel. Yup, a barrel.
• **Hydrate** • 3458 N Halsted St
773-975-9244
Just what Boystown needs—a gay-friendly fern bar!
• **Kit Kat Lounge** • 3700 N Halsted St
773-525-1111
Live drag queen shows.
• **Monsignor Murphy's** • 3019 N Broadway St
773-348-7285
Irish pub with plenty of board games.
• **Progress Bar** • 3359 N Halsted St
773-697-9268
Boystown bar featuring visual lighting installation.
• **Rocks Lakeview** • 3463 N Broadway St
773-472-0493
Microbrews, good whisky list, and excellent bar food.
• **Roscoe's** • 3356 N Halsted St
773-281-3355
Cavernous mingling for the gay sweater set.
• **Sidetrack** • 3349 N Halsted St
773-477-9189
Popular showtune sing-a-longs!
• **Town Hall Pub** • 3340 N Halsted St
773-472-4405
Unassuming, mixed clientele, live music.
• **Wilde** • 3130 N Broadway St
773-244-0404
Classy bar for bookish set.

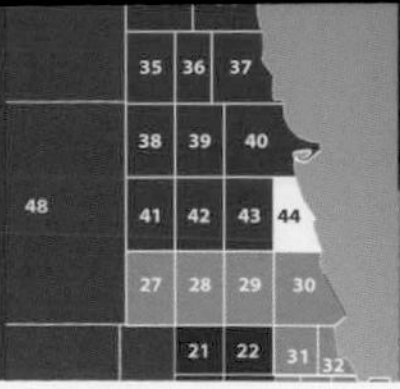

Map 44

Restaurants

- **Angelina Ristorante** • 3561 N Broadway St
773-935-5933 • $$$
Casual, romantic Italian.
- **Ann Sather** • 3415 N Broadway St
773-305-0024 • $
Airy branch of local comfort food chain.
- **The Bagel** • 3107 N Broadway St
773-477-0300 • $
Great deli fare.
- **The Chicago Diner** • 3411 N Halsted St
773-935-6696 • $$
A vegetarian institution.
- **Chilam Balam** • 3023 N Broadway St
773-296-6901 • $$
Yummy organic, small plate Mexican.
- **Clark Street Dog** • 3040 N Clark St
773-281-6690 • $
24-hour hot dogs and cheese fries.
- **Drew's** • 3201 N Halsted St
773-244-9191 • $$$$
Great wine list.
- **Flub A Dub Chub's** • 3021 N Broadway St
773-857-6500 • $
Hot dogs Chicago-style. No ketchup.
- **Half Shell** • 676 W Diversey Pkwy
773-549-1773 • $$$
Casual raw bar.

- **Joy's Noodles & Rice** • 3257 N Broadway St
773-327-8330 • $$
Standard noodles, soup, or fried rice; impressively simple.
- **La Creperie** • 2845 N Clark St
773-528-9050 • $$
Live French music. Shabby, but cute.
- **Ping Pong** • 3322 N Broadway St
773-281-7575 • $$$
Always busy BYOB, hit or miss Asian fusion.
- **Stella's Diner** • 3042 N Broadway St
773-472-9040 • $
Can you say diner?
- **Wakamono** • 3313 N Broadway
773-296-6800 • $$
Sushi and Japanese small plates.

East Lakeview's nightlife is unquestionably the most fun you'll have in the city. Dining options run the gauntlet from ultra chic to comfortably casual. The neighborhood is stacked with gay nightclubs and bars like **Roscoe's** and **Sidetrack**. No Saturday night visit to Boystown is complete without a drag show. You'll go (Lady) Gaga for the queens at the **Kit Kat Lounge & Supper Club**. Parking is rough in this busy borough, but it's a cinch to hail a cab at any hour.

Shopping

- **Bookman's Corner** • 2959 N Clark St
  773-929-8298
  Chicago's most surprising bookstore, last of a dying breed.
- **Century Shopping Centre** • 2828 N Clark St
  773-248-7759
  Most notable occupants include the cinema and Bally's Fitness.
- **Gramaphone Records** • 2843 N Clark St
  773-472-3683
  DJ's shop here for the latest wax.
- **Johnny Sprockets** • 3001 N Broadway
  773-244-1079
  Catering to all your bicycle needs.
- **Kozy's Cyclery** • 3712 N Halsted St
  773-281-2263
  East Lakeview branch of Chicago bike chain.

- **Ragstock** • 812 W Belmont Ave
  773-868-9263
  Vintage resale and trendy off-price clothes.
- **Reckless Records** • 3126 N Broadway St
  773-235-3727
  Oldies and new releases on vinyl.
- **Spare Parts** • 2949 N Broadway St
  773-525-4242
  Cool bags, purses, and man purses.
- **Unabridged Bookstore** • 3251 N Broadway St
  773-883-9119
  Helpful bookstore with great travel, kids, and gay sections.
- **Windy City Sweets** • 3308 N Broadway St
  773-477-6100
  Old-fashioned candy shop with homemade fudge.

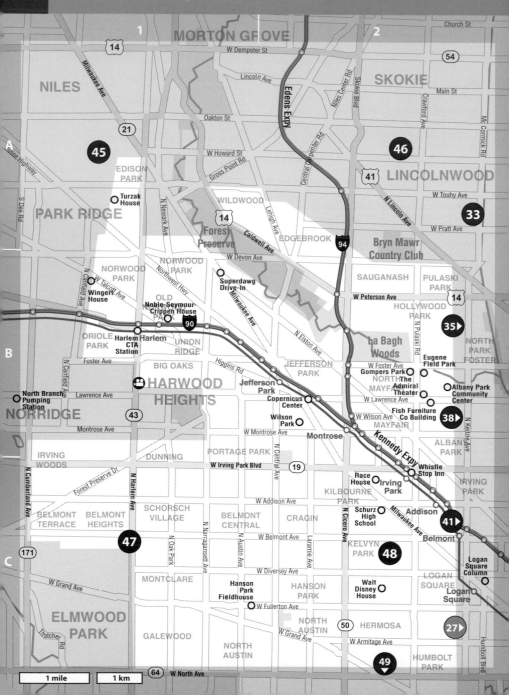

Greater Chicago · **Northwest**

1

14

2

Church St

MORTON GROVE

W Dempster St

Lincoln Ave

NILES

Milwaukee Ave

Edens Expy

54

Main St

SKOKIE

Niles Center Rd

Skokie Blvd

Central Carpenter Rd

Crawford Ave

McCormick Rd

21

Oakton St

A

45

46

41

LINCOLNWOOD

N Lincoln Ave

W Touhy Ave

S Dee Rd

PARK RIDGE

Turzak
House

EDISON
PARK

W Howard St

Gross Point Rd

WILDWOOD

14

Lehigh Ave

Caldwell Ave

EDGEBROOK

94

Bryn Mawr
Country Club

33

W Pratt Ave

Forest
Preserve

W Devon Ave

Grosse Highway

NORWOOD
PARK

N Canfield Ave

W Talcott Ave

Wingert
House

NORWOOD
PARK

Northwest Hwy

Old

Superdawg
Drive-In

Milwaukee Ave

N Elston Ave

SAUGANASH

W Peterson Ave

HOLLYWOOD
PARK

La Bagh
Woods

PULASKI
PARK

N Pulaski Rd

14

35▶

NORTH
PARK
FOSTER

Noble-Seymour-
Crippen House

90

B

ORIOLE
PARK

Harlem Harlem
CTA
Station

UNION
RIDGE

N Canfield Ave

Foster Ave

BIG OAKS

**HARWOOD
HEIGHTS**

Higgins Rd

JEFFERSON
PARK

Eugene
Field Park

Gompers Park

NORTH
MAYFAIR

The
Admiral
Theater

Albany Park
Community
Center

N Kedzie Ave

North Branch
Pumping
Station

Lawrence Ave

Jefferson
Park

W Foster Ave

W Lawrence Ave

Fish Furniture
Co Building

38▶

NORRIDGE

43

Copernicus
Center

Wilson
Park

Montrose Ave

W Montrose Ave

Montrose

W Wilson Ave

MAYFAIR

ALBANY
PARK

D

IRVING
WOODS

N Cumberland Ave

DUNNING

Forest Preserve Dr

N Harlem Ave

PORTAGE PARK

W Irving Park Blvd

N Central Ave

19

Kennedy Expy

Whistle
Stop Inn

IRVING
PARK

BELMONT
TERRACE

BELMONT
HEIGHTS

SCHORSCH
VILLAGE

N Oak Park

BELMONT
CENTRAL

N Narragansett Ave

N Austin Ave

CRAGIN

Laramie Ave

W Addison Ave

W Belmont Ave

Race
House

Irving
Park

N Cicero Ave

Schurz
High
School

KILBOURNE
PARK

Milwaukee Ave

Addison

41▶

47

171

C

W Diversey Ave

KELVYN
PARK

48

Belmont

Logan
Square
Column

MONTCLARE

Hanson
Park
Fieldhouse

HANSON
PARK

Walt
Disney
House

LOGAN
SQUARE

Logan
Square

Logan Blvd

27▶

**ELMWOOD
PARK**

Thatcher Rd

GALEWOOD

NORTH
AUSTIN

W Fullerton Ave

NORTH
AUSTIN

50

HERMOSA

W Grand Ave

W Armitage Ave

Humbolt Blvd

HUMBOLT
PARK

49▼

171

W Grand Ave

64

W North Ave

1 mile

1 km

If there's one thing you can count on in Northwest Chicago, it's that you can count on just about everything. Compared to other sections of the city, the Northwest is a bastion of stability. Most of the people and the businesses have been around forever, and even typically transitory ethnic enclaves—in this case Eastern European, Middle Eastern, North African, Korean, and Italian—are fairly entrenched. That said, the slow but steady growth of the northwest side communities of Jefferson Park, Mayfair, and Edison Park is notable, as more young families discover the affordable housing and excellent school districts offered here. Additionally, Northwest Chicago is blessed with an abundance of small parks and field houses, as well as a large hunk of forest preserve, giving much of the area a bucolic, suburban feel.

○ Landmarks

- **Admiral Theater** • 3940 W Lawrence Ave
- **Copernicus Center** • 5216 W Lawrence Ave
- **Eugene Field Park** • 5100 N Ridgeway Ave
- **Fish Furniture Co. Building** • 3322 W Lawrence Ave
- **Gompers Park** • 4222 W Foster Ave
- **Hanson Park Fieldhouse** • 5501 W Fullerton Ave
- **Harlem CTA Station** • 5550 N Harlem Ave
- **National Veterans Art Museum** • 4041 N Milwaukee Ave
- **Noble-Seymour-Crippen House** • 5624 N Newark Ave

- **North Branch Pumping Station** • W Lawrence Ave & NE River Rd
- **North Park Village Nature Center** • 5801 N Pulaski Rd
- **Race House** • 3945 N Tripp Ave
- **Schurz High School** • 3601 Milwaukee Ave
- **Superdawg Drive-In** • 6363 N Milwaukee Ave
- **Turzak House** • 7059 N Olcott Ave
- **Walt Disney House** • 2156 N Tripp Ave
- **Whistle Stop Inn** • 4200 W Irving Park Rd
- **Wilson Park** • 4630 N Milwaukee Ave
- **Wingert House** • 6231 N Canfield Ave

Northwest Chicago wears its blue-collar ethnic proclivities on its sleeve. Local shops and restaurants don't go out of their way to attract clientele outside their own, and even the staff at the area's abundant Korean and Eastern European businesses make little effort to communicate in English. Adventuresome diners and cooks rise to the challenge—some of the city's best restaurants and ethnic grocers can be found here, including Thai vegan spot **Amitabul** and Korean **Joong Boo Market. American Science and Surplus** has you covered for telescopes, army gear, UV spy pens, and (to say the least) more. Farther south, Logan Square's young contingent is sprawling out along a quiet stretch of Armitage at Kedzie thanks to a new crop of bars and restaurants.

🍸 Nightlife

- **Babe's** • 4416 N Milwaukee Ave
- **Belmont Tap** • 6101 W Belmont Ave
- **The Burlington** • 3425 W Fullerton Ave
- **The Double** • 3545 W Fullerton Ave
- **Edison Park Inn** • 6715 N Olmsted Ave
- **Emerald Isle** • 6686 N Northwest Hwy
- **Fifth Province Pub** • 4626 N Knox Ave
- **Ham Tree Inn** • 5333 N Milwaukee Ave
- **Jimmy Mack Bar** • 5581 N Northwest Hwy
- **Moretti's** • 6727 N Olmsted Ave
- **Rabbits** • 4945 W Foster Ave
- **Rosa's Lounge** • 3420 W Armitage Ave
- **Three Counties Irish Pub** • 5856 N Milwaukee Ave
- **Vaughan's Pub & Grill** • 5485 N Northwest Hwy
- **Weegee's Lounge** • 3659 W Armitage Ave
- **West on North** • 2509 W North Ave

🍴 Restaurants

- **Amarind's** • 6822 W North Ave
- **Amitabul** • 6207 N Milwaukee Ave
- **BRGRbelly** • 5739 W Irving Park Rd
- **Café Con Leche** • 2714 N Milwaukee Ave
- **Café Prague** • 6710 W Belmont Ave
- **Chai Asian Bistro** • 4748 W Peterson Ave
- **Chicago Kalbi** • 3752 W Lawrence Ave
- **Chocolate Shoppe Ice Cream** • 5337 W Devon Ave
- **Dimaggio** • 7326 W Lawrence Ave
- **Eat First** • 3337 W Belmont Ave

- **El Cubanito** • 2555 N Pulaski Rd
- **Elliott's Seafood Grille & Chop House** • 6690 N Northwest Hwy
- **Friendship Chinese Restaurant** • 2830 N Milwaukee Ave
- **Gale Street Inn** • 4914 N Milwaukee Ave
- **Great Sea Chinese Restaurant** • 3253 W Lawrence Ave
- **Grota Smorgasbord** • 3112 N Central Ave
- **Hiromi's** • 3609 W Lawrence Ave
- **La Villa Restaurant** • 3638 N Pulaski Rd
- **Lawrence Fish Market** • 3920 W Lawrence Ave
- **Mirabell** • 3454 W Addison St
- **Pasta D'Arte** • 6311 N Milwaukee Ave
- **Red Apple Buffet** • 6474 N Milwaukee Ave
- **Ristorante Agostino Gustofino** • 2817 N Harlem Ave
- **Russell's Barbecue** • 1621 N Thatcher Ave
- **Shokran** • 4027 W Irving Park Rd
- **Smak-Tak** • 5961 N Elston Ave
- **Smoque** • 3800 N Pulaski Rd
- **Sol de Mexico** • 3018 N Cicero Ave
- **Staropolska Restaurant** • 3030 N Milwaukee Ave
- **Tre Kronor** • 3258 W Foster Ave
- **Wellfleet** • 4423 N Elston Ave
- **Zebda** • 4344 N Elston Ave

🛍 Shopping

- **American Science & Surplus** • 5316 N Milwaukee Ave
- **Discovery Clothing** • 3348 W Belmont Ave
- **Fantasy Costumes** • 4065 N Milwaukee Ave
- **FishGuy Market** • 4423 N Elston Ave
- **Galos Caves** • 6501 W Irving Park Rd
- **H & B True Value** • 5329 N Milwaukee Ave
- **Harlem Irving Plaza** • 4104 N Harlem Ave
- **Joong Boo Market** • 3333 N Kimball Ave
- **Kurowski's Sausage Shop** • 2976 N Milwaukee Ave
- **Montrose Deli** • 5411 W Montrose Ave
- **Old Town Tap** • 3313 W Irving Park Rd
- **Perfume Outlet** • 3608 W Lawrence Ave
- **Promise Data Recovery** • 3525 W Peterson Ave
- **Rolling Stones** • 7300 W Irving Park Rd
- **Rudy's Cycle and Fitness** • 5711 W Irving Park Rd
- **The Sweden Shop** • 3304 W Foster Ave
- **Unique Thrift Store** • 6560 W Fullerton Ave
- **Viking Ski Shop** • 3422 W Fullerton Ave
- **Village Discount Outlet** • 3301 W Lawrence Ave
- **Village Discount Outlet** • 4635 N Elston Ave
- **Whole Foods** • 6020 N Cicero Ave
- **Wig Bags** • 4621 N Lawndale Ave

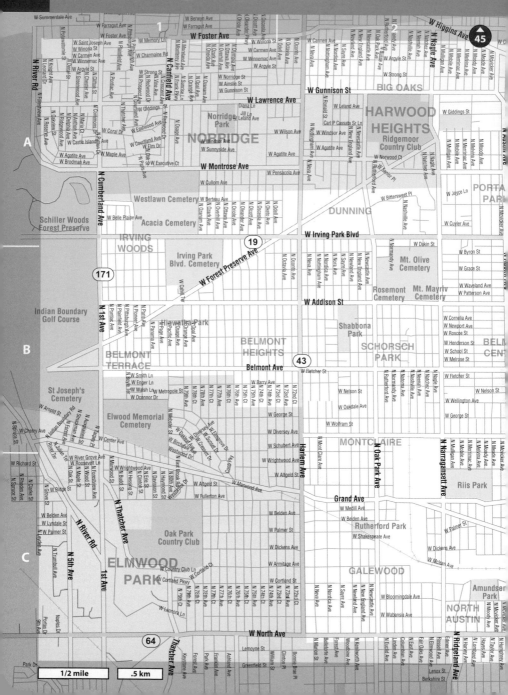

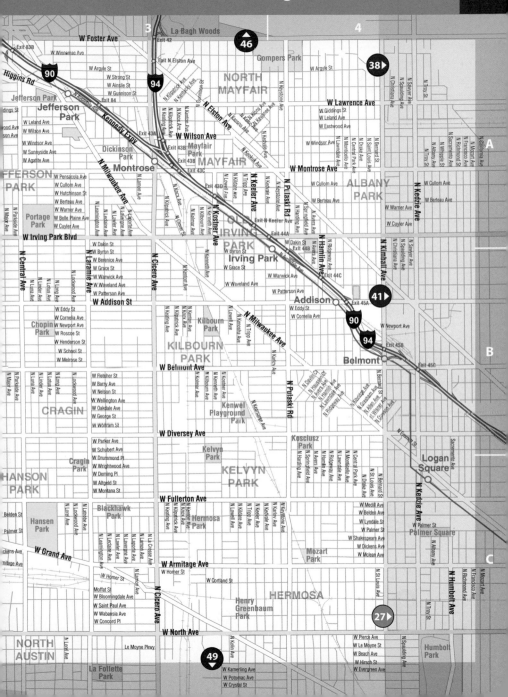

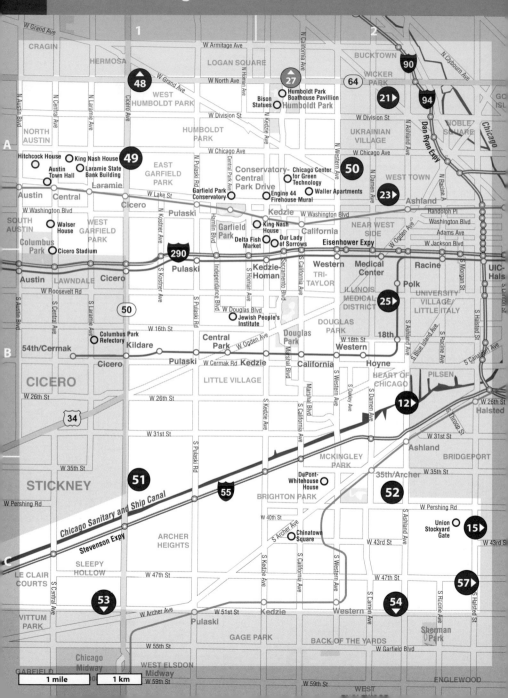

1

CRAGIN

W Grand Ave

HERMOSA

LOGAN SQUARE

W Armitage Ave

W North Ave

48

W Grand Ave

WEST HUMBOLDT PARK

27

64

BUCKTOWN

WICKER PARK

90

Humboldt Park
Boathouse Pavillion

21

94

Bison
Statues

Humboldt Park

NOBLE SQUARE

Chicago

W Division St

HUMBOLDT PARK

NORTH AUSTIN

W Division St

UKRAINIAN VILLAGE

A

W Chicago Ave

Hitchcock House

King Nash House

49

Austin
Town Hall

Laramie State
Bank Building

EAST GARFIELD PARK

Laramie

Conservatory-
Central
Park Drive

Chicago Center
for Green
Technology

50

W Chicago Ave

WEST TOWN

23

Austin

Central

W Lake St

Cicero

Garfield Park
Conservatory

Engine 44
Firehouse Mural

Waller Apartments

Ashland

Randolph Pl

Pulaski

Kedzie

W Washington Blvd

Washington Blvd

W Washington Blvd

Adams Ave

SOUTH AUSTIN

Walser
House

WEST GARFIELD PARK

King Nash
House

California

NEAR WEST SIDE

W Jackson Blvd

Racine

Columbus
Park

Cicero Stadium

Garfield
Park

Delta Fish
Market

Our Lady
of Sorrows

Eisenhower Expy

290

Austin

LAWNDALE

Cicero

Pulaski

**Kedzie-
Homan**

Western

**Medical
Center**

Racine

**UIC-
Hals**

W Roosevelt Rd

**TRI-
TAYLOR**

Polk

**UNIVERSITY
VILLAGE/
LITTLE ITALY**

50

**ILLINOIS
MEDICAL
DISTRICT**

25

Columbus Park
Refectory

Kildare

Central
Park

**DOUGLAS
PARK**

18th

B

54th/Cermak

Cicero

Pulaski

W Cermak Rd

Kedzie

California

Hoyne

Western

W Douglas Blvd

Jewish People's
Institute

Douglas
Park

W 18th St

CICERO

LITTLE VILLAGE

**HEART OF
CHICAGO**

PILSEN

W 26th St

W 26th St

12

W 26th St
Halsted

34

W 31st St

Ashland

BRIDGEPORT

W 35th St

STICKNEY

51

DuPont-
Whitehouse
House

**McKINGLEY
PARK**

35th/Archer

W 35th St

52

W Pershing Rd

55

BRIGHTON PARK

W Pershing Rd

Union
Stockyard
Gate

15

W 40th St

**ARCHER
HEIGHTS**

Chinatown
Square

W 43rd St

W 43rd St

**LE CLAIR
COURTS**

**SLEEPY
HOLLOW**

W 47th St

W 47th St

57

C

**VITTUM
PARK**

53

W Archer Ave

54

W 51st St

Kedzie

Western

Pulaski

GAGE PARK

**Sherman
Park**

W 55th St

WEST ELSDON

W Garfield Blvd

**Chicago
Midway**

**Chicago
Midway**

| 1 mile | 1 km |

W 59th St

GARFIELD

WEST

ENGLEWOOD

2

Despite the turf between Humboldt and Columbus Park's lush greens, idyllic lagoons and historic buildings being some of Chicago's roughest, the city's west side is home to spirited folk. 26th Street is the commercial artery of Little Village's thriving Mexican population, and Puerto Rican pride prevails along Division Street and North Avenue through vibrant public art and a jubilant annual parade. **Garfield Park Conservatory** is a popular spot to tie the knot. Brighton Park and Archer Heights epitomize the classic Chicago blue collar ethic, where labor unions rule and the Old Style flows freely.

○ Landmarks

- **Austin Town Hall** • 5610 W Lake St
- **Bison Statues in Humboldt Park** •
  1400 N Sacramento Ave
- **Chicago Center for Green Technology** •
  445 N Sacramento Blvd
- **Chinatown Square** • 2133 S China Pl
- **Columbus Park Refectory** • 5701 W Jackson Blvd
- **Delta Fish Market** • 228 S Kedzie Ave
- **DuPont-Whitehouse House** • 3558 S Artesian Ave
- **Engine 44 Firehouse Mural** • 412 N Kedzie Ave

- **Garfield Park** • 100 N Central Park Ave
- **Garfield Park Conservatory** • 300 N Central Park Ave
- **Hitchcock House** • 5704 W Ohio St
- **Humboldt Park Boathouse Pavilion** •
  1400 N Humboldt Dr
- **Jewish People's Institute** • 3500 W Douglas Blvd
- **JJ Walser House** • 42 N Central Ave
- **King-Nash House** • 3234 W Washington Blvd
- **Laramie State Bank Building** • 5200 W Chicago Ave
- **Our Lady of Sorrows** • 3121 W Jackson Blvd
- **Union Stock Yard Gate** • Peoria St & Exchange Ave
- **Waller Apartments** • 2840 W Walnut St

Try **Flying Saucer** for healthy, hearty breakfasts tailored to vegans and meat eaters alike. Vinyl collectors scour **Out of the Past Records**' mountainous collection of blues, soul, jazz, and gospel recordings. Down in McKinley Park, **La Palapa**'s thatched umbrellas and mariscos will transport you to Mexico. (Just turn your chair away from Damen Avenue.)

🍸 Nightlife

- **Archie's** • 2600 W Iowa St
- **The Beetle** • 2532 W Chicago Ave
- **Illinois Bar & Grill** • 4135 W 47th St
- **La Justicia** • 3901 W 26th St
- **Rootstock Wine & Beer Bar** • 954 N California Ave

🍴 Restaurants

- **Bacchanalia** • 2413 S Oakley Ave
- **Birria Huentitan** • 4019 W North Ave
- **Birrieria Zaragoza** • 4852 S Pulaski Rd
- **Bruna's Ristorante** • 2424 S Oakley Ave
- **Coleman's** • 5754 W Chicago Ave
- **Falco's Pizza** • 2806 W 40th St
- **Feed** • 2803 W Chicago Ave
- **Flying Saucer** • 1123 N California Ave
- **Huck Finn Donuts** • 3414 S Archer Ave
- **Ignotz** • 2421 S Oakley Ave
- **La Cebollita** • 4343 W 47th St
- **La Encantada** • 3437 W North Ave
- **La Palapa** • 2000 W 34th St
- **Lindy's and Gertie's** • 3685 S Archer Ave
- **MacArthur's** • 5412 W Madison Ave
- **Nellie's** • 2458 W Division St
- **The Submarine Piers** • 4048 S Archer Ave
- **Taqueria Atotonilco** • 3916 W 26th St
- **Taqueria Los Comales** • 3141 W 26th St
- **Taqueria Los Gallos 2** • 4252 S Archer Ave

🛍 Shopping

- **Ashley Stewart** • 800 N Kedzie Ave
- **Buyer's Flea Market** • 4545 W Division St
- **Dulcelandia** • 3300 W 26th St
- **Family Dollar** • 5410 W Chicago Ave
- **Family Dollar** • 1360 N Pulaski Rd
- **Humboldt House** • 1045 N California Ave
- **Out of the Past Records** • 4407 W Madison St
- **Swap-O-Rama** • 4100 S Ashland Ave
- **Village Discount Outlet** • 2514 W 47th St
- **Village Discount Outlet** • 4020 W 26th St
- **Watra Church Goods** • 4201 S Archer Ave
- **West Town Bikes / Ciclo Urbano** • 2459 W. Division
- **Working Bikes Cooperative** • 2434 S Western Ave

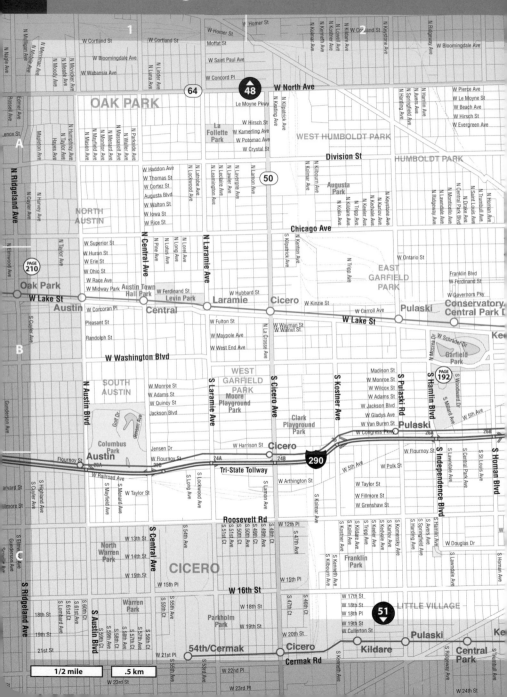

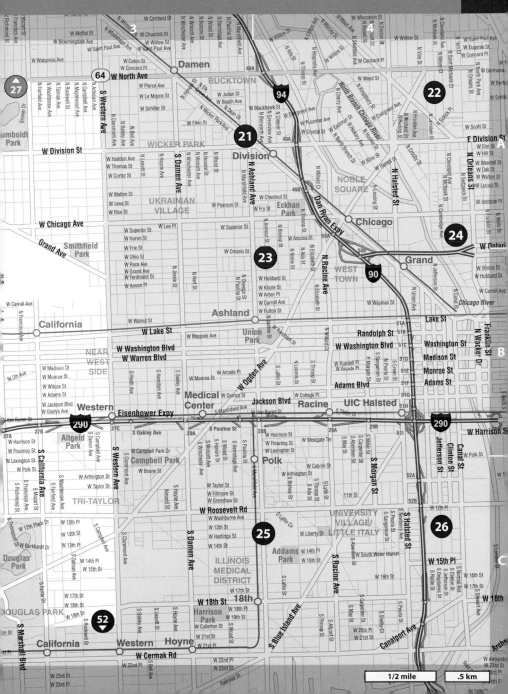

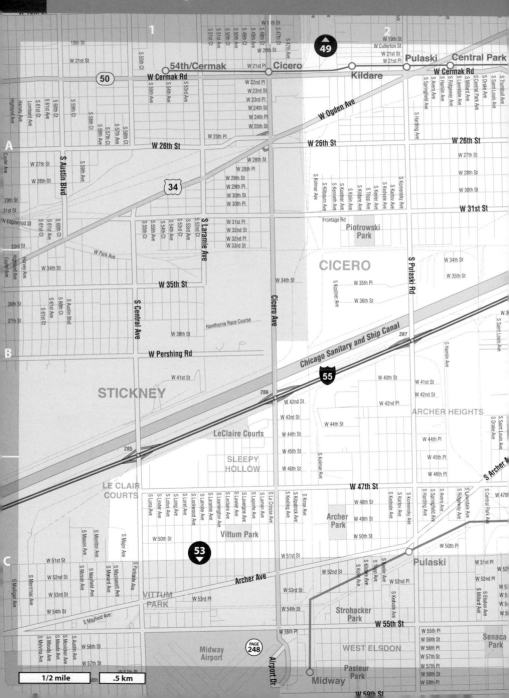

CICERO

STICKNEY

ARCHER HEIGHTS

LeClaire Courts

SLEEPY HOLLOW

LE CLAIR COURTS

Vittum Park

VITTUM PARK

WEST ELSDON

Senaca Park

Pasteur Park

Strohacker Park

Archer Park

Piotrowski Park

Hawthorne Race Course

Chicago Sanitary and Ship Canal

Midway Airport

Midway

PAGE 248

54th/Cermak   Cicero   Pulaski   Central Park

Kildare

Pulaski

1/2 mile   .5 km

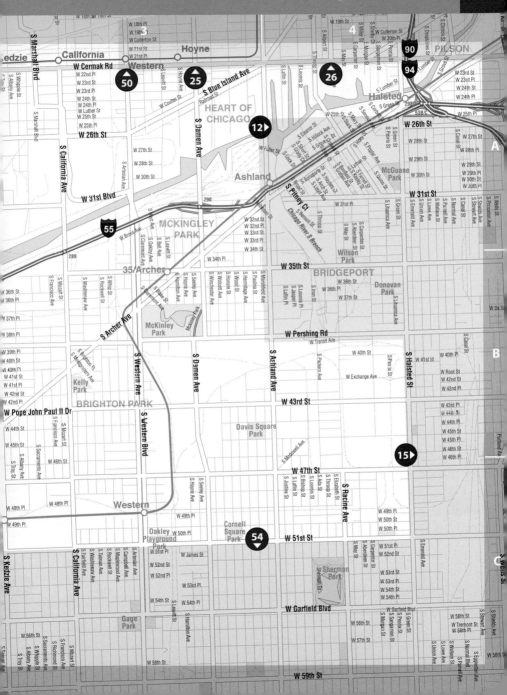

55

Adlai E Stevenson Expy

W 47th St

1

ARCHER HEIGHTS

2

W 47th St

51 ▲

Pulaski

W Archer Ave

Kedzie

Western

52 ▲

BACK OF THE YARDS

W 51st St

GARFIELD RIDGE

GAGE PARK

Sherman Park

18 ▶

PAGE **248**

W Archer Ave

W 55th St

WEST ELSON

W 55th St

S Central Ave

W Garfield Blvd

CLEARING

Chicago Midway Airport

Midway Airport

W 59th St

CHICAGO LAWN

S California Ave

Graffiti Mural

ENGLEWOOD

A

W 63rd St

Capital Cigar Store

W 63rd St

WEST ENGLEWOOD

Ashland/ 63rd

W 65th St

S Cicero Ave

WEST LAWN

MARQUETTE PARK

Marquette Rd

Marquette Park

Halsted

53

54

57 ▶

BEDFORD PARK

S Pulaski Rd

FORD CITY

S Kedzie Ave

W 71st St

S Western Ave

S Damen Ave

S Ashland Ave

S Racine Ave

S Halsted St

43

BURBANK

State Ave.

W 79st St

ASHBURN

WRIGHTWOOD

WEST CHATHAM

SCOTTSDALE

MARYCREST

PARKVIEW

GRESHAM

B

W 87th St

S Central Ave

EVERGREEN PARK

Campbell House

William MR French Ho

12 **20**

W 95th St

Original Rainbow Cone

Edwin C Young House

Adams House

OAK LAWN

Bronzeville Children's Museum

Evans House

Karge House

Ridge Park

S Bev Pkwy

Oakdale Park

Horton Mansion

Edward L Roberts House

S Ridgeland Ave

TALLY'S CORNER

W 99th St

McDonnell House

Givens Irish Castle

Bell Tower

JB Condos Metra Station

57 🐾

294

W 103rd Rd

S Cicero Ave

S Pulaski Rd

Chambers House

McComber Hou

103rd

How Ho

Burhans-Ellinwood Model House

Ridge Historical S

55

MOUNT GREENWOOD

56

Frank Anderson House

Gately House

Harris House

Blackwelder House

Hopkinson House

Lackmore House

Ferguson House

W 111th St

MOUNT GREENWOOD HEIGHTS

Beverly Arts Center

Metra Station 111th

Bohn Park

Arnett Chapel

W 111

Holy Name of Mary Church

C

W 115th St

Godspeed House

St. Walter Catholic Church

S Kedzie Ave

Morgan Park Apostolic Church

W 115t

ALSIP

S Western Ave

S Vincennes St

Dan Ryan Expy

59 ▶

Tri-State Tollway

Calumet Sag Rd

W 119th St

W 127th St

1 mile

1 km

Vermont

The Southwest side comprises several communities steeped in Chicago's ethnic blue collar history, including a large Lithuanian population, Italians, Arab Americans, African Americans, and the Irish. This cultural diversity has not come without conflict—Marquette Park was once a gathering spot for white supremacy groups. Today, the park is better known for its fishing pond, golf course, and occasional outbursts of gang violence. Southernmost in the southwest side, the Beverly and Morgan Park areas are chockablock with historic homes and civic pride.

o Landmarks

- **Adams House** •
  9625 S Longwood Dr
- **Arnett Chapel AME Church** •
  11218 S Bishop St
- **Bell Tower Condos** •
  10317 S Longwood Dr
- **Blackwelder Summerlin House** •
  10910 S Prospect Ave
- **The Body of Lake Michigan** •
  5700 S Cicero Ave
- **Bohn Park** • 1966 W 111th St
- **Burhans-Ellinwood Model House** •
  10410 S Hoyne Ave
- **Campbell House** •
  9250 S Damen Ave
- **Edward L. Roberts House** •
  10134 S Longwood Dr
- **Edwin C. Young House** •
  9215 S Pleasant Ave
- **Ferguson House** •
  10954 S Prospect Ave
- **Frank Anderson House** •
  10400 S Longwood Dr

- **Gately House** • 10655 S Hoyne Ave
- **Givens' Irish Castle** •
  10244 S Longwood Dr
- **Goodspeed House** •
  11216 S Oakley Ave
- **Harris House** •
  10856 S Longwood Dr
- **Holy Name of Mary Church** •
  11159 S Loomis St
- **Hopkinson House** •
  10820 S Drew St
- **Horton Mansion** •
  10200 S Longwood Dr
- **Howe House** • 10208 S Wood St
- **JB Chambers House** •
  10330 S Seeley Ave
- **Karge House** • 2035 W 99th St
- **Lackore House** •
  10956 S Prospect Ave
- **McCumber House** •
  10305 S Seeley Ave
- **Metra 103rd/Washington Heights Rock Island District Branch Line Station** •
  W 103rd St & S Vincennes Ave

- **Metra Rock Island Main Line**
  111th St/Monterey Ave Station •
  W 111th St & W Monterey Ave
- **Midway International Airport** •
  5700 S Cicero Ave
- **Morgan Park Apostolic Pentecostal Church** •
  11401 S Vincennes Ave
- **Morgan Park United Methodist Church** • 11030 S Longwood Dr
- **Oakdale Park** • 956 W 95th St
- **Original Rainbow Cone** •
  9233 S Western Ave
- **Raymond W. Evans House** •
  9914 S Longwood Dr
- **Ridge Historical Society** •
  10621 S Seeley Ave
- **Ridge Park** • 9625 S Longwood Dr
- **St. Walter Catholic Church** •
  11722 S Oakley Ave
- **William MR French House** •
  9203 S Pleasant Ave

We're still lamenting the reform of the nation's largest, sloppiest St. Paddy's Day parade into a more wholesome day of family fun. If you're still looking to be reckless in this neck of the woods, the collection of neighborhood pubs dotting Western Avenue won't turn you away.

🐂 Nightlife

- **Bobby G's** • 6843 W Archer Ave
- **Cookie's Cocktail Lounge** •
  1024 W 79th St
- **Cork & Kerry** • 10614 S Western Ave
- **Groucho's** • 8355 S Pulaski Rd
- **Halina's Pub** • 7023 W Archer Ave
- **Lagunitas Brewing Company** •
  2607 W 17th St
- **Lanigan's Irish Pub** • 3119 W 111th St
- **O'Rourke's Office** •
  11064 S Western Ave
- **Patrick's Tavern** • 6296 S Archer Ave
- **Sean's Rhino Bar** •
  10330 S Western Ave
- **Tom's Tap** • 6707 W Archer Ave
- **Wrong's Tap** • 10014 S Western Ave

🍴 Restaurants

- **Birrieria de la Torre** •
  6724 S Pulaski Rd
- **Fox's Restaurant** •
  9956 S Western Ave
- **Lumes House of Pancakes** •
  11601 S Western Ave
- **New China Tea** • 4024 W 55th St
- **Nicky's Grill and Yogurt Oasis** •
  10500 S Western Ave
- **Original Rainbow Cone** •
  9233 S Western Ave
- **Top Notch Beef Burgers** •
  2116 W 95th St
- **Uncle Joe's Jerk** •
  10210 S Vincennes Ave
- **Vito and Nick's Pizzeria** •
  8433 S Pulaski Rd

🛍 Shopping

- **Beverage Art Brewer & Winemaker Supply** • 9030 S Hermitage Ave
- **Beverly Cigar Co.** •
  10513 S Western Ave
- **Beverly Rare Records** •
  11612 S Western Ave
- **Bookie's Paperbacks & More** •
  10324 S Western Ave
- **Calabria Imports** • 1905 W 103rd St
- **County Fair** • 10800 S Western Ave
- **Ford City Mall** • 7601 S Cicero Ave
- **Optimo Fine Hats** •
  51 W Jackson Blvd
- **Southwest Ace Hardware** •
  6908 W Archer Ave
- **Southwest Book & Video** •
  7733 S Cicero Ave
- **Village Discount Outlet** •
  6419 S Kedzie Ave

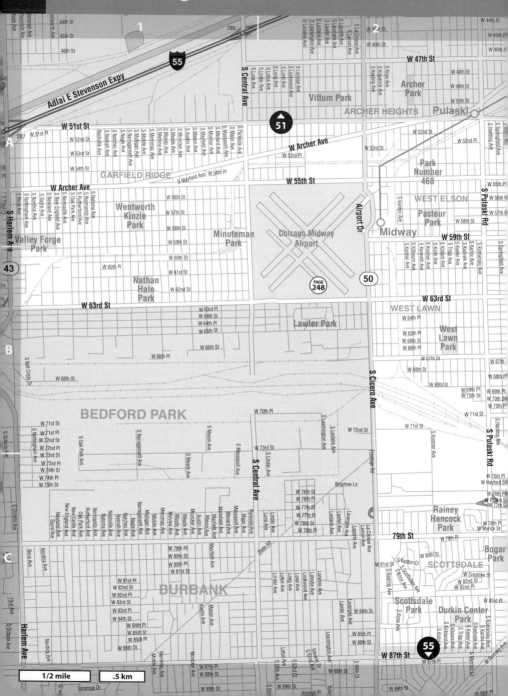

1/2 mile   .5 km

Park

3

W 45th St
W 46th St
W 46th St

4

W 45th St
W 46th St

W 47th St

W 47th St

Kedzie

Western

W 48th St
W 48th Pl

W 49th St
W 49th Pl

W 50th St

Cornell Square Park

W 51st St

BACK OF THE YARDS

52

15

GAGE PARK

W 52nd St
W 52nd Pl

W 53rd St
W 54th St

Sherman Park

W 53rd Pl
W 54th Pl

S Halsted St

S Wentworth Ave

S Lafflin St

A

Gage Park

W 55th St

W 56th St
W 57th St
W 58th St

S Kedzie Ave

S California Ave

S Western Ave

S Damen Ave

S Ashland Ave

S Racine Ave

W Garfield Blvd

Hermitage Park

W 59th St

W Tremont St
W 57th St
W 58th St

S Emerald Ave

CHICAGO LAWN

W 59th Pl
W 60th St
W 60th Pl
W 61st St
W 61st Pl
W 62nd St
W 62nd Pl

Lindblum Park

W 60th St
W 61st St

W 62nd St

ENGLEWOOD

W 60th St
W 61st St

W Englewood Ave

S Union Ave

W 63rd St

Ashland/63rd

Halsted

S Halsted Pkwy

W 63rd St
W 63rd Pl

B

W 63rd Pl
W 64th St
W 64th Pl
W 65th St
W 65th Pl
W 66th St
W 66th Pl

WEST ENGLEWOOD

Oakley Playlot

Odgen Park

W 64th St

W 65th St
W 65th Pl
W 66th St

18

Montgomery Park

W Marquette Rd

Marquette Park

Mann Dr

Kams Dr

Redfield Dr

No 44 Playlot

W Lithuanian Plaza Ct

W 68th St
W 69th St
W 70th St

W 71st St

W 71st Pl
W 72nd St
W 72nd Pl
W 73rd St
W 73rd Pl

Hamilton Park

Murray Playground Park

W 74th St

W 75th St
W 76th St
W 77th St
W 78th St

57

W 76th

C

ASHBURN

WRIGHTWOOD

Dawes Park

W 79th St

W 79th Pl
W 80th St

GRESHAM

WEST CHATHAM

W 80th St
W 81st St

S Eggleston Ave

S Vincennes Ave

W 82nd St
W 83rd St

MARYCREST

Ashburn Park

O' Hallaren Park

Foster Park

W 83rd St
W 83rd Pl
W 84th St
W 84th Pl

Dan Ryan Woods

W 85th Pl
W Seipp St
W 86th St
W 86th Pl

W 82nd St

W 84th St
W 85th St
W 86th St

Evergreen Cemetery

W 87th St

56

W Hopkins St

| 1/2 mile | .5 km |

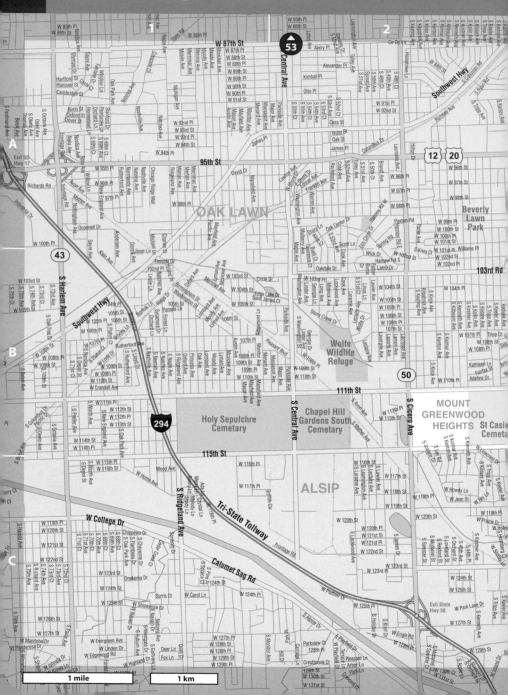

E 51st St
Hyde Park Blvd

1

2

Garfield
Garfield Blvd
Garfield

W 55th St
E 59th St

Washington
Park

Jackson
Park

Ban Ryan Expy

ILLINOIS

INDIANA

18

63rd

East 63rd/
Cottage
Grove

19

20

E 63rd St

E Hayes Dr

Lake Michigan

Halsted

WEST
WOODLAWN

E 67th St

Oak Woods
Cemetery

A

E Marquette Rd

69th

PARK
MANOR

E 71st St

WOODLAWN

SOUTH
SHORE

Kenna
Apartments

South Shore
Cultural Center

58

HAMILTON
PARK

E 74th St
E 75th St

ENGLEWOOD
Auburn Park

E 75th St

E 76th St

CHATHAM

Miller House

Vincennes Ave

State St

GRAND
CROSSING

S Stony Island Ave

S Jeffery Blvd

New Regal
Theatre

41

E 79th St
79th

MARYNOOK

E 79th St

SOUTH CHICAGO

S South Shore Dr

54

E 83rd St

57

STONY
ISLAND
PARK

S Chicago Ave

S Yates Blvd

S Mackinaw Ave

S Commercial Ave

Calumet River

87th

BURNSIDE

E 87th St

Chicago
Skyway

CALUMET
HEIGHTS

S Cottage Grove Ave

S Lafayette Ave

PRINCETON
PARK

WEST
CHESTERFIELD

94

PILL
HILL

Peoples
Gas
South
Chicago

S Ewing Ave

S Avenue O

90

B

Carter G Wooden
Regional
Library

E 95th St

Trinity United
Church of Christ

95th/Dan Ryan

Chicago State
University

Robert S.
Abbott Park

COTTAGE GROVE
HEIGHTS

12 **20**

JEFFERY
MANOR

S Stony Island Ave

S Colfax Ave

E 95th St

E 100th St

SOUTH
DEERING

S Ewing Ave

57

LONGWOOD
MANOR

ROSEMOOR

W 103rd St

E 103rd St

E 106th St

60

WASHINGTON
HEIGHTS

S Halsted St

Lilydale Progressive
Missionary Baptist

59

S King Dr

Pullman
Clock
Tower

Hyde Park

S Torrence Ave

Eggers
Woods

FERNWOOD

ROSELAND

E 111th St

E 113th St

Market

Palmer Hall
Park

Lake Calumet

Calumet River

Wolf Lake
Park

S Avenue O

Chicago Skyway

Indianapolis Blvd

Calumet Ave

41

Lilydale First
Baptist Church

56

West Pullman
Elementary
School

Foster
House &
Stable

E 115th St

S State St

PULLMAN

Wolf Lake

ILLINOIS

INDIANA

C

W 119th St

WEST PULLMAN

West Pullman Park

Cedar Park Cemetery
& Funeral Home

W 127th St
Vermont Ave

E 127th St

S Indiana Ave

Ford Freeway

912

GOLDEN
GATE

W 130th St

E 130th St

ALTGELD
GARDENS

RIVERDALE

Forest
Preserve

Little Calumet River

S Saginaw Ave

S Brainard Ave

HEGEWISCH

1 mile   1 km

Former lifeblood of the South Side economy, US Steel Company left behind expansive, desolate acreage decades ago. But despite squashed Olympic development hopes, transit artery Lake Shore Drive is currently being extended south, and solid plans for housing and infrastructure may become reality over the next few years. Still, life goes on in the South Side, one of the most crime-riddled areas in the city between Garfield Boulevard and Englewood, as well as the comfortable middle-class enclaves of South Shore to Chatham to Burnside, a bungalow belt that defies the area's rough-and-tumble reputation.

○ Landmarks

- **Abbott Park** • 49 E 95th St
- **Allan Miller House** • 7121 S Paxton Ave
- **Bronzeville Children's Museum** • 9301 S Stony Island Ave
- **Cedar Park Cemetery & Funeral Home** • 12540 S Halsted St
- **Chicago Skyway** • 8801 S Anthony Ave
- **Chicago State University** • 9501 S King Dr
- **Foster House & Stable** • 12147 S Harvard Ave
- **Historic Pullman** • 11141 S Cottage Grove Ave
- **Kenna Apartments** • 2214 E 69th St
- **Lilydale First Baptist Church** • 649 W 113th St
- **Lilydale Progressive Missionary Baptist Church** • 10706 S Michigan Ave
- **Market Hall** • E 112th St & Champlain Ave
- **The Nation of Islam National Center** • 7351 S Stony Island Ave
- **New Regal Theatre** • 1641 E 79th St
- **Oak Woods Cemetery** • 1035 E 67th St
- **Palmer Park** • 201 E 111th St
- **Peoples Gas South Chicago** • 8935 S Commercial Ave
- **Pullman Clock Tower** • 11141 S Cottage Grove Ave
- **South Shore Cultural Center** • 7059 South Shore Dr
- **Trinity United Church of Christ** • 400 W 95th St
- **West Pullman Elementary** • 11941 S Parnell Ave
- **West Pullman Park** • 401 W 123rd St
- **Woodson Regional Public Library** • 9525 S Halsted St

75th Street is a major hub of South Side action: South Shore's **Jeffery Pub** offers a friendly haven for the South Side's GLBTQ folks. South Deering received its 15 minutes of fame when the smoked fish offerings of **Calumet Fisheries** were featured on Anthony Bourdain's *No Reservations*.

🍸 Nightlife

- **Jeffery Pub** • 7041 S Jeffery Blvd
- **Red's the New Generation** • 6926 S Stony Island Ave
- **South Shore Inn** • 13611 S Brainard Ave

🍴 Restaurants

- **5 Loaves Eatery** • 405 E 75th St
- **BJ's Market & Bakery** • 8734 S Stony Island Ave
- **Cal Harbor Restaurant** • 546 E 115th St
- **Calumet Fisheries** • 3259 E 95th St
- **Daddy O's Jerk Pit** • 7518 S Cottage Grove Ave
- **Dat Donut** • 8251 S Cottage Grove Ave
- **Hienie's Shrimp House** • 10359 S Torrence Ave
- **Jamaican Jerk Spice** • 6500 S Cottage Grove Ave
- **Lem's BBQ** • 311 E 75th St
- **Old Fashioned Donuts** • 11248 S Michigan Ave
- **Soul Veg City** • 203 E 75th St
- **That's-A-Burger** • 8301 S Stony Island Ave
- **Yassa African Restaurant** • 3511 S King Dr

🛍 Shopping

- **A&G International Fresh Market** • 5630 W Belmont Ave
- **The African Hedonist** • 8128 S Cottage Grove Ave FL #1
- **Hagen's Fish Market** • 5635 W Montrose Ave
- **Hyman's Hardware** • 8614 S Commercial Ave
- **Jordan's Beauty Supply** • 1911 E 79th St
- **K & G Fashion Superstore** • 7540 S Stony Island Ave
- **The Underground Bookstore** • 1727 E 87th St

Garfield
Garfield

W 52nd St
W 53rd St
W 53rd Pl
W 54th St
W 54th Pl

E Garfield Blvd
E 54th Pl

Washington Park

E 53rd St
E 54th St

W 55th Pl

E 55th St

1

2

Englewood

E 59th St

W 57th St
W 58th St
W 59th Pl
W 60th St
W 60th Pl
W 61st St
W 61st Pl
W 62nd St

18

Washington Park Lagoon

Midway Plaisance

19

S Lake Shore Dr

20

Jackson Park

A

63rd St

63rd

King Dr

East 63rd - Cottage Grove

E 63rd Pl

WOODLAWN

PAGE 198

South Lagoon

Halsted

WEST WOODLAWN

E Marquette Rd

69th

PARKE MANOR

GRAND CROSSING

90

SOUTH SHORE

E 71st St

54

W 74th St

MARYNOOK

E 75th St

Rosenblum Park

E 75th St

B

W 75th St
W 76th St

Grand Crossing Park

79th

CHATHAM

E 79th St

94

W 83rd St

Avalon Park

STONY ISLAND PARK

SOUTH CHICAGO

Chicago Skyway

87th

WEST CHESTERFIELD

E 87th St

CALUMENT HEIGHTS

Owens Park

PRINCETON PARK

Tuley Park

BURNSIDE

59

12 **20**

PILL HILL

95th

E 95th St

| 1 mile | | 1 km |

A

B

C

Lake Michigan

Rainbow
Park

E 79th St

Chicago Skyway
Service Area

Russell
Square
Park

SOUTH
CHICAGO

E 84th St

E 85th St

E 86th St

E 87th St

Bessemer
Park

90

S Chicago Ave

PILL HILL

12 **20**   **60**   E 95th St

E Foreman Dr   S Walton Dr

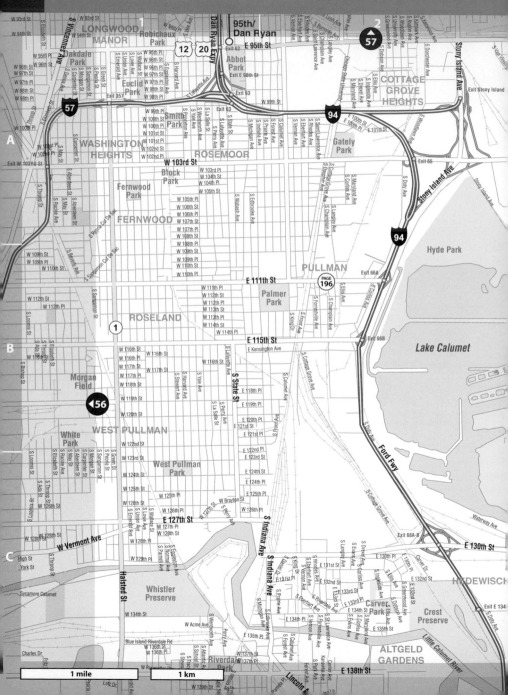

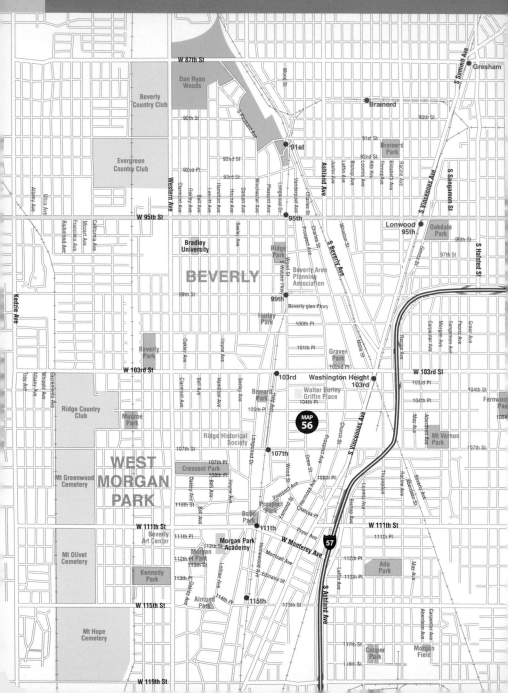

Overvew

Beverly Hills, best known simply as Beverly, is the stronghold of Chicago's heralded "South Side Irish" community. An authentic medieval castle, baronial mansions, rolling hills, and plenty of pubs compose Chicago's Emerald Isle.

Once populated by Illinois and Potawatomi Indian tribes, Beverly became home to clans of Irish-American families after the Great Chicago Fire. Famous residents include Andrew Greeley, Brian Piccolo, George Wendt, the Schwinn Bicycle family, and decades of loyal Chicago civil servants. Proud and protective of their turf, these close-knit South Siders call Beverly and its sister community, Morgan Park, "the Ridge." The integrated neighborhood occupies the highest ground in Chicago, 30 to 60 feet above the rest of the city atop Blue Island Ridge. Although the Ridge is just 15 miles from the Loop, most North Siders only trek there for the South Side Irish Parade (www.southsideirishparade.org), which attracts hundreds of thousands of people each year around St. Patrick's Day.

And there is more to Beverly than green beer and *craic*. The Ridge Historic District is one of the country's largest urban areas on the National Register of Historic Places. Beverly and Morgan Park encompass four landmark districts including the Ridge Historic District, three Chicago Landmark Districts, and over 30 Prairie-style structures.

Architecture

Within approximately a nine-mile radius, from 87th Street to 115th Street and Prospect Avenue to Hoyne Avenue, one can view a vast collection of homes and public buildings representing American architectural styles developed between 1844 and World War II. The 109th block of Prospect Avenue, every inch of Longwood Drive, and the Victorian train stations at 91st Street, 95th Street, 99th Street, 107th Street, 111th Street, and 115th Street are all great Chicago landmarks. Walter Burley Griffin Place on W 104th Street has Chicago's largest concentration of Prairie School houses built between 1909 and 1913 by Griffin, a student of Frank Lloyd Wright and designer of the city of Canberra in Australia.

Beverly Area Planning Association (www.bapa.org) provides a good architectural map, plus events and shopping information for the district. History buffs and researchers should get in contact with the Ridge Historical Society (www.ridgehistoricalsociety.org), which hosts talks and events from time to time.

Culture & Events

The Beverly Arts Center is the epicenter of Ridge culture. The $8 million facility provides visual and performance art classes for all ages as well as events and festivals (2407 W 111th St, 773-445-3838; www.beverlyartcenter. org). Historic Ridge homes open their doors to the public in the fall for the annual Home Tour, Chicago's oldest such tour. Sites are chosen for their diverse architectural styles and historical significance. The Home Tour is organized by the Beverly Area Planning Association (www.bapa.org), and guided trolley tours are also offered for an additional fee.

Where to Eat

• **Rainbow Cone**, 9233 S Western Ave
773-238-9833
Ice cream. People line up day and night in the summer.
• **Top Notch Beefburger**, 2116 W 95th St
773-445-7218
Burgers really are top notch at this '50s-style grill.

Where to Drink

• **Lanigan's Irish Pub**, 3119 W 111th St
773-233-4004
Live celtic music from time-to-time.

Where to Shop

• **Bev Art Brewer and Winemaker Supply**
9030 S Hermitage Ave
773-233-7579
Everything you need to brew and bottle it yourself.
• **Calabria Imports**, 1905 W 103rd St
773-396-5800
Imported Italian gourmet foodstuffs.
• **Optimo Hat Co**, 51 W Jackson Blvd
312-922-2999
Custom made men's hats.

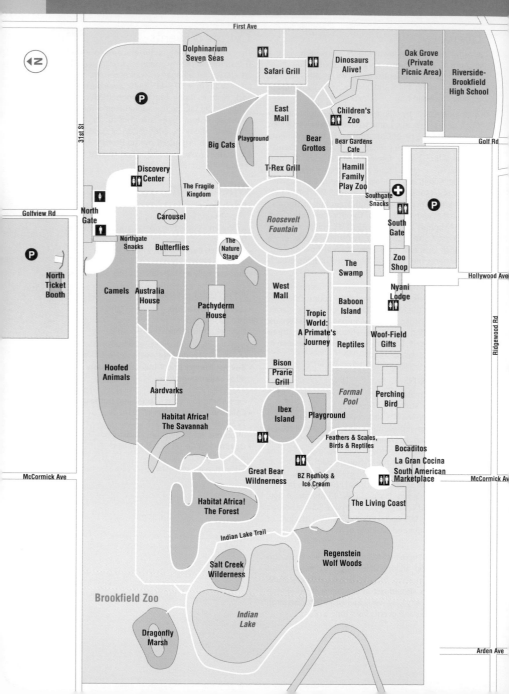

General Information

Address: 31st St & First Ave, Brookfield, IL 60513
Phone: 708-688-8000
Website: www.brookfieldzoo.org or @brookfield_zoo
Hours: Open daily from 10 am-5 pm (6 pm weekends)
Admission: $16.95 adults, $11.95 children 3-11, seniors over 65, free for children 2 and under.

Overview

While Lincoln Park Zoo is free, Brookfield offers a far more comprehensive wild animal experience with a strong emphasis on conservation education. 216 acres of creepy critters make for a memorable day trip. We'll skip the analogy with the Joliet Riverboat Casino.

Hamill Family Play Zoo

This interactive play area is dedicated solely to kids (just what a zoo needs: more kids). Children get to interact in a variety of ways, including donning costumes to play "zoo keeper" or "ring-tailed lemur," creating and frolicking in their own simulated habitats, planting seeds in the greenhouse, or spotting creepy insects in the outdoor bug path. Think a grownup would look silly dressed like a lemur? We want to play! Admission $2.50.

Regenstein Wolf Woods

The zoo's impressive wolf exhibit allows visitors to follow the progress of a small pack of endangered male wolves as they do the wolfy things wolves do—when they're not sleeping, of course. One-way glass allows spectators to get up close and personal with the wolves without freaking them out. So far, the mirrors have been 100% unsuccessful in detecting any wolf shoplifting.

Other Exhibits

Of course the zoo is full of exhibits, some more fascinating than others. Among them are the seasonal butterfly exhibit and the dragonfly marsh. Here are some other worthwhile sights:

• **Habitat Africa**: This is broken up into two sections: The Rainforest, with its zebras and African millipedes (heebie-jeebies), and The Savannah, with our favorite, the giraffes.

• **Tropic World**: Visit Kamba, the gorilla born in front of a captivated, slightly disgusted crowd of zoo visitors (mother Koola now knows how Marie Antoinette felt when she shared the delivery of her offspring with the French peasantry) and Bakari, who was born to mother Binto.

• **Stingray Bay**: 50 cownose rays swim in a 16,000-gallon saltwater tank, ready for slimy cuddles! Get up close and personal with the creatures as they glide underneath your fingertips. Admission is $4 for adults, $2.50 for seniors 65 and over and children 3 to 11.

• **Feathers and Scales**: Birds and Reptiles: We're pretty sure there are bats in there, but we've blocked the traumatic memory from our unstable minds. Enter at your own risk.

• **Big Cats**: Visit lions, tigers, and snow leopards as they prance, purr, and prowl. Part of The Fragile Kingdom exhibit, the Big Cats are impressive and beautiful in their natural habitat.

• **Great Bear Wilderness**: The Great Bear Wildness features two iconic North American animals: Polar bears and Grizzly Bears.

How to Get There

By Car: From the Eisenhower or Stevens Expressway, exit at First Avenue. From there, signs will direct you the short distance to the zoo. Lot parking is $10.

By Train: From downtown Chicago, take the Burlington Northern Metra line to Zoo Stop/Hollywood Station.

By Bus: Pace buses 304 and 331 stop right at the zoo's gates.

If you're coming in from out of town, consider staying at one of the zoo's hotel partners, which offer Brookfield Zoo packages including one admission to the zoo and three admissions to special shows and extras. Details and booking information can be found on Brookfield Zoo's website.

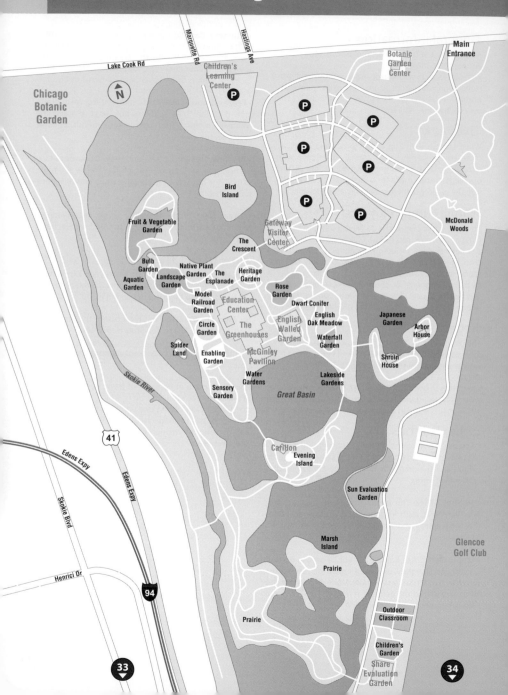

Lake Cook Rd

Marquette Rd

Hastings Ave

Botanic
Garden
Center

Main
Entrance

Children's
Learning
Center

Chicago
Botanic
Garden

N

Bird
Island

McDonald
Woods

Fruit & Vegetable
Garden

Gateway
Visitor
Center

The
Crescent

Bulb
Garden

Native Plant
Garden

Heritage
Garden

Aquatic
Garden

Landscape
Garden

The
Esplanade

Rose
Garden

Model
Railroad
Garden

Education
Center

Dwarf Conifer

English
Oak Meadow

Japanese
Garden

Circle
Garden

The
Greenhouses

English
Walled
Garden

Arbor
House

Spider
Land

Enabling
Garden

McGinley
Pavilion

Waterfall
Garden

Shroin
House

Water
Gardens

Lakeside
Gardens

Sensory
Garden

Great Basin

Carillon

Evening
Island

Sun Evaluation
Garden

Skokie River

41

Edens Expy

Edens Expy

Skokie Blvd

Marsh
Island

Prairie

Glencoe
Golf Club

Henrici Dr

94

Prairie

Outdoor
Classroom

Children's
Garden

Share
Evaluation
Garden

33

34

General Information

Address: 1000 Lake Cook Rd, Glencoe, IL 60022
Phone: 847-835-5440
Website: www.chicagobotanic.org or @chicagobotanic
Hours: Open 365 days, hours vary seasonally based on daylight
Admission: Free

Overview

Occupying 385 acres, the serene and lovely Chicago Botanic Garden has been the backdrop for many a chi-chi wedding since they opened the gates in 1972. The Botanic Garden is comprised of 26 gardens and four natural area. Among them are a specialized Japanese garden, a rose garden, a bulb garden, a greenhouse full of tropical vegetation, a waterfall garden, and several beds solely dedicated to indigenous plants and flowers. Constructed around nine islands with six miles of lake shoreline, the Botanic Garden is one of a select group of public gardens accredited by the American Association of Museums.

The Garden hosts changing exhibits and events, including its popular Model Railroad Garden, which features American landmarks made from plant material. Both the Ikebana Society and Macy's sponsor flower shows throughout the year; check the events schedule online to see what's going on before visiting. The Chicago Botanic Garden also offers lifestyle/wellness classes, including yoga and tai chi. Availability and times vary; check the website or call for more information.

The Botanic Garden serves food at the Garden View Café, which offers breakfast and café fare with a focus on local and sustainable, plus barista-helmed coffee. The Garden Grille serves up burgers and other grillables in season. Also in season, enjoy a beverage overlooking the roses at the Rose Terrace Café. Picnicking is allowed in the Picnic Glen, by Parking Lot 2.

How to Get There

By Car: Take I-90/94 W (The Kennedy) to I-94 (The Edens) and US 41. Exit on Lake Cook Road, then go a half-mile east to the garden. Parking costs $25 per car and $10 for seniors on Tuesdays.

By Train: Take the Union Pacific North Line to Braeside Metra station in Highland Park. Walk west about one mile along Lake Cook Road (aka County Line Road). If you ride the train to the Glencoe station, you can take a trolley directly to the garden. Round-trip tickets cost $2, free for children five and under.

By Bus: The Pace bus 213 connects at Davis Street in Evanston, and the Park Avenue Glencoe and Central Street Highland Park Metra stops. Buses don't run on Sundays and holidays.

By Bicycle: The Chicago Bikeway System winds through the forest preserves all the way up to the garden. Join it near the Billy Caldwell Golf Club at 6200 N Caldwell. A bicycle map is available on the Botanic Garden website.

Ravinia Festival

Address: 200 Ravinia Park Rd, Highland Park, IL 60035
Phone: 847-266-5100
Website: www.ravinia.org or @RaviniaFestival

Overview

The Ravinia Festival, the nation's oldest outdoor concert venue, has been hosting classical music concerts since 1904. The summer home of the Chicago Symphony Orchestra, Ravinia's crowded summer schedule also features pop, rock, and jazz, as well as top names from opera and world music.

The Pavilion—Those who are serious about the music experience pay a premium for one of the 3,200 seats in this covered, open-air pavilion, affording them a view of the stage and better acoustics.

The Lawn—Although you can't see the stage, great outdoor acoustics bring the concert to you on the lawn, where blanket rights for CSO residency concerts come cheap—typically $10 a pop. Just add picnic.

The Martin Theatre—The only remaining building original to the Festival, the 1904 Martin Theatre now hosts Martinis at the Martin, a cabaret series celebrating the Great American Songbook.

Eating at Ravinia

Ravinia is well known for lawn picnickers who compete to outdo each other with elaborate spreads, including roll-up tables, table linens, candelabras, champagne, and caviar. For those less ambitious, Ravinia offers picnic fare via its Picnic Box option, ice cream and other sweet treats at Carousel Ice Cream Shop, or you can make reservations to eat in at their fine-dining restaurant, Mirabelle. Ravinia Market offers eclectic food, from grilled skewers to brick-oven pizzas. The Park View and Mirabelle restaurants offer full-service dining options before the show. Wine, beer, and soft drinks are also available at concession stands throughout the park.

How to Get There

By Car: I-94 and I-294 have marked exits for Ravinia. Skip traffic back-ups on Lake Cook Road by exiting at Deerfield, Central, or Clavey Roads, and following directions to Park and Ride lots, which offer free parking and shuttle buses to Ravinia. The West Lot, Ravinia's closest parking spot, costs $10 for classical concerts and $20 for pop & jazz shows; parking fills up early for the most popular concerts.

By Train: During festival season, Metra offers the "Ravinia Special" along the Union Pacific North Line. For $7 round-trip, the train departs the Ogilvie Transportation Center at Madison and Canal and arrives at Ravinia's west gate in 40 minutes including stops at Clybourn, Ravenswood, Rogers Park, and Evanston. Trains depart for the city 15 minutes after the concert's end.

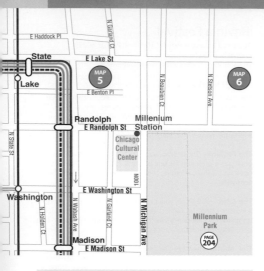

General Information

NFT Maps: 5, 6

Address: 78 E Washington St, Chicago, IL 60602

Website: www.chicagoculturalcenter.org or @ChiCulturCenter

Hours: Mon–Thurs 9 am–7 pm, Fri 9 am–6 pm, Sat 9 am–6 pm, Sun 10 am–6 pm

Overview

The Chicago Cultural Center is the Loop's public arts center. Free—that's right, we said FREE—concerts, theatrical performances, films, lectures, and exhibits are offered daily. Admission to the Cultural Center and its art galleries are all free, too, as is its WiFi, in case you're in a bind.

The building itself, constructed in 1897, is a neoclassical landmark featuring intricate glass and marble mosaics on its walls and grand stairways. Once the city's central public library, the Cultural Center boasts the world's largest Tiffany dome in Preston Bradley Hall. Free (there's that lovely word again) 45-minute architectural tours are held on Wednesdays, Fridays, and Saturdays at 1:15 pm. Tours meet at the Randolph Street lobby and are limited to the first 20 people. The building is also home to one of the city's popular Visitor Information Centers, which provide custom itineraries for tourists, multilingual maps, and concierge services. You can also find "InstaGreeters" from the Chicago Greeter Program, who will give on-the-spot walking tours. The Greeters also offer free two- to four-hour walking tours with chatty and knowledgeable guides around one of any number of neighborhoods throughout the city; book in advance via www.chicagogreeter.com.

Performances

The Chicago Cultural Center offers a number of daytime concerts around the year for all ages in various genres in its Preston Bradley Hall.

Art Galleries

A permanent exhibit in the Landmark Gallery, "Stand Up for Landmarks! Protests, Posters & Pictures" is a stunning black-and-white photographic survey of Chicago architecture. Five additional galleries regularly rotate exhibits, showcasing work in many media by renowned and local artists. Tours of current exhibits are ongoing.

How to Get There

By Car: Travel down Michigan Avenue to Randolph Street. From Lake Shore Drive, exit at Randolph Street.

By Train: From the Richard B. Ogilvie Transportation Center, travel east to Michigan Avenue on CTA buses 20, 56, 60, and 157. From Union Station, take CTA buses 151 and 157. From the Randolph Street station below Millennium Park, walk west across Michigan Avenue.

By L: Take the Green, Brown, Orange, Purple, or Pink Line to the Randolph stop. Walk east one block.

By Bus: CTA buses 3, 145, 147, 151 stop on Michigan Avenue in front of the Cultural Center.

General Information

NFT Map: 5
Address: 400 S State St, Chicago, IL 60605
Phone: 312-747-4300
Website: www.chipublib.org or @chipublib
Hours: Mon–Thurs 9 am–9 pm, Fri–Sat 9 am–5 pm, Sun 1 pm–5 pm

Overview

The massive Harold Washington Library Center is named for Harold Washington (1925–1987), Chicago's first African American mayor, who served from 1983 until he died in office (literally in office—he was in meeting about school issues at the time) in 1987. Said to be the world's largest public library, the 756,640-square-foot neoclassical architectural monstrosity has over 70 miles of shelves storing more than 9 million books, microforms, serials, and government documents. Notable works of sculpture, painting, and mosaics liven up the building's ample wall space and open areas.

Harold Washington's popular library, containing current general titles and bestsellers, is easy to find on the ground floor. The library's audio-visual collection (including an impressive collection of books on tape as well as videos, DVDs, and popular music CDs) is also housed here. The second floor is home to the children's library, and the general reference library begins on the third floor where the circulation desks are located. Among the notable features of the library is the eighth floor Music Information Center housing sheet music and printed scores, 150,000 recordings, the Chicago Blues Archives, eight individual piano practice rooms, and a chamber music rehearsal room. The ninth floor Winter Garden, with its olive trees and soaring 100-foot high ceilings is a popular site for special events. If you have your sights set on getting hitched here, leave your priest or rabbi at home—the library's status as a civic building precludes religious services on its premises.

Frequent free public programs are held in the lower level's 385-seat auditorium, video theater, exhibit hall, and meeting rooms; check the online Events page for more details.

Research Services

To check the availability or location of an item, search the library's Online Catalog on www.chipublib.org. The Chat With a Librarian feature is available Mon–Fri 9 am–12 noon, or try emailing (response within two days). For faster answers to common research questions, check out the website's selection of free online resources.

Computer Services

The Chicago Public Library's High Speed Wireless Internet System provides free access; all you need is a wireless enabled laptop computer, tablet PC, or PDA. The Library's network is open to all visitors free of charge and without filters. No special encryption settings, user names, or passwords are required.

The library's computers with Internet access and word processing, desktop publishing, graphic presentation, and spreadsheet applications are located on the third floor in the Computer Commons. Computer use is free and available on a first-come-first-served basis. You can reserve computers online and for up to two one-hour sessions per day. For downloads, bring your own flash drive or purchase one at the library for a fee. Laser printing is also provided for 15 cents a page.

Thomas Hughes Children's Library

The 18,000-square-foot Thomas Hughes Children's Library on the second floor serves children through eighth grade. A British citizen and member of Parliament, Thomas Hughes was so taken by news of the tragic Chicago Fire that he started a book collection for Chicago. His collection resulted in the 8,000 titles that composed the first Chicago Public Library. In addition to more than 120,000 children's books representing 40 foreign languages, there is a reference collection on children's literature for adults. Computers with Internet connections are also available. Children's programs are hosted weekly.

Special Collections

The library's Special Collections & Preservation Division's highlights include: Harold Washington Collection, Civil War & American History Research Collection, Chicago Authors & Publishing Collection, Chicago Blues Archives, Chicago Theater Collection, World's Columbian Exposition Collection, and Neighborhood History Research Collection. The collections' reading room is closed Wednesday, Thursday, and Sunday.

How to Get There

By Car: The library is at the intersection of State Street and Congress Parkway in South Loop. Take I-290 E into the Loop.

By L: The Brown, Purple, Orange, and Pink Lines stop at the Library Station. Exit the Red Line and O'Hare Airport Blue Line at Van Buren Station; walk one block south. Change from the Harlem/Lake Street Green Line to the northbound Orange Line at Roosevelt Road station; get off at Library Station.

By Bus: CTA buses that stop on State Street in front of the library are the 2, 6, 10, 29, 36, 62, 151, 145, 146, and 147.

Overview

Bordering the city to the north and surrounded by beautiful lakeshore scenery and affluent suburbs, Evanston may seem a world away. Truth be told, this town is only 12 miles from Chicago's bustling Loop. Spacious Victorian and Prairie Style homes with mini-vans and Mercedes parked on tree-lined streets overlook Lake Michigan and surround the quaint college town's downtown. Unlike other development-minded and sub-divided suburbs, Evanston still maintains a Chicago-esque feel and remains one of its most attractive bordering municipalities. Of course, Evanston residents still walk with their noses in the air and even charge their city neighbors to visit their beaches. We wonder what their tax base would look like without the city. Once home to Potawatami Indians, Evanston was actually founded after the establishment of the town's most well-known landmark, Northwestern University. Plans for the school began in 1851, and after the university opened for business four years later, its founder John Evans (along with a bunch of other Methodist dudes) proposed the establishment of the city, and so the town was incorporated as the village of Evanston in 1863. Today, residents are as devoted to cultural and intellectual pursuits as the morally minded patriarchs were to enforcing prohibition. The sophisticated, racially diverse suburb of roughly 75,000 packs a lot of business and entertainment into nearly eight square miles. Superb museums, many national historic landmarks, parks, artistic events, eclectic shops, and theaters make up for any subpar seasons by Northwestern University's Wildcats in the competitive Big Ten conference.

Culture

Evanston has several museums and some interesting festivals that merit a visit. Besides Northwestern's Block Museum of Art (www.blockmuseum. northwestern.edu), the impressive Mitchell Museum of the American Indian (www.mitchellmuseum.org) showcases life of the Midwest's Native Americans. The 1865 home of Frances E. Willard, founder of the Women's Christian Temperance Union and a women's suffrage leader, is located at 1730 Chicago Avenue (www.franceswillardhouse.org). Tours of the historic home are offered on the afternoons of every first and third Sunday of each month. Admission costs $10 for adults and $5 for children 12 and under.

Festivals & Events

• April: Evanston goes Baroque during Bach Week, 847-293-6686, www.bachweek.org.

• June: Fountain Square Arts Festival and free Starlight Concerts hosted in many of the city's parks through August

• July: Ethnic Arts Festival

Nature

Evanston is blessed with five public beaches open June through Labor Day. Non-residents should remember their wallets to pay for beach passes. For hours, fees, and boating information, contact the City of Evanston's Recreation Division (www. cityofevanston.org). The town's most popular parks encircle its beaches: Grosse Point Lighthouse Park, Centennial Park, Burnham Shores Park, Dawes Park, and South Boulevard Beach Park. All are connected by a bike path and fitness trail. On clear days, Chicago's skyline is visible from Northwestern's campus. West of downtown, McCormick, Twiggs, and Herbert Parks flank the North Shore Channel. Bicycle trails thread along the shore from Green Bay Road south to Main Street. North of Green Bay Road is Canal Shores Golf Course, a short 18-hole, par 60 public links at 1031 Central Street (www. canalshores.org) and the Evanston Ecology Center and Ladd Arboretum, located at 2024 McCormick Boulevard (www.evanstonenvironment.org).

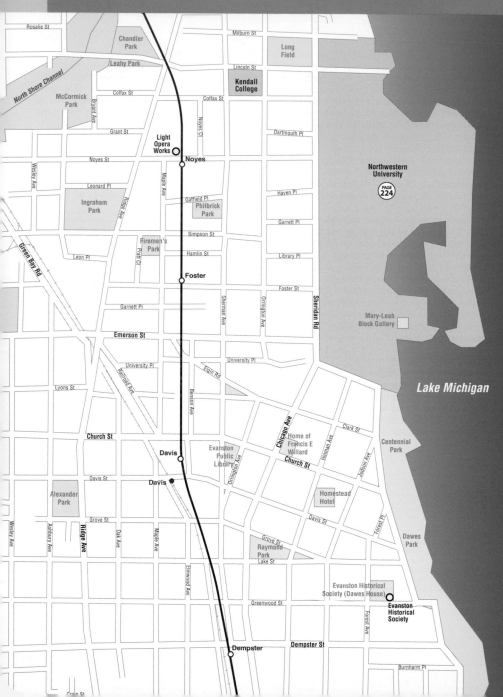

Rosalie St

Chandler Park

Milburn St

Long Field

Leahy Park

Lincoln St

North Shore Channel

Kendall College

McCormick Park

Colfax St

Colfax St

Bryant Ave

Grant St

Dartmouth Pl

Noyes St

Light Opera Works

Noyes

Noyes Ct

Wesley Ave

Leonard Pl

Northwestern University

PAGE 224

Ingraham Park

Ridge Ave

Maple Ave

Gaffield Pl

Haven Pl

Philbrick Park

Garrett Pl

Simpson St

Firemen's Park

Pratt Ct

Hamlin St

Library Pl

Leon Pl

Foster

Green Bay Rd

Foster St

Garnett Pl

Sherman Ave

Orrington Ave

Sheridan Rd

Emerson St

Mary-Leah Block Gallery

University Pl

University Pl

Elgin Rd

Railroad Ave

Lyons St

Lake Michigan

Church St

Benson Ave

Chicago Ave

Clark St

Davis

Centennial Park

Evanston Public Library

Home of Francis E Willard

Hinman Ave

Judson Ave

Davis St

Davis

Church St

Alexander Park

Homestead Hotel

Orrington Ave

Wesley Ave

Ashbury Ave

Ridge Ave

Oak Ave

Maple Ave

Grove St

Davis St

Forest Pl

Dawes Park

Grove St

Raymond Park

Lake St

Elmwood Ave

Evanston Historical Society (Dawes House)

Evanston Historical Society

Greenwood St

Forest Ave

Dempster

Dempster St

Burnharm Pl

Crain St

How to Get There

By Car: Lake Shore Drive to Sheridan Road is the most direct and scenic route from Chicago to Evanston. Drive north on LSD, which ends at Hollywood; then drive west to Sheridan and continue north. Near downtown, Sheridan becomes Burnham Place briefly, then Forest Avenue. Go north on Forest, which turns into Sheridan again by lakefront Centennial Park.

Parking: Watch how and where you park. The rules and regulations are strict and fiercely enforced. Remember...Evanston police do not have much to do.

By Train: Metra's Union Pacific North Line departing from the Richard B. Ogilvie Transportation Center in West Loop stops at the downtown Davis Street CTA Center station, 25 minutes from the Loop. This station is the town transportation hub, where Metra and L trains and buses interconnect.

By L: The CTA Purple Line Express L train travels direct to and from the Loop during rush hours. Other hours, ride the Howard-Dan Ryan Red Line to Howard Street, and transfer to the Purple Line for free.

By Bus: From Chicago's Howard Street Station, CTA and Pace Suburban buses serve Evanston.

○ Landmarks

- **Evanston Historical Society** · 225 Greenwood St
- **Music Theater Works** · 516 4th Street; Wilmette
- **Northwestern University** · 633 Clark St

▼ Nightlife

- **Prairie Moon** · 1635 Chicago Ave

🍴 Restaurants

- **Blind Faith Café** · 525 Dempster St
- **Buffalo Joe's** · 812 Clark St
- **Dozika** · 601 Dempster St
- **Hecky's Barbeque** · 1902 Green Bay Rd
- **Joy Yee's Noodles** · 533 Davis St
- **Kansaku** · 1514 Sherman Ave
- **Mt. Everest** · 630 Church St
- **Noodles & Company** · 930 Church St
- **Tapas Barcelona** · 1615 Chicago Ave
- **Trattoria Demi** · 1571 Sherman Ave

🛍 Shopping

- **Art + Science Salon** · 811 Church St
- **Campus Gear** · 1722 Sherman Ave
- **Coucou** · 1716 Sherman Ave

W Kinzie St

Carroll Dr

N Central Park Ave

W Carroll Ave

N St Louis Ave

N Homan Ave

W Fulton St

N Avers Ave

P

Garfield Park Conservatory

W Fulton Blvd

Conservatory Dr

W Walnut St

Gold Dome Building

Conservatory Central Park Drive

Pulaski

N Pulaski Rd

N Harding Ave

W Lake St

Kedz

W Maypole Ave

N Hamilton Ave

W West End St

N McCrea Dr

Lagoon

P

W Maypole Ave

W Washington Blvd

Garfield

W Washington Blvd

MAP 49

Warren Dr

W Warren Ave

Park

W Madison St

W Madison St

S Pulaski Rd

S Springfield Ave

S Hamilton Blvd

S Woodward Dr

S Central Park Ave

S St Louis Ave

S Homan Ave

S Spaulding Ave

W Monroe St

Cusic Ct

W Monroe St

W Wilcox Ave

W Adams Ave

W Adams St

Tennis Courts

Independence Blvd

W Jackson Blvd

W Jackson Blvd

S Christiana Ave

W Gladys Ave

S Trumbull Ave

W Van Buren St

W Fifth Ave

S Millard Ave

W Gladys Ave

Pulaski

W Congress Pkwy

290

Dwight D Eisenhower Expy

W Harrison St

Overview

Since 1908 the historic West Side has been home to an equally historic botanical gem—Garfield Park Conservatory. The mid 1990s saw major restoration efforts, along with the creation of The Garfield Park Conservatory Alliance, an organization that has raised money for various programs involving the Conservatory. The rest of the vast 185-acre park boasts fishing lagoons, a swimming pool, an ice rink, baseball diamonds, and basketball and tennis courts. Garfield Park's landmark Gold Dome Building houses a gymnasium, fitness center, boxing center, grand ballroom, and various meeting rooms.

Garfield and its sister parks—Humboldt Park (1400 N Sacramento Ave, 312-742-7549) and Douglas Park (1401 S Sacramento Dr, 773-762-2842)—constitute a grand system of sprawling green spaces linked by broad boulevards designed in 1869 by William Le Baron Jenney (better known as the "father of the skyscraper"). However, Jenney's plan didn't bear fruit until almost 40 years later (after the uprooting of corrupt park officials), when Danish immigrant and former park laborer Jens Jensen became chief landscape architect. In 1908, Jensen completed the parks and consolidated their three small conservatories under the 1.8-acre Garfield Park Conservatory's curvaceous glass dome meant to evoke a "great Midwestern haystack."

Garfield Park Conservatory

Address: 300 N Central Park Ave, Chicago, IL 60624
Phone: 773-638-1766
Website: www.garfield-conservatory.org or @ gpconservatory
Hours: 9 am–5 pm daily, Wed until 8 pm
Admission: FREE

One of the nation's largest conservatories, Garfield Park has six thematic plant houses with 1,000 species and more than 10,000 individual plants from around the world. Plants Alive!, a 5,000-square-foot children's garden, has touchable plants, a soil pool for digging, a Jurassic Park-sized bumble bee, and a two-story, twisting flower stem that doubles as a slide. School groups often book the garden for field trips, so check first to determine public access hours. Annual Conservatory events include the Spring Flower Show, Azalea/Camellia Show, Chocolate Festival, Summer Tropical Show, Chrysanthemum (Chicago's city flower) Show, and Holiday Garden Show. Visit online for program scheduling. There is a farmers market at the park on Sundays 11 am–4 pm from June through October.

Fishing

Garfield Park's two lagoons at Washington Boulevard and Central Park Avenue and those at Douglas and Humboldt Parks are favorite West Side fishing holes. Seasonally, they are stocked with bluegill, crappie, channel catfish, and largemouth bass. Eating the fish is another matter. Kids can participate in free fishing sessions at the park lagoons during the summer through the Chicago Park District.

Nature

The Chicago Park District leads free nature walks and has created marked trails with information plaques at the city's bigger parks, Garfield, Douglas, and Humboldt Parks included. Seasonally, visitors can view as many as 100 species of colorful butterflies at the formal gardens of the three parks. The parks' lagoons are officially designated Chicago birding parks, so take binoculars (see also the Chicago Ornithological Society for more information: www.chicagobirder.org). Picnics for 50 people or more, or tent set-up, require party-throwers to obtain permits issued by the Chicago Park District.

How to Get There

By Car: Garfield Park is ten minutes from the Loop. Take I-290 W; exit on Independence Boulevard and drive north. Turn east on Washington Boulevard to Central Park Avenue. Go north on Central Park Avenue two blocks past the Golden Dome field house and Lake Street to the Conservatory. A free parking lot is on the building's south side, just after Lake Street. Street parking is available on Central Park Avenue, Madison Street, and Washington Boulevard.

By L: From the Loop, take the Green Line west to the Conservatory-Central Park Drive stop, a charming renovated Victorian train station at Lake Street and Central Park Avenue.

By Bus: From the Loop, board CTA 20 Madison Street bus westbound. Get off at Madison Street and Central Park Avenue. Walk four blocks north to the Conservatory.

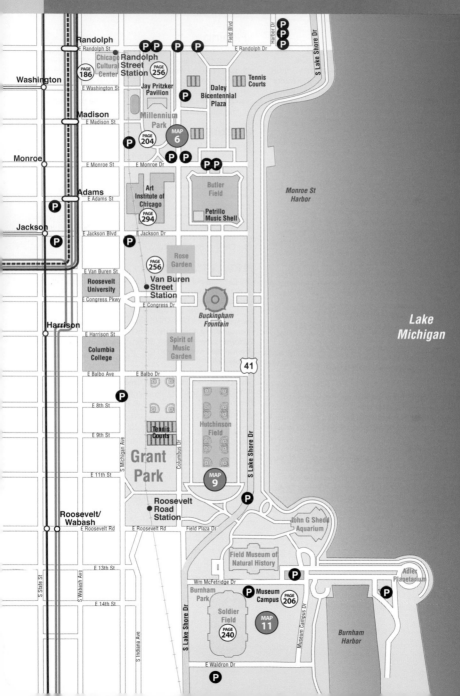

Overview

Grant Park, where grass meets glass, is Chicago's venerable "front lawn." Spanning the Lake Michigan shoreline from N Randolph Street to S Roosevelt Road and west to Michigan Avenue, it's safe to say there's not a more trafficked park this side of New York City's Central Park. Grant Park is a study in contrasts: on the one side featuring massive summer festivals (such as the annual homage to obesity known as Taste of Chicago) that turn the park into Chicago's dirty doormat; but during the rest of the year, a quiet place to relax, play, and count the number of panhandlers who ask if you can "help them out with a dollar."

The park's history can be traced back to 1835 when concerned citizens lobbied to prevent development along their pristine waterfront. Little did they know that when the State of Illinois ruled to preserve the land as "public ground forever to remain vacant of buildings" this meant for everyone, including the wealthy elite who were literally perched on the lofty balconies of the tawny palaces that lined the downtown shores of Lake Michigan. Be careful what you wish for, yes? Architect and city planner Daniel Burnham laid the groundwork for the park and made plans to erect museums, civic buildings, and general park attractions along the waterfront. This plan got somewhat sidetracked by the Great Chicago Fire of 1871. Interestingly enough, remaining debris from the fire was pushed into the lake and now forms part of the foundation for much of Grant Park and Chicago's famous shoreline. Chicagoans can thank local land-lover and legendary mail-order magnate Aaron Montgomery Ward for pressuring the State of Illinois in 1911 to preserve the land as an undeveloped open space.

Nature

Grant Park's lawns, gardens, lakefront, and bench-lined paths attract a mixed crowd of lunching office workers, exercise fanatics, readers, gawking tourists, homeless and not-so-homeless vagabonds, and just your run-of-the-mill idiots. South and north of famous Buckingham Fountain are the formal Spirit of Music Garden and Rose Garden, respectively. There are also a multitude of sculptures, ranging in form and style, strewn with abandon throughout the park, so expect to see art appreciators and imitators alike milling about as well.

Sports

Much of the sports areas in Grant Park are on the south end of the park. Baseball diamonds and tennis courts are available on a first-come basis unless they are reserved for league play. There is also a skate park, volleyball courts and a field house.

Maggie Daley Park

Covering 20 acres in Grant Park's northeast corner, the evolution of what had been Daley Bicentennial Plaza into Maggie Daley Park—named in honor and memory of Chicago's beloved former first lady—came about after the garage underneath needed substantial renovations that necessitated removing the existing plaza. A growing Lakeshore East population and proximity to Millennium Park to the north informed the new park's design, which seamlessly links some of Chicago's top attractions while providing recreation and open space opportunities for Lakeshore residents. Among other things, the plan contains a rock climbing area, a curvy ice skating "ribbon," skate park, and a boffo brilliant "play garden" ("ground" just seems so...beneath us!) that blows minds with its multi-themes, oversize equipment, slide crater, and water area.

Buckingham Fountain

Buckingham Fountain is Grant Park's spouting centerpiece at the intersection of Congress Parkway and Columbus Drive, and was the original starting point of Route 66. Designed by Edward Bennett, the fountain is an homage to Lake Michigan and houses four statues that represent the Lake's four surrounding states (Illinois, Indiana, Michigan, and Wisconsin, ya big idiot). It has been showering onlookers with wind-blown spray since 1927 and, unfortunately, is notable for its role in the opening sequence of the sitcom *Married...with Children*. In warm weather months, the center basin blasts water 150 feet into the air every 20 minutes all day long. Lights and music accompany the skyrocketing water display during evening hours. Food concessions and restrooms can be found nearby.

Festivals & Events

Chicagoans used to gather at the Petrillo Music Shell for free Grant Park Orchestra and Chorus concerts during the summer months. Now they go to the Jay Pritzker Pavilion in Millennium Park, located between Michigan and Columbus Avenues that, in and of itself, is worth a visit. Concerts take place June through August (www.grantparkmusicfestival. com or @gpmf). You can't always pass up a free headliner concert at Grant Park's monstrous summer festivals. If at all possible, avoid the gut-to-gut feeding frenzy that is the Taste of Chicago. If you must go, hit it on a weekday afternoon; go on the weekend and you'll understand why. In June, get your groove on at the Chicago Blues Fest. If you're really a diehard fan, spend a full paycheck for a three-day pass to Lollapalooza in August. Extra deodorant required. For a complete event schedule, contact the Chicago Department of Cultural Affairs and Special Events at www.cityofchicago. org/dcase.

How to Get There

By Car: Exits off Lake Shore Drive west to Grant Park are Randolph Street, Monroe Drive, Jackson Drive, Balbo Drive, and Roosevelt Road. Also, enter the park from Michigan Avenue heading east on the same streets. The underground East Monroe Garage is off Monroe Drive. Columbus Drive runs through Grant Park's center and has metered parking.

By Train: From the Richard B. Ogilvie Transportation Center, travel east to Michigan Avenue and Grant Park on CTA buses 20, 56, 60, and 157. From Union Station, board CTA buses 7 and 126.

Metra trains coming from the south stop at the Roosevelt Road station on the south end of Grant Park before terminating at the underground Millennium Station at Randolph Street.

By L: Get off at any L stop in the Loop between Randolph Street and Van Buren Street. Walk two blocks east to Grant Park.

By Bus: CTA buses 3, 4, 6, 7, 126, 147, and 151 stop along Michigan Avenue in front of Grant Park.

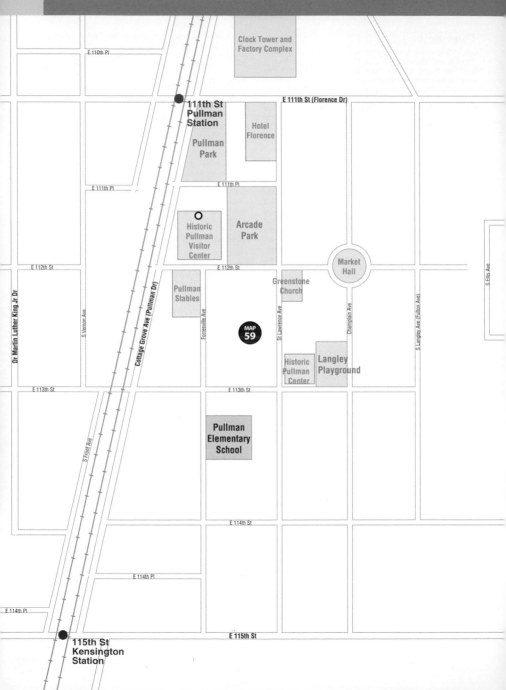

E 110th Pl

Clock Tower and
Factory Complex

E 111th St (Florence Dr)

111th St
Pullman
Station

Hotel
Florence

Pullman
Park

E 111th Pl

E 111th Pl

Historic
Pullman
Visitor
Center

Arcade
Park

E 112th St

E 112th St

Market
Hall

Pullman
Stables

Greenstone
Church

MAP
59

Historic
Pullman
Center

Langley
Playground

E 113th St

E 113th St

Pullman
Elementary
School

E 114th St

E 114th St

E 114th Pl

E 114th Pl

E 115th St

115th St
Kensington
Station

Dr Martin Luther King Jr Dr

S Vernon Ave

Cottage Grove Ave (Pullman Dr)

S Front Ave

Forrestville Ave

St Lawrence Ave

Champlain Ave

S Langley Ave (Fulton Ave)

S Ellis Ave

General Information

Historic Pullman Foundation: www.pullmanil.org
Historic Pullman Visitor Center: 11141 S Cottage Grove Ave, 773-785-8901
Hours: Tues–Sun, 11 am–3 pm
Admission: $5 adults, $4 students under 18, $4 seniors

Overview

Although railroad magnate George Pullman's Utopian community went belly-up, the Town of Pullman he founded 14 miles south of the Loop survives as a National Landmark Historic District. Built between 1880 and 1885, Pullman is one of America's first planned model industrial communities.

The "workers' paradise" earned Pullman humanitarian hoorahs, as well as a 6% return on his investment. Pullman believed that if laborers and their families lived in comfortable housing with gas, plumbing, and ventilation—in other words, livable conditions—their productivity would increase, as would his profits. Pullman was voted "the world's most perfect town" at the Prague International Hygienic and Pharmaceutical Exposition of 1896.

All was perfect in Pullman until a depression incited workers to strike in 1894, and the idealistic industrialist refused to negotiate with his ungrateful workers. While George Pullman's dream of a model community of indentured servitude died with him in 1897, hatred for him lived on. Pullman's tomb at Graceland Cemetery is more like a bomb shelter. To protect his corpse from irate labor leaders, Pullman was buried under a forest of railroad ties and concrete.

The grounds and buildings that make up Pullman went through most of the twentieth century stayed intact until 1998, when a man who heard voices in his head torched several of the site's primary buildings. Fortunately, die-hard Pullmanites have banded together to maintain the remaining structures, and for anyone interested in labor history or town planning, the city is worth a train or bus ride down from the Loop.

Architecture & Events

Architect Solon Beman and landscape architect Nathan Barrett based Pullman's design on French urban plans. Way back when, Pullman was made up of mostly brick row houses (95% still in use), several parks, shops, schools, churches, and a library, as well as various health, recreational, and cultural facilities.

Today, the compact community's borders are 111th Street (Florence Drive), 115th Street, Cottage Grove Avenue (Pullman Drive), and S Langley Avenue (Fulton Avenue). If you're interested in sightseeing within the historic district, we suggest you start at the Pullman Visitor Center, housed in the historic Arcade Building. There you can pick up free, self-guided walking tour brochures and watch an informative 15-minute film on the town's history. Check online for additional specialty tour information and lecture details.

Along with self-guided tours, the Visitor Center offers 90-minute guided tours on the first Sunday of the month from May to October; key tour sites include Hotel Florence, Greenstone Church (interior), Market Square, the stables, and the fire station. Tours start at 1:30 and cost $10 for adults, $7 for seniors, and $7 for students. Reservations not required. The annual House Tour in mid-October is a popular Pullman event where several private residences open their doors to the public from 11 am to 5 pm on Saturday and Sunday.

Where to Eat

Cal Harbor Restaurant (546 E 115th St, 773-264-5435): Omelettes, burgers, etc. at this family grill.

How to Get There

By Car: Take I-94 S to the 111th Street exit. Go west to Cottage Grove Avenue and turn south, driving one block to 112th Street to the Visitor Center surrounded by a large, free parking lot.

By Train: Metra's Electric Main Line departs from Millennium Station (underground) at Michigan Avenue between S Water Street and Randolph Street. Ride 30 minutes to Pullman Station at 111th Street. Walk east to Cottage Grove Avenue, and head south one block to 112th and the Visitor Center.

By L: From the Loop, take the Red Line to the 95th Street station. Board CTA 111 Pullman bus going south.

By Bus: CTA 4 bus from the Randolph Street Station travels south to the 95th Street and Cottage Grove stop. Transfer to 111 Pullman bus heading south, which stops at the visitors center.

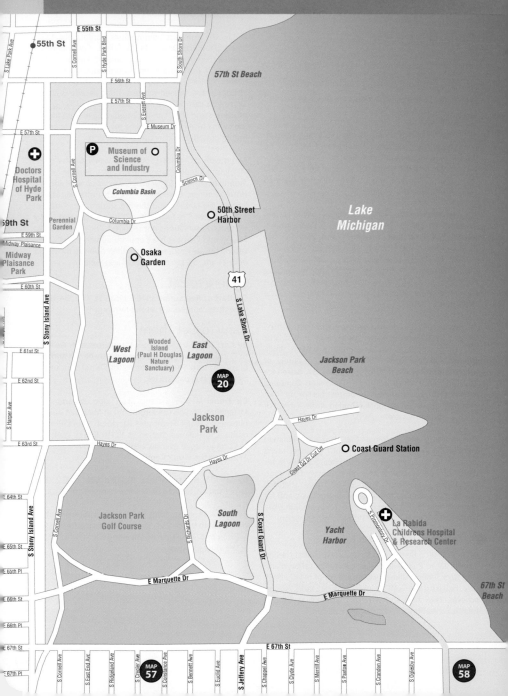

55th St

E 55th St

57th St Beach

E 56th St

E 57th St

E Museum Dr

P

Museum of
Science
and Industry

Columbia Dr

Doctors
Hospital
of Hyde
Park

Columbia Basin

Science Dr

59th St

Perennial
Garden

Columbia Dr

50th Street
Harbor

Lake
Michigan

E 59th St

Midway Plaisance

Midway
Plaisance
Park

Osaka
Garden

41

E 60th St

S Stony Island Ave

S Lake Shore Dr

E 61st St

West
Lagoon

Wooded
Island
(Paul H Douglas
Nature
Sanctuary)

East
Lagoon

Jackson Park
Beach

E 62nd St

S Harper Ave

MAP
20

E 63rd St

Hayes Dr

Jackson
Park

Hayes Dr

Coast Guard Station

Hayes Dr

S Cornell Ave

Coast Gd Dr Cut Off

S Stony Island Ave

E 64th St

Jackson Park
Golf Course

S Richards Dr

South
Lagoon

S Coast Guard Dr

Yacht
Harbor

S Promontory Dr

La Rabida
Childrens Hospital
& Research Center

E 65th St

E 65th Pl

E Marquette Dr

E 66th St

E Marquette Dr

67th St
Beach

E 66th Pl

S Cornell Ave

S East End Ave

S Ridgeland Ave

S Cregier Ave

S Constance Ave

S Bennett Ave

S Euclid Ave

S Jeffery Ave

S Chappel Ave

S Clyde Ave

S Merrill Ave

S Paxton Ave

S Crandon Ave

S Oglesby Ave

E 67th St

E 67th St

E 67th Pl

MAP
57

MAP
58

Overview

Historic Jackson Park, named for Mary Jackson, original owner of the land and cousin to president Andrew Jackson, borders Lake Michigan, Hyde Park, and Woodlawn, and was, for a long time, an unused tract of fallow land. The 543-acre parcel was eventually transformed into a real city park in the 1870s thanks to Frederick Law Olmsted and Calvert Vaux of Central Park fame. The Midway Plaisance connects Jackson Park to Washington Park.

Jackson Park experienced its 15 minutes of worldwide fame in 1893 when it played host to the World's Fair Columbian Exposition. Today, the Museum of Science and Industry and La Rabida Children's Hospital and Research Center occupy two of the former fair structures. Situated along the lake, the park features three harbors and beaches. The park is also home to the first golf course west of the Allegheny Mountains.

Museum of Science and Industry

Address: 57th St & Lake Shore Dr, Chicago, IL 60637
Phone: 773-684-1414
Website: www.msichicago.org or @msichicago
Hours: 9:30 am–4 pm daily, with extended hours until 5:30 during high-traffic times
Admission: $18 for adults, ($15 for Chicagoans); $11 for children 3-11, ($10 for Chicagoans); $17 for seniors, ($14 for Chicagoans) (Note: The Museum offers free admission to Illinois residents on what seem to be arbitrary days, and hours vary month to month, so check the website regularly.)

The 1893 World's Fair Arts Palace is home to the Museum of Science and Industry. The mammoth 350,000-square-foot bastion is one of the largest science museums in the world. Generations of Chicagoans and visitors have been wowed by a vast array of exhibits, including hatching baby chicks, U-505 (the only World War II German submarine captured), and the Walk-Through Heart. The model railroad, another favorite exhibit, has been expanded to the now 3,500-square-foot Great Train Journey, which depicts the route from Chicago to Seattle. Other popular attractions include the coal mine, the Fairy Castle, and the Omnimax Theater's five-story, domed, wrap-around theater.

Nature

Two lagoons surround Wooded Island, a.k.a. Paul H. Douglas Nature Sanctuary. Osaka Garden, a serene Japanese garden with an authentic tea house and entrance gate, sits at the island's northern tip. The ceremonial garden, like the golden replica of Statue of the Republic on Hayes Avenue, recalls the park's 1893 Exposition origins. The Chicago Audubon Society (www.chicagoaudubon.org) conducts bird walks in the park. These sites and the Perennial Garden at 59th Street and Cornell Drive are also havens for butterflies.

Sports

Back in the very beginning of the 20th century, the Jackson Park Golf Course (312-245-0909 or jacksonpark.cpdgolf.com) was the only public course in the Midwest. Today, the historic 18-hole course is certified by the Audubon Cooperative Sanctuary and has beautiful wilderness habitats. (Or are those scruffy fairways?) Greens fees are $28 during the week and $31 on weekends (all rates are discounted for residents). A driving range is adjacent to the course.

The city's park fitness facilities are a great deal, the facility at the Jackson Park field house included. The fitness center is open Mon–Fri 9 am–9:30 pm, Sat 9 am–4:30 pm, and Sun 11 am–4:30 pm. Adult membership passes cost $17 a month or $150 for the year. From Hayes Drive north along Cornell Avenue are outdoor tennis courts, baseball diamonds, and a running track. Tennis courts are on the west side of Lakeshore Drive at 63rd Street. Jackson Park's beaches are at 57th Street and 63rd Street (water playground, too). Inner and Outer Harbors allow shore fishing.

Neighboring Parks

North of Jackson Park at 55th Street and Lake Shore Drive is Promontory Point, a scenic lakeside picnic spot. Harold Washington Park, 51st Street and Lake Shore Drive, has a model yacht basin and eight tennis courts on 53rd Street.

To the west, 460-acre Washington Park (5531 S Martin Luther King Dr, 773-256-1248) has an outdoor swimming pool, playing fields, and nature areas. It's also worth stopping by to see Lorado Taft's 1922 Fountain of Time sculpture and the DuSable Museum of African American History (740 E 56th Pl, 773-947-0600; www.dusablemuseum.org).

At 71st Street and South Shore Drive are South Shore Beach, with a harbor, bird sanctuary, and South Shore Cultural Center (7059 South Shore Dr, 773-256-0149). South Shore Golf Course is a nine-hole public course. Greens fees are $17 weekdays and $19 on weekends (southshore.cpdgolf.com).

How to Get There

By Car: From the Loop, drive south on Lake Shore Drive, exit west on 57th Street. From the south, take I-94 W. Exit on Stony Island Avenue heading north to 57th Drive. The museum's parking garage entrance is on 57th Drive. The Music Court lot is behind the museum. A free parking lot is on Hayes Drive.

By Bus: From the Loop, CTA buses 6 and 10 (weekends and daily in summer) stop by the museum.

By L: (the quickest way to get to Jackson Park): Take the Green Line to the Garfield Boulevard (55th Street) stop; transfer to the eastbound 55 bus.

By Train: Sporadic service. From the Loop's Millennium Station at Randolph Street and Van Buren Street stations, take Metra Electric service. Trains stop at the 55th, 56th, and 57th Street Station platform. Walk two blocks east.

Overview

The largest of Chicago's 500-plus parks, Lincoln Park stretches 1,208 acres along the lakefront from the breeder cruising scene at the North Avenue Beach to the gay cruising scene at Hollywood Beach. The park boasts one of the world's longest bike trails, but thanks to an ever-increasing abundance of stroller pushers, leashless dogs, and earbud-wearing wheely-doodlers, the path proves treacherous for cyclists and pedestrians alike. Nonetheless, sporty types and summertime dawdlers still find satisfaction indoors and out at Lincoln Park. Take a break from winter inside the Lincoln Park Conservatory, a tropical paradise full o' lush green plants no matter what the thermometer reads. Public buildings, including animal houses at the Lincoln Park Zoo, Café Brauer, Peggy Notebaert Nature Museum, and vintage beach bath houses, make the park as architecturally attractive as it is naturally beautiful.

Much of southern Lincoln Park is open green space populated by football, soccer, dog play, and barbecue grills. Paths shaded by mature trees lead to stoic statues. Until the 1860s, Lincoln Park was nothing more than a municipal cemetery filled with the shallow graves of cholera and smallpox victims, and it was concern about a public health threat that instigated the creation of the park. Although the city attempted to relocate all the bodies in the cemetery-to-park conversion of 1869, digging doggies may unearth more than picnickers' chicken bones.

Nature

In spring, bird watchers flock to Lincoln Park's ponds and nature trails. Addison Bird Sanctuary Viewing Platform north of Belmont Harbor overlooks five fenced-in acres of wetlands and woods. Birding programs around North Pond are run by the Lincoln Park Conservancy (www.lincolnparkconservancy.org) and the Chicago Ornithological Society (www.chicagobirder. org). More than 100 species of birds have been identified at the 10-acre pond. Free guided walks are held on most Wednesdays during the year starting at 7 am. Bring binoculars and a canteen of coffee. The Fort Dearborn Chapter of the Illinois Audubon Society hosts park and zoo bird walks (www. fortdearbornaudubon.org). Migratory birds gather around the revamped 1889 Alfred Caldwell Lily Pool at Fullerton Parkway and North Cannon Drive. Next to the Conservatory, Grandmother's Garden and the more formal French-style garden across the street are favorites for both wedding party photos and the homeless during the warmer months.

Sports

Baseball diamonds on the park's south end are bordered by La Salle Drive and Lake Shore Drive, next to the field house and NorthStar Eatery. Bicyclists and runners race along Lincoln Park Lagoon to the footbridge over Lake Shore Drive to North Avenue Beach, Chicago's volleyball mecca. To reserve courts and rent equipment, go to the south end of the landmark, boat-shaped bath house. Just north of the bath house is a seasonal rollerblade rink and fitness club. North of Montrose Harbor on the North Wilson Drive lakefront is a free skateboard park.

The 9-hole Sydney R. Marovitz Public Golf Course (3600 Recreation Dr) hosts hackers year-round. Snail-slow play allows plenty of time to enjoy skyline views from this lakefront cow pasture, which is always crowded. Greens fees are $26 weekdays, $29 on weekends, and you can rent clubs. Reserve tee times online at sydneymarovitz.cpdgolf.com or show up at sunrise. The starter sits in the northeast corner of the clock tower field house. For those who want to take it even more leisurely, check out the Diversey Miniature Golf Course (diversey.cpdgolf.com), which offers an 18-hole course complete with waterfalls and footbridges. Diversey mini-golf rates are $10 adults, $8 juniors/seniors. Also nearby is the Diversey Golf Range (141 W Diversey Ave), open year-round (large bucket $16, small bucket $10).

Four clay tennis courts, the last ones left in Chicago, are open 7 am–8 pm and cost $18 per hour; tennis shoes are required. For reservations and further information, call 312-742-7821. There courts on Recreation Drive at Waveland are free, and first come, first, uh, served.

An archery range on the north end of Belmont Harbor is where the Lincoln Park Archery Club (www.lincolnparkarcheryclub. org) meets. They offer a number of clinics throughout the summer for newcomers to the sport.

Members of the Lincoln Park Boat Club row in Lincoln Park Lagoon. Rowing classes for the public are offered May through September (www.lpbc.net).

The Nature Boardwalk surrounds the South Pond at the Lincoln Park Zoo. Take a walk or jog through the urban oasis which acts as a natural haven for native birds, frogs, fish, and turtles. The Patio at Café Brauer (2021 North Stockton) is sunny spot to take in the view and sip on a specially brewed Boardwalk Blue blueberry-infused golden ale from Goose Island.

Green City Market

Address: 1817 N Clark St, Chicago, IL 60614
Phone: 773-880-1266
Website: www.chicagogreencitymarket.org or @greencitymarket
Hours: May–October, Wed & Sat 7 am–1 pm (off-season every other Saturday at Peggy Notebaert Nature Museum)

No Lincoln Park experience would be complete without visiting a quintessential yuppie hotspot—the farmers market. What began in an alley next to the Chicago Theatre in 1998 has since become Chicago's only year round sustainable market, showcasing local farmers selling everything from organic produce and cheese to elk meat and microgreens. Free chef demonstrations take place every Wednesday and Saturday at 10:30 am, a different fruit or vegetable is featured every month according to what's in season.

Lincoln Park Zoo

Address: 2001 N Clark St, Chicago, IL 60614
Phone: 312-742-2000
Website: www.lpzoo.org or @lincolnparkzoo
Hours: April-May 10 am-5 pm; Memorial Day-Labor Day 10 am-5 pm on weekdays, 10 am-6:30 pm on weekends; September-October 10 am-5 pm; November-March 10 am-4:30 pm
Admission: FREE

Lions and tigers and bears and kids, oh my! We're not sure which scares us most. Established in 1868, Lincoln Park Zoo is the country's oldest free zoo, and still a leader in wildlife conservation. National TV shows *Zoo Parade* and *Ray Rayner's Ark in the Park* were filmed here. Look for some family (or, at least, in-law) resemblance at the 29,000-square-foot Regenstein Center for African Apes. Come early and hear the white-cheek gibbons, the smallest of the ape family, mimic car alarms in their morning song to mark their territory. You may even catch one peeing off his tree before a captivated audience. Flanking the zoo's northwest side is the free Lincoln Park Conservatory, a fantastic source of oxygen renewal recommended for hangover sufferers. The Pritzker Family Children's Zoo simulates a North American woods.

Peggy Notebaert Nature Museum

Address: 2430 N Cannon Dr, Chicago, IL 60614
Phone: 773-755-5100
Website: www.naturemuseum.org or @NatureMuseum
Hours: Mon–Fri 9 am–5 pm, Sat–Sun 10 am–5 pm
Admission: $9 adults, $7 seniors & students, $6 children ages 3–12; Thursdays suggested donation for Illinois residents

The Peggy Notebaert Nature Museum succeeds in making Illinois' level landscape interesting. The contemporary version of the 1857 Chicago Academy of Sciences, this hands-on museum depicts the close connection between urban and natural environments and represents global environmental issues through a local lens. A flowing water lab and flitting butterfly haven invite return visits. A must-see for anyone with a passion for taxidermy and/or Silence of the Lambs. You can also discover how pollutive you are in your everyday life—and how to change it in their Extreme Green House exhibit. Get back to nature with a full class and summer camp schedule.

Chicago History Museum

Address: 1601 N. Clark St & North Ave, Chicago, IL 60614
Phone: 312-642-4600
Website: www.chicagohistory.org or @ChicagoMuseum
Hours: Mon–Sat 9:30 am–4:30 pm, Sun 12 noon–5 pm
Admission: $14 adults, $12 seniors & students, children under 12 free; Free days for Illinois residents vary, visit website for full schedule

The Chicago History Museum holds over 20 million primary documents relating to the history of the Chicago area. Exhibits about the city's pioneer roots, architecture, music, fashion, neighborhoods, windy politics, and oral histories breathe life into an otherwise dry history. Locals can access the excellent research center (open Tuesday through Friday, $10/day; students through grade 12 are free) for genealogical information and housing history. North & Clark Café explores Chicago's love of food.

Performances

Lincoln Park Cultural Center (2045 N Lincoln Park W, 312-742-7726) stages plays, theater workshops, and family-friendly performances year-round. While Theater on the Lake (Fullerton Ave & Lake Shore Dr, 312-742-7994) is best known for its summer schedule of alternative drama, it hosts events throughout the calendar year. Lincoln Park Zoo hosts outdoor summer concerts and events as well. See their events calendar online.

How to Get There

By Car: Lake Shore Drive exits to Lincoln Park are Bryn Mawr Avenue, Foster Avenue, Lawrence Avenue, Wilson Drive, Montrose Drive, Irving Park Parkway, Belmont Avenue, Fullerton Avenue, and North Avenue.

Free parking lots are at Recreational Drive near Belmont Harbor and Simonds Drive near Montrose Harbor. Paid lots are located at North Avenue Beach, Chicago Historical Society, Lincoln Park Zoo, and Grant Hospital Garage. Stockton Drive and Cannon Drive have free street parking. A metered lot is on Diversey Parkway, next to the golf range.

By Bus: CTA buses 151, 156, and 146 travel through Lincoln Park.

By L: Get off the Red Line at any stop between Fullerton and Bryn Mawr Avenues, then head one mile east. On the Brown Line, all stops between Sedgwick and Belmont are about a mile east of the park as well.

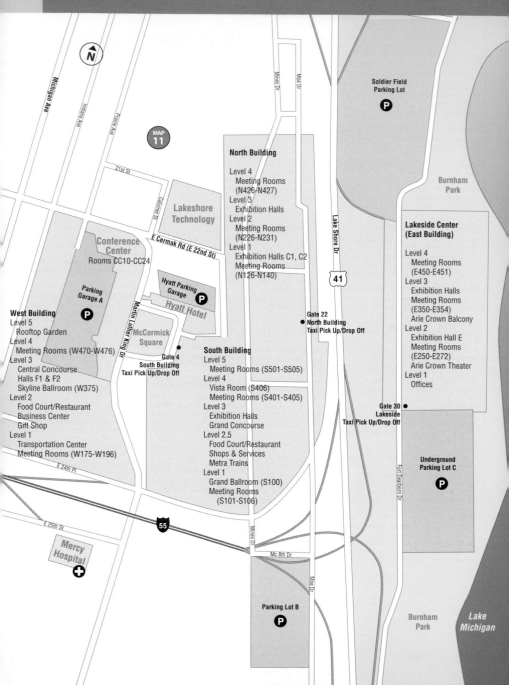

N

MAP
11

21st St

Soldier Field
Parking Lot
P

North Building

Level 4
  Meeting Rooms
  (N426-N427)
Level 3
  Exhibition Halls
Level 2
  Meeting Rooms
  (N226-N231)
Level 1
  Exhibition Halls C1, C2
  Meeting Rooms
  (N126-N140)

Burnham
Park

**Lakeside Center
(East Building)**

Level 4
  Meeting Rooms
  (E450-E451)
Level 3
  Exhibition Halls
  Meeting Rooms
  (E350-E354)
  Arie Crown Balcony
Level 2
  Exhibition Hall E
  Meeting Rooms
  (E250-E272)
  Arie Crown Theater
Level 1
  Offices

Lakeshore
Technology

E Cermak Rd (E 22nd St)

**Conference
Center**
Rooms CC10-CC24

Hyatt Parking
Garage
P

Parking
Garage A
P

Hyatt Hotel

41

Gate 22
● North Building
Taxi Pick Up/Drop Off

West Building
Level 5
  Rooftop Garden
Level 4
  Meeting Rooms (W470-W476)
Level 3
  Central Concourse
  Halls F1 & F2
  Skyline Ballroom (W375)
Level 2
  Food Court/Restaurant
  Business Center
  Gift Shop
Level 1
  Transportation Center
  Meeting Rooms (W175-W196)

McCormick
Square

Gate 4
South Building
Taxi Pick Up/Drop Off

South Building
Level 5
  Meeting Rooms (S501-S505)
Level 4
  Vista Room (S406)
  Meeting Rooms (S401-S405)
Level 3
  Exhibition Halls
  Grand Concourse
Level 2.5
  Food Court/Restaurant
  Shops & Services
  Metra Trains
Level 1
  Grand Ballroom (S100)
  Meeting Rooms
  (S101-S106)

Gate 30 ●
Lakeside
Taxi Pick Up/Drop Off

**Underground
Parking Lot C**
P

E 24th Pl

E 25th St

55

Mercy
Hospital
✚

Mc 8th Dr

Parking Lot B
P

Burnham
Park

*Lake
Michigan*

General Information

NFT Map: 11
Mailing Address: 2301 S King Dr, Chicago, IL 60616
Phone: 312-791-7000
Website: www.mccormickplace.com or @McCormick_Place
South Building: Exhibit Hall A
North Building: Exhibit Halls B and C; Metra Train Station
Lakeside Center (East Building): Exhibit Halls D and E; 4,267-seat Arie Crown Theater (Level 2)
West Building: Exhibit Hall F; Transportation Center; Parking Lot A

Overview

When it comes to the convention business, size matters. With 2.6 million square feet of exhibit space spread over four buildings, McCormick Place is the largest convention center in the country and one of the largest in the world. The center hosts more than three million visitors every year for trade shows, including the Chicago Auto Show, and public exhibitions in the South Building, North Building, Lakeside Center (East Building) and West Building. McCormick Place also includes the Arie Crown Theatre, one of the largest theaters in Chicago according to seating capacity, which hosts a variety of plays, concerts, and seminars. McCormick Place's growth continues to bolster the rapid development of South Loop, and with each expansion the complex's overall aesthetic appeal steadily improves. But despite major renovations, Chicagoans still refer to the complex as "the mistake on the lake." Mayor Daley called the black boxy behemoth the "Berlin Wall" that separates Chicagoans from their beloved lakefront.

Finding Your Way Around

Getting to McCormick Place is the easy part. Then you have to navigate the inside. The main entrance is off Martin Luther King Drive, next to the Hyatt Hotel. Here's how to crack the code names for meeting rooms and exhibit halls:

All meeting room locations start with E (Lakeside Center/East Building), N (North Building), S (South Building), or W (West Building). The first numeral represents the floor level, and the last two digits specify which room. Room numbers are never duplicated among the complex's three buildings.

Exhibit halls are named by consecutive letters starting with the South Building where Hall A (Level 3) is located. North Building houses Halls B (Level 3) and C (Level 1). Exhibit Halls D (Level 3) and E (Level 2) are in Lakeside Center. Exhibit Hall F (Level 3) is in the West Building.

Restaurants & Services

Connie's Pizza and McDonald's Express are in the North Building (Level 2). The Fine Print Restaurant has a full-service dining option. The West Building has a large food court on the second floor. Level 2.5 of the South Building has many options, including La Brea Bakery and Jamba Juice. The Grand Concourse in the South Hall (Level 2.5 and 3) also has shops, shoe shine, and massage services. ATMs are available in each building: Level 2.5 in the South Building in the Convenience Center; Level 2 in the North Building near McDonalds; Level 1 in the West Building near the Transportation Center; and Level 2 in the Lakeside/East Building, near the Arie Crown Theater box office. There are Starbucks located in the concourse of the West Building, on Level 2.5 of the South Building, and Level 3 of the North Building. If you're totally lost, there are Visitor Information Centers in each building. Good luck finding them.

How to Get There

By Car: From the Loop, take Lake Shore Drive south; from the southeast, travel north on Lake Shore Drive. Signage to McCormick Place on Lake Shore Drive is frequent and clear. There are three main lots: Parking Lot A is for events in the North, South and West Buildings; Lot B serves the South Building and offers a pre-paid express pass option; Lot C is for events at Lakeside Center and Arie Crown Theater. There is also parking at the Hyatt and an additional lot north of McCormick Place at Soldier Field.

By Bus: From the Loop and within walking distance of many hotels, CTA bus 3 stops at McCormick Place. From Richard B. Ogilvie Transportation Center, take buses 20, 56, 60, or 157 to Michigan Avenue; transfer to a southbound 3. From Union Station, board eastbound bus 7 to Michigan Avenue; transfer to a southbound 3.

During major shows, countless charter buses circle downtown hotels, transporting conventioneers to McCormick Place for free. Charter buses travel on an express busway from Randolph Street to the South Building in less than ten minutes. For schedules, check with the hotels and at McCormick Place information desks.

By Train: A Metra train ride from the Loop's Millennium Station at Randolph Street and Van Buren Street stations to the McCormick Place Station takes nine minutes. Escalators to the train platform are on the west side of the Grand Concourse (Level 2.5).

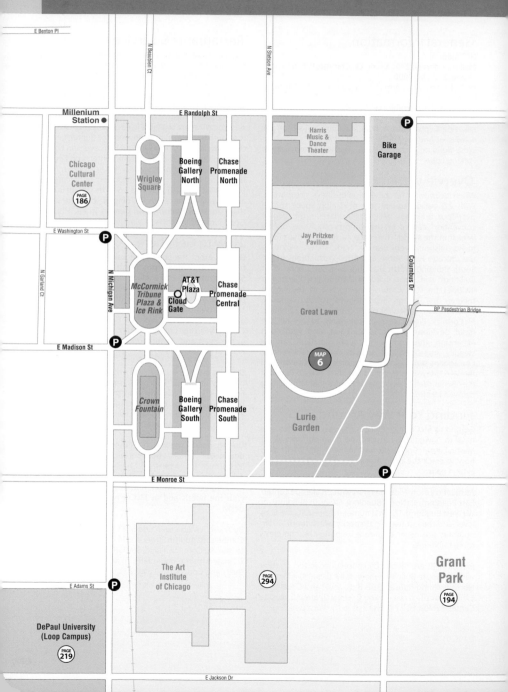

E Benton Pl

N Beaubien Ct

N Stetson Ave

Millenium Station ●

E Randolph St

Harris Music & Dance Theater

Bike Garage

Chicago Cultural Center

PAGE 186

Wrigley Square

Boeing Gallery North

Chase Promenade North

Jay Pritzker Pavilion

E Washington St

P

N Garland Ct

N Michigan Ave

Columbus Dr

McCormick Tribune Plaza & Ice Rink

AT&T Plaza

Cloud Gate

Chase Promenade Central

Great Lawn

BP Pedestrian Bridge

E Madison St

P

MAP 6

Crown Fountain

Boeing Gallery South

Chase Promenade South

Lurie Garden

E Monroe St

P

The Art Institute of Chicago

PAGE 294

Grant Park

PAGE 194

E Adams St

P

DePaul University (Loop Campus)

PAGE 219

E Jackson Dr

Overview

Only four years behind schedule (who's counting?) and hundreds of millions of dollars over budget (okay, this we counted), Millennium Park finally launched itself in July 2004 as the cultural epicenter Mayor Daley promised us it would be back in 1997. Even if it did take myriad stopgap funding measures resembling yesteryear Al Capone strong-arm tactics to eternally endow us with the AT&T Plaza, McCormick Tribune Plaza & Ice Rink, and the Chase Promenade, locals and tourists alike agree it was well worth it. Even staunch, longtime local naysayers have come to acknowledge that, when all is said and done, the end result really is an amazing addition to Grant Park's north point and is, without a doubt, one of downtown Chicago's crowning jewels.

The park is built on land that was controlled by the Illinois Central Railroad from the 19th century until 1997. In some ways, the wait was worth it: the park's design is entirely modern and completely unmoored from "classic" park design. The starchitects and artists involved have contributed some of their most high-profile, impressive work. The overall experience is fun and vital, and it's not for nothing that Millennium Park immediately became one of the city's most visited attractions. And if you're visiting for the first time, a good starting point is the park's Welcome Center, which is open daily and located at 201 E Randolph Street.

Jay Pritzker Pavilion

The centerpiece of Millennium Park is the Pritzker Pavilion. It seems the whole park may have very well been conceived to give Frank Gehry's architectural masterpiece an appropriate setting. The pavilion's innovative trellis structure of stainless steel ribbons doubles as the sound system, which replicates the acoustics of an indoor space. The pavilion's stage area is as big as Orchestra Hall across the street and can accommodate a 120-person orchestra and a 150-person choir. Seating for the free concert events includes a 4,000-seat terrace and an additional 95,000-square-foot lawn area that can accommodate 7,000 picnickers. The pavilion is the home of the summer-long Grant Park Music Festival, which features a full-slate of classical concerts.

Harris Theater for Music & Dance

Several dance and theatrical troupes share the 1,500-seat underground space behind Gehry's behemoth bandshell, including Hubbard Street Dance Chicago (not to be missed, but good luck getting tickets!), the Chicago Children's Choir, and the Jazz Institute of Chicago. Two underground parking garages flank the theater, and as with all parking in this area, it's first come/first served and a bit of a mess on the weekends. Tickets and schedule available at www.harristheaterchicago.org

Nature & Sculpture

The park has several different defined spaces: Wrigley Square, with its neoclassical epistyle; the Chase Promenade, gearing up to house art fairs and ethnic festivals; and the AT&T Plaza (between the skating

rink and promenade), which is home to Anish Kapoor's 100-ton stainless steel jelly-bean sculpture, Cloud Gate (be sure to take a picture of yourself staring into it—not exactly original, but so hard to resist). Flanking the skating rink to the south is the modernist Crown Fountain, which features two glass brick towers, 50 feet in height, with projected video images of the faces of actual Chicago residents. The Lurie Garden, a ridiculously conceptual assemblage of seasonal foliage, offers a beautiful public gathering space as well as more contemplative environments. The BP Bridge, a 925-foot-long winding bridge—Frank Gehry's first—connects Millennium Park to Maggie Daley Park just east of the park. Clad in brushed stainless steel panels, the BP Bridge complements the Pritzker Pavilion in function as well as design by creating an acoustic barrier for traffic noise. It's well worth the walk.

Sports

The 15,910-square-foot McCormick Tribune Ice Rink opens annually in November. On Saturdays in the summer, take part in free fitness classes on the Great Lawn. The options range from tai chi to yoga, with some more danceable aerobics as well. The park also houses a state-of-the-art, heated bicycle garage, which provides parking for 300 bikes, showers, a repair facility, and a café.

Dining

The 300-seat Park Grill (consistently one of the top burgers in the city) overlooking the skating rink offers burgers, steaks, and salads year-round. In the summer, carry-away grub is available from a variety of kiosks throughout the park.

How to Get There

No matter your mode of travel, approach the area around Millennium Park with patience and allow extra time.

By Car: Exits off Lake Shore Drive west to Millennium Park are at Randolph Street and Monroe Drive. Also, enter the park from Michigan Avenue heading east on the same streets. If you choose to drive, underground parking is available in several areas. Access the Grant Park North Garage from Michigan Avenue. Enter Millennium Park Garage from the lower levels of Randolph Street and mid-level of Columbus Drive. Parking is also available at the Grant Park South and East Monroe Garages.

By Train: Metra trains coming from the south terminate at the underground Millennium Park Station at Randolph Street. From the Richard B. Ogilvie Transportation Center, travel east to Michigan Avenue and Millennium Park on CTA buses 20, 56, 60, and 157. From Union Station, board CTA buses 60 or 151.

By L: Get off at any L stop in the Loop between Randolph Street and Monroe Street. Walk two (or three) blocks east to Millennium Park.

By Bus: CTA buses 3, 4, 6, 14, 20, 56, 60, 124, 151, 157, and 173 serve the park.

Grant
Park

PAGE
194

41

Water Taxi
Dock

Fed Underpass

E Roosevelt Rd

Main
Entrance
Handicap
Entrance

Shedd
Aquarium

North Main
Entrance

Group
Entrance

North
Entrance

Adler
Planetarium

S Columbus Dr

Handicap
Entrance

The Field
Museum

South Main
Entrance

Solidarity Dr
Solidarity Dr

P

Planetarium Lot

P

Group & Handicap
Entrance

McFetridge Dr

P

North Garage

P

Burnham
Harbor

Lynn White Dr

12th St
Beach

Museum Campus Dr

Soldier
Field

PAGE
240

Northerly
Island
Park

Waldron Dr

S Lake Shore Dr

MAP
11

Waldron Garage

P

Burnham
Park

Merrill C Meigs
Field

S Prairie Ave

S Calumet Ave

18th St
Station

Main Museum
Visitor Entrance

E 18th St

South Lot

P

E Cullerton St

E 21st St

Lake
Michigan

200E

300E

E Cermak Rd

S Dr Martin L King Jr Dr

S Dr Martin L King Jr Dr

Arie Crown
Theater

S Cottage Grove Ave

E 23rd St

400E

E 23rd Dr

23rd St
McCormick
Place
Station

S Calumet Ave

S Prairie Ave

McCormick
Place

PAGE
202

E 24th St

E 24th Pl

E 24th Pl

Burnham
Park

Stevenson Expy

55

E 25th St

Overview

Museum Campus is the ultimate destination for educational field trips. South of Grant Park at the intersection of Roosevelt Road and Lake Shore Drive, Museum Campus's 57 acres of uninterrupted lakefront parkland connect three world-renowned Chicago institutions: The Field Museum, Shedd Aquarium, and Adler Planetarium & Astronomy Museum. You've got Mayor Daley to thank for all of this beautiful space; it was the bossman himself who championed the rerouting of Lake Shore Drive to the west to consolidate the land around Museum Campus, which opened in 1998. Chicagoans, take note: although none of the museums that make up the museum campus are shouting from rooftops about it, all three offer reduced admission rates to locals. Be sure to ask for it.

The Field Museum

Address: 1400 S Lake Shore Dr, Chicago, IL 60605
Phone: 312-922-9410
Website: www.fieldmuseum.org or @FieldMuseum
Hours: Open daily 9 am–5 pm, except Christmas
Admission: Basic admission is $18 Adults, $15 students & seniors, $13 children ages 3–11. Additional admission fees apply for full museum experience. Free days for Illinois residents vary, visit website for full schedule.

The massive, Greek Revival-style museum constructed in 1921 houses over 20 million artifacts. From dinosaurs, diamonds, and earthworms to man-eating lions, totem poles, and mummies, there is just too much to savor in a single visit. The permanent *Evolving Planet* exhibit features an interactive stroll through 4 billion years of evolution, from single-celled organisms through dinosaurs, hominids, and finally to human beings. Another noteworthy permanent exhibit is Sue, the largest, most complete, and best preserved Tyrannosaurus Rex discovered to date. Complete with a half-smoked pack of Marlboros, since we now know that's what killed the dinosaurs. As with most museums, some temporary exhibits cost additional bucks on top of normal museum fees. Free museum tours are available; check website for times.

John G. Shedd Aquarium

Address: 1200 DuSable Lake Shore Dr, Chicago, IL 60605
Phone: 312-939-2438
Website: www.sheddaquarium.org or @shedd_aquarium
Hours: Memorial Day–Labor Day: Daily, 9 am–6 pm; Labor Day–Memorial Day: Mon–Fri, 9 am–5 pm; Sat–Sun: 9 am–6 pm. Closed Christmas.
Admission: Basic admission is $8 adults, $6 children ages 3–11. Additional admission fees apply for full museum experience. Free days for Illinois residents vary, visit website for full schedule.

Opened in 1929, the Beaux Arts-style aquarium's six wings radiate from a giant, circular coral reef tank. The museum features revolving exhibits with a special focus on marine ecology and preservation. Popular favorites include Wild Reef, where you can get up close and personal with the sharks. During the summer the Shedd hosts weekly "Jazzin at the Shedd" events featuring live jazz, cocktails overlooking the downtown skyline, fireworks, and full access to the aquarium until 10 pm.

Burnham Park

Burnham Park, the site of the 1933 Century of Progress exhibition, encompasses McCormick Place, Burnham Harbor, the former Merrill C. Meigs Airport (closed in a political coup by Mayor Daley in 2003), and Soldier Field. A free skateboard park is located at Lake Shore Drive and 31st Street. The 12th Street Beach, especially popular with swimmers and divers because of the deep water east of the beach, is on Northerly Island. Other beaches are at 31st Street and 49th Street. Outdoor basketball courts are east of Lake Shore Drive around 35th Street and 47th Street. Fishing is welcome along Solidarity Drive and Burnham Harbor shore. The wilderness Nature Area at 47th Street attracts butterflies and birds.

Adler Planetarium

Address: 1300 S Lake Shore Dr, Chicago, IL 60605
Phone: 312-922-7827
Website: www.adlerplanetarium.org or @adlerskywatch
Hours: Mon–Fri 9:30 am–4 pm, Sat–Sun 9:30 am–4:30pm; Third Thursdays (21+ Adler After Dark) 6:30 pm–10:30 pm; check website for special extended summer hours
Admission: Basic admission is $12 adults, $8 children 3–11. Additional admission fees apply for full museum experience. Free days for Illinois residents vary, visit website for full schedule.

The Adler Planetarium & Astronomy Museum offers interactive exhibits explaining space phenomena and intergalactic events; its 2,000 historic astronomical and navigational instruments form the western hemisphere's largest collection. On the first Friday of every month, weather permitting, amateur astronomers young and old are invited to bring their own telescopes to the Planetarium lawns. Roving scientists offer tips and instructions on telescope usage and observational features. Come summer, the 21+ Adler After Dark events are great, nerdy date nights featuring both kinds of cosmos. Chicago skyline views from the planetarium grounds are out of this world any day of the week, and are always worth the trip.

How to Get There

By Car: From the Loop, take Columbus Drive south; turn east on McFetridge Drive. From the south, take Lake Shore Drive to McFetridge Drive. Area parking lots are near Soldier Field, Field Museum, Adler Planetarium, and McCormick Place. Standard $19 rate for parking in the lot adjacent to the Adler and $19 in the Soldier Field lot. Fees are higher on days when there's Park District-sponsored special events. Metered parking is available on Solidarity Drive.

By Bus: CTA buses 2, 6, 10, 12, 14, 127, 130, and 146 serve the area.

By L: Ride the Orange, Red, or Green Lines to the Roosevelt Road stop. Walk east through the pedestrian underpass at Roosevelt Road.

By Train: From Richard B. Ogilvie Transportation Center, travel east on CTA bus 20 to State Street; transfer to the 146. From Union Station take CTA bus 1, 126, or 151; transfer at State Street to the 10 or 146. From La Salle Street station, take the 146. South Shore and Metra trains stop at the Roosevelt Road station.

On Foot: Walk south through Grant Park past bobbing boats and the gushing Buckingham Fountain to the Museum Campus.

Water Taxis: Seasonally, water taxis operate between Navy Pier and Museum Campus (312-222-9328; www.shorelinesightseeing.com).

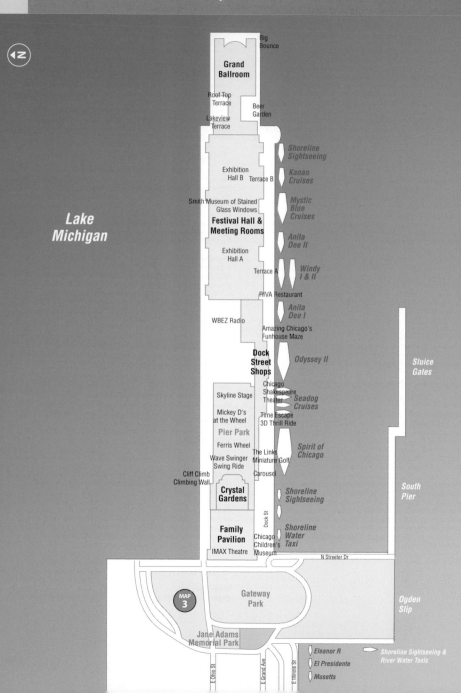

N

Lake
Michigan

Big
Bounce

**Grand
Ballroom**

Roof Top
Terrace

Beer
Garden

Lakeview
Terrace

*Shoreline
Sightseeing*

Exhibition
Hall B   Terrace B

*Kanan
Cruises*

Smith Museum of Stained
Glass Windows

*Mystic
Blue
Cruises*

**Festival Hall &
Meeting Rooms**

Exhibition
Hall A

*Anita
Dee II*

Terrace A

*Windy
I & II*

RIVA Restaurant

WBEZ Radio

*Anita
Dee I*

Amazing Chicago's
Funhouse Maze

**Dock
Street
Shops**

Odyssey II

*Sluice
Gates*

Chicago
Shakespeare
Theater

Skyline Stage

*Seadog
Cruises*

Mickey D's
at the Wheel

Time Escape
3D Thrill Ride

Pier Park

Ferris Wheel

The Links
Miniature Golf

*Spirit of
Chicago*

Wave Swinger
Swing Ride

Cliff Climb
Climbing Wall

Carousel

**Crystal
Gardens**

*Shoreline
Sightseeing*

*South
Pier*

Dock St

**Family
Pavilion**

Chicago
Children's
Museum

*Shoreline
Water
Taxi*

IMAX Theatre

N Streeter Dr

MAP
3

Gateway
Park

*Ogden
Slip*

Jane Adams
Memorial Park

E Ohio St

E Grand Ave

E Illinois St

● *Eleanor R*

● *El Presidente*

● *Musetts*

◗ *Shoreline Sightseeing &
River Water Taxis*

General Information

NFT Map: 3
Address: 600 E Grand Ave Chicago, IL 60611
Phone: 312-595-7437
Website: www.navypier.com or @NavyPier
Pier Hours: Summer, 10 am–10 pm Sun–Thur, 10 am–10 pm Fri–Sat; Off-season 10 am–8 pm Sun–Thur, 10 am–10 pm Fri–Sat (winter closes 7 pm Sun). Closing times of restaurants, shops, and attractions vary by season, holiday, and public exhibitions/events.
Skyline Stage: 1,500-seat outdoor performance pavilion in Pier Park, performances are May through September
IMAX Theatre: 312-595-5629 or @NavyPierIMAX
Free Fireworks: Memorial Day to Labor Day, Wednesdays (9:30 pm) & Saturdays (10:15 pm)
WBEZ Radio: NPR local affiliate, 312-948-4600; www.wbez.org or @WBEZ
Exhibit Space: Festival Hall, Lakeview Terrace, Ballroom Lobby, Grand Ballroom; 36 meeting rooms

Overview

With nine million visitors a year, Navy Pier is the quintessential Chicago tourist attraction. Yet save for an occasional Skyline Stage concert, speed-boat ride, or high-end nosh at Riva, most Chicagoans reserve Pier visits for those times when you have either very elderly or very young relatives in town. Knocked for years as a glorified mall on the lake, Navy Pier is undergoing a multi-multi-million-dollar "reimagining" that intends to refocus the visitor experience toward something more diverse, local-friendly, sustainable and in touch with the waterfront. With a boutique hotel. Phase I is scheduled for completion in 2015, with funding to follow for subsequent work.

Opened to the public in 1916 as a municipal wharf, the pier has also done time as a) the University of Illinois at Chicago's campus, b) a hospital, c) a military training facility, d) a concert venue, and e) a white elephant. In 1989, the Metropolitan Pier and Exposition Authority invested $150 million to transform the crumbling pier into an uninspired entertainment-exhibition complex that still somehow attracts three times as many visitors than the Art Institute of Chicago and Willis Tower combined. In addition to convention space (home to the annual Chicago Flower and Garden Show), Navy Pier also houses two museums, the Shakespeare Theater, the Crystal Gardens, an outdoor concert pavilion, a vintage grand ballroom, a 15-story Ferris wheel, an IMAX Theatre, and, just for the hell of it, a radio station.

Chicago Shakespeare Theater

The Chicago Shakespeare Theater has a 510-seat, courtyard-style theater and a 180-seat studio theater that are Chicago's sole venues dedicated to performing wordsmith Willy's works. In addition to the season's plays, the theater produces Shakespeare "shorts" for younger patrons. A bookstore and teacher resource center are also located on-site (312-595-5600; www.chicagoshakes.com or @chicagoshakes).

Chicago Children's Museum

The Chicago Children's Museum features daily activities, a creative crafts studio, and 15 interactive exhibits ranging from dinosaur digs and waterworks to a toddler tree house, safety town, and construction zone. The museum is open daily from 10 am to 5 pm, and Thursday until 8 pm. Admission is $14 for adults and children, $13 for seniors and children under one. Children 15 and under get in free on the first Sunday of every month under the Free First Sundays program, and Thursdays 5 pm to 8 pm is free admission for all. (312-527-1000; www.chicagochildrensmuseum.org or @childrensmuseum).

Smith Museum of Stained Glass Windows

Smith Museum is the first stained-glass-only museum in the country. The 150 windows installed in the lower level of Festival Hall are mainly from Chicago-area buildings and the city's renowned stained glass studios. Windows representing over a century of artistic styles include works by Louis Comfort Tiffany, Frank Lloyd Wright, Louis Sullivan, and John LaFarge. The free museum is open during Pier hours.

Getting There

By Car: From the north, exit Lake Shore Drive at Grand Avenue; proceed east. From the southeast, exit Lake Shore Drive at Illinois Street; go east. Parking garages are located on the Pier's north side, and plenty of parking lots are just west of Lake Shore Drive in Streeterville.

By Bus: CTA buses 29, 65, 66, and 124 serve Navy Pier.

By L: Take the Green or Red Line to Grand Avenue. Board eastbound CTA Bus 29, or take the free trolley.

By Train: From Richard B. Ogilvie Transportation Center or Union Station, take CTA bus 124.

By Trolley: Free, daily trolleys that typically run every 20 minutes travel between Navy Pier and State Street along Grand Avenue and Illinois Street from Memorial Day to Labor Day. Pick-up points are indicated by "Navy Pier Trolley Stop" signs along the route.

By Boat: Seasonal water shuttles travel between Navy Pier and the Museum Campus and along the Chicago River to the Sears Tower (312-222-9328; www.shorelinesightseeing.com or @ShorelineSights).

Coffee

• **Starbucks** • 600 E Grand Ave

General Information

Visit Oak Park: 888-625-7275;
www.visitoakpark.com or @VisitOakPark

Overview

You can thank Oak Park for Prairie Style architecture, *A Moveable Feast*, McDonald's, and, yes, *Tarzan*. The creators of each called this charming suburb their home: Frank Lloyd Wright, Ernest Hemingway, Ray Kroc, and Edgar Rice Burroughs, respectively. Best known for its architectural gems and strong public schools, Oak Park is a happy hunting ground for home buyers seeking upscale, integrated living ten miles from the Loop. Less impressed than most with his picture-perfect hometown, Hemingway famously described Oak Park as "a village of wide lawns and narrow minds."

Architecture

Oak Park harbors the nation's largest concentration of Frank Lloyd Wright buildings, 25 in the village and another six in neighboring River Forest. The village's must-see sites are located in a compact area bordered by Division Street, Lake Street, Forest Avenue, and Ridgeland Avenue. Designs by Wright, William Drummond, George W. Maher, John Van Bergen, and E. E. Roberts are represented throughout.

You can ground yourself in Prairie Style architectural principles at the brilliant Frank Lloyd Wright Home and Studio. Maintained by the Frank Lloyd Wright Trust, guided tours of the designer's personal space are offered daily 10 am–4 pm (951 Chicago Ave, 312-994-4000; flwright.org or @FLWTrust). Tickets can be purchased on the foundation's website or on-site (early arrival recommended) at a cost of $17 for adults, $15 for students, seniors and military, and free for children 3 and under (photography allowed with extra $5 pass). Excellent walking tours of the surrounding streets are also offered: $15 for adults, $12 students, seniors and military, and free for children 3 and under. Worth every penny.

Completed in 1908, Unity Temple (875 Lake St, 708-383-8873; www.utrf.org) was Wright's first commissioned public building; today it houses Oak Park's Unitarian-Universalist congregation. Guided tours and self-guided audio tours of Unity Temple are offered Monday through Saturday through the Frank Lloyd Wright Trust (flwright.org): $15 for adults, $12 students, seniors and military, and free for children 3 and under. Designed by George W. Maher, Historic Pleasant Home (217 S Home Ave, 708-383-2654; www.pleasanthome.org or @PleasantHomeOP) aptly illustrates the architectural evolution from Victorian design to early Prairie Style with tours held Thursday through Sunday at 12:30 pm, 1:30 pm, and 2:30 pm ($10 adults, $8 for students and seniors, $5 children; free self-guided Walk In Wednesdays tours for Illinois residents Wed 10 am–12 pm).

The Oak Park Visitors Center (1010 Lake St, 708-848-1500) offers maps, books and souvenirs and tickets to the Hemingway's Birthplace Home and Museum, and Pleasant Home.

Culture & Events

Once a year in May, the public gets to snoop inside Wright-designed private residences during the popular Wright Plus Housewalk organized by the Frank Lloyd Wright Trust (flwright. org).

Get your fill of he-man author Hemingway at the Hemingway Birthplace Home & Museum (www.ehfop.org or @EHFOP). The museum, housed in the Arts Center of Oak Park, is open Sunday through Friday 1 pm–5 pm, and Saturday 10 am–5 pm (200 N Oak Park Ave, 708-848-2222; $10 adults, $8 students and seniors). His birthplace, also included with the price of admission, is located just up the street at 339 N Oak Park Avenue. For a one-stop confab with both of Oak Park's favorite sons, stroll three blocks north and two west to the 600 block of N. Kenilworth Ave, where Wright's Balch House (611) stands across the street from the Prairie Style home (600) to which Hemingway's family moved when he was 5 years old.

Summer evenings, catch Shakespeare's works performed outdoors in Austin Gardens by the Oak Park Festival Theatre company (708-445-4440; oakparkfestival.com or @OakParkFestival). The lush Oak Park Conservatory, originally built in 1929 to provide a place for all of the exotic plants Oak Park residents collected on their travels abroad, is located at 615 Garfield Street (708-725-2400; www.pdop.org or fopcon. org; suggested $2 donation) and definitely worth a visit.

○ Landmarks

• **Frank Lloyd Wright Home and Studio** • 951 Chicago Ave

🍸 Nightlife

• **Avenue Ale House** • 825 S Oak Park Ave

🍴 Restaurants

• **Buzz Café** • 905 S Lombard Ave
• **Cucina Paradiso** • 814 North Blvd
• **Jerusalem Café** • 1030 Lake St
• **Khyber Pass** • 1031 Lake St
• **Mama Thai** • 1112 W Madison St
• **New Rebozo** • 1116 Madison St
• **Pete's Red Hots** • 6346 W Roosevelt Rd
• **Petersen's Ice Cream** • 1100 Chicago Ave
• **Poor Phil's** • 139 S Marion St

🛍 Shopping

• **Barnard's Schwinn** • 6109 W North Ave
• **Pumpkin Moon** • 1028 North Blvd

General Information

Address: 1 Great America Pkwy, Gurnee, IL 60031
Phone: 847-249-1776
Website: www.sixflags.com/greatamerica or @SFGreat_America
Hours: Open May through October, 10:30 am until the evening (as late as 10 pm in middle of summer), but check calendar on website for specific hours and dates.
Entry: Full price tickets are $66.99 for adults and $46.99 for kids under 54"; online discounts available.

Overview

Metropolitan Chicago's Six Flags Great America is the seventh facility in the Six Flags amusement park empire, which began in Texas in 1961. Great America opened in 1976 (thus the "Great America") as a Marriott property, and was sold to Six Flags in 1984. Known for its thrill rides, the park is home to the Whizzer, an original park feature that has received recognition from the American Coaster Enthusiasts group.

Tickets

Reduced rates are available for advanced purchase through the website and via promo codes and other promotions throughout the season. "The Flash" passes are available for impatient riders, offering cuts in line (and, for a price, even deeper cuts) for an extra fee. For die-hard thrill seekers, or if you plan to go more than once a year, season passes offer the best deal.

For the Kiddies

The kiddo sections of Great America are divided into KIDZOPOLIS and Camp Cartoon. Both offer easy-going rides and games for tykes, while various Looney Tunes figures amble around for photo-ops. The water park has its own kid-friendly attractions as well. The double-decker classic Columbia Carousel, another original park feature, is located just past the park's main entrance; it actually may be too tame for young 'uns hopped up on funnel cake and Tweety-pops. If your kids are a little older and more badass (but still too weak-kneed to experience the real deal), take them on the Whizzer, mini-coaster and quintessential training wheels for every 'tween. Other rides the height-challenged set can get on include the Orbit and the Whirligig—spinning fun guaranteed to make hearts soar and tummies flip, and also provoke the occasional mid-ride retch. Then there's also the good old-fashioned flume-tastic Logger's Run.

Thrill Rides

Every few years, Six Flags tries to outdo itself with an even more death-defying and harrowing ride. Case in point: the Superman-Ultimate Flight ride in which passengers soar through the air head-first as though they were flying, nearly brushing the ground below them on the giant loop-de-loop. Other thrills include the Raging Bull "hyper-twister," where you drop at incredible degrees and speeds into subterranean depths. Batman The Ride allows your feet to dangle free, while riders remain standing, supported by a bicycle seat between the legs (men who desire children, be wary). Also try the equally frightening Vertical Velocity, V2 for short, which propels riders backward and forward up a corkscrew at 70 mph in less than four seconds, suspended by the same paltry harness that barely staves off fatality. Meanwhile, the classic wooden American Eagle coaster offers vintage, but no-less-worrisome, rickety thrills. The Viper, newer and sexier cousin to the geriatric American Eagle, provides a similar timber ride and is modeled after Coney Island's Cyclone. Try The Demon if you're interested in forgetting your name and address. Buccaneer Battle is a pirate-themed raft ride that allows you to soak other people with super-powered soak guns. Cool.

Hurricane Harbor Water Park

Opened in 2005, Great America's adjoining Hurricane Harbor water park features pools and various thrill slides in case you want to bring your trunks to the park. Open until around 6 p.m. through most of the summer, Hurricane Harbor costs an extra $5 (free for season pass holders) and includes access to shower facilities. Lockers are available for rent. Attractions include Skull Island, a supersoaker interactive water play structure highlighted by a 1,000-gallon-plus water drop that dumps itself upon unsuspecting children every so often. The park has miles of water rides, including the twisty tunnels of Hurricane Mountain and the high-speed tube and bowl slides of Vortex and Typhoon. Tornado, a combination tube and bowl slide, allows four riders to experience spinning in the 60-foot-wide funnel together. An adventure river, Castaway Creek, offers both exciting adventures complete with geysers, as well as leisurely relaxation under waterfalls and mists.

Fright Fest

Avoid the heat and long lines of the summer season and creep into the park during the month of October (mostly on weekends) among the Halloween-themed décor, haunted houses, and scary music playing over the P.A. This is, by far, our favorite time to go and worth the price of a season pass for the convenience of just dropping by for a few thrills whenever the heck you feel like it (the park is open until midnight on most Saturday nights during Fright Fest). Water rides (dyed blood red—bwahahaha!) in the park are usually less crowded, so take advantage of those to get the pasty white complexion and blue-tinged lip effect that will help you fit in, especially since costumes aren't allowed.

Make a Night of It

Six Flags partners with many area hotels, including several either within walking distance or accessible via a shuttle bus—saving on parking and avoiding having to drive under the influence of pure joy. See, for example, Grand Hotel & Suites (5520 Grand Ave, 847-249-7777), Hampton Inn (5550 Grand Ave, 847-662-1100), Holiday Inn Gurnee (6161 West Grand Ave, 847-336-6300), KeyLime Cove Indoor Waterpark Resort (1700 Nations Dr, 877-713-4951), or Econo Lodge (3740 Grand Avenue, 224-441-3270). Various other nearby accommodations in neighboring towns also provide shuttle bus service, and some also offer discount tickets. Check the Six Flags website for more details.

How to Get There

By Car: Take I-94 or I-294 west, exit at Grand Avenue. Typical driving time is about 45 minutes from Chicago. Be aware that traffic is very congested in July and August! Arrive extra early or extra late to beat the crowds.

By Train & Bus: Take the Metra Union Pacific North Line to Waukegan, where you can catch the Pace bus 565 to Great America. Pace also offers express bus service from Schaumburg and Rosemont on Fridays and weekends during the summer. Note: Public transportation to Great America from the Ogilvie Transportation Center and Madison and Canal takes just over two hours each way.

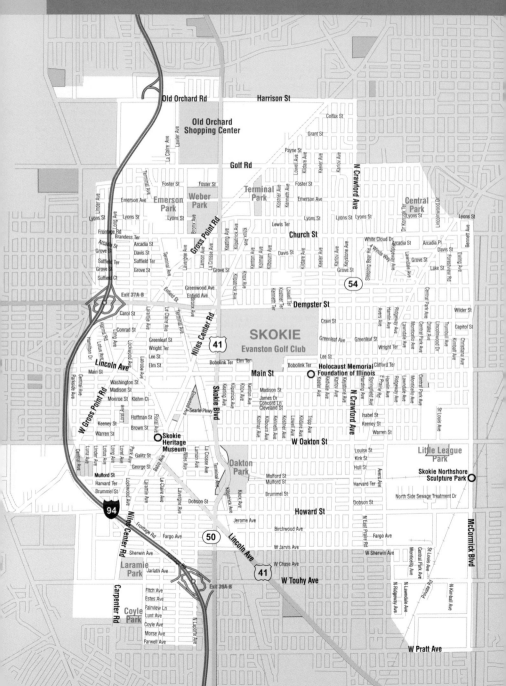

SKOKIE

Evanston Golf Club

Old Orchard Shopping Center

Emerson Park

Weber Park

Terminal Park

Central Park

Oakton Park

Little League Park

Laramie Park

Coyle Park

Holocaust Memorial Foundation of Illinois

Skokie Heritage Museum

Skokie Northshore Sculpture Park

Old Orchard Rd · Harrison St · Colfax St · Grant St · Golf Rd · Payne St · Foster St · Lewis Ter · Church St · White Cloud Dr · Arcadia St · Arcadia Pl · Davis St · Lake St · Emerson Ave · Lyons St · Davis St · Grove St · Greenwood Ave · Enfield Ave · Dempster St · Crain St · Greenleaf Ave · Wright Ter · Wilder St · Capitol St · Lincoln Ave · Main St · Bobolink Ter · Lee St · Washington St · Madison St · Monroe St · James Dr · Concord Ln · Cleveland St · W Oakton St · Keeney St · Warren St · Hoffman St · Brown St · Mulford St · Harvard Ter · Brummel St · George St · Galitz St · Louise St · Kirk St · Hull St · Harvard Ter · Dobson St · Howard St · Jerome Ave · Birchwood Ave · Fargo Ave · W Jarvis Ave · W Chase Ave · W Touhy Ave · Sherwin Ave · Jarlath Ave · Fitch Ave · Estes Ave · Fairview Ln · Lunt Ave · Coyle Ave · Morse Ave · Farwell Ave · W Pratt Ave

N Crawford Ave · Gross Point Rd · Niles Center Rd · Skokie Blvd · W Gross Point Rd · Lincoln Ave · McCormick Blvd · Carpenter Rd

94 · 50 · 41 · 54

Exit 37A-B · Exit 39A-B

General Information

www.skokie.org

Overview

When Skokie was first incorporated under the moniker Niles Centre in 1888, it was considered to be the rowdy neighbor of temperate Evanston due to the large number of taverns within its borders. By 1940, residents were clamoring for a name change and a PR facelift. In November of that year, the village was renamed Skokie after the nearby Skokie River and canals, which themselves were named after an old Native American word for "swampland." Personally, we'd be more attracted to a party town, but nonetheless, the facelift was a success. With the completion of the Edens Expressway in the 1950s, residential development in Skokie was booming.

A chunk of the growth comprised Eastern European refugees from World War II, many of whom were Jewish. It is estimated that between 1945 and 1955, 3,000 Jewish families resettled in Skokie. Synagogues and Jewish services followed, and the village soon developed a self perpetuating reputation as a thriving Jewish enclave. Skokie made international headlines in 1977–78 when it contested plans by the National Socialist Party of America, a branch of the American Nazi Party, to march on the village square. The NSPA was defended by the ACLU in a divisive case that brought the contest between free expression and freedom against hate speech into the international fore. As far as the NSPA was concerned, the decision to march in Skokie was an act of political manipulation. Chicago had denied the Nazis' right to march in SW Chicago's Marquette Park, which was the NSPA's home turf. The group then threatened to relocate their planned assembly to Skokie. When the Village of Skokie lost their bid to ban the march, Chicago finally conceded, allowing the Nazis to gather at Marquette Park in June 1978. A handful of Nazis showed up, countered by thousands of anti-Nazi protesters.

As if being the head of a neo-Nazi movement and threatening to march on the front lawns of concentration camp survivors doesn't already make you the world's biggest jackass/creep, NSPA leader Frank Collin secured the title in 1979 when he was arrested and incarcerated on child molestation charges.

Culture & Events

In 1988, an urban renewal project to restore the North Shore's decrepit Chicago River waterfront resulted in the two-mile Skokie Northshore Sculpture Park (sculpturepark.org), an outdoor recreation area with walking paths, picnic areas, and featuring more than 60 sculptures by artists of local, national, and international renown. The park, sandwiched between McCormick Blvd and the north branch of the Chicago River, runs the two miles from Touhy to Dempster.

Time travel through history at the Skokie Heritage Museum (8031 Floral Ave, 847-674-1500), an assemblage of historical photos, papers, and artifacts painstakingly gathered by the Skokie Historical Society. The museum, housed in a restored 1887 firehouse, also features the history of Skokie's firefighters. Behind the museum, an authentic 1840s log cabin relocated to this location allows kids a glimpse into the town's pioneer past.

Skokie is the home of the Illinois Holocaust Museum & Education Center (9603 Woods Dr, 847-967-4800; www.ilholocaustmuseum.org or @ihmec). Opened in 2009, the facility is not only on a mission to educate future generations about the horrors of the Holocaust but also an attempt to close an upsetting chapter in Skokie's history. The two wings and their respective architecture are meant to evoke the hard edges of the historical record and the soft arches of a hopeful future. It's open to the public weekdays 10 am–5 pm and Thursday evening until 8 pm. Saturday and Sunday from 11 am-4pm. Museum closed Thanksgiving, Christmas, and major Jewish holidays. Admission is $12 for adults, $8 for seniors and students aged 12-22, $6 for children 5-12.

North Shore Center for the Performing Arts

Home to the Skokie Valley Symphony Orchestra, the Centre East Theater, and, most notably, the highly acclaimed Northlight Theater, the North Shore Center for the Performing Arts (9510 Skokie Blvd, 847-673-6300; www.northshorecenter.org or @NSCPAS) is a state-of-the-art performance venue. Touring artists perform here, world class theater (sometimes featuring ensemble members from Steppenwolf) is mounted here, and it's also a North Shore venue for exhibits and trade shows. Designed by architect Graham Gund in 1996, the North Shore Center for the Performing Arts has given Northeast Illinois culture seekers a reason to come to Skokie besides bagels and lox.

Where to Drink

Despite its alcohol-fueled history, Skokie is not really known as a place to imbibe socially. Young residents head to youthful watering holes in the vicinity of the Northwestern campus in formerly tee-totaling Evanston (will the ironies never end?). Meanwhile, local drunks hang out at anonymous corner taverns just like anywhere else. Retail workers, middle managers, and the secretarial set mingle and mate at the food and booze joints adjacent to Old Orchard.

Where to Eat

Old Orchard Shopping Center is filled with family-friendly chain options. Happily, Skokie still houses enough locally owned, independent restaurants to add interest and diversity to their dining scene. Folks travel from all over Chicagoland for local delis and kosher fare ever debating the superiority of Kaufman's v. New York Bagel and Bialy as THE place for a bagel and shmear.

How to Get There

By Car: Take the Edens Expressway (I-94), and exit at Dempster.

By L: The Skokie Swift Yellow Line runs non-stop between the Howard Street Red Line terminus and the Dempster-Skokie station at 5001 Dempster St. Trains run approximately every 10-15 minutes between 5 am and 11 pm.

🍴 Restaurants

- **Grecian Kitchen Delight** • 3938 Dempster St
- **Hub's** • 3727 Dempster St
- **Kaufman's Delicatessen & Bakery** • 4905 Dempster St
- **Ruby of Siam** • 9420 Skokie Blvd
- **Shallots Bistro** • 7016 Carpenter Rd
- **Zad** • 3910 Dempster St

Columbia College Chicago

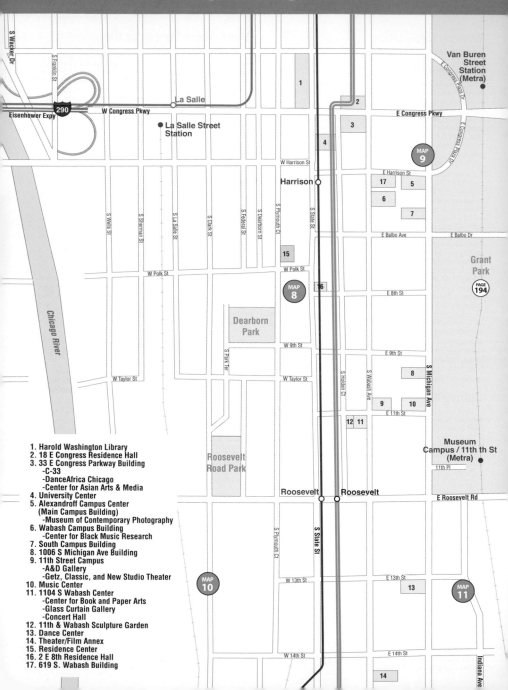

1. Harold Washington Library
2. 18 E Congress Residence Hall
3. 33 E Congress Parkway Building
   -C-33
   -DanceAfrica Chicago
   -Center for Asian Arts & Media
4. University Center
5. Alexandroff Campus Center
   (Main Campus Building)
   -Museum of Contemporary Photography
6. Wabash Campus Building
   -Center for Black Music Research
7. South Campus Building
8. 1006 S Michigan Ave Building
9. 11th Street Campus
   -A&D Gallery
   -Getz, Classic, and New Studio Theater
10. Music Center
11. 1104 S Wabash Center
    -Center for Book and Paper Arts
    -Glass Curtain Gallery
    -Concert Hall
12. 11th & Wabash Sculpture Garden
13. Dance Center
14. Theater/Film Annex
15. Residence Center
16. 2 E 8th Residence Hall
17. 619 S. Wabash Building

General Information

NFT Maps: 8, 9, 11
Address: 600 S Michigan Ave, Chicago, IL 60605
Phone: 312-369-1000
Website: www.colum.edu or @ColumbiaChi
Event Information: www.colum.edu/calendar
Enrollment: 10,142 (2013)
Endowment: $123 million (2013)

Overview

Named in honor of the World's Columbian Exposition, Columbia College Chicago first opened in 1890 as a women's speech academy. Over time, it has become one of America's most diverse private arts and media schools. It is best known for its film, television, and fiction departments, which turn out prominent professionals. Columbia alumni played key writing and production roles in *Barbershop*, *Real Women Have Curves*, *Analyze This*, *Schindler's List*, and *Leaving Las Vegas*. They win Emmy Awards (for art direction on *Alias*, special effects on *Star Trek: Enterprise*, animation on *Samurai Jack*, and cinematography on *Carnivale*). And they write acclaimed books; celebrated scribblers Joe Meno, Don DeGrazia, and Sam Weller all returned to Columbia's fiction writing department as faculty. Other programs include photography, dance, theater, music, art and design, journalism, fashion design, poetry, education, and management for the arts, entertainment, and media. Columbia's campus is the bustling South Loop, and its colorful student body immerse themselves in the city.

Tuition

Tuition for full-time undergrads hovers around $23,000. There's fees, books, art supplies, CTA passes, and obligatory museum visits, too. And have you heard about the Superdorm (525 S State St)? There, you can live in the middle of the Loop with more than 1,700 of your closest friends. Hey, college is a perpetual slumber party.

Culture

Columbia College is one of Chicago's most esteemed cultural arts presenters; more than 300,000 visitors attend Columbia events each year. The college hosts a regular slate of innovative dance performances throughout the year. The Museum of Contemporary Photography is one of just a handful of fully accredited photography museums in the United States. The Story Week Festival of Writers, held in the spring, is among Chicago's top literary draws. The college brings in authors, editors, agents, and publishers for a week of readings, panels, and special events, such as a rock-related literature night at the Metro. Spring also brings Fashion Columbia and the Manifest Urban Arts Festival, celebrating graduate achievements. The college's galleries and theaters feature the work of students alongside notable outside artists. The school's Media Production Center (MPC), located at 1600 S State St, opened in early 2010. Designed by local architects Studio Gang, it's a 35,000 sq. ft. state-of-the-art facility—containing studios, labs and classrooms—which allows for cross-disciplinary collaboration unlike anywhere else in the U.S. at the college/university level.

• Museum of Contemporary Photography
600 S Michigan Ave
312-663-5554
www.mocp.org or @MoCP_Chicago

• ShopColumbia
619 S Wabash Ave
312-369-8616
https://shop.colum.edu/

• Glass Curtain Gallery
1104 S Wabash Ave, 1st Fl
312-369-6643

• C33 Gallery
33 W Ida B. Wells Dr
312-369-6856

• Dance Center
1306 S Michigan Ave
312-369-8300
www.colum.edu/dance_center or @Dance_Center

• Getz, Classic, and New Studio Theaters
72 E 11th St
312-369-6126
www.colum.edu/theater_center

• Concert Hall
1014 S Michigan Ave
312-369-6240

• Center for Black Music Research
618 S Michigan Ave, 6th Fl
312-369-7559
www.colum.edu/cbmr

• Media Production Center (MPC)
1600 S State St
312-369-3314

Department Contact Information

Undergraduate Admissions: 312-369-7130
Graduate Admissions: 312-369-7260
School of Fine and Performing Arts: 312-369-7964
School of Media Arts: 312-369-8211
School of Liberal Arts and Sciences: 312-369-8211

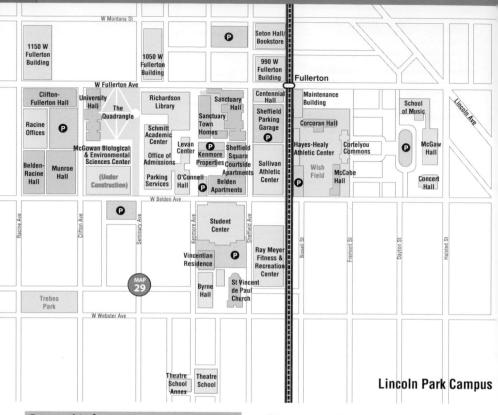

Lincoln Park Campus

General Information

Lincoln Park Campus: Welcome Center, 2400 N Sheffield Ave, Chicago, IL 60614
Phone: 773-325-7000 x5700
Loop Campus: 1 E Jackson Blvd, Chicago, IL 60604
Phone: 312-362-8000
Naperville Campus: 312-476-4500/630-548-9378
Oak Forest Campus: 312-476-3000/708-633-9091
O'Hare Campus: 312-476-3600
Website: www.depaul.edu or @DePaulU
Enrollment: 24,414 (2013)
Endowment: $384 million (2013)

Overview

Established in 1898 by the Vincentian Fathers as a school for immigrants, DePaul has become the country's largest Catholic university (with over 24,000 students) and the biggest private educational institution in Chicago, offering nearly 300 undergraduate and graduate programs of study. Of the university's seven campuses in the Chicago area, the Lincoln Park and Loop campuses serve as the core locations. The highly acclaimed Theatre School, College of Liberal Arts

and Sciences, School of Music, and School of Education hold down the 36-acre Lincoln Park campus amid renovated historic homes on tree-lined streets.

DePaul's Loop Campus at Jackson Boulevard and State Street is where you'll find the College of Commerce, College of Law, and School of Computer Science, Telecommunications, and Information Systems. Nationally respected Kellstadt Graduate School of Business and DePaul's thriving continuing education program, the School of New Learning, can also be found on the Loop Campus. The heart of the Loop campus is DePaul Center, located in the old Goldblatt Brothers Department Store, now grounded by a university-sanctioned Barnes and Noble. Most students in the Loop campus are adults, so popular hangouts include the Brown Line L, Red Line L, and Metra stations while they're all waiting for the train home. Prominent DePaul alumni include Chicago father-son mayors Richard M. Daley and his dad, the late Richard J. Daley; McDonald's Corporation's former CEO Jack Greenberg; Pulitzer Prize-winning composer George Perle; and actors Gillian Anderson and John C. Reilly.

Tuition

Full-time undergraduate tuition hovers around $34,000.

Sports

The DePaul Blue Demons might be named a bit oddly as the athletic ambassadors of the largest Catholic university in the United States, but their teams are strong despite any identity confusion. The Blue Demons play in the Big East Conference and DePaul's teams include men's and women's basketball, cross-country, soccer, tennis, and track and field, men's golf, and women's softball and volleyball. Its men's basketball team often has solid years and standout players often move on to the NBA.

For tickets, visit the ticket office at the Sullivan Athletics Center (2323 N Sheffield Ave, 773-325-7526, depaulbluedemons.com). The Blue Demons play at McGrath-Phillips Arena (volleyball, 2323 N Sheffield Ave), Wintrust Arena (men's and women's basketball, 200 E Cermak Rd, 312-791-6900; wintrustarena.com), and Wish Field and Cacciatore Stadium (men's and women's soccer and softball, respectively, both on the 900 block of Belden Ave).

Culture on Campus

DePaul's vibrant Theatre School is the oldest of its kind in the Midwest. Founded in 1925 as the Goodman School of Drama, the school stages over 150 performances during its season. The Theatre School performs contemporary and classic plays at its 1,325-seat Merle Reskin Theatre, a French Renaissance-style theater built in 1910 and located at 60 E Balbo Drive in the South Loop. Chicago Playworks and the School of Music's annual opera are also performed at the Merle Reskin Theatre. Best of all, tickets are reasonable—all under $20. For directions and parking garage locations, call 312-922-1999 or go to theatre.depaul.edu. Take the Red Line to the Harrison Street or Jackson Street stops just southwest of the theater. CTA buses 29, 36, 151, and 146 also stop nearby.

The DePaul Art Museum (museums.depaul.edu), located at 935 W Fullerton, is open Wed–Sun and offers free admission to all visitors. Permanent collections of sculpture and oil paintings from local and international artists adorn the galleries. A pay parking lot is located one block east of the library on N Sheffield Avenue. DePaul's John T. Richardson Library and Loop campus library in DePaul Center (library.depaul.edu) are open to the public year-round, 7 am–11 pm. Take plenty of change for the copy machines as check-out privileges are reserved for students and faculty.

Department Contact Information

Lincoln Park Campus Admissions Office: 773-325-7500
Loop Campus Admissions Office: 312-362-8300
College of Commerce: 312-362-6783
College of Law: 312-362-8701
College of Liberal Arts & Sciences: 773-325-7300
John T Richardson Library: 773-325-7862
Loop Campus Library: 312-362-8433
Kellstadt Graduate School of Business: 312-362-8810
School for New Learning: 312-362-8001
College of Computing and Digital Media: 312-362-8381
School of Music: 773-325-7260
Theatre School: 773-325-7917

Illinois Institute of Technology

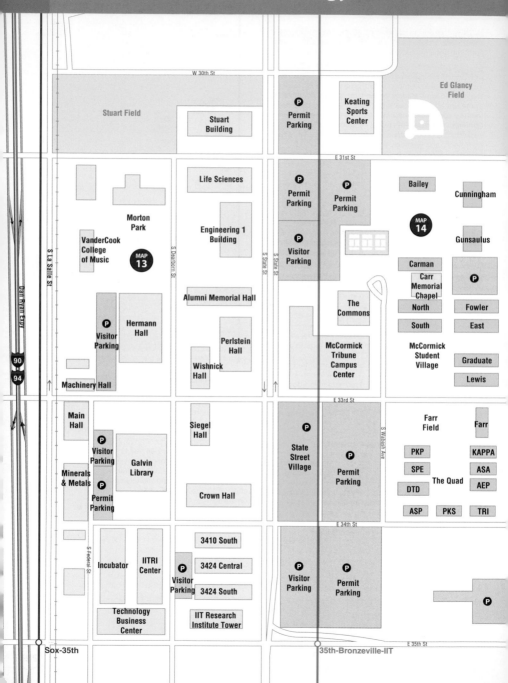

Illinois Institute of Technology

General Information

NFT Map: 13, 14
Main Campus: 3300 S Federal St, Chicago, IL 60616
Phone: 312-567-3000
Website: www.iit.edu or @illinoistech
Enrollment: 7,850 (2013)
Endowment: $194 million (2013)

Overview

In the 19th century, when higher education was reserved for society's upper crust, meat magnate Philip Danforth Armour put his money to good use and funded an institution dedicated to students who wished to learn a variety of industrial arts. The Armour Institute carried his name until a merger with the engineering school Lewis Institute in 1940 changed the name to Illinois Institute of Technology. Over the next 40 years, the college continued to merge with other small technical colleges, resulting in the IIT we know today. The school is as notable for its Mies Van Der Rohe-designed campus (although it is arguably not his best work) as for its groundbreaking work in aeronautics research. The student center, designed by Dutch architect Rem Koolhaas, includes a space-aged metallic tube through which the local L train travels.

Chicago-Kent College of Law, Stuart School Graduate School of Business, and the Master of Public Administration program are all based in the Loop. The Institute of Design is located near Merchandise Mart. The Rice campus, in west suburban Wheaton, offers undergraduate continuing education and degree programs to working professionals. The National Center for Food Safety and Technology, located on the Moffett Campus in the southwest suburbs, and the IIT Research Institute, housed in IIT's tallest building on its main campus in Bronzeville, are just two of the many research organizations IIT has incorporated since 1936 to serve various needs of private industry and government. IIT grants PhDs and other professional degrees in a vast array of areas including science, mathematics, engineering, architecture, psychology, design, business, and law.

Tuition

Undergrads pay around $40,000 per academic year plus room and board, books, and various fees. Graduate, law and business school tuition varies by program.

Sports

IIT competes in NCAA Division III. The Scarlet Hawks field teams in an array of sports, including men's and women's swimming and diving, cross-country, track and field, basketball, soccer, and men's baseball, women's lacrosse, and women's volleyball.

Developments on Campus

Most first-year students live on IIT's architecture-rich campus. The State Street Village student residence, located at State and 33rd Streets, was designed by well-known Chicago-based architect Helmut Jahn. Jahn, a graduate of IIT himself, created the six-building complex across the street from Van Der Rohe's historical landmark, the S.R. Crown Hall. When not diving deep into all manner of stuff that 98 percent of the rest of civilization barely comprehends, IIT students also participate in more than 120 student clubs and organizations and Greek life is not shunned or frowned upon (an IIT fun fact: around 8% of all Greeks get a 4.0 GPA each semester; Bluto Blutarsky these cats ain't). Also, all of Chicago and all it has to offer is accessible via the Red and Green L lines.

Department Contact Information

Undergraduate Admissions: 312-567-3025
Graduate Admissions: 312-567-3020
Alumni Office: 312-567-5000
Armour College of Engineering: 312-567-3009
Office of Professional Development: 630-682-6035
Chicago-Kent College of Law: 312-906-5000
College of Architecture: 312-567-3260
College of Science: 312-567-3800
Keating Sports Center: 312-567-3296
Institute of Design: 312-595-4900
Lewis College of Human Sciences: 312-567-3956
Stuart School of Business: 312-906-6500

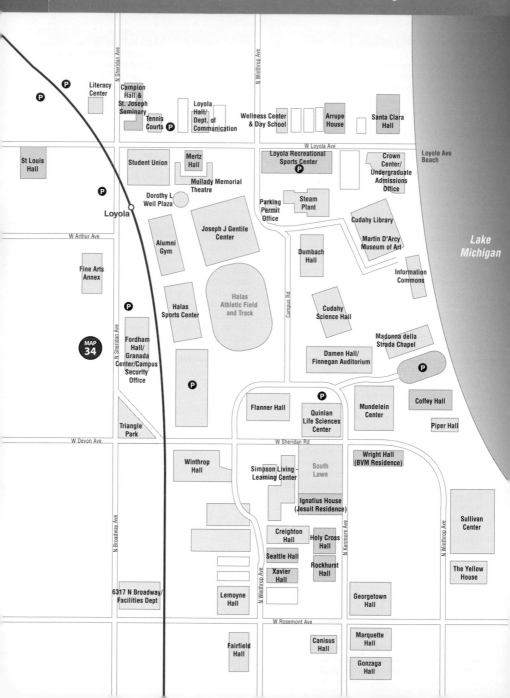

Loyola University (Lake Shore Campus)

Literacy Center
Campion Hall & St. Joseph Seminary
Tennis Courts
Loyola Hall/ Dept. of Communication
Wellness Center & Day School
Arrupe House
Santa Clara Hall

N Sheridan Ave
N Winthrop Ave

W Loyola Ave
Loyola Ave Beach

St Louis Hall
Student Union
Mertz Hall
Mullady Memorial Theatre
Loyola Recreational Sports Center
Crown Center/ Undergraduate Admissions Office

Dorothy L Weil Plaza
Loyola

W Arthur Ave

Joseph J Gentile Center
Parking Permit Office
Steam Plant
Cudahy Library
Martin D'Arcy Museum of Art

Alumni Gym
Dumbach Hall
Information Commons

Fine Arts Annex

Lake Michigan

Halas Sports Center
Halas Athletic Field and Track
Campus Rd
Cudahy Science Hall

MAP 34

Fordham Hall/ Granada Center/Campus Security Office
Madonna della Strada Chapel

Damen Hall/ Finnegan Auditorium

N Sheridan Ave

Flanner Hall
Quinlan Life Sciences Center
Mundelein Center
Coffey Hall
Piper Hall

Triangle Park

W Devon Ave
W Sheridan Rd

Winthrop Hall
Simpson Living - Learning Center
South Lawn
Wright Hall (BVM Residence)

N Broadway Ave

Ignatius House (Jesuit Residence)

N Winthrop Ave
N Kenmore Ave
N Winthrop Ave

Sullivan Center

Creighton Hall
Holy Cross Hall

Seattle Hall
Rockhurst Hall
The Yellow House

6317 N Broadway/ Facilities Dept
Xavier Hall

Lemoyne Hall
Georgetown Hall

W Rosemont Ave

Fairfield Hall
Canisus Hall
Marquette Hall

Gonzaga Hall

General Information

Lake Shore Campus: 1032 W Sheridan Rd, Chicago, IL 60626
Phone: 773-274-3000
Water Tower Campus: 820 N Michigan Ave, Chicago 60611
Phone: 312-915-6000
Health Sciences Campus: 2160 S First Ave, Maywood, IL 60153
Phone: 708-216-9000
Website: www.luc.edu or @LoyolaChicago
Enrollment: 15,957 (2014)
Endowment: $463 million (2014)

Overview

Loyola University, one of the largest Jesuit universities in the United States, is known throughout the Midwest for its first-rate schools of business and law, as well as for its Medical Center (a well-respected research institution). It was originally established in 1870 as St. Ignatius College and was re-named in 1909.

Lake Shore Campus, the largest campus of Loyola's four campuses, is on the lake in Rogers Park and houses the College of Arts & Sciences, the Graduate School, Niehoff School of Nursing, Mundelein College Adult Education Program, and Cudahy Library. The university's Water Tower campus downtown on Michigan Avenue is home to the Schools of Business, Education, Law, and Social Work and some College of Arts & Sciences courses. Loyola operates the Stritch School of Medicine and the Master's degree programs through the Niehoff School of Nursing at its suburban Maywood campus. The university also has a campus in Rome, one of the largest American campuses in Western Europe, as well as centers in Beijing on the campus of Beijing University and Vietnam. Notable graduates include Sho Yano, who ranks first in the world with the highest known I.Q. Other notable grads include Chicago Bears owner George S. Halas Jr., actor/comedian Bob Newhart, and celebrated authors Sandra Cisneros and Stuart Dybek.

Tuition

Undergraduate tuition costs just over $37,000 (give or take a couple hundred dollars depending on the program of study), including most added fees. All first – and second-year students are required to live on campus and participate in a meal plan.

Sports

Represented by their mascot the LU Wolf, the Loyola Ramblers compete in the NCAA Division I Atlantic 10 Conference. Loyola rambles in varsity sports such as men's and women's basketball, cross-country, golf, soccer, track and field, and volleyball and women's softball. The Ramblers men's volleyball program won consecutive national titles in 2014 and 2015, and the men's basketball squad reached the Final Four of the 2018 NCAA Tournament. Catch basketball at the Joseph J. Gentile Center on the Lake Shore Campus. For tickets, visit the box office, call 773-508-WOLF or visit www.loyolaramblers.com.

Culture on Campus

Founded in 2005, the Loyola University Museum of Art (LUMA) showcases the famous Martin D'Arcy collection of Medieval, Renaissance and Baroque art. Paintings by masters Tintoretto, Guercino, Bassano, and Stomer, plus sculpture, furniture, jewelry, decorative arts, and liturgical vessels, are part of the over 500-piece collection dating from 1150 to 1750. The museum, located at 820 N Michigan Avenue, Is housed In the historic Lewis Towers building on Mag Mile. General admission is $8, $6 for seniors and $2 for non-Loyola students under age 25 (free on Tuesdays and every day with Loyola ID) Hours: Tues, 11 am–8 pm; Wed–Sun: 11 am–6 pm. For more information, call 312-915-7600 or visit www.luc.edu/luma.

The university's Cudahy Library, Lewis Library at the Water Tower Campus, Science Library, Health Sciences Library, and Graduate Business School Library are all open to the public. Checkout privileges, however, are reserved for the university's students and faculty.

The Loyola University Theatre performs at the Kathleen Mullady Theatre (1125 W Loyola Ave, 773-508-3847) in the Centennial Forum/Mertz Hall building on the Lake Shore campus. A second studio stage is active with student productions during the fall and spring term, and a number of Loyola arts alumni events take place every year on campus.

The Loyola Campus also offers a variety of media options for its students. Printwise, there is *Inside Loyola*, *Loyola Magazine* and the *Loyola Phoenix* student newspaper. WLUW (88.7 FM) hosts a variety of shows.

Department Contact Information

Undergraduate Admission Office: 312-915-6500
School of Continuing and Professional Studies: 312-915-8900
College of Arts & Sciences: 773-508-3500
Quinlan School of Business: 312-915-8900
School of Education: 312-916-6800
School of Law: 312-915-7120
Stritch School of Medicine: 708-216-3229
Niehoff School of Nursing: 773-508-3249
John Felice Rome Center: 773-508-2760
School of Social Work: 312-915-8900
Graduate School of Business: 312-915-6124
The Graduate School: 773-508-3396
University Libraries: 773-508-2632

Northwestern University (Evanston Campus)

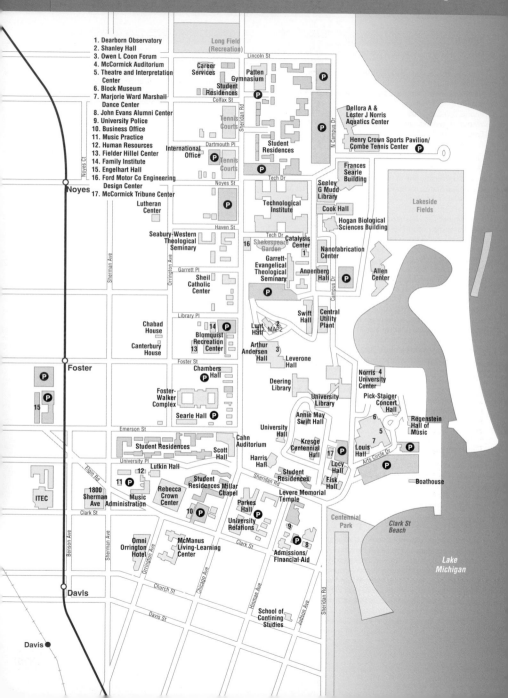

General Information

Evanston Campus: 633 Clark St, Evanston, IL 60208
Phone: 847-491-3741
Chicago Campus: Abbott Hall, 710 N Lake Shore Dr, Chicago, IL 60611
Phone: 312-503-8649
Website: www.northwestern.edu or @NorthwesternU
Enrollment: 21,000 (2014)
Endowment: $7.9 billion (2013)

Overview

Northwestern University, along with the University of Chicago, likes to think of itself as part of the "Ivy League of the Midwest." While this might seem a little snooty, NU is certainly the cream of the crop in the Big Ten Conference. 21,000 full- and part-time students attend Northwestern's 12 schools and colleges, located in Evanston and downtown Chicago, a far cry from the two original faculty members and ten students in attendance when the school opened in 1855. NU's campus in Doha, Qatar opened in 2008 and offers communication and journalism degrees, along with a certificate in Middle East studies and a minor in politics and media.

Founded in 1851, Northwestern University was established in Evanston by many of the same Methodist founding fathers of the town itself, including the founder of Chicago's Board of Trade. The University's name was derived from its founders' desire to service the citizens of the former Northwest Territory. The 240-acre lakefront campus is bordered roughly by Lincoln Street to the north and extends south to Clark Street and west to Sheridan Road. The Evanston campus houses the Weinberg College of Arts and Sciences; McCormick School of Engineering and Applied Science; the Schools of Music, Communication, Education and Social Policy; the Graduate School; Medill School of Journalism; and J.L. Kellogg School of Management.

The university did a bit of branching out when it purchased land for the Chicago campus in 1920. Located on a 25-acre lot between the lake and Michigan Avenue in the Streeterville neighborhood, the Chicago campus houses the Schools of Law, Medicine, and Continuing Studies. Graduate school and Kellogg courses are also offered at the Chicago campus. Several excellent hospitals and medical research institutions affiliated with the university dominate the northern edge of Streeterville. The Robert H. Lurie Medical Research Center at Fairbanks Court and Superior Street, completed in 2004, has expanded the university's research abilities with nine floors of laboratory space. The Prentice Women's Hospital, completed in 2007, continues to offer comprehensive and innovative treatments bolstering women's and infants' health.

Tuition

The university charges around $47,000 for undergrad tuition only. Room and board rates hover around $15,000 for an undergraduate student living in a double room and on a 14-meal-per-week plan.

Sports

The only private school in the Big Ten conference, Northwestern fields eight men's and eleven women's intercollegiate teams along with a host of club teams. A rare powerhouse outside the northeast, the women's lacrosse team won the NCAA national championship seven times between 2005 and 2012, going undefeated in two of those seasons. The Wildcats' football fortune has been looking up ever since the purple-clad boys broke an epic 33-year losing streak in 2004; subsequent years have seen bowl games and an occasional Top 25 ranking. The Wildcats' home is Ryan Field at 1501 Central Avenue, about three blocks west of the Central stop on the elevated Purple Line of the CTA. Basketball games are held at the Welsh-Ryan Arena behind the stadium. For tickets, visit www.nusports.com or call 888-467-8775 (i.e., "888-GO-PURPLE"). Northwestern students get free admission to any home game with valid NU WildCARD ID.

Culture on Campus

The Mary and Leigh Block Museum of Art on the Evanston campus (40 Arts Circle Dr; 847-491-4000; www.blockmuseum. northwestern.edu or @NUBlockMuseum) has 4,000 items in its permanent collection, including Old Masters' prints, architectural drawings, contemporary photographic images, and modern sculpture. The Block is also home to the state-of-the-art Pick-Laudati Auditorium that hosts film festivals and contemporary classics, as well as cinema series and lectures throughout the year. Hours: Tues, 10 am–5 pm; Wed–Fri, 10 am–8 pm; weekends, 10 am–5 pm. Admission is always free, but a suggested donation is appreciated.

The Pick-Staiger Concert Hall (50 Arts Circle Dr, 847-491-5441; www.pickstaiger.com or @pickstaiger), is not only the main stage for the university's musical performances but it is also home to several professional performance organizations such as the Chicago Chamber Musicians, Chicago Philharmonic, Northshore Concert Band, Evanston Symphony Orchestra, and others. Each year, Pick-Staiger Concert Hall also hosts the Segovia Classical Guitar Series and the Winter Chamber Music Festival. Call 847-467-4000 or visit www.pickstaiger.com to purchase tickets.

Student-led A & O Productions (www.aoproductions.net or @aoproductions) has been programming events, hosting films, and bringing comedians, speakers, and bands to campus since 1969. Past performers have included Lupe Fiasco, Tracy Morgan, Snoop Dogg, and Sarah Silverman.

For the upper echelon student interested in art or vandalism, one can visit the famed "Rock" that students began defacing in the 1940s. "Go Cats!," "Rich Kids Can Tag As Well!" and "I'm wasting my parent's money!" have all made brief appearances. Northwestern University also runs a student newspaper, The Daily Northwestern, and a student-run radio station, WNUR 89.3 FM (www.wnur.org or @WNUR893).

Department Contact Information

Undergraduate Admissions: 847-491-7271
Graduate School (Evanston): 847-491-5279
Weinberg College of Arts and Sciences: 847-491-3276
Feinberg School of Medicine: 312-503-8649
Kellogg School of Management: 847-491-3308
Medill School of Journalism: 847-467-2050
School of Communication: 847-491-7023
School of Professional Studies: 312-503-6950
School of Education and Social Policy: 847-491-8193
McCormick School of Engineering and Applied Science: 847-491-5220
School of Law: 312-503-3100
School of Music: 847-491-7575

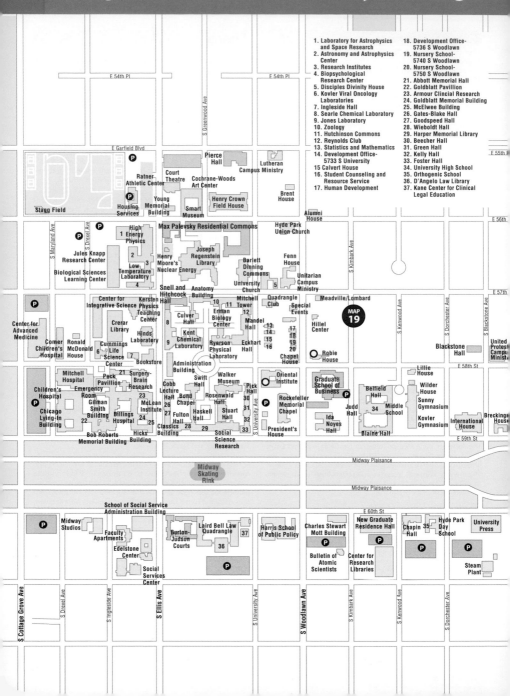

1. Laboratory for Astrophysics and Space Research
2. Astronomy and Astrophysics Center
3. Research Institutes
4. Biopsychological Research Center
5. Disciples Divinity House
6. Kovler Viral Oncology Laboratories
7. Ingleside Hall
8. Searle Chemical Laboratory
9. Jones Laboratory
10. Zoology
11. Hutchinson Commons
12. Reynolds Club
13. Statistics and Mathematics
14. Development Office- 5733 S University
15. Calvert House
16. Student Counseling and Resource Service
17. Human Development
18. Development Office- 5736 S Woodlawn
19. Nursery School- 5740 S Woodlawn
20. Nursery School- 5750 S Woodlawn
21. Abbott Memorial Hall
22. Goldblatt Pavillion
23. Armour Clincial Research
24. Goldblatt Memorial Building
25. McElwee Building
26. Gates-Blake Hall
27. Goodspeed Hall
28. Wieboldt Hall
29. Harper Memorial Library
30. Beecher Hall
31. Green Hall
32. Kelly Hall
33. Foster Hall
34. University High School
35. Orthogenic School
36. D'Angelo Law Library
37. Kane Center for Clinical Legal Education

MAP 19

General Information

NFT Map: 19
Mailing Address: Edward H. Levi Hall, 5801 S Ellis Ave, Chicago, IL 60637
Phone: 773-702-1234
Website: www.uchicago.edu or @UChicago
Enrollment: 15,000 (2014)
Endowment: $6.7 billion (2013)

Overview

Located amid the pleasant tree-lined streets of Hyde Park just seven miles south of downtown Chicago, the University of Chicago is a world-renowned research institution with a winning tradition in Nobel prizes. More than 80 Nobel laureates have been associated with the university as faculty, students or researchers. The university prides itself on its rigorous academic standards and top-ranked programs, while its students thrive in an environment that encourages creative exploring, taking risks, intellectual rigor, and determining the direction and focus of one's own education.

While its business, law, and medical schools are renowned for cranking out brainy gurus with assembly line efficiency, the university also has a long alumni list filled with artists, writers, politicians, film directors, and actors. To name a few: Studs Terkel, Sara Paretsky, Carol Moseley-Braun, Kurt Vonnegut, Susan Sontag, David Auburn, Ed Asner, Saul Bellow, Katharine Graham, Philip Glass, Saul Alinsky, Paul Goodman, Mike Nichols, and Second City improv theater founders Bernard Sahlins and Paul Sills.

Established in 1890, the University of Chicago was founded and funded by John D. Rockefeller. Built on 200 acres donated by Marshall Field and designed by architect Henry Ives Cobb, the university's English Gothic buildings of ivy-clad limestone ooze old money and intellectual achievements. Rockefeller described the university as "the best investment I ever made." We just hope parents footing the bill for their kids' education feel the same.

The University of Chicago operates on a trimester schedule rather than the more common two-semester academic year. Chicago has about 15,000 students, 5,000 of which are undergraduates. About 2,000 of the graduate students attend classes at the downtown riverfront campus Gleacher Center (450 N Cityfront Plaza Dr, 312-464-8787; www.gleachercenter.com), where the popular Graham School of Continuing Liberal and Professional Studies holds most of its continuing education classes.

Tuition

Undergraduate tuition is inching up toward $50,000 a year, not including room and board, although the university makes an effort to graduate two-thirds of its students debt free.

Sports

A long time ago, the famous nickname "Monsters of The Midway" belonged to The University of Chicago's football team (not "da Bears"), and the institution garnered football trophies right along with Nobel Prizes. The Maroons racked up seven Big Ten Football championships between 1899 and 1924, but the gridiron glory of yore faded and losing teams became the norm. The bleachers at Stagg Field, where fans once flocked to witness athletic triumphs, earned more fame as the site where Enrico Fermi and university scientists split the atom on Dec. 2, 1942. Four years later, President Robert Maynard Hutchins put in the university's walking papers from the Big Ten and abolished the football team. Perhaps this was a step towards prioritizing scholarly pursuits over athletic achievement, however the catastrophic results of the "controlled release of nuclear energy" might be to blame. But the school hasn't totally abandoned sports. Varsity football, reinstated in 1969, is back, albeit in a different form. UChicago is a member of NCAA Division III's University Athletic Association and hosts 19 varsity athletic sports in a conference comprised of some of the nation's leading research institutions, and since 1990 has won team championships in men's basketball, women's cross country, football, men's and women's soccer, softball, men's indoor track & field, and wrestling. The campus also boasts over 45 club sports and hundreds of intramural teams.

Culture on Campus

The Reva and David Logan Center for the Arts is the University of Chicago's state-of-the art multidisciplinary arts center. Opened in 2012, the 184,000-square-foot building integrates a dynamic mix of spaces to create a rich environment for arts and scholarship for the university, the South Side and greater Chicago. Visit logan.uchicago.edu for the calendar of events.

The Robie House, located at 5757 S Woodlawn Ave, is Frank Lloyd Wright's residential ode to all things horizontal and structurally organic (312-994-4000; flwright.org). This Prairie-style masterpiece is considered one of the most important buildings in the history of American architecture. Adult tickets cost $17, students and seniors pay $14.

Two must-see but often overlooked free museums on campus are the Oriental Institute Museum (1155 E 58th St, 773-702-9520; oi.uchicago.edu or @orientalinst) and the Smart Museum of Art (5550 S Greenwood Ave, 773-702-0200; smartmuseum.uchicago.edu or @SmartUChicago). Showcasing ancient treasures from university digs since the 1900s (and yes, Indiana Jones did his undergraduate studies at U of C), the Oriental Institute houses permanent galleries devoted to ancient Egypt, Nubia, Persia, Mesopotamia, Syria, Anatolia, the ancient site of Megiddo, along with a rotation of special exhibits. The Smart Museum boasts a permanent collection of 10,000 fine art objects spanning five millennia of both Western and Eastern civilizations—so yes, it'll be enough to look at for that afternoon you have to kill.

To satisfy your inner cineaste, take in a picture show at Doc Films (Ida Noyes Hall, 1212 E 59th St, 773-702-8574; docfilms.uchicago.edu or @DocFilmsChicago), the largest continuously running student film society in the nation. The screenings at their state-of-the-art theater range from foreign art house fare to documentaries to Hollywood classics, and feature companion lectures and Q &A with professors, actors, directors, and producers. If you're jonesing for a music fix, University of Chicago Presents is one of the city's landmark classical music presenters and features a variety of performers in the elegant, Victorian-style Mandel Hall (chicagopresents.uchicago.edu or @chicagopresents).

The university's Equity playhouse Court Theater continues its national reputation of staging critically acclaimed contemporary and classical productions by renowned playwrights (5535 S Ellis Ave, 773-753-4472; www.courttheatre.org or @courtchicago).

Department Contact Information

Undergraduate Student Admissions: 773-702-8650
Divinity School: 773-702-8200
Booth School of Business: 773-702-7743
Graham School of Continuing Liberal and Professional Studies: 773-702-1722
Harris Graduate School of Public Policy Studies: 773-702-8400
Law School: 773-702-9494
Pritzker School of Medicine: 773-702-1939

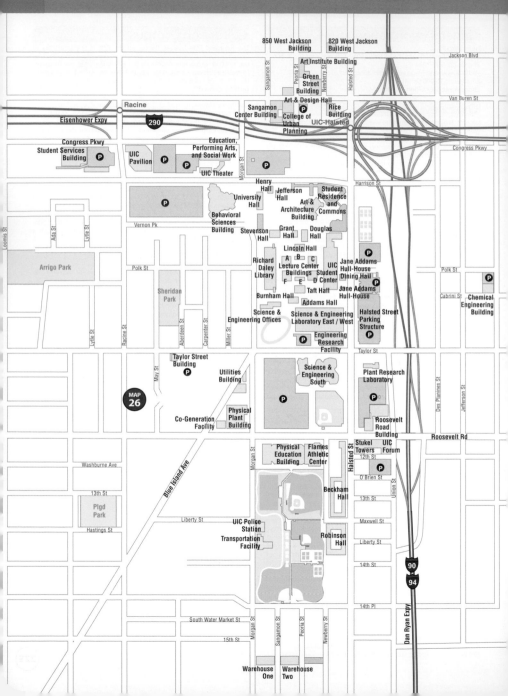

General Information

NFT Map: 26
Address: 1200 W Harrison St, Chicago, IL 60680
Phone: 312-996-7000
Website: www.uic.edu or @UICnews
Enrollment: 28,000 (2014)
Endowment: $675 million (2013)

Overview

With over 27,000 students, the University of Illinois at Chicago (UIC) is the largest university in the city. Located on the Near West Side, UIC is ethnically diverse and urban to the core. It is a leading public research university and home to the nation's largest medical school. Its legacy as a builder in Chicago, however, is a bit spotty. In the mid-1960s, the school leveled most of what was left of a vibrant Italian-American neighborhood to build its campus next to the Eisenhower Expressway.

Today, UIC continues to consume city blocks south of Roosevelt Road in further developing the South Campus. The expansions have all but erased the colorful, landmark Maxwell Street flea market area (this bustling mess of market now takes place only on Sundays along nearby S Canal Street). Of course, not everyone is crying over the loss of the eyesore market or the decrepit, crumbling buildings and homes that comprised the area, although we question whether a community of pricey cookie-cutter townhomes really constitutes much of an improvement. One thing that everyone seems to agree on is that many of the campus' original, ugly cement slab structures are kissing the wrecking ball as well. Even with the multi-million-dollar improvements, the campus is still fairly average; unless you're going to class or the doctor, a lone trip to UIC to see the Jane Addams Hull-House Museum is sufficient.

Tuition

In-state undergraduate tuition and fees ranges from approximately $11,000 to $14,000 .

Sports

The UIC Flames, named after the Great Chicago Fire of 1871, are, uh, hot these days. The men's basketball team has competed in the NCAA tournament, and the women's gymnastics, tennis squad, and softball teams have all advanced to NCAA tournament play in the past two decades. Other Flames men's and women's teams include swimming & diving and cross-country/track & field. UIC also has men's tennis, gymnastics, baseball, and soccer, as well as women's basketball and volleyball. Basketball games and women's volleyball matches are played at UIC Pavilion at the corner of S Racine Avenue and Harrison Street. For tickets, call 312-413-8421, or visit www.uicflames.com.

The campus has its own bowling alley located at 750 S Halsted Street (312-413-5170) where the public is welcome to sling balls and swig beers with students.

Culture on Campus

Jane Addams Hull-House (800 S Halsted St, 312-413-5353; www.uic.edu/jaddams/hull or @JAHHM), America's first settlement house, opened in 1889. The free museum documents the pioneering organization's social welfare programs that supported the community's destitute immigrant workers. Jane Addams was cool. Way cool. Museum hours are 10 am to 4 pm Tuesday through Friday and noon to 4 pm on Sunday, closed on Mondays and Saturdays.

Department Contact Information

Admissions and Records: 312-996-4350
Graduate College: 312-413-2550
School of Architecture: 312-996-3335
College of Applied Health Sciences: 312-996-2079
College of Business Administration: 312-996-2700
College of Education: 312-996-4532
College of Engineering: 312-996-2400
College of Liberal Arts and Sciences: 312-413-2500
College of Medicine: 312-996-3500
College of Nursing: 312-996-7800
College of Pharmacy: 312-996-7240
School of Public Health: 312-996-6620
College of Social Work: 312-996-7096
College of Urban Planning and Public Affairs: 312-413-8088
Office of Continuing Studies: 312-996-8025
University of Illinois Medical Center: 800-842-1002

Continuing Education in Chicago

Whether you want to change careers or just your waistline, learn a foreign language or learn more about the one you already know, Chicago is a great city to channel your inner student.

Get to the point of the matter with fencing classes from Midwest Fencing Academy. Turn off the Food Network, and learn to do it yourself at Kendall College, The French Pastry School, or The Chopping Block. Learn to put your foot down with style at the Flamenco Arts Center. Find out why laughter truly is the best medicine at The Second City Training Center or Comedy Sportz. Run away and join the circus after trapeze classes from Trapeze School Chicago. And discover that you really can teach an old dog new tricks at AnimalSense.

Continuing Education and Professional Development

Adler University, www.adler.edu or @AdlerUniversity, 312-662-4000, 17 N Dearborn St, 60602

City Colleges of Chicago (various locations), www.ccc.edu or @ChiCityColleges, 773-265-5343

The French Pastry School, www.frenchpastryschool.com or @PastrySchool, 312-726-2419, 200 S Wacker Dr, 60606

John Marshall Law School, www.jmls.edu or @JMLSChicago, 312-427-2737, 300 S State St, 60604

Kendall College, www.kendall.edu or @KendallCollege, 888-905-3632, 18 S Michigan Ave 3rd Floor, 60603

Pacific College of Oriental Medicine, www.pacificcollege.edu or @PCOMChicago, 773-477-4822, 65 E Wacker Pl, 21st Flr, 60601

Roosevelt University, www.roosevelt.edu or @RooseveltU, 312-341-3500, 430 S Michigan Ave, 60605

School of the Art Institute of Chicago, www.saic.edu or @saic_news, 800-232-7242, 36 S Wabash Ave, 60603

School of Professional Studies at Northwestern University, sps.northwestern.edu or @NorthwesternSPS, 847-491-5611, 405 Church St, 60201

Spertus College (Jewish culture), www.spertus.edu or @Spertus, 312-322-1700, 610 S Michigan Ave, 60605

Tribeca Flashpoint Media Arts Academy, www.tfa.edu or @TribecaChicago, 312-506-0600, 28 N Clark St, Ste 500, 60602

A Little Bit of Everything

AnimalSense, www.animalsense.com or @AnimalSense, 312-564-4570, various locations.

The Discovery Center, www.discoverycenter.cc or @dcenterchicago, 773-348-8120, 4318 N Elston Ave 2nd fl, 60641

The Feltre School (English grammar, writing, public speaking), www.feltre.org, 312-445-0516, 641 W Lake St, 60661

Kayak Chicago, www.kayakchicago.com, 312-852-9258, 1220 W LeMoyne Ave, 60622

Motorcycle Riding School, www.motorcyclelearning.com, 773-968-7433, 1680 N Ada St, 60642

Ride Chicago Motorcycle School, www.ride-chicago.com, 773-878-7433, 2509 W Fullerton Ave, 60647

StoryStudio Chicago, www.storystudiochicago.com or @StoryStudio, 773-477-7710, 4043 N Ravenswood, Ste 222, 60613

The Writers' Loft, www.thewritersloft.com, 1450 W Waveland Ave, 60613

Arts and Lifestyle

Annoyance Theatre (comedy improv classes), www.annoyanceproductions.com or @The_Annoyance, 773-697-9693, 851 W Belmont Ave, 60657

Chicago Dramatists, www.chicagodramatists.org, 312-633-0630, 1105 W Chicago Ave, 60642

Comedy Sportz, www.comedysportzchicago.com, 773-549-8080, 929 W Belmont Ave, 60657

Fire Arts Center of Chicago, www.firearts.org, 773-544-9908, 1830 N Kostner Ave, 60639

Lillstreet Art Center, www.lillstreet.com or @Lillstreet, 773-769-4226, 4401 N Ravenswood Ave, 60640

Old Town School of Folk Music, www.oldtownschool.org, 773-728-6000, 4544 N Lincoln Ave, 60625

Palette & Chisel Academy of Fine Art, www.paletteandchisel.org, 312-642-4400, 1012 N Dearborn, 60610

The Second City Training Center, www.secondcity.com or @TheSecondCity, 312-664-3959, 1608 N Wells St f4, 60614

WoodSmyth's (woodworking classes), www.woodsmythschicago.com, 773-477-6482, 5750 W Grand Ave, 60639

Athletics and Dance

All About Dance, www.allaboutdance.org or
@AAD_Chicago, 773-572-8701, 501 W North Ave, 60610

Chicago Sailing Club, www.chicagosailing.com or
@chisail, 773-871-7245, 3550 N Recreation Dr, 60657

Degerberg Academy Martial Arts,
www.degerbergacademy.com, 773-728-5300,
4717 N Lincoln Ave, 60625

Latin Street Dancing, www.laboriqua.com, 312-427-2572,
600 Roosevelt Rd #2w, 60607

Midwest Fencing Academy,
www.midwestfencingacademy.com, 224-715-5941,
6100 N Cicero Ave, 60646

The School of Ballet Chicago, www.balletchicago.org or
@BalletChicago, 312-251-8838, 17 N State St, 19th Flr, 60602

Thousand Waves (martial arts), www.thousandwaves.org or
@TWSeido, 773-472-7663, 1220 W Belmont, 60657

Together We Tri (triathalon training), www.togetherwetri.com

Trapeze School Chicago, chicago.trapezeschool.com or
@TSNYChicago, 773-484-8861

Food and Wine

City Winery, www.citywinery.com/chicago or
@CityWineryCHI, 312-733-9463, 1200 W Randolph St, 60607

The Chopping Block, www.thechoppingblock.net or
@TheChoppingBloc, 773-472-6700, 4747 N Lincoln Ave;
312-644-6360, The Merchandise Mart Plaza, Ste 107, 60654

The Wooden Spoon, www.woodenspoonchicago.com,
773-293-3190, 5047 N Clark St, 60640

Foreign Languages

Alliance Francaise de Chicago, www.af-chicago.org or
@AllianceChicago, 312-337-1070, 810 N Deaborn St, 60610

Chicago Mandarin Chinese Center, www.chicagomcc.com,
312-316-6038, 33 N Dearborn St Suite 1000, 60602

Goethe Institut, www.goethe.de/chicago or @GI_Chicago,
312-263-0472, 150 N Michigan Ave, Ste 200, 60601

Instituto Cervantes Chicago, chicago.cervantes.es or
@Chicago_IC, 312-335-1996, 31 W Ohio St, 60610

Italian Cultural Institute of Chicago, www.iicchicago.esteri.it
or @IIC_Chicago, 312-822-9545,
500 N Michigan Ave, Ste 1450, 60611

General Information

Active Transportation Alliance: 35 E Wacker Pl #1782, www.activetrans.org or @activetrans; 312-427-3325
Chicago Cycling Club: www.chicagocyclingclub.org or @ccc_scoop; 773-509-8093
Divvy Bikes: www.divvybikes.com or or @DivvyBikes; 855-553-4889
DOT Chicago Complete Streets: www.chicagocompletestreets.org
The Chainlink: www.thechainlink.org

Overview

During the Emanuel administration, the city set forth a comprehensive strategy to make Chicago the best big city for bicycling. By 2020, the plan is for a 645-mile network of biking facilities in order to provide a bicycle accommodation within a half-mile of every Chicagoan. In addition, the plan calls for more bikeways where more people live and to build more infrastructure where ridership is high, while establishing a strong backbone of infrastructure where ridership is currently lower.

In short, the bicycling situation in Chicago has improved, but there is still a long way to go. Bike riders still need to carefully navigate the city streets and trails as residents learn to adjust to the city's bicycle initiatives. Currently, Chicago has more than 200 miles of bike lanes—and not just painted lanes on busy thoroughfares where double parking is endemic but also on-street protected and buffered lanes; a recent initiative was to make a two-way, protected bike lane on Dearborn Street through the Loop. There are more than 36 miles of trails, including the 18.5 mile Lakefront Trail, which does not always require you battle headphone-wearing roller bladers, leashless dogs, and shoulder-to-shoulder stroller pushers. Chicago also has more than 13,000 bike racks—more than most big cities—and sheltered, high-capacity bike parking areas at many CTA rail stations, and even a state-of-the-art bike parking garage in Millennium Park (complete with showers!).

Divvy, the city's bike share system, debuted in the spring of 2013. The system is planned for 4,750 bikes available for sharing at 475 locations across the city. Bikes are available 24 hours a day, 7 days a week, 365 days a year for short point-to-point trips. Users pick up a bike from a self-service docking station and return it to any other station nearest their destination. Yearly membership is $75 and day passes are $7, allowing for unlimited trips of up to 30 minutes each. Users can learn more and enroll at www.divvybikes.com.

If you are a cyclist in Chicago, bear in mind that bicycles, like other vehicles of the roads, are subject to the same laws and rights as drivers. You might feel like you're the only biker in the city who comes to a full stop at a sign, but fastidiously sticking to the laws is a good way to make a case for drivers to accept bikers. This includes the right to take a lane and the obligation to hand signal for turns. It goes without saying that you should always ride defensively (but don't ride on sidewalks: you can be ticketed). Helmets are still optional, but you'd have to have a pretty thick head to tempt fate without one. The many white "ghost bikes" set up throughout the city serve as vigils for fallen bikers, and remind riders of the need to buy and wear a helmet. Besides, one of the many perks of cycling is that no matter how goofy you may feel in your gear, there is always someone who looks much, much stupider beside you. The same goes for an adequate assortment of chains and u-locks, as bike thievery is rampant in every neighborhood in the city. The police department offers a bike registration service, so you'll have legal recourse if you stumble upon your stolen bike somewhere out there. The Active Transportation Alliance does its best to raise awareness with events like Bike the Drive in May (no cars on Lake Shore Drive for a whole morning!) and Bike to Work Week in June.

Bikes Onboard Mass Transit

Bicycles are permitted (free) on all L trains at all times except rush hour (7 am–9 am and 4 pm–6 pm on weekdays). Use the accessible turnstile or ask an attendant to open an access gate. Don't try to take your bike through the tall steel gates—not least of which because it will get stuck. Only two bikes per carriage are allowed, so check for other bikes before you get on. The CTA has equipped all of its buses with front exterior bike racks, which are much less intimidating to use than they appear. If your bike is the first to be loaded, lower the rack and place it in position with the front wheel facing the curb. If there is already a bike on the rack, place your bike's rear wheel toward the curb. If two bikes are already loaded, wait for the next bus (whenever that may be). Bus-traveling bicyclists be warned, horror stories abound about bikes falling off racks, and there are even hit-by-bus-while-trying-to-remove-bike rumors. Always tell the driver that you are going to be loading or removing your bike, and ask for help if you need it—not all bus drivers are as gruff as they appear. On Metra commuter trains, bikes are allowed on all weekday trains arriving in Chicago after 9:30 am and leaving Chicago before 3 pm and after 7 pm, and on all weekend trains (with the exception of some major events). There is a maximum number of bikes allowed per rail car (it varies by line—check the Metra website for your planned route), so follow the conductor's instructions if he or she asks you to board a different car.

Bike Shops	Address	Phone	Map
Bike and Roll Chicago – Riverwalk	239 E Randolph St	312-729-1000	2
Bike and Roll Chicago – Navy Pier	700 E Grand Ave	312-729-1000	3
Bike and Roll Chicago – Ohio St Beach	400 N Lake Shore Dr	312-729-1000	3
Bike and Roll Chicago – Millennium Park	239 E Randolph St	312-729-1000	6
Cycle Bike Shop	1465 S Michigan Ave	312-987-1080	11
Blue City Cycles	3201 S Halsted St	312-225-3780	13
Bike and Roll Chicago – DuSable Museum	740 E 56th Pl	312-729-1000	18
Blackstone Bicycle Works	6100 S Blackstone Ave	773-241-5458	19
Quick Release Bike Shop	1527 N Ashland Ave	773-871-3110	22
Boulevard Bikes	2769 N Milwaukee Ave	773-235-9109	27
Smart Bike Parts	3031 W Armitage Ave	773-384-3010	27
BFF Bikes	2056 N Damen Ave	773-666-5153	28
Cycle Smithy	2468 N Clark St	773-281-0444	30
Bike and Roll Chicago – Oak St Beach	N Lake Shore Dr & E Oak St	312-729-1000	31
Village Cycle Center	1337 N Wells St	312-751-2488	31
Gary's Cycle Shop	6317 N Clark St	773-743-4201	37
Uptown Bikes	4653 N Broadway St	773-728-5212	40
Roscoe Village Bikes	2016 W Roscoe	773-477-7550	42
Heritage Bicycles	2959 N Lincoln Ave	773-245-3005	43
Johnny Sprockets	3140 N Broadway	773-244-1079	44
Kozy's Cyclery	3712 N Halsted St	773-281-2263	44

Billiards

The city's affluent "nesters" may be more interested in big-screen TVs than pool tables these days. But you'd rather mix your pleasure with strategy, a convivial game of billiards is still a fine way of turning strangers into friends…€¦ not to mention learning the angles above the angles above the angles. Many bars, from the seedy to the swanky, have a table or four. Chicago is also home to a good number of establishments that cater specifically to pool sharks. Have a good one, and don't get hustled.

The game's popularity goes in cycles. It spiked in the '80s thanks largely to *The Color of Money*, the pool-themed film starring Paul Newman and Tom Cruise, part of which was shot at **Chris's Billiards (Map 48)**. With two-dozen tables, no booze and no nonsense, this Jefferson Park institution remains the most credible spot among Chicago's seasoned players, although it sometimes intimidates newcomers. (We wouldn't call it "sleazy," but we wouldn't eat off the floor, either.) Uno Billiards **(Map 38)** is an oasis of seediness in the otherwise upscale Albany Park area. The equipment's not in tip-top shape, but cut this place and it bleeds character. Chicago Billiards **(Map 35)** is also a hike from downtown, but it's a more family-oriented room with a full food menu. If you're looking for snooker, a billiards variation wildly popular in Britain, they've got the hook-up here.

Somewhat hipper environs can be found at City Pool Hall Food & Spirits **(Map 1)**, a well-kept room also noted for its delectable burgers. If racking the balls ever gets seriously trendy again, you can bet that the folks at G Cue Billiards **(Map 24)** will be the first to know. Professional player Tom Karabatsos runs this two-level lounge, which accommodates more hangers-out than pool purists.

For an even more gloriously inauthentic pool adventure, you can usually find a table at one of Chicago's bowling alleys. Diversey-River Bowl **(Map 42)** may be better known for its blacklights and throbbing pop soundtrack, but for those who can't shoot straight sober, it's got a game room with a full-service bar. It's open 'til 3 am on weekends. Waveland Bowl **(Map 42)** has tables all night, every night, though there's often a wait, and it's hard to focus when high school and college kids keep distracting us with their air hockey and their Dance Dance Revolution. Southport Lanes **(Map 43)** is a mite classier, with lovely Brunswick tables in a welcoming back area. Table rates at all of Chicago's pool halls vary by time of day and number of players. To save money, show up early—many halls offer discounts for pre-5 pm players.

A few major music venues also have tables, where musicians can be found relieving their road-warrior angst between sound checks. Show up early at the Double Door or the Empty Bottle (See Nightlife Map 21), and you might get to hustle the people who wrote your favorite song. South Loop blues joint Buddy Guy's also offers pool, and although the cover may be a bit intimidating, there is nothing quite like shooting stick while some of Chicago's saddest songsters wail next door.

Billiards	Address	Phone	Fee	Map
City Pool Hall	640 W Hubbard St	312-491-9690	$12 per hour	1
G Cue Billiards	157 N Morgan St	312-850-3170	$14 per hour	24
Waveland Bowl	3700 N Western Ave	773-472-5900	$8-15 per hour	42

Bowling

Bowling is supposed to be the most blue-collar of all sports, so in the City of Big Shoulders, you'd expect comb-overs, beer frames, unfashionable wrist guards, and visible plumber's cracks to abound. In the '90s, several local alleys jazzed it up for the teenagers with rock music and late night fog and-light shows, and we can live with that. Lately, however, the trend is toward atmosphere-conscious boutique spots that treat strikes and spares as an afterthought. These are nice places to take a date, but we're a little scared when so-called bowling alleys advertise "small plates."

But if you're intrigued by the idea of high-end lounges that mash-up retro kitsch with modern glam, head to **10 Pin Bowling Lounge (Map 2)**, where you can sip a trend-'tini on a cushy couch with an urban professional crowd. And the upscale, Hollywood-themed chain, **Lucky Strike Lanes (Map 3)**, is a good place to kill time if you're waiting to catch a movie at the adjacent AMC River East.

If you prefer not to define your bowling experience as "sophisticated" or "cutting edge," we recommend the newly-renovated **Lincoln Square Lanes (Map 38)**, the city's only second-floor alley, which has been open since 1918. Climb a flight of stairs above Matty K's Hardware store and you'll get twelve lanes with old-school wood floors, live blues and rockabilly music on weekends, and a balcony from which to watch the action. Other good choices for an authentic Chicago bowling adventure include **Diversey-River Bowl (Map 42)**, where there's an eclectic mix of league fanatics and hipster rockers ordering bottles of Bud shaped like bowling pins, or the only-slightly-grungy **Waveland Bowl (Map 42)**, which has been open 24 hours a day, seven days a week since 1969.

For a place that successfully maintains a vibe of "real deal" authenticity while welcoming newcomers, head to the **Timber Lanes (Map 39)**, where hand scoring still reigns amid wood-paneled walls, a pinball machine, and a well-stocked bar. Owner Bob is a ubiquitous presence during league play, bowling left-handed to maintain the pretense of fairness. Since opening 1945, they've had leagues for men, women, mixed, gay and lesbian, and the blind. They've also hosted full-contact, Mexican wrestling-style bowling and nude nights—though shoes were still required. The cost to crush pins at each of these destinations varies based on time of day and whether you'll be bringing your own stylish shoes. Our advice: call ahead to make sure lanes are available and inquire about fees.

Bowling	Address	Phone	Map
10 Pin Bowling Lounge	330 N State St	312-644-0300	2
Lucky Strike Lanes	322 E Illinois St	312-245-8331	3
Fireside Bowl	2646 W Fullerton Ave	773-486-2700	27
Timber Lanes	1851 W Irving Park Rd	773-549-9770	39
Diversey River Bowl	2211 W Diversey Pkwy	773-227-5800	42
Waveland Bowl	3700 N Western Ave	773-472-5900	42

Weather permitting, golfers can tee up all year round in Chicago. The Chicago Park District's public courses are open daily, dawn to dusk. At **Jackson Park**'s **(South)** premier 18-hole facility, the scenery alone will make you forget the bustle of the city. The nine-hole **Sydney R. Marovitz (Waveland) Golf Course (Map 43)** is usually busy, but it has great views of the lake. And **Robert A. Black**'s **(Map 34)** nine-hole, 2,339-yard, par-33 layout was designed by the renowned Dick Nugent. In addition, the park district operates three driving ranges and three learning centers, including one for juniors at Douglas Park.

The Forest Preserve District of Cook County offers 11 public courses in and around the city. **Indian Boundary**'s **(Northwest)** huge fairways and fast-moving greens make for fun play and golfers often catch glimpses of visiting deer. At **Edgebrook (Northwest)**, bordered by mature trees along the Chicago River, the signature fifth hole—a 93-yard par three with an elevated green—offers a serious test of skill. Just 10 minutes from downtown, **Billy Caldwell**'s **(Northwest)** sharply undulating greens make it a great place to play a quick nine. Many of the city's courses offer twilight specials, so bring your glow-in-the-dark balls if you're looking to save some cash.

And, for a real urban golf experience, the privately owned **Harborside International (South)**, host to some Illinois PGA events, offers two tricky 18-hole, Scottish-links courses open to the public in season. Private courses in the city include the **Beverly, Ridge,** and **Ridgemoor** country clubs and **Riverside Golf Club**. However, if you want to see Tiger Woods play, you'll have to head out to the suburbs; the PGA tour visits clubs like **Cog Hill** in southwest Lemont and the members-only **Medinah Country Club** in the western 'burbs.

If you prefer your golf a little smaller, in-the-know mini-golfers head to the Park District's exceptionally cheap miniature golf course at **Diversey (Map 44)**, or head down south to the ultimate in windmill-dodging action, supernatural-themed **Haunted Trails Amusement Park (Southwest)**. **Navy Pier (Map 3)** also has a course, but the throngs of tourists with multi-colored balls makes it hard to recommend for the putt-putt purist.

Golf Courses

	Address	Phone	Map	Weekdays	Weekends
Robert A. Black Golf Course	2045 W Pratt Blvd	773-596-2581	34	$16.25	$17.75
Sydney R. Marovitz Golf Course	3701 N Recreation Dr	773-661-0140	44	$26	$29
Edgebrook Golf Course	6100 N Central Ave	773-763-8320	NW	$24	$28
Indian Boundary Golf Course	8600 W Forest Preserve Ave	773-625-9630	NW	$28	$30
Columbus Park Golf Course	5701 W Jackson Blvd	773-673-5016	W	$14.50	$15.75
Marquette Park Golf Course	6700 S Kedzie Ave	773-526-5040	SW	$15.25	$16.50
South Shore Country Club	7059 S South Shore Dr	773-496-5043	S	$17	$19
Harborside International Golf Center	11001 S Doty Ave	312-782-7837	S	$80	$92
Jackson Park Golf Course	6401 S Richards Dr	773-496-5015	S	$28	$31
Canal Shores Golf Course	1031 Central St	847-475-9173	Evanston	$20	$25

Driving Ranges

	Address	Phone	Map	Fees
Diversey Driving Range	141 W Diversey Dr	773-661-0105	3	Large bucket $16, club rental available
Marquette Park Golf Course	6700 S Kedzie Ave	773-526-5040	SW	
Harborside International Golf Center	11001 S Doty Ave	312-782-7837	S	$10/100 balls
Jackson Park Golf Course	6401 S Richards Dr	773-496-5015	S	Small bucket $6, large bucket $9 (no fee for clubs)

Mini Golf Courses

	Address	Phone	Map	Fees
Diversey Miniature Golf	141 W Diversey Pkwy	773-661-0105		Adults $9.00, Juniors/Seniors $7
Douglas Park	1401 S Sacramento Dr	866-223-5564		Free
Haunted Trails Amusement Park	7759 S Harlem Ave	708-598-8580		Adults $6, 12 & under $4.50
Navy Pier Mini Golf	600 E Grand Ave	312-595-7437		$15

General Information

Chicago Park District: 312-742-PLAY (7529);
www.chicagoparkdistrict.com

Overview

Due to the temperature extremes that Chicago experiences, its residents can enjoy both ice skating and inline skating at various times of the year. Ice skating can be a fun, free, winter activity if you have your own skates, and if you don't, many rinks rent them. Skateboarding is also a popular pastime and a number of parks throughout the city are equipped with skating facilities.

Inline Skating

Paths and streets fill up in the summertime with these one-row rollers. Similar to bike riding, inline skating in Chicago serves dual purposes. If you plan on strapping on the blades to get from A to B, be super-careful navigating the streets. As it is, Chicago drivers tend to have difficulty seeing cyclists, and chances are they won't notice you until you've slammed into their open car door. Wear protective gear whenever possible, especially a helmet, and learn to shout loudly so that people can anticipate your approach. If recreational skating is more your speed, Chicago has many recreational paths with cool places to skate.

Roller Derby

If watching skating seems far more interesting than actually lacing up, catch the Windy City Rollers, Chicago's premier all-female roller derby league (www.windycityrollers.com or @windycityroller). Featuring tattooed beauties beating the crap out of each other while skating the circular track, the WCR is unlike any other Chicago sporting event out there. Plenty of beer is served, and the atmosphere is fun and loose, while still retaining the competitive spirit that makes the Derby the Derby.

Skate Parks

If you're more interested in adrenaline than exercise, grab your blades or board and a couple of buddies and head down to the magnificent Burnham Skate Park (east of Lake Shore Drive at 31st St). With amazing grinding walls and rails, vert walls, and banks, Burnham Park presents hours of fun and falls. Logan Blvd Skate Park (N Western Ave and Logan Blvd) is a shared board-bike facility, and features a bowl corner with a spine, smaller quarters with hips, funbox with small flat and down rail, smaller spine and some hips. There are also places to skate in Lincoln, Piotrowski, and Grant Parks.

Ice Skating

The Park District's seven outdoor rinks offer free admission and reasonably priced skate rentals, making ice skating an excellent way to turn bitterly frozen winter lemons into recreational lemon ice. The city-owned McFetridge Sports Complex offers indoor skating year-round (3843 N California Ave, 773-478-2609, mcfetridgesportscenter.com; $5 admission and $3 rental).

The Olympic-sized skating rink and warming-house complex at Midway Plaisance offer a South Side venue for dropping precise one-footed salchows on an unsuspecting public. Located at 59th and Woodlawn, the rink, like all city rinks, has $3 admission and $6 rentals ($7 rental/admission; children and students free). During the summer, the facility is used for rollerskating and other entertainment. Other ice skating rinks are located seasonally at Mt. Greenwood, Riis, Rowan, Warren, West Lawn, Wentworth, and McKinley Parks.

If you, like the rest of Chicago, have recently caught hockey fever, try your hand at one of the many adult and child leagues run year-round at Johnny's Ice House, 1350 W Madison St (312-226-5555, www.johnnysicehouse.com). Close to downtown, Johnny's offers times and skill levels for any aspiring puckster. An interior bar guarantees a good time, regardless of game results. See also Johnny's Ice House West at 2550 W Madison St (312-243-4441).

The McCormick Tribune Ice Rink at Millennium Park (55 N Michigan Ave) is another option: admission is free and rentals run $10. The Winter Wonderfest at Navy Pier also features a seasonal rink (www.winterwonderfest.com), as does Wrigley Field's The Rink at Wrigley (1060 W Addison St, 773-525-1638).

Gear

If you're after skateboard gear, check out Uprise Skateboard Shop at 1820 N Milwaukee Ave (773-342-7763, www.upriseskateboards.com). For inline skating equipment, Londo Mondo (www.londomondo.com) has two locations: 1100 N Dearborn Street at W Maple St, 312-751-2794; and 2148 N Halsted St, 773-327-2218.

General Information

Chicago Park District: 312-742-PLAY (7529); www.chicagoparkdistrict.com or @ChicagoParks

The Chicago Park District operates more than 50 outdoor pools and more than 25 indoor pools, many of which are equipped with ramps or lifts for disability access. At the top of our list is the 500-person-capacity outdoor wonderment at **Washington Park (Map 18)**, a 50-meter pool that's connected to a large, oval, side pool where fountains spray into a zero-depth entrance. Even better—it's got a 36-foot, theme-park-style water slide. It's overrun with pool rats during open swim periods, but grown folks like the designated lap times, water aerobics classes, and adult swims.

We also like the 30-meter outdoor pool at **River Park (Map 38)**, an Albany Park spot that boasts a diving well, a spacious deck with lounge chairs and umbrella tables, and an interactive kids' water playground. And when the weather gets cold, there's great lap swimming at the **Ida Crown Natatorium** at Eckhart Park **(Map 24)**. What's a natatorium? It's a pool inside its own building, and this one looks like it might have been designed by Eero Saarinen, but it wasn't.

All outdoor pools are free for the summer (mid-June to Labor Day). During the year, lap swim fees for indoor pools are $25 a month or $40 for three months. Get a complete list of facilities and register for aquatic exercise, diving, lifeguard, underwater hockey, and water polo classes at www.chicagoparkdistrict.com.

Outdoor Pools

	Address	Phone	Map
Wentworth Gardens Park	3770 S Wentworth Ave	312-747-6996	13
Taylor Park	41 W 47th St	312-747-6728	15
Washington Park	5531 S MLK Dr	773-256-1248	18
Pulaski Park	1419 W Blackhawk St	312-742-7559	22
Union Park	1501 W Randolph St	312-746-5494	24
Dvorak Park	1119 W Cullerton St	312-746-5083	26
Holstein Park	2200 N Oakley Ave	312-742-7554	28
Wrightwood Park	2534 N Greenview Ave	312-742-7816	29
River Park	5100 N Francisco Ave	312-742-7516	38
Chase Park	4701 N Ashland Ave	312-742-7518	40
McFetridge Sports Center (California Park)	3843 N California Ave	773-478-2609	41
Hamlin Park	3035 N Hoyne Ave	312-742-7785	42
Douglas Park	1401 S Sacramento Dr	866-223-5564	West

Indoor Pools

	Address	Phone	Map
McGuane Park	2901 S Poplar Ave	312-747-6497	12
Clemente Park	2334 W Division St	312-742-7538	21
Eckhart Park/Ida Crown Natatorium	1330 W Chicago Ave	312-746-5490	24
Harrison Park	1824 S Wood St	312-746-5491	25
Kelly Park	2725 W 41st St.	312-747-6197	West
Sheridan Park	910 S Aberdeen St	312-746-5369	26
Stanton Park	618 W Scott St	312-742-7896	31
Mather Park	5941 N Richmond St	312-742-7501	35
Welles Park	2333 W Sunnyside Ave	312-742-7511	39
Winnemac Park	5001 N Leavitt St.	312-742-5101	39
Gill Park	825 W Sheridan Rd	312-742-7802	43

While we admit we're suckers for any sport that includes the word "love" in its scoring system, we try not to think of the significance that it means "zero" in tennis talk. Find love and more at these Chicago tennis courts.

Indoor Facilities
McFetridge Sports Center (Map 41) is the only indoor public facility in the system. All tennis courts free and open to the public on a first-come-first-served basis. Courts are open daily—check each park for individual hours. **Midtown Athletic Club (Map 28)** offers lessons and competitive programs for kids and adults.

Outdoor Facilities
In the summer, opt for tennis with a view at several lakeside facilities, including reconstructed courts in Grant Park's Maggie Daley Park. Waveland Park's Tennis on the Lake provides daily instruction from April through October. A full listing of the Chicago Park District's 120+ facilities is available at www.chicagoparkdistrict.com.

Tennis Courts	Address	Phone	Fees	Map
Maggie Daley Park	337 E Randolph St	312-742-3918	$7/hr; reservations required	6
Grant Park	331 E Randolph St	312-742-3918		6
Roosevelt Park	62 W Roosevelt Rd	312-742-3918		8
Mandrake Park	3858 S Cottage Grove Ave	312-747-9938		12
McGuane Park	2901 S Poplar Ave	312-747-6497		12
Armour Square Park	3309 S Shields Ave	312-747-6012		13
Ellis Park	3520 S Cottage Grove Ave	773-285-7099		14
Fuller Park	331 W 45th St	312-747-6144		15
Metcalfe Park	4134 S State St	312-747-6728		16
Kenwood Community Park	1330 E 50th St	312-747-6286		17
Washington Park	5531 S Dr Martin Luther King Jr Dr	773-256-1248		18
Jackson Park	6401 S Stony Island Ave	773-256-0903		20
Clemente Park	2334 W Division St	312-742-7538		21
Union Park	1501 W Randolph St	312-746-5494		24
Harrison Park	1824 S Wood St	312-746-5491		25
Sheridan Park	910 S Aberdeen St	312-746 5369		26
Midtown Athletic Club	2444 N Elston Ave	773-796-6523		28
Jonquil Playlot Park	1023 W Wrightwood Ave	312-742-7816		29
Oz Park	2021 N Burling St	312-742-7898		30
Lake Shore Park	808 N Lake Shore Dr	312-742-7891		32
Lerner Playlot Park	7000 N Sacramento Ave	773-761-0380		33
Rogers Park	7345 N Washtenaw Ave	773-381-6274		33
Indian Boundary Park	2500 W Lunt Ave	773-764-0338		33
Warren Park	6601 N Western Ave	773-262-6314		33
Loyola Park	1230 W Greenleaf Ave	773-262-8605		34
Pottawattomie Park	7340 N Rogers Ave	773-262-5835		34
Touhy Park	7348 N Paulina St	773-262-6737		34
Green Briar Park	2650 W Peterson Ave	773-761-0582		35
Legion Park at the Chicago River	3103 W Peterson Ave	312-742-7529		35
Mather Park	5941 N Richmond St	312-742-7501		35
Emmerson Park	1820 W Granville Ave	773-761-0433		36
Horner Park	2741 W Montrose Ave	773-478-3499		38
River Park	5100 N Francisco Ave	312-742-7516		38
Welles Park	2333 W Sunnyside Ave	312-742-7511		39
Chase Park	4701 N Ashland Ave	312-742-7518	$5/hr	40
Brands Park	3259 N Elston Ave	773-478-2414		41
Revere Park	2509 W Irving Park Rd	773-478-1220		41
McFetridge Sports Center	3843 N California Ave	773-478-2609	$16–$24/hr	41
Hamlin Park	3035 N Hoyne Ave	312-742-7785		42
Diversey Clay Courts	2800 N Lake Shore Dr	312-742-7821	$18/hr; reservations must be made in person	44
Waveland Tennis Center	3650 N Recreation Dr	773-278-8877	$7/hr; reservations required	44
Douglas Park	1401 S Sacramento Dr	866-223-5564		West

Even though the city seemingly perennially ranks among the fattest in the country, Chicagoans aren't completely unfamiliar with the concept physical fitness, which is saying something in the land of deep dish pizza and Italian beef. Leagues aren't just limited to stalwarts like basketball and home-grown 16-inch softball; dodgeball and kickball leagues abound, and if you can organize the squad and raise the money necessary to participate, you won't even notice you're working out as you pelt some unsuspecting lame-o in the face with an inflated rubber ball.

General Tips

If you're interested in finding a specific league or group for a particular sport, a good place to start is Chicago Athlete magazine. This free publication is also available online at www.mychicagoathlete.com and is distributed around town.

If you're a beginner, before you go spending a ton of money on your sport of choice, check out what the Chicago Park District (www.chicagoparkdistrict.com) has to offer. They offer loads of clubs, training groups, and classes on a wide range of sports from archery to weightlifting to yoga—all on the cheap. Their handy online program guide lets you search by age group, parks, program type, or zip code. The latter is particularly handy if you don't know where to find your local park district building.

Multiple Sports Leagues and Clubs

Chicago Sport and Social Club (www.chicagosocial.com) is the mother of all of the Windy City leagues. Offering volleyball, basketball, football, floor hockey, soccer, dodge ball, dance, bowling, running, kickball, yoga, softball, rock climbing, kayaking, tennis, boot camp and boxing fitness, and even bar games (such as euchre, darts, and pool), this league has it all. Even if you're not interested in joining, you can watch the league's be-thonged hardbodies spike the ball around every summer at Oak Street Beach or North Avenue Beach or vicariously take in an aerobics class while you burn your hide to a crisp.

The non-profit Chicago Metropolitan Sports Association (chicagomsa.leagueapps.com) is the largest gay and lesbian sports organization in the Midwest, offering badminton, bowling, flag football, soccer, co-ed and women's softball, tennis, and volleyball. Even if you're not interested in playing, it's still fun to watch.

Running

By far, most of the area sports groups and clubs are focused on running. If you're training for a running event—everything from your first 5K to the Chicago Marathon—the Chicago Area Runner's Association (www.cararuns.org) has you covered. This organization is for all levels of runners—from the seasoned marathoner to the amateur looking to begin running for the first time. With group runs, clinics, training programs, and a monthly newsletter, this organization has it all for anyone wanting to feel the gravel beneath their New Balances, the wind in their hair, and the lakefront gnats in their teeth.

Triathlon

When you're ready to, er, "tri" something a little more intense you can set your sights on a triathlon. The city offers tons of opportunities to get involved with this swim-bike-run race. Clubs run the gamut from volunteer-driven organizations to professional training for a fee. Check out Chicago Endurance Sports (www.chicagoendurancesports.com), Chicago Tri Club (www.chicagotriclub.com), Lakeview YMCA Triathlon Club (www.ymcachicago.org/lakeview), or Together We Tri (www.togetherwetri.com). With any of these groups, you can expect to join a group that will tailor your workouts to your needs, find a supportive team environment, attend clinics on transitions and the individual sports, and get a training schedule that you can use on your non-group workout days.

Rugby

If rugby's your game, Chicago has opportunities to join in the fun and violence. Two women's teams dominate the Chicago scene—North Shore Women's Rugby (www.northshorerugby.com) and Chicago Women's Rugby (www.cwrfc.org). For the men, Chicago offers more opportunities: Chicago Griffins Rugby Club (www.chicagogriffins.com), Chicago Lions Rugby Football Club (www.chicagolions.com), Lincoln Park Rugby Football Club (www.lprfc.com), and the South Side Irish (www.southsideirishrugby.com).

General Information

Chicago Park District: www.chicagoparkdistrict.com or @ChicagoParks, 312-742-PLAY (7529)
Active Transportation Alliance: www.activetrans.org or @activetrans, 312-427-3325
Chicago Area Runner's Association: www.cararuns.org or @CARARuns, 312-666-9836

Overview

Greater Chicago offers more than 250 recreational off-road paths that allow bikers, skaters, walkers, and joggers to exercise without worrying about vehicular traffic. In addition to recreational paths in the city's parks, designated off-street trails line the Lakefront, North Shore Channel, North Branch Trail along the Chicago River, Burnham Greenway, and Major Taylor Trail.

Lakefront Trail

Chicago has one of the prettiest and most accessible shorelines of any city in the US—this is the 500-pound gorilla of recreational paths in Chicago. Use one of Lake Shore Drive's over/underpasses (generally available every half mile or so) and you'll discover 15 miles of bathing beaches and over 20 miles of bike paths—just don't anticipate being able to train for the Tour de France during summer weekends, when the sheer number of people makes it impossible to bike along the path at faster than a snail's pace. But thanks to Burnham and Bennett's 1909 "Plan for Chicago," at least we can count on the shoreline remaining non-commercial, with great cycling, jogging, blading, skating, and swimming opportunities for all.

Major Taylor Trail

If you've ever wanted to take in a slice of Chicago's southwestern-most corner (and let's face it, who hasn't?), try the six-mile bike route that begins at Dawes Park at 81st and Hamilton Streets near Western Avenue. The route incorporates an abandoned railroad right-of-way and runs to the southeast through Beverly and Morgan Park, ending up at the Cook County Forest Preserve near 130th and Halsted Streets. The trail was named in honor of cycling legend Marshall "Major" Taylor, one of the first African American cyclists, who lived out the final years of his life in a YMCA in Chicago.

North Branch Trail

To access the northern end of the trail, take Lake Cook Road to the Chicago Botanic Garden, located east of I-94. You can also start from any of the forest preserves as the path winds southward. To access the southern end of the trail in Chicago, take Milwaukee Avenue to Devon Avenue and head a short way east to the Caldwell Woods Preserve. The North Branch winds along the Chicago River and the Skokie Lagoons, but unlike most of the other trails, this one crosses streets, so be careful and look out for cars as you approach.

Still, it represents a great way to get out of the city—and if you make it all the way to the Botanic Garden, admission is free as you won't have to pay for parking!

Burnham Greenway

The 11-mile stretch of the Burnham Greenway, which extends from 104th Street on the city's south side all the way down to Lansing in the south suburbs, has a bit of a checkered past (the former railroad right-of-way was once cited for major pollution), but now the paved route is great for biking, skating, and pedestrians. Expect to find all of northern Illinois' major ecosystems, from wetlands to prairies to a Ford Motor plant in close proximity to one another.

North Shore Channel Trail

This trail follows the North Shore Channel of the Chicago River from Lawrence Avenue through Lincolnwood, Skokie (where you'll find a bizarre sculpture park lining the trail), and Evanston to Green Bay Road at McCormick Boulevard. Not all of the seven miles of the trail are paved bike paths and you'll have to switch back and forth between path and street. Skokie paved the trail segment between Oakton and Howard Streets, but there are still many missing links in the route, much to the chagrin of Friends of the Chicago River (FOCR), who are trying to extend and improve the Channel Trail. The Green Bay Trail branches off to the north from the North Shore Channel Trail and will take you past multi-million dollar houses, cute suburban downtowns, and the Ravinia Festival.

Chicago Park District

Many of the parks under the jurisdiction of the Chicago Park District have paths dedicated to cycling, jogging, walking, rollerblading, and skating. The Chicago Area Runner's Association is so committed to lobbying for runners' rights that it successfully petitioned to have the Lincoln Park running paths plowed and salted through the winter so they could continue their running activities (though prepare to find water fountains that are shut off and bathrooms that are locked). This calls into question the sanity of such masochistic dedication, but we can only assume that the entire year is needed to prepare for the Chicago Marathon, held annually in October.

The 606 Trail

The long-awaited elevated path is slated to open in June 2015 on the tracks of the former Bloomingdale Line. The corridor adds nearly three miles of safe, recreational green space to Wicker Park, Bucktown, Logan Square and Humboldt Park. As construction progresses and gentrification spreads west, real estate developers are already tripping over themselves to build, gut or reno every property within view of the trail.

General Information

NFT Map: 11
Address: 1410 Special Olympics Dr,
Chicago, IL 60605
Phone: 312-235-7000
Lost & Found: 312-235-7202
Website: www.soldierfield.net
Box Office: 847-615-BEAR (2327)
Bears Website: www.chicagobears.com
Ticketmaster: 312-559-1212;
www.ticketmaster.com

Overview

The gleaming hunk of stadium with the mismatched Doric columns out front is the second iteration of Soldier Field, which first opened October 9, 1924—the 53rd anniversary of the Chicago Fire. Planned just after World War I, the facility was originally known as Municipal Grant Park Stadium before being rechristened in 1925 as Soldier Field. Although it is probably best known as the home of Da Bears, the football team did not even start using Solider Field until 1971. Indeed, the stadium has seen its share of events, from college football to NASCAR to a Martin Luther King, Jr. rally to stadium shows by The Rolling Stones, U2, Madonna, Bruce Springsteen, and Bon Jovi.

In 1985 Soldier Field was listed on the National Register of Historic Places, a sentimental pick. Soon enough, however, with the stadium needing major repair and lacking the requisite pro football amenities like ginormoscreens and luxury boxes, officials began the delicate task of figuring out exactly how to update the landmark. The solution was to basically gut the inside and preserve some of the stadium's distinctive column facade. In 2006 Soldier Field was delisted from the National Register of Historic Places.

Originally constructed for $13 million, the 2003 renovation of Soldier Field cost $632 million. Although the Bears lost to the Green Bay Packers in their first game at the renovated stadium, the finished product was lauded for its forward-looking design. Also, there was more sideline seating, concession stands, and bathrooms—the last of which you can never have too many. And of course the ginormoscreens: two 82-foot-by-23-foot behemoths, which, at 1,886 square feet, offer more space than many American homes.

Public tours are available Mon–Fri 9 am–5 pm. Tours include access to the field, south courtyard, Doughboy statue, grand concourse, colonnades, Skyline Suite and visitors' locker room. Tours cost $15 for adults and $10 for students 10 and over.

How to Get Tickets

Single-game tickets are available in July via Ticketmaster. Set your alarm. Season tickets are nearly impossible to come by, unless you're related somehow to Bill Swerski, in which case see if 'ol Uncle Bill will chip in for your Personal Seat License, whose prices seem to rival a freaking taxi medallion.

The best way to get great seats (other than by having them left to you in a will) is to use the various online ticket exchanges, either the officially sanctioned Ticketmaster Ticket Exchange resale site or an entity like StubHub.

How to Get There

By Car: From the north or south, take Lake Shore Drive; follow the signs to Soldier Field. For parking lots, exit at E McFetridge, E Waldron, E 14th Boulevard, and E 18th Drive. From the west, take I-55 E to Lake Shore Drive, turn north, and follow the signs. Travel east on I-290, then south on I-90/94 to I-55; get on I-55 E to Lake Shore Drive. On non-game days, expect to pay around $22 for the parking lots surrounding Soldier Field, less for Adler Lot, and you can reserve a spot online before you arrive. Rates rise significantly on game days; suffice it to say, you don't even want to know. Visit www.soldierfieldparking.com for detailed information or call the Soldier Field Parking Hotline at 312-235-7701. Two parking and game-day tailgating lots are located south of Waldron Drive. There are also lots on the Museum Campus off McFetridge Drive and near McCormick Place off 31st Street and E 18th Street.

By Train: On game days, CTA Soldier Field Express bus 128 runs non-stop between the Ogilvie Transportation Center and Union Station to Soldier Field. Service starts two hours before the game, runs up to 30 minutes after kickoff, and up to one hour post-game.

By L: Take the Red, Orange, or Green Lines to the Roosevelt station stop. Board eastbound CTA bus 146 to the Museum Campus, and then walk south to Soldier Field. Walking from Roosevelt station would take approximately 15 minutes… an alternative to waiting for the bus.

By Bus: CTA bus 146 stops on McFetridge Drive near Soldier Field. Buses 3, 4, 12, and 18 stop somewhat near the stadium.

General Information

NFT Map: 13
Address: 333 W 35th St
Chicago, IL 60616
General Info: 312-674-1000
Ticket Sales: 866-SOX-GAME
Website: https://www.mlb.com/
whitesox/ballpark

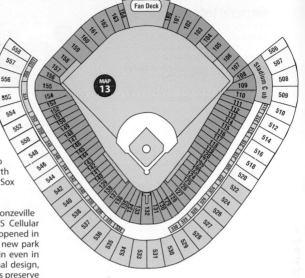

Overview

Both of Chicago's major league ballparks are named for corporations (one famous for gum, the other famous for mortgages) but the similarities end there. Any White Sox fan will tell you: tourists pay big bucks to watch ivy grow in the little place on the North Side, real baseball fans head to see the White Sox play at Guaranteed Rate Field.

Straddling the Bridgeport and Bronzeville neighborhoods on Chicago's south side, US Cellular Field, now known as Guaranteed Rate Field, opened in 1991 to replace the old Comiskey Park. The new park was built for $167 million—a relative bargain even in 1991. Cost-cutting meant altering the original design, though, and not for the better (though it does preserve a replica of Bill Veeck's signature exploding firework scoreboard from the old yard). What the park lacks in beauty, it makes up for with its friendly staff, terrific sightlines (although the park itself faces the wrong way, wedged uncomfortably between 35th Street and an elementary school) and fabulous food—perennially rated among the best in Major League Baseball. Meat-eaters: follow your nose to the grilled onions and say "Polish with." Better yet, say "Polish witt"—you'll get a sublimely good Polish sausage smothered in caramelized onions. And for the vegetarian, as long as you keep your voice down, you can snag a very tasty veggie dog at several of the Sox's many concession stands. Indeed, look around and you'll notice that most Sox fans do enjoy their food at the ballpark. And if you're hoping to hear about fashion, or business deals, or coffee shops, this ain't the place. Fans here talk about baseball. They love the game, and they love the team that finally brought a World Series trophy to Chicago back in 2005.

How to Get Tickets

Purchase tickets through the team's website (www.whitesox.com) or at the Guaranteed Rate Field Box Office (weekdays: 10 am 6 pm, weekends: 10 am–4 pm). Children shorter than the park's turnstile arm (approximately 36 inches) are admitted free, but must share your seat. Attendance is generally abysmal, so take advantage of desperate specials such as Half-Price Monday tickets, available on select Monday home games (except for big ticket matchups, e.g., Yankees, Cubs). Check the website for Value Days schedules. Pet check is located between Gates 2 and 3, for a $3 fee.

How to Get There

By Car: Guaranteed Rate Field is located at the 35th Street exit off the Dan Ryan Expressway. Take I-90/94, stay in the local lanes, and exit at 35th Street. If you're parking, exit at 35th Street. Follow signs to "Sox Parking" at lots E, F, and L on the stadium's south side. Fans with red, prepaid season parking coupons exit at 31st Street, and follow signs for "Red Coupons" to lots A, B, and C just north of the stadium. If the 35th Street exit is closed due to heavy traffic, which is often the case on game days, proceed to the 39th Street exit; turn right for "Sox Parking" and left for "Red Coupons." The handicapped parking and stadium drop-off area is in Lot D, west of the field and accessible via 37th Street. If you're planning to tailgate, the lots open two hours before the game and close 30 minutes after everything is said and done.

By Bus: CTA buses 24 and 35 stop closest to the park. Others stopping in the vicinity are the 29, 44, and 39.

By L: Ride the Red Line to the 35th Street-Sox stop just west of the ballpark. Another good option, especially heading north after the game, is the Green Line. The 35th-Bronzeville-IIT (Illinois Institute of Technology) Station is a little longer walk that the 35th Street-Sox stop, but always less crowded.

Sports • United Center

General Information

NFT Map: 23
Address: 1901 W Madison St
Chicago, IL 60612
Phone: 312-455-4500
Website: www.unitedcenter.com
Ticketmaster: 312-559-1212;
www.ticketmaster.com
Chicago Bulls: 312-455-4000
Bulls Website: www.bulls.com
Chicago Blackhawks:
312-455-7000
Blackhawks Website:
www.chicagoblackhawks.com

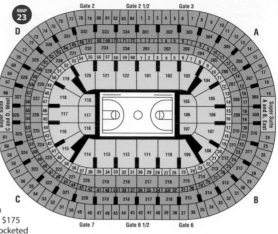

Overview

The commanding crown of Chicago's West Town District, the United Center is home to both the NHL's Blackhawks and the NBA's Bulls. The stadium, which seats about 20,000 for both hockey and basketball, is also a theater, convention hall, and concert venue. Opened in 1994, the $175 million stadium was privately funded by deep-pocketed Blackhawks owner William Wirtz and penny-pinching Bulls majority owner Jerry Reinsdorf (a privately funded and owned stadium—what a concept!) and built to replace the beloved but aging Chicago Stadium. The new arena borrows from the old Madhouse on Madison, which stood across the street until 1995: the old building's exterior and even its acoustics are alluded to and echoed in the new facility. As an experience, the level of theatrics and delicious way-above-average food, make a night at the United Center unlike anything else in the city. And just in case you forget whose "house" this is, the impressive statue of Michael Jordan posterizing an anonymous bronze mass located in front of the main entrance to the United Center is there to remind you (although Blackhawk legends Stan Mikita and Bobby Hull also are honored with statues along Madison, and Jordan wingman Scottie Pippen and coach/broadcaster Johnny "Red" Kerr have bronzes inside the building). When the United Center isn't reveling in all those rings and hoisted cups, it serves as the city's go-to venue for arena rock acts like Springsteen, The Rolling Stones, and U2. In 1996 it hosted the Democratic National Convention.

How to Get Tickets

Book tickets over the phone or online with Ticketmaster, or visit the United Center box office at Gate 4. On non-game days, box office hours are generally Monday to Saturday, 11 am to 6 pm (Sat until 4 pm). On game days, the box office is open until the first intermission or halftime.

How to Get There

By Car: From the Loop, drive west on Madison Street to United Center. From the north, take I-90/94 and exit at Madison Street; head west to the stadium. From the southwest, take I-55 N to the Damen/Ashland exit; head north to Madison Street. From the west, take I-290 E to the Damen Avenue exit; go north to Madison Street.

Parking lots surround United Center, as do countless cops. General public parking in Lots A, E, J, D and F is $24–$40. Lot H on Wood Street is closest to the stadium and is reserved for VIPs. Disabled parking is in Lots G on Damen Avenue.

By L: Take Orange, Green, Purple, or Brown lines to Madison and switch to westbound 20 bus. Or, take the Forest Park Branch of the Blue line to the Medical Center-Damen Avenue Station. Walk two blocks north to United Center.

By Bus: CTA bus 19 United Center Express is the most efficient choice. In service only on event and game days, this express bus travels from Randolph Street south down Michigan Avenue, then west along Madison Street to the United Center. No stops are made between Halsted and the United Center. Service begins 90 minutes before events and continues for one hour after events end. CTA bus 20 also travels Madison Street beginning at Wabash Avenue and has "owl service."

General Information

NFT Map: 43
Address: 1060 W Addison St
Chicago, IL 60613
Cubs Box Office Phone: 773-404-2827
Tickets.com: 800-THE-CUBS (843-2827)
Lost & Found: 773-404-4185
Website: www.cubs.com

Overview

Built in 1914 and originally known as Weeghman Park, the stadium was renamed Wrigley Field in 1926 to honor chewing gum mogul and former Cub owner William Wrigley, Jr. It is the second-oldest ballpark in Major League Baseball (a few years behind Boston's Fenway Park) and is (along with Fenway, in certain years, at least) sometimes more interesting for its rich history than for what's taking place on the field. With its signature ivy-covered walls, manual scoreboard, and view-obstructing columns, Wrigley harks back to a bygone era of baseball stadia—night games weren't even possible at Wrigley until 1988 when lights were finally installed. That said, a multi-hundreds-of-millions-dollar multi-year renovation project will add seating, hoodely-doo amenities, and an adjacent multi-use development. The most un-Wrigley update debuted for the 2015 season: a massive 3,900-square-foot videoboard in the outfield. And while the good news is that the changes will be privately financed, the trade-off will be more on-field advertising to help pay for it.

Quirks abound at Wrigley. Strange lake-effect wind patterns wreak havoc on batters, especially in the early months of the season. Invading seagulls sometimes make the infield look like a cross between an aviary and Hitchcock's *The Birds*. And about those nearby buildings with the seats on them—until the 1990s, it was a time-honored tradition for the club to share sightlines. Then building owners got a little greedy, erecting bleacher seats and actually charging people to sit up there. The Cubs retaliated, even going as far as trying to block the view, until all parties agreed to share a portion of the profits with the team.

Wrigley has hosted its share of historic moments: Ernie Banks' 500th career home run in 1970, Kerry Wood's twenty strikeouts in 1998, and Sammy Sosa's sixty home runs in 1998, 1999, and 2001. A day at Wrigley is like no other experience in the world, and a must-see for any self-respecting Chicagoan/baseball fan, and there is nothing—nothing!—like singing "Take Me Out to The Ballpark" during the seventh inning stretch inside the friendly confines. Because no matter the score, we will "root, root, root for the Cubbies."

How to Get Tickets

Individual game tickets can be purchased from the Cubs' website, by calling 800-843-2827, or in person at Wrigley Field outside of Gate F at the corner of Clark and Addison Streets; open weekdays from 8 am to 6 pm and weekends from 9 am to 4 pm. You can usually score discount tickets to afternoon games Monday through Thursday in April, May, and September, or by waiting around the ballpark until the game starts. Especially when they are in the typical six-game losing skid. Children aged three and up require tickets.

How to Get There

By Car: If you must. Remember the old days when Wrigleyville hillbillies used to let you park on their front lawns for five bucks? Well, today traffic on game days is horrendous, and parking prices are sky-high. Post-game spill-out from local bars and dozens of mindless cab drivers freeze traffic as police do their best to prevent drunken revelers from stumbling into the streets. From the Loop or south, take Lake Shore Drive north; exit at Irving Park Road, and head west to Clark Street; turn south on Clark Street to Wrigley Field. From the north, take Lake Shore Drive to Irving Park Road; head west to Clark Street, and turn south. From Chicago's West Side, take I-290 E or I-55 N to Lake Shore Drive, then follow directions above. From the northwest, take I-90 E and exit at Addison Street; travel east three miles. From the southwest side, take I-55 N to I-90/94 N. Exit at Addison Street; head east to the park.

Street parking around Wrigley Field is heavily restricted, nearly impossible and insanely expensive. The Cubs operate several garages around the area, and advance reservations are available up to 24 hours in advance by calling 800-843-2827. On game nights, tow trucks cruise Wrigleyville's streets nabbing cars without a resident permit sticker. On night and weekend games, park smart at the team's free remote lot, which has 1,000 spaces and a free shuttle to Wrigley.

By L: Take the Red line direct to Wrigley Field, get off at the Addison Street stop one block east.

By Bus: CTA buses 22, 8, and 152 stop closest to Wrigley Field.

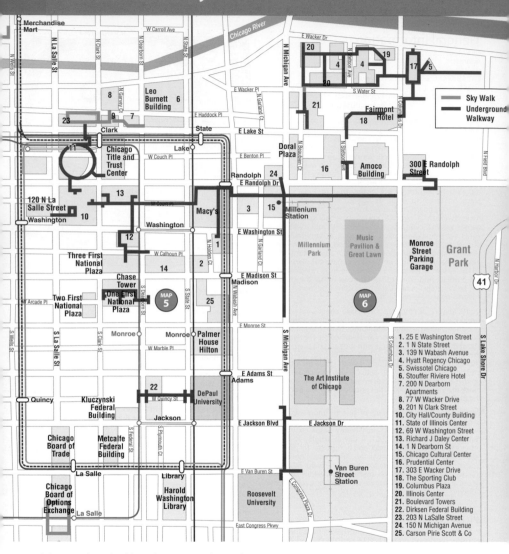

While a number of cold-weather cities are known for their above-ground walkways, Chicago is known for its Pedway, a 40-block network of tunnels and overhead bridges that connects important public, government, and private sector buildings with retail stores, major hotels, rapid transit stations, and commuter rail stations. A subterranean city with shops, restaurants, services, and public artworks, the Pedway is a welcome alternative to navigating trafficked intersections on foot and walking outdoors in Chicago's frigid winters. The underground walkway system is open 24 hours; however, access to a number of the buildings is limited after standard business hours. The first Pedway links were built in 1951 to connect the State Street and Dearborn Street subways at Washington Street and Jackson Boulevard. Today, Chicago's Pedway continues to grow as city government and the private sector cooperate to expand it. Those planning on making a subterranean trip to experience the Pedway in its glory would do well to click on over to www.spiegl.org/pedway/pedway.html for a map of the whole lair.

General Information

Address:	10000 W O'Hare
	Chicago, IL 60666
Phone:	773-686-2200 / 800-832-6352
Website:	www.ohare.com
Ground Transportation:	773-686-8040
Lost & Found:	773-894-8760
Parking:	773-686-7530
Traveler's Aid:	773-894-2477
Police:	773-686-2385
Customs Information:	773-894-2900

Overview

Named for Butch O'Hare, the superstar US Navy fighter pilot who earned a Medal of Honor during World War II, O'Hare International Airport is one of the busiest airports in the world, handling more than 66 million passengers each year. For many around the country, O'Hare serves as the source of B-roll for news reports about crazy-making weather-related travel delays, often during the holidays, and for good reason: of the top metropolitan statistical areas in the US, Chicago is probably the one with the worst winter weather. So there's that. But don't let worries of delays and frozen runways keep you grounded.

The airport, located just 17 miles northwest of the Loop, is so close to town that it's actually within Chicago city borders. That said, allow plenty of time to get to the airport, but don't stress too hard about security lines unless you're going to Europe. Or if it's Christmas. Or if you're going to Europe on Christmas. Or if you're taking a puddle jumper to Dubuque. Keep in mind if you're taking a red-eye flight that most eateries and shops are closed at night and early morning, so bring snacks and a novel. A good one.

Expansion spells relief, and the O'Hare modernization and expansion plan begun under former Mayor Daley is currently entering its final phases under Mayor Rahm Emanuel, having already opened an additional runway while reconfiguring the existing seven runways. Along with other improvements, when the program is complete, O'Hare's capacity should be doubled, helping the airport keep busy well into the 21st century.

Psst. We'll tell you a secret that will make picking up guests at the airport a lot more pleasant. Sign up online for the airline to notify you of flight information and changes via your cellphone, then park your car, and head to the Hilton bar (located in the airport) to wait out the arrival. Better yet, avoid the stress of driving by taking the train in, then waiting at the Hilton bar for Aunt Sally, and load her and yourself into a cab. You probably shouldn't be driving at this point, anyway.

How to Get There

By Car: Strongly consider taking public transit to O'Hare, peek a few inches forward for information on the L. But if you absolutely must drive, pay close attention here. To be on the safe side, allow over an hour just for the drive (more during rush hours). From the Loop to O'Hare, take I-90 W. From the north suburbs, take I-294 S. From the south suburbs, take I-294 N. From the west suburbs, take I-88 E to I-294 N. Get off all of the above highways at I-190, which leads you directly to the airport. All of the major routes have clear signage, easily legible when you're moving at a snail's pace.

Parking: O'Hare Airport's parking garage reflects its hometown's passion for sports. All levels of the Main Parking Garage are "helpfully" labeled with Chicago sports teams' colors and larger-than-life logos (Wolves, Bulls, Blackhawks, White Sox, Bears, and Cubs). Annoying elevator muzak whines each team's fight song. If this isn't enough to guide you to your car, we can't help you, because the garage's numbering-alphabetical system is more aggravating than the tinny elevator tunes. If you're parking for less than three hours, go to Level 1. Parking costs $5 for the first 3 hours, and $10 for up to 4 hours.

Overnight parking close to Terminals 1, 2, and 3 on Levels 2 through 6 of the garage or in outside lots B and C costs $35 a day ($34 on weekends). For flyers with cash to burn, valet parking is available on Level 1 of the garage for $10 for the first hour, or $53 per day (8-24 hours). Parking in the International Terminal 5's designated Lot D costs $2 for the first hour, jumping to $10 for four hours and rising steadily from there to a daily rate of $60 (13-24 hours; $59 on weekends). Incoming international passengers always disembark in Terminal 5 (even if the airline departs from another terminal) because passengers must clear customs.

The long-term parking lots are Economy Lots E ($17) and F ($9). From Lot E, accessible via free shuttles to the free Airport Transit System (ATS) train station serving all terminals.

By Bus: Pace Suburban bus routes 250 (with connections to CTA Yellow and Purple Lines) and 330 (connecting with Amtrak/Metra BNSF Line La Grange Road Station) both stop at the airport.

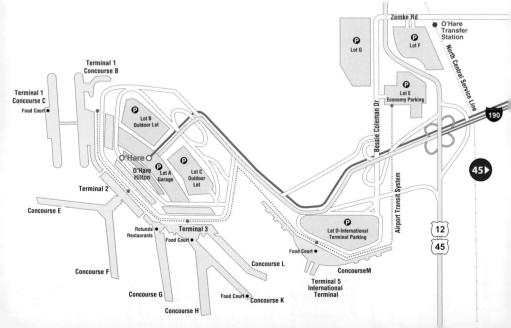

By Train: As a train with an inbound/outbound rush hour-focus, the odds of the Metra North Central Line schedule conveniently coinciding with your flight time are slim, but it could be worth it if you plan in advance. The North Central Line departs Union Station for Antioch, with a stop at the O'Hare Transfer station several times a day (weekdays only). Fare from Union Station is $4.75 one-way. Travel time is approximately 30 minutes.

By L: The CTA Blue Line train is the easiest and most efficient way to get to O'Hare. Trains run frequently between downtown Chicago and O'Hare 24 hours a day. Travel time from the Loop is 45 minutes. The station is located on the lower level of Terminal 2. From there use the Airport Transit System to reach other terminals. The full fare from O'Hare is $5 (back outbound you'll pay the standard single-ride rate).

By Cab: Join the cab queue at the lower level curb-front of all terminals. There are no flat rates, as all of the cabs run on meters, but you probably won't have to spend more than $40. Beware if you're traveling to certain suburbs, though: fare rules allow cabbies to raise your fare for these routes; ask what the fare will be when you enter the cab. Shared ride service is available to downtown ($24 per person), McCormick Place ($24 per person), and Midway International Airport ($37 per person). Cab companies serving O'Hare include American United, 773-327-6161; Flash Cab, 773-561-1444; Yellow Cab, 773-907-0020; and Sun Taxi, 773-736-3883.

By Kiss & Fly: The Kiss & Fly is a convenient drop-off and pick-up point for "chauffeurs" who want to avoid the inevitable chaos at the terminal curb-side. Flyers should leave enough time for the ATS transfer to their terminals. The Kiss & Fly zone is off Bessie Coleman Drive. Take I-190 to the International Terminal exit to Bessie Coleman Drive. Turn left at the light and follow Bessie Coleman Drive north to the Kiss & Fly entrance and ATS stop.

By Shuttle: Go Airport Express (888-284-3826 or www. airportexpress.com) provides shared-ride, door-to-door shuttle service between O'Hare and downtown hotels/attractions daily from 4 am until 11:30 pm. Shuttles depart every 10 to 15 minutes from Terminals 1E, 3F, 2D, and 5E. Expect to pay about $30. No reservations necessary (reservations required for other destinations).

Tri State/United Limo (800-248-8747, www.coachusa.com/ tristateunitedlimo) offers hourly service between O'Hare and Midway from early morning to evening. The shuttle leaves from the International Terminal's outside curb by Door 5E and from the airport's Bus Shuttle Center in front of the O'Hare Hilton Hotel by Door 4. Allow at least an hour for travel time between the airports and expect to pay $24 for a one-way fare. Tri State/United Limo also serves nearby communities on the South Side and Northwest Indiana, including Notre Dame.

By Limousine: Sounds pricey, but depending on where you're going and how many people you are traveling with, it may be cheaper to travel by limo than by cab or shuttle. Advance reservations recommended.

Airlines

Airline/Terminal
Aer Lingus 5
Aero Mexico 5
Air Berlin 3 (dep), 5 (arr)
Air Canada 2
Air Canada Jazz 2
Air Choice One 3
Air France 5
Air India 5
Alaska Airlines 3
Alitalia 5
All Nippon 1,5
American Airlines 3 (dep), 5 (int'l arr)
Asiana Airlines 5
Austrian Airlines 5
Avianca Airlines 5
British Airways 5
Cathay Pacific Airways 5
Cayman Airways 5
Copa Airlines 5
Delta and Delta Shuttle 2
Etihad Airways 5
Frontier Airlines 3 (dep), 5 (int'l arr)
Hainan Airlines 5
Iberia Airlines 3 (dep), 5 (arr)
Japan Airlines (JAL) 3 (dep), 5 (arr)
JetBlue 3
KLM Royal Dutch Airlines 5
Korean Air 5
LOT Polish Airlines 5
Lufthansa 1 (dep), 5 (arr)
Qatar Airways 5
Royal Jordanian 5
Scandinavian Airlines (SAS) 5
Spirit Airlines 3
SWISS 5
Turkish Airlines 5
United & United Express 1 & 2 (dep), 5 (int'l arr)
US Airways 3
USA 3000 5
Virgin America 3
Virgin Atlantic 5
Volaris Airlines 5
Westjet Airlines 3

Car Rental

Advantage: 2170 Mannheim Rd, 847-635-8031
Alamo: 560 Bessie Coleman Dr, 888-826-6893
Avis: 10000 Bessie Coleman Dr, 888-849-0277
Budget: 10000 Bessie Coleman Dr, 800-621-2380
Dollar: 10000 Bessie Coleman Dr, 866-434-2226
Easy Parking: 4000 N Mannheim Rd, 877-822-3872/800-323-3221
Enterprise: 6400 N Schilling Rd, 847-928-3320
Hertz: 10000 Bessie Coleman Dr, 773-686-7272
National: 560 Bessie Coleman Dr, 888-826-6890/773-694-4640
Payless: 4000 N Mannheim Rd, 224-220-0604
Thrifty: 3901 N Mannheim Rd, 877-283-0898

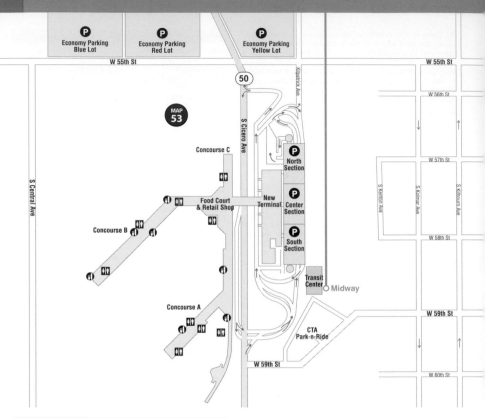

General Information

Address:	5700 S Cicero Ave
	Chicago, IL 60638
Phone:	773-838-0600
Website:	www.midwayairport.org
Police:	773-838-3003
Parking:	773-838-0756
Customs:	773-948-6330

Overview

Named to commemorate the Battle of Midway during World War II, Midway International Airport is located just ten miles southwest of downtown Chicago. Once the world's busiest airport, by the 1960s, Midway eventually lost that title to upstart O'Hare. That said, Midway still ranks as one of the 30 busiest airports in the US, serving 20 million passengers per year. Now considered the city's outlet mall of airports, Midway primarily serves budget carriers like Southwest Airlines. On the positive side, it is an easy alternative to the bigger, badder O'Hare. Plus the bars for pre-flight entertainment aren't as crowded.

The "International" in Midway International Airport returned in 2002 after a 40-year absence, the result of a $739 million terminal development project that added a new terminal building, concourses, parking, and customs facility. The rental car building on 55th Street opened in 2013, and consolidates rental agencies in one spot.

Superstitious travelers beware of flying December 8th. On this date in 1972, a Boeing 737 crashed into a residential area during landing. In 2005, exactly 33 years later another Boeing slid off the runway in a landing attempt on December 8. Spooky.

How to Get There

By Car: From downtown, take I-55 S. From the northern suburbs, take I-290 S to I-55 N. From the southern suburbs, take I-294 N to I-55 N. From the western suburbs, take I-88 E to I-294 S to I-55 N. Whether you're traveling north or south along I-55, look for the Cicero Avenue/South/Midway Airport exit.

By Bus: CTA buses 47, 54B, 55, 55A, 55N, 62N, 62H, 63, and 63W all serve the airport. Take the Green Line or the Red Line to the Garfield Station and transfer to bus 55 heading west. If you're coming from the south on the Red Line, get off at the 63rd Street stop and take bus 63 westbound. In addition, Pace suburban routes 379, 382, 383, 384, 385, 386, and 390 travel to the airport.

By L: The most convenient and cost-effective method of travel between Midway Airport and the Loop is a 20–30 minute train ride on the CTA Orange Line. Midway is the terminus of the Orange Line, which circles around the Loop and heads back to the airport. Trains run between 4–4:30 am and approximately 1 am. Trains run frequently during rush hours (approximately every five minutes), less so in the middle of the day, and every 10–15 minutes in the evening and late evening hours. The Orange Line conveniently drops you off inside Midway Airport (a huge plus in winter time!)--allow about 15 minutes to cart yourself and all your belongings to the security checkpoint.

By Cab: Cabs depart from the lower levels of the terminals and are available on a first-come-first-served basis. There are no flat rates (all cabs run on meters), but you can plan on paying around $30 to get to the Loop. Shared ride service is available to downtown ($18 per person), McCormick Place ($18 per person), and O'Hare International Airport ($35 per person). Cab companies serving Midway include American United, 773-327-6161; Flash Cab, 773-561-1444; Yellow Cab, 773-907-0020; and Sun Taxi, 773-736-3883.

By Shuttle: Go Airport Express (888-284-3826 or www.airportexpress.com) provides shared ride, door-to-door shuttle service between Midway and downtown hotels/attractions daily from 6 am until 11:30 pm. Shuttles depart approximately every 15 minutes outside the Lower Level Arrivals door #3. Expect to pay about $27 to get to the city.

Tri State/United Limo (800-248-8747, www.coachusa.com/tristateunitedlimo) offers hourly service between O'Hare and Midway from early morning to evening. The shuttle leaves from the Lower Level Arrivals door #3. Allow at least an hour for travel time between the airports and expect to pay $24 for a one-way fare. Tri State/United Limo also serves nearby communities on the South Side and Northwest Indiana, including Notre Dame.

By Limousine: Sounds pricey, but depending on where you're going and how many people you are traveling with, it may be cheaper to travel by limo than by cab or shuttle. Advance reservations recommended.

Parking

Short-term, hourly parking is located on Level 1 of the parking garage, with convenient access to the Terminal building. Parking is free for the first 10 minutes, then $2 for 10-30 minutes, and $5 for 30 minutes to 1 hour. The rates increase incrementally with each additional hour, up to $60 for 24 hours ($59 weekends). Daily parking is available on levels 2, 4, 5, and 6; rates are the same as short-term parking up to 4 hours, after which the fee levels off to $32 per day ($31 weekends). Long-term/economy lots and a garage are $15 a day--just be sure to allow extra time to get to the terminal. 24-hour complimentary shuttle service is available seven days a week between terminal and the economy lots, which are just east of Cicero Avenue and a quarter mile west of Cicero on 55th Street, and the economy garage at 55th and Laramie.

Airlines

Concourse A
Air Tran
Delta
Porter Airlines
Southwest Airlines
Volaris Airlines

Concourse B
Southwest Airlines

Concourse C
Frontier
Public Charters
Sun Country Airlines

Car Rental

Alamo: 800-327-9633
Avis: 800-331-1212
Budget: 800-527-7000
Dollar: 800-800-4000
Enterprise: 800-566-9249
Hertz: 800-654-3131
National: 800-227-7368
Thrifty: 800-527-7075

Chicago Water Taxi

Spring through fall, commuters can enjoy a convenient and scenic way of getting about via Wendella's Chicago Water Taxi (312-337-1446, www.chicagowatertaxi.com or @chgowatertaxi), which links Ogilvie Transportation Center to North Michigan Avenue and Chinatown. Chicago Water Taxis operate seven days a week and tickets may be purchased on board the boat, at the Wendella ticket office at 400 N Michigan Ave, at Trump Plaza, or at the Madison Street and Michigan Avenue dockside kiosks. Fares start at $3 one-way, with options for one-day and multiple ride passes available.

Shoreline Water Taxi

From Union Station, commuters can hop aboard a Shoreline Water Taxi (312-222-9328, www.shorelinesightseeing.com/water-taxi or @ShorelineSights), which makes stops at North Michigan Avenue, Navy Pier, and the Museum Campus, and offers a weekday rush hour commuter service between between Erie Street Dock at Erie and Larrabee Streets and Union Station. Fares are $2 one-way or $15 for a ten-ride pass. Tickets may be purchased from dockside kiosks.

General Information

Mailing address:
Chicago Transit Authority
567 W Lake St.
Chicago, IL 60661
Phone: 312-664-7200
CTA information: 888-YOUR CTA (968-7282)
Website: www.transitchicago.com

Overview

We may never find a system of public transit free from flaws, but if you need a quick, socially responsible way to get from A to Wrigley, CTA's your guy. Once you figure out its complicated card system, CTA service will get you relatively close to where you need to go (most of the time), and sometimes the city's trains and buses are even on schedule! For location-to-location CTA directions and schedules, we honestly and without irony, recommend the useful CTA trip planner at tripsweb.rtachicago.com. It is useful in that it includes Pace suburban buses.

Fares and Ventra

While buses accept cash and coin, you must use a Ventra card to ride the L. Fare on the L is $2.25. Bus fare is $2 with Ventra card and $2.25 with cash (no transfers with cash fare). On both bus and L, transfers cost 25 cents, up to two additional rides within two hours.

The Ventra Card is a payment system that allows customers to use a single fare card for regional transit through the Chicago area. This means it can be used on CTA and Pace.

There are three ways to use the Ventra system:

Ventra Card: Any amount of money can be loaded on to a Ventra Card with cash or online

Ventra Ticket: A disposable, paper card, the Ventra Ticket is for single ride use and day pass unlimited-ride tickets.

Personal bank issued credit cards: Link your personal credit or debit card with RFID chip technology (look for the four nesting parentheses, the universal symbol for information transmitted wirelessly through the ether) to your Ventra account and you add value or purchase passes so you can use your own card as a fare card.

Ventra Cards will have a one-time cost fee of $5 that is refunded as transit value. Disposable, single ride Ventra tickets cost $3, which includes the $2.25 fare, a $.25 transfer and a $.50 limited use ticket fee (since you pay for a transfer whether you take one or not, and you're getting penalized for a single ticket with that $.50, the rational choice is to just get the $5 Ventra Card). You can also use the Ventra Card as a prepaid debit card; just keep in mind the requisite fees associated with most prepaid debit cards.

Ventra Cards are available at Ventra Vending Machines, located at all L stations and at CTA headquarters at 567 West Lake Street. Vending machines are also located at Chicago Union Station, Ogilvie Transportation Center, Millennium Station, Navy Pier, and the Museum of Science & Industry. In addition, retailers across the city both sell and add value to Ventra Cards; check www.ventrachicago.com for a full list of retailers.

Unlimited passes often offer the best value:

• 1-Day CTA Pass for $10
• 3-Day CTA Pass for $20
• 7-Day CTA Pass for $28
• 7-Day CTA/Pace Pass for $33
• 30-Day CTA/Pace Pass for $100

One-day passes are available as a disposable one-time-only Ventra Card, but other passes require a Ventra Card, though the $5 fee can be applied to the pass cost, depending on how and when you sign up for an account.

Reduced Fares: Reduced fares are available for qualified passengers--people with disabilities, senior citizens, students (during school days/hours only) and children aged 7 through 11 (children under 7 ride free).

CTA Buses

CTA's buses cart about one million sweaty, crabby passengers around Chicago and its surrounding suburbs everyday; the fleet is the second-largest public transportation system in the US. CTA's 120-plus bus routes mirror Chicago's efficient grid system. The majority of CTA routes run north-south or east-west, and in areas where the streets are numbered, the bus route is usually the same as the street.

The entire CTA bus fleet meets ADA accessibility standards. All buses kneel (or tilt to make the first step less steep). All buses are equipped with wheelchair lifts and secure wheelchair seating. Additionally, as a boon to the visually impaired and those too busy gawking at Chicago's skyscrapers to read the signs on the front of each bus, all buses clearly and loudly announce the bus number and direction at every stop.

Bus Tracker is a helpful online resource helping riders determine "exactly" when a bus will arrive. Accessible via www.ctabustracker.com or via text message, the Bus Tracker gives a damn good estimate of arrival times, cutting down wait times by a significant margin. You'll be grateful in December. And January. And February. And March…

Bus Stops: CTA stops are clearly marked with blue and white signs displaying the name and number of the route, as well as the final destination. Most routes operate from the early morning until 10:30 pm. Night routes, called "Night Owls," are identified on bus stop signage by an owl picture. Owl service runs approximately every half-hour through the night. All bus stop signs are labeled with a "Stop ID number" that you can use to get arrival times by text message. Simply text ctabus [stopID] to 41411 on your cell phone and the bus tracker will text you back with estimated arrival times for all buses at that stop.

Bicycles Onboard: All CTA buses are equipped with bike racks mounted on front grills to carry up to two bikes. The CTA website features tutorial videos that explain how to load a bicycle with the two different systems buses use. Locking your bike to the rack is not allowed, but you are encouraged to sit near the front and keep an eye on your ride.

Transit • The L

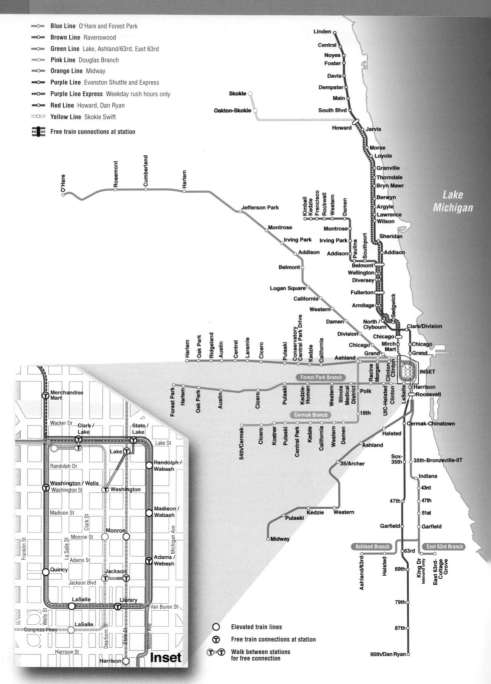

- **Blue Line** O'Hare and Forest Park
- **Brown Line** Ravenswood
- **Green Line** Lake, Ashland/63rd, East 63rd
- **Pink Line** Douglas Branch
- **Orange Line** Midway
- **Purple Line** Evanston Shuttle and Express
- **Purple Line Express** Weekday rush hours only
- **Red Line** Howard, Dan Ryan
- **Yellow Line** Skokie Swift
- **Free train connections at station**

Lake Michigan

Linden
Central
Noyes
Foster
Davis
Dempster
Main
South Blvd
Howard
Jarvis
Morse
Loyola
Granville
Thorndale
Bryn Mawr
Berwyn
Argyle
Lawrence
Wilson
Sheridan
Addison
Belmont
Wellington
Diversey
Fullerton
Armitage
North / Clybourn
Clark/Division

Skokie
Oakton-Skokie

O'Hare
Rosemont
Cumberland
Harlem

Jefferson Park
Montrose
Irving Park
Addison
Belmont
Logan Square
California
Western

Kimball
Kedzie
Francisco
Rockwell
Western
Damen
Montrose
Irving Park
Addison
Paulina
Southport

Damen
Division
Chicago
Chicago
Grand

Mirch Mart
Chicago
Grand
INSET

Sedgwick
Clark/Division

Harlem
Oak Park
Ridgeland
Austin
Central
Laramie
Cicero
Pulaski
Conservatory Central Park Drive
Kedzie
California
Ashland

Racine
Morgan
Clinton
Clinton
UIC-Halsted
LaSalle

Harrison
Roosevelt

Forest Park Branch

Forest Park
Harlem
Oak Park
Austin
Cicero
Pulaski
Kedzie-Homan
Western
Illinois Medical District
Polk
18th

Cermak Branch

Cermak-Chinatown

54th/Cermak
Cicero
Kostner
Pulaski
Central Park
Kedzie
California
Damen
Western
Ashland
Halsted

Sox-35th
35th-Bronzeville-IIT
Indiana
43rd
47th
51st
Garfield
63rd
69th
79th
87th
95th/Dan Ryan

35/Archer
47th

Kedzie   Western
Pulaski
Midway

Garfield

Ashland Branch
Ashland/63rd
Halsted

East 63rd Branch
King Dr
Inbound only
East 63rd-
Cottage Grove

Inset

Merchandise Mart
Wacker Dr
Clark / Lake
State / Lake
Lake St
Randolph Dr
Randolph / Wabash
Washington / Wells
Washington St
Washington
Madison St
Madison / Wabash
Monroe
Monroe St
Adams St
Adams / Wabash
Jackson
Quincy
Jackson Blvd
LaSalle
Library
Van Buren St
LaSalle
Congress Pkwy
Harrison St
Harrison
Inset

Franklin St
Wells St
LaSalle St
Clark St
Dearborn St
State St
Michigan Ave
Wabash Ave

○ Elevated train lines
Ⓣ Free train connections at station
Ⓣ↔Ⓣ Walk between stations for free connection

Overview

Whether traveling underground, on street level, or above the sidewalk, Chicagoans refer to their elevated rapid transit system as the "L" (though some prefer to call it the "Smell.") No matter what you call it, nothing says Chicago as loud and clear as the high-pitched whine, guttural grumble, and steely grind of the train itself. L tracks lasso Chicago's heart, creating The Loop, where five of the seven L lines ride side-by-side above the pulsating business and financial district.

L trains run on 242.2 miles of track and serve 144 stations in the Chicago Metropolitan Area. The numerous track delays and stalls in service are a burden to thousands of daily commuters. That said, due to the general directness of the L routes, easy station-to-station transfers, and the difficulties of parking (especially near popular destinations such as Grant Park and Wrigley Field), the benefits of L transportation usually outweigh the discomforts and inconveniences.

Fares

All L trips require a Ventra Card, Chicago's universal fare card. To use cards, tap the reader on top of the turnstile. Standard fare on CTA trains is $2.25, and a 25 cent transfer allows two additional rides within two hours of issuance. Transfer rates are automatically deducted from your fare card when reused within the time limit. Transferring within the rail network is free at determined, connected transfer stations.

Frequency of Service

CTA publishes schedules that say trains run every 3 to 12 minutes during weekday rush hours and every 6 to 20 minutes all other times. Nice idea, but the truth is service can be irregular, especially during non-rush hours, after-hours, and in bad weather. While the system is relatively safe late at night, buses with Owl night service may be better options in the wee hours. The CTA's Train Tracker app gives station-specific ETAs, making it possible to minimize the number of times you lean over the platform looking in vain for your train.

L Lines

Blue Line: Its 24-hour O'Hare and Forest Park branches service the West and Northwest sides, including getting travelers to and from O'Hare Airport in a jiffy.

Pink Line: Chicago's newest elevated rail line took over the Blue Line's former Cermak/Douglas route with service to the near Southwest Side. The first trains leave the 54th/Cermak terminus at 4:05 am weekdays, and the last train from the Loop leaves 1:30 am daily.

Red Line: Runs north-south from the Howard Street station down to the 95th Street/Dan Ryan station; operates 24-hours.

Brown Line: Starts from the Kimball Street station and heads south with service to the Loop and sometimes just to Belmont Avenue, where you can connect with the 24-hour Red Line. On weekdays and Saturdays, the first Loop-bound train leaves Kimball at 4 am; the last Kimball-bound train leaves the Loop at 1:30 am. Truncated service to and from Belmont continues to run until 2 am on weekdays and Saturdays, with the last Kimball-bound train departing Belmont at 2:25 am. Sunday morning Brown Line service begins at 5 am but only to Belmont; Loop-bound trains don't start running until 6:30 am on Sundays, and go until 11:50 pm; after that, you can catch the northbound Brown Line at Belmont until 12:55 am.

Orange Line: Service from Midway Airport and Chicago's Southwest Side to and from the Loop. Trains depart Midway at 4 am on weekdays, and 4:30 am on Saturdays and Sundays. The last train leaves the Loop for Midway at 1:25 daily.

Green Line: Covers portions of west and south Chicago. The Harlem/Lake Street branch travels straight west to suburban Oak Park, while the Ashland/63rd Street and Cottage Grove branches go south and split east and west. Daily service begins between 4 and 5 am, depending on the branch, and run until about 12–1 am.

Purple Line: Shuttles north/south between Linden Place in suburban Wilmette and Chicago's northernmost L station at Howard Street. Service runs at 4:50 am–1:45 am on weekdays, 4:50 am–2:15 am on Fridays, 5:30 am–2:15 am on Saturdays, and 6:30 am–1:45 am on Sundays/holidays. An express service runs from Linden to the Loop, with no stops between Howard and Belmont, during weekday rush hours. Purple Line Express trains leave Linden 5:20 am–9:30 am, and 2:30 pm–6:30 pm each weekday. The last northbound Purple Line Express train leaves the Loop at 10:15 am during morning rush and 7:10 pm in the evenings.

Yellow Line: Also known as the "Skokie Swift," the Yellow Line runs between the north suburban Skokie Station and Chicago's Howard Street station, with one intermediate stop at Oakton Street. Weekday service runs 5 am–11:15 pm, and 6:30 am–11:15 pm on Saturdays and Sundays.

Bicycles

Bicycles ride free and are permitted on board at all times except weekdays from 7 am to 9 am and 4 pm to 6 pm. Only two bikes are allowed per car, so survey the platform for other bikes and check out the cars as they pull into the station for two-wheelers already on board. When entering a station, either use the turnstile, or ask an attendant to open the gate. Don't try to take your bike through the tall steel gates, because it will get stuck. There is usually bicycle parking available at stations, either at the stations themselves or on the street.

PACE Suburban—Chicago Buses

General Information
Phone: 847-364-7223
RTA Travel Info: 836-7000 (any Chicago or suburban area code)
Website: www.pacebus.com or @PaceSuburbanBus

Overview

Pace buses serve nearly 40 million passengers in the Chicago suburbs and some parts of the city. With over 200 routes covering 3,446 square miles, Pace provides a vital transportation service to commuters traveling between suburbs, within suburbs, to Metra train stations, and into the city. Buses usually run every 20–30 minutes, and service stops by mid-evening. Special express service is offered to Chicago-area entertainment and cultural venues.

Park-n-Ride Stations: Pace owns 12 Park-n-Ride stations, most with free parking, located throughout Pace's six-county coverage area.

Fares: Pace fares cost $1.75 for both regular and local or feeder service. Transfers are $.25 and include two transfers in a two hour window. The one-way fare on express routes costs $4. Pace buses use the Ventra Card. Pass options include the Pace 30-Day Pass, which allows unlimited Pace rides for $60. A combined CTA/Pace 30-day unlimited ride pass costs $100 and can be used on all Pace buses and CTA trains and buses.

Greyhound Buses

Greyhound (800-231-2222, www.greyhound.com or @GreyhoundBus) is the rock-bottom traveler's best friend. The bus line offers dirt-cheap fares, the flexibility drifters prefer, "basic" station "amenities," and the gritty, butt-busting experience of traveling America's scenic blue-line highways and rural byways with some colorful characters. You'll get the most out of "the Dog" by remembering a few key bits of advice: 1) above all, BYO toilet paper and/or disposable wipes; 2) cushions, pillows, air freshener, and earplugs rise above the level of mere travel store accoutrements; 3) pack a cooler, then padlock it (about which the less said, the better); 4) and for Pete's sake, charge your devices…or bring a book.

Stations: Greyhound's main train station is south of Union Station at 630 W Harrison St in West Loop (312-408-5821). CTA buses 60, 125, 156, and 157 make stops near the terminal. The closest L stop is on the Blue Line's Forest Park Branch at the Clinton Street Station on Congress Parkway. Additional Chicago-area Greyhound stations are located within L train stations: 14 W 95th St in the Red Line's 95th Street/Dan Ryan Station (312-408-5999), and 5800 N Cumberland Ave on the Blue Line's O'Hare Branch in the Cumberland Station (773-693-2474).

Shipping Services: Greyhound Package Express (www.shipgreyhound.com) offers commercial and personal shipping services and is available at all three Chicago bus stations. Packages are held at the station for pick-up.

Fares: Tickets can be purchased on the phone or online with a credit card, or at a station with cash, travelers' checks, or credit cards.

Regular fare pricing applies for both individual advance ticket sales and minutes-before-departure sales. Tickets can be used for travel to the designated destination on any day or at any departure time. Because Greyhound does not reserve seats, boarding occurs on a first-come-first-served basis, so get in line at the boarding zone for a choice seat. Greyhound does offer priority boarding for a small surcharge. Often if a significant number of passengers turn out for the same bus, Greyhound rolls another bus, or two, or three out on the spot. Good dog.

Discounts are available for children under 12 (up to 25% off regular fares), seniors 62 and older (5% discounts), and military members (10% discounts). Students and veterans can receive discounts via respective membership cards (with associated fees). The cost for an individual return ticket is always deeply discounted if it is purchased at the same time as a departure ticket. Tickets purchased three days in advance earn up to two reduced companion ticket (no age restrictions). Check website for web only specials. Passengers accompanying someone with a disability always ride at a reduced rate.

Megabus.com

Roll over Greyhound, there's a new dog in town, and a cheaper one at that! An import from the UK, Megabus.com (us.megabus.com or @megabus) buses travel between most major Midwest cities, including Minneapolis, Detroit, Milwaukee, St. Louis, Cleveland, Indianapolis, and beyond, and a host of smaller destinations across the Midwest.

Fares: Ticket prices are determined by how far in advance you buy your tickets, how popular the route is, and what day of the week you travel on. If your Fairy Godmother is on your side, it is possible that you could take a trip to, say, Kansas City, for as low as $1. Of course, as the service becomes more popular, the fares go up. And if you're like us, you don't buy your fares months ahead of time, which adds to the cost. But even so, most fares don't go too much higher than $20 each way. Still a sweet deal, even by Greyhound standards.

Stations: Megabus doesn't have stations, per se. But you'll see the line snaking outside Union Station as you approach. Union Station in downtown Chicago is the arrival and departure stop for all buses out of Chicago. Park yourself at the east side of South Canal Street, between Jackson Blvd and Adams Street, and try to get there early. It's first come, first serve seating.

Other important logistics: You can order your Megabus ticket online up to 45 days in advance. You can only bring one piece of luggage (up to 50 pounds) to stow under the bus and one small carry-on. No bikes allowed. Megabus is more or less wheelchair accessible, just make sure you call and let them know, and they can accommodate you.

Transit • Metra Train Lines

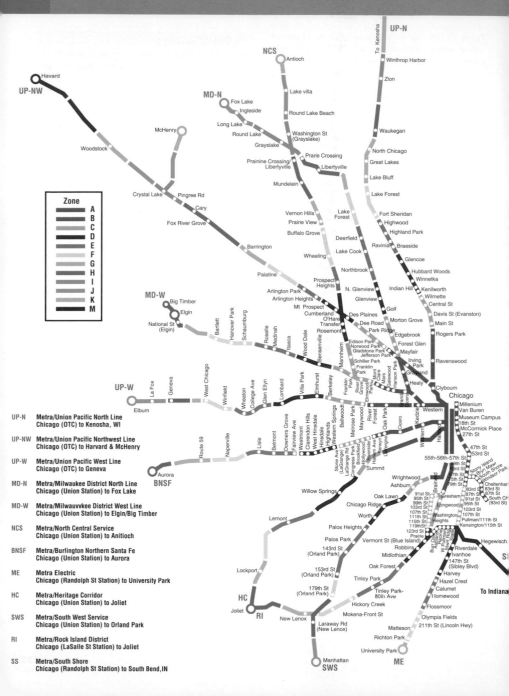

Zone
- A
- B
- C
- D
- E
- F
- G
- H
- I
- J
- K
- M

UP-N   **Metra/Union Pacific North Line**
Chicago (OTC) to Kenosha, WI

UP-NW   **Metra/Union Pacific Northwest Line**
Chicago (OTC) to Harvard & McHenry

UP-W   **Metra/Union Pacific West Line**
Chicago (OTC) to Geneva

MD-N   **Metra/Milwaukee District North Line**
Chicago (Union Station) to Fox Lake

MD-W   **Metra/Milwauvvkee District West Line**
Chicago (Union Station) to Elgin/Big Timber

NCS   **Metra/North Central Service**
Chicago (Union Station) to Anitioch

BNSF   **Metra/Burlington Northern Santa Fe**
Chicago (Union Station) to Aurora

ME   **Metra Electric**
Chicago (Randolph St Station) to University Park

HC   **Metra/Heritage Corridor**
Chicago (Union Station) to Joliet

SWS   **Metra/South West Service**
Chicago (Union Station) to Orland Park

RI   **Metra/Rock Island District**
Chicago (LaSalle St Station) to Joliet

SS   **Metra/South Shore**
Chicago (Randolph St Station) to South Bend, IN

General Information

Metra Address: Metra Passenger Services
547 W Jackson Blvd
Chicago, IL 60661
Phone: 312-322-6777
Website: www.metrarail.com
Metra Passenger Service: 312-322-6777
South Shore Metra Lines: 800-356-2079
RTA Information Center: 312-836-7000;
www.rtachicago.com

Overview

With 11 lines and roughly 495 miles of track, Metra does its best to serve Cook, DuPage, Lake, Will, McHenry, and Kane counties with 241 stations scattered throughout the city and 'burbs. The rails, branching out from four major downtown stations, are lifelines for commuters traveling to and from the Loop.

The good news for Metra is that ridership is strong; the sheer multitude of folks who live in the suburbs but work in the city (and hate to deal with rush hour) means that Metra will always have a job. The bad news for riders is that parking at popular stations is difficult, if not impossible, and most people don't live close enough to Metra stations to walk. In an attempt to resolve its parking issues, Metra is purchasing land surrounding many suburban stations and constructing new parking facilities.

Loop Stations

There are four major Metra train stations in the Loop which 11 train lines feed into:

Station/Line

Ogilvie Transportation Center: Union Pacific/North Line, Union Pacific/Northwest Line, Union Pacific/West Line

Union Station: Milwaukee District/North Line, Milwaukee District/West Line, North Central Service, BNSF Railway, Heritage Corridor, SouthWest Service

LaSalle Street Station: Rock Island District

Millennium Station: Metra Electric District (Main Line, South Chicago, and Blue Island Branches) and South Shore Line

Fares

Depending on the number of the 12 Metra fare zones you traverse, one-way, full-fare tickets cost between $2.75 and $9.25. Tickets may be purchased through a ticket agent or vending machine at select stations, or on board the train (with a $3 surcharge if the station at which you boarded the train had a ticket agent or ticket vending machine). There is no reserved seating.

The ten-ride ticket provides no discount, but Metra offers a monthly unlimited ride pass which is the economical choice for commuters who use Metra service daily. If your commute includes CTA and/or Pace bus services, consider purchasing a Link-Up Pass ($55) for connecting service on CTA during weekday rush hours (6:30 am–9:30 am and 3:30 pm–7 pm) and on anytime on Pace buses. Metra's Weekend Pass costs $7 and includes unlimited rides on Saturday and Sunday, with the exception of the South Shore route. You can buy all the aforementioned tickets in person, through the mail, or online. Children under age seven ride free and kids ages 7 to 11 ride for half-price weekdays. Weekend family fares allow up to three children 11 and under to ride free with an adult. Students, senior citizens, people with disabilities and US military personnel are all eligible for reduced fares.

Before You Board

Bicycles are permitted on weekday off-peak hours (inbound before 6:31 am and after 9:30 am and outbound before 3 pm and after 7 pm) and at all times on weekends. Large, bulky items like skis, non-folding carts, water buffaloes, and other large items are not allowed on trains. Pets, with the exception of service animals, are also prohibited aboard trains.

General Information

Loop Station Address: Millennium Station at 151 E Randolph St, Chicago, IL 60601
Website: www.nictd.com
Lost & Found: 219-874-4221 x205

Overview

Service on the historic South Shore Line began in 1903. Service to South Bend was added in 1908. In 1992, an extension was added to South Bend Airport, completing the current 90-mile route, which takes about 2.5 hours from start to finish. The Northern Indiana Commuter Transportation District (NICTD) oversees the line and its modern electric trains, which serve as a vital transportation link for many northwest Indiana residents working in the Loop. Although a separate entity from Metra, the South Shore Line travels to Millennium Station along Metra tracks, making stops in Chicago at 63rd Street, 57th Street, McCormick Place, Museum Campus, and Van Buren Street.

The South Shore's commuter service reflects its Indiana ridership. Outbound heading from the Loop, there are limited stops before the Hegewisch station, close to the Indiana state line. When traveling by train to Chicago's South Side, you're better off on an outbound Metra Electric Line train departing from the Millennium Station. A trip on the South Shore is a cheap post-industrial voyeuristic thrill, as a complete round-trip from the Loop all the way to South Bend can be had for not much more than a deep dish pie at Lou Malnati's. Along the way you will pass by dozens of antiquated factories, one of the longest stretches of sand dunes in the Great Lakes region, and, of course, Gary, Indiana.

Fares

Regular one-way fares can be purchased at the stations (with cash or personal check), on board trains (cash only), or online (Visa and Mastercards accepted). Ticket prices vary with distance traveled. Tickets purchased on board are assessed a $1 surcharge if the station's ticket windows were open at the time of departure.

Special South Shore fares and packages include 10-Ride and 25-Ride tickets and a monthly pass good for unlimited travel. These can be purchased in person at stations staffed with ticket agents, station vending machines, and via the mail. Senior citizens/disability fares offer savings for persons aged 65 and older with valid identification and for disabled passengers. Youth fares include free passage for infants under two years (who must sit in a paying passenger's lap) and half off a regular fare for children aged two to 13 years. Family fares are available on weekends and holidays as well as off-peak times on weekdays. Each fare-paying adult (minimum age 21) may take one child (age 13 and under) with them free of charge. Additional children will be charged the reduced youth fare. Active duty military personnel in uniform may request reduced fares with their Common Access Cards (CAC).

Before You Board

Any accompanying baggage must be placed in the overhead racks. No bicycles are permitted on board. Apart from small animals in carry-on cages, the only pets allowed on board are service dogs accompanied by handlers or passengers with disabilities. Animals must not occupy seats.

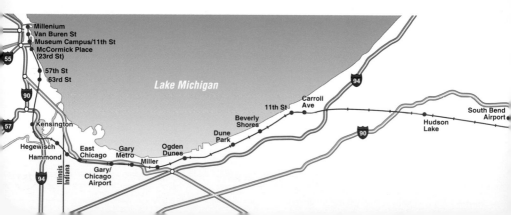

General Information

Phone: 800-872-7245
Website: www.amtrak.com or @Amtrak
Union Station: 225 S Canal St, Chicago, IL 60606
Union Station Information: www.chicagounionstation.com

Overview

The best city in America for riding the rails, Chicago hubs Amtrak's 500-station national railroad network, which covers every state but Alaska, Hawaii, South Dakota, and Wyoming. Departing from Union Station, Amtrak trains head west to Los Angeles, San Francisco, Portland and Seattle; east to Washington, DC, New York City and Boston; north to Milwaukee and Minneapolis; and south to New Orleans and San Antonio, Texas.

Fares

Amtrak offers affordable fares for regional travel, with travel times comparable to flying when you factor in today's early airport check-ins. Their prices can't compete with airfares on longer hauls, but just as airlines offer deeply discounted fares, so does Amtrak. Ask sales agents about special fares and search Amtrak's website for the best deals. (Booking in advance does present some savings.) We recommend the website, as callers risk being on hold longer than it takes to ride a train from Chicago to Los Angeles.

Amtrak offers special fares year-round for seniors, veterans, students, children under 16, and groups. The "Hot Deals" page on Amtrak's website lists sale fares. Amtrak has also hooked its cars up with plenty of travel partners to create interesting "Amtrak Vacations" packages, including air-rail deals, whereby you rail it one way and fly back the other—attractive for long-distance travel. The prices listed below are approximate, likely to change and don't include upgrades like sleeper cars. Check with Amtrak for updates.

Service

Someday, high-speed rail may come to the Midwest. Meanwhile, only a lucky few can claim to have arrived on time when traveling the longer routes on Amtrak, so tell whoever is picking you up you'll call them on your cell phone when you get close.

Pack food for your ride, as dining car fare is mediocre and pricey. On the upside, Amtrak's seats are comfortable and roomy; some have electric sockets for computer hookups; bathrooms are in every car; and the train is almost always clean.

And you don't have to travel light. Your ticket lets you carry on two bags and check two for free, each weighing up to 50 pounds. Check an additional two bags and items such as bicycles, golf bags, baby strollers, musical instruments, and skis with handling fees of $5 to $20 each. Amtrak's default liability for checked baggage tops out at $500, so if your designer duds are worth more than that you'll want to ante up for extra coverage. Weapons; large, sharp objects; corrosive or dangerous chemicals; and the like are all prohibited, just like on planes; check for current regs before you pack.

Within Illinois and to Missouri: Amtrak's Illinois Service trains travel to 28 downstate cities from Chicago daily: "The Illinois Zephyr" and "The Carl Sandburg" travel to Quincy (on the Mississippi); "Illini Service" and "The Saluki" roll between Chicago and Carbondale; "The Lincoln Service" goes through corn and soybean country to St. Louis. Also running daily, "The Southwest Chief" stops in Kansas City five hours into its trip to Albuquerque and Los Angeles. "City of New Orleans" makes a number of downstate stops, too.

To Milwaukee and Minneapolis: Frequent enough for commuters, "Hiawatha Service" (www.amtrakhiawatha.com) runs seven round-trip trains a day (six on Sunday) to Sturtevant, Wisconsin (near Racine); Milwaukee's Mitchell Airport; and downtown Milwaukee, leaving Chicago about every two hours and stopping en route in suburban Glenview. The 90-minute trip costs about $25 each way (a good alternative to driving on busy weekends and rush hours). En route to the northwest, "The Empire Builder" also stops in Milwaukee, as well as Minneapolis; it takes some eight and a half hours to reach the Twin Cities.

To Michigan: Skip scary driving through the "Snow Belt" by taking the train. Three lines offer daily service to the Winter Water Wonderland: "The Pere Marquette" heads to Grand Rapids; "The Blue Water" takes passengers to Port Huron; and "The Wolverine" goes to Ann Arbor and Detroit, among other places. The ride to the Motor City takes about six hours.

To the East Coast: "The Capitol Limited" runs daily through Cleveland and Pittsburgh to Washington, DC, an 18-hour trip, while "The Cardinal" takes 26.5 hours to get to New York via Indianapolis, Cincinnati, Philadelphia, and Washington three days a week. The "Lake Shore Limited" passes through Albany, NY, and goes to New York City (19 hours) and Boston (22 hours).

To Seattle or Portland: The "Empire Builder" takes passengers to Seattle and Portland and everywhere in between. With the journey to Seattle taking around 46 hours, we definitely recommend dropping some additional dollars on a sleeper car.

To San Francisco: You'll spend two solid days and then some riding the rails during the 52-hour journey on the "California Zephyr" to San Francisco (Emeryville). The "Zephyr" passes through Denver, Salt Lake City, and Sacramento, and makes a host of small-town America stops along the way.

To Los Angeles: You'll have plenty of time to study your map to the Hollywood stars on the "Southwest Chief," which departs for LA daily via Albuquerque, takes almost 42 hours.

To San Antonio: The mighty "Texas Eagle" doesn't exactly glide to the Alamo. It stops at 40 cities on its way from the Midwest through Texas to the Southwest, 32-plus hours to San Antonio.

To New Orleans: The train Chicago's Steve Goodman made famous, "City of New Orleans," runs from Chicago via Memphis to The Big Easy in roughly 19 hours. Good morning, America, how are you?

Union Station

Location: 225 S Canal St at E Adams St and E Jackson Blvd
Amtrak: 800-872-7245 or www.amtrak.com
Metra Rail: 312-322-6777 or metrarail.com
General Information: www.chicagounionstation.com or @ChiUnionStation

An innovation for both design and travel, Chicago's Union Station is the "Grand Dame" of rail service in a city once considered to be the undisputed rail center of the United States. Designed by the architects Graham, Anderson, Probst, and White and built between 1913 and 1925, Union Station is a terminus for six Metra lines and a major hub for Amtrak's long-distance services. In its peak during the 1940s, this local transportation treasure handled as many as 300 trains and 100,000 passengers on a daily basis. While today's volume is just half that, this monumental station stands as the last remaining grand station still in use in the City of Chicago and was given landmark status in 2002. Most commuters don't take the time to gaze skyward when rushing through the Great Hall of Union Station (who really has the time to stop and assess their surroundings beyond that of their intended use?), but by not doing so, they are missing something special. Take the time to look up at the magnificent light-swathed ceiling and maybe then it will become clear why Union Station's ornate Great Hall is considered one of the United States' great interior public spaces. Union Station is also a premiere location for formal functions as it annually plays host to a multitude of private affairs and black-tie gatherings.

Both Metra's and Amtrak's train services are on the Concourse Level (ground floor) of the station. This level is then further divided into the North Concourse and South Concourse. There is an information desk located between the concourses on this level. And while there is signage throughout Union Station, the many escalators, stairways, and multiple entrances/exits can make navigating the block-long building somewhat of a challenge.

Ticket Windows: The easiest way to get to Metra ticket agents is to enter Union Station at the Clinton Street entrance near East Jackson Boulevard and go down into and through the Grand Hall. Metra's ticket agents will be on your left in the North Concourse. Metra's ticket office is open daily 6 am–11 pm. Metra Lines that terminate at Union Station are Milwaukee District North and West Lines, North Central Service, Burlington Northern Santa Fe (BNSF), Heritage Corridor, and SouthWest Service.

To get to the Amtrak action, enter Union Station off Canal Street, take the escalator down into the Grand Hall, and turn left. Amtrak's attractive, vintage ticket agent desk straddles the two concourses and is open daily 6 am–9:20 pm.

Services: On the Mezzanine/Street Level, there is a plethora of convenience stores, newsstands, and eateries. ATMs are located in both concourses on this level.

Public Transportation: The closest L stop to Union Station is Clinton Street on the Blue Line, which stops two blocks south of the station. The Orange, Brown, and Purple Lines stop three blocks east of the station at the Quincy stop on Wells Street. CTA buses 7, 37, 60, 124, 126, 151, 156, 157 all stop at Union Station. Most commuters heading to work in the Loop enter and exit the station from the Madison Street, Adams Street, and Jackson Boulevard doorways where cabs line up.

Richard B. Ogilvie Transportation Center

Location: 500 W Madison St at S Canal St
Lost & Found: 312-496-4751
MetraMarket: www.metramarket.com

Built in 1911 and known locally as the North Western or Madison Street Station, the Metra's Union Pacific Lines originate from the Richard B. Ogilvie Transportation Center, which serves approximately 40,000 passengers each day. Where Union Station is about form and function, Ogilvie focuses solely on function. Overtly stark and sterile, the tall, smoky-glass-and-green-steel-girder building replaced what was once a classic grand train station similar to the ornate, Beaux Arts-inspired Union Station. Though most of the historic fixtures have been removed, some of the original clocks remain and serve as a reminder of earlier days. The empty space under the tracks is now MetraMarket, which is filling up with thousands of square feet of shops and restaurants to serve the West Loop/Fulton River District area.

Ticket Windows: Metra's ticket office is on the upper level, across from the entrance to the train platform and is open 5:30 am–12:40 am Monday–Saturday, and 7 am–12:40 am Sundays.

Services: MetraMarket has many vendors, large and small, including the Chicago French Market, various artisanal food shops and boutiques, and a CVS. There is also a food court in the Citigroup Center lobby that is open from 5 am–12 am weekdays and 7 am–11 pm on weekends. Restrooms are available.

Public Transportation: The closest L station is the Clinton Street stop at Lake Street on the Pink and Green Lines, several blocks north of the station. CTA buses 20, 56, and 157 board at Washington and Canal Streets and travel to North Michigan Avenue and the Loop. Coming from the Loop, take the same bus lines west across Madison Street. If you're after a cab, you'll find other like-minded commuters lining up in front of the main entrance on Madison Street between Canal and Clinton Streets.

Millennium Station

Location: 151 E Randolph St at N Michigan Ave
Lost & Found: 312-322-7819
Website: www.millenniumstation.com

Back when it was just Randolph Street Station, this facility was not much to look at. Now that it sits under one of Chicago's major attractions, it has been spiffed up with new shops and a charming blue-terrazzo floor. The underground station, centrally located in the Loop, serves up to 100,000 commuters daily. This is also the station where the South Shore Line to South Bend, Indiana originates. Schedules for all are somewhat sporadic except during weekday rush hour commutes. (The Van Buren Street Station also serves both the Metra Electric and South Shore Lines and is located at East Jackson Boulevard and Van Buren Street.)

Ticket Windows: Enter the Millennium Station at East Randolph Street and North Michigan Avenue. The ticket office is immediately visible upon descending the steps off Michigan Avenue or entering via the Pedway, which tunnels around the Loop and east under Michigan Avenue, ending at the station. Ticket office hours are 5:55 am–12:50 am (Sunday, 7 am–12:50 am). The waiting room is open 5 am–12:50 am daily.

Services: Millennium Station offers amenities such food and retail shops, including an outpost of a certain very, very large coffee chain, and ATMs. On an upbeat note, the bathrooms are rather clean, which is a most welcome find in the Loop.

Public Transportation: Millennium Station is served by over a half dozen CTA bus routes, including the 3, 4, 56, 145, 147, 151, and 157. One block west of the train station is the CTA's Randolph/Wabash elevated station, which is served by the Orange, Green, Purple, Pink, and Brown Lines.

LaSalle Street Station

Location: 414 S La Salle St at E Congress Pkwy
Lost & Found: 312-322-8957

The La Salle Street Station, located underneath the Chicago Stock Exchange, serves the Metra Rock Island District Line's passengers. This former behemoth of a station has been greatly reduced in both size and stature, handling roughly 15,000 commuters daily on the line out toward Joliet.

Ticket Windows: Enter the station off LaSalle Street, take the escalator one floor up, and walk through the slim corridor to an open-air area where the tracks are. To your right you'll see the ticket office. Agents are on duty 6:15 am–9 pm weekdays and 11 am–7:30 pm on Saturday.

Services: A convenience stand is open 8 am–8 pm weekdays. Restrooms are available. The waiting room is open 6 am–12 am daily.

Public Transportation: The Blue Line's La Salle Street stop at Congress Parkway and the Orange, Purple, and Brown Lines La Salle Street stop at Van Buren Street drop L riders right in front of the train station. CTA buses 7, 36, 126, and 151 stop near the station, as well.

General Information

City of Chicago Department of Transportation (DOT):
www.cityofchicago.org/Transportation or @ChicagoDOT
Illinois Department of Transportation (IDOT): www.dot.state.il.us
or www.gettingaroundillinois.com or @IDOT_Illinois
WBBM-AM 780: Traffic updates every ten minutes on the 8s

Orientation

Anyone who says baldness is hereditary has never found him/
herself in a Chicago traffic jam, pulling out his/her hair to pass the
time and calm the nerves. We highly recommend taking public
transportation whenever possible, especially since Chicago has
such strong bus and rail systems. But if you must drive in the city,
Chicago's grid system makes it relatively easy to navigate.

The intersection of State and Madison Streets in the Loop serves
as the base line for both Chicago's street and house numbering
system. Running north and south is State Street--the city's east/
west dividing line. Madison Street runs east and west and divides
the city into north and south. Street and building numbers
begin at "1" at the State and Madison Streets intersection and
numerically increase going north, south, east, and west to
the city limits. Street signs will let you know in what direction
you're heading. The city is divided into one-mile sections, or
eight square blocks, each with a consecutively higher series of
"100" numbers. For example, Western Ave, sitting at 2400 W, is
further west than Ashland Ave, located at 1600 W. In addition,
Chicagoans numerically refer to street locations such as Irving
Park Road as "40 hundred north" rather than "four thousand
north." An interesting historical tidbit about the city's three
primary diagonal streets: Milwaukee, Elston, and Lincoln Avenues
all used to be Native American trails.

Buildings with even number addresses are on the north and west
sides of streets; odd numbers sit on the south and east sides.
Chicago's diagonal streets also follow the grid numbering system,
most of which receive north or south addresses. East-west streets
north of Madison are named, as in Fullerton or Belmont; south
of Madison they are generally numbered, as in 31st or 79th, with
several major streets being named. Once you get out of the city
limits, good luck. Often times you will find that our suburban
friends like to refer to the same road by two different names.
Roads will also magically turn into something different for no
apparent reason. And sometimes they don't bother putting up
street signs at all.

Bridge Lift Season

While bridges spanning the Chicago River contribute to the city's
architectural fame, they also serve as a major source of traffic
congestion. Boating season demands that bridges lower and
rise, so as to allow Chicago's elite access between Lake Michigan
and storage yards via the Chicago River. On scheduled days from
early April until June the Chicago Department of Transportation
raises the movable bridges along the Main and South Branches
of the river. Bridges are raised one at a time, in order, and each
lift takes about ten minutes. In all, 27 bridges are raised, from the
Ashland Avenue Bridge on the South Branch to Lake Shore Drive.
Lifts generally begin in the morning, either 8 am or 9:30 am and
affect the entire downtown area between 11:30 am and 1 pm.
The Chicago Department of Transportation announces details in
advance; check website for details.

Snow Routes

The Department of Streets and Sanitation manages the ice and
snow removal on Chicago's streets. Since failure to efficiently
handle city snow removal seals the re-election fate of Chicago's
mayors, snow events are a serious business. Thus, Chicago doesn't
have mere snow plows--instead the mayor oversees a fleet of

nearly 300 "Snow Fighting Trucks." From the city's 911 center, the
"Snow Command" utilizes modern urban surveillance systems to
zero in on the (literal) facts on the ground. The Chicago Shovels
site (www.chicagoshovels.org) is the go-to for updates and real-
time, GPS-enhanced plow information.

Between December 1 and April 1 a Winter Overnight Parking
Ban is in place for 107 miles of priority arteries daily from 3 am
until 7 am, whether or not snow is present. Parking restrictions
will also be in effect for another 500 miles of designated snow
routes when snow is piled at least two inches on the pavement.
Unfortunately, the two-inch snow routes are a crap-shoot. Tow
trucks will enforce these restrictions by their own rules, it seems.
On a snow route, you will either find your car gone or buried by
a passing plow. Safety dictates you keep your car off of these
routes even if only an inch and a half are predicted.

Major Expressways and Tollways

While the city's grid system is logical, the interstate highway
system feeding into the city is confusing for those who don't
travel it often. Chicago has free expressways and tollways which
require paying a fee. The expressways are generally referred to by
their names, such as "The Kennedy" or "The Eisenhower." When
venturing to Indiana, one can experience the Chicago Skyway,
a stretch of elevated road that connects I-94 and the Indiana Toll
Road that soars 120 feet above the Calumet River. When using
the tollways, which includes the Skyway, I-PASS speeds up the
process and can be purchased through the Illinois State Toll
Highway Authority (800-824-7277 or www.illinoistollway.com).

DMVs

The Illinois Department of Motor Vehicles (DMV) is one of life's
unavoidable hassles. But you'd be pleasantly surprised to see
how many of your car-related responsibilities (like renewing
your driver's license, getting vehicle registrations, etc.) can
be completed online (www.cyberdriveillinois.com). While the
Secretary of State has made vast improvements to the efficiency
of all DMV locations, the facility tucked behind the food court of
the James R. Thompson Center **(Map 5)** truly earns its "express"
status.

Chicago DMVs/Map/Hours
100 W Randolph St, Concourse Level (Map 5);
Mon–Fri, 8 am–5 pm
69 W Washington St, Concourse Level (Map 5);
Mon–Fri, 8 am–5 pm
17 N State St, Ste 1000 (Map 5); Mon–Fri: 8:30 am–5 pm
5401 N Elston Ave (Map 46); Mon-Fri, 8:30 am–5 pm
4642 W Diversey St (Map 48); Tues–Fri, 8 am–5:30 pm;
Sat, 7:30 am–12 pm
5301 W Lexington St (Map 49); Tues–Fri, 8 am–5:30 pm;
Sat, 7:30 am–12 pm
9901 S Martin Luther King Dr (Map 59); Mon–Fri, 8:30 am–5 pm

Car Share

Chicago is blessed with good public transportation, and it's of
course possible to get along without a car. That said, there are
times--laundry, groceries, beer runs--when a private conveyance
becomes temporarily necessary. Thankfully, Chicago has been a
pioneer in car sharing. Several companies, including Zip Car (www.
zipcar.com), Enterprise Car Share (www.enterprisecarshare.com),
and Hertz 24/7 (www.hertz247.com), offer a fleet of vehicles at
subscribers' disposal for short errands or all-day rental. Cars are
parked at convenient locations throughout the city. Peer-to-
peer car share is also an option;. Relay Rides (relayrides.com) and
Getaround (www.getaround.com) are two such entities where
owners rent out their vehicles. Rates for all services hover around
$10 an hour, give or take a buck or two.

General Information

Office of the City Clerk: City Hall, 121 N La Salle St,
Rm 107, Chicago, IL 60602
Phone: 312-744-6774
Hours: Weekdays, 8 am–5 pm
Website: www.chicityclerk.com or @chicityclerk
Department of Finance: PO Box 6289, Chicago IL 60680-6289
Website: www.cityofchicago.org/finance
Parking Ticket Assistance & "Boot" Inquiries: 312-744-PARK (7275)
Auto Pound Headquarters (for towed vehicles): 312-744-4444

Overview

Parking in Chicago has never been what we would call a joyous experience. Between neighborhood permit-only parking zones, snow routes, and a constant rotation of street fairs, street cleaning, street construction, and parking spot "dibs" in the winter, figuring out where and how to park in the city requires an advanced degree in Asininity. Some areas, like Lincoln Park, Lakeview, and Wicker Park, would test the nerves and the patience of the Dalai Lama. These areas are all easily accessible by public transit, and taxi cabs are plentiful, so unless you want to be part of the problem and not the solution, transport yourself accordingly.

In 2009, former Mayor Daley added to the problem by leasing all of Chicago's parking meters to a private firm (a 75 year lease!), causing fares to increase each year, and allowing for changes like expanded metered parking hours. Maybe the ONE positive side of the meter fiasco is the advent of Pay Boxes. These handy contraptions at least do you the courtesy of allowing you to pay with a credit card--of course through the nose, or whatever other orifices through which money shoots. The days of saving your quarters are over; now just start a separate bank account for parking. And for further convenience, the ParkChicago app allows you to pay using your smart phone, so when your meter expires there's no need to hightail it back to your car to replenish.

City Stickers

Residents of Chicago who own motor vehicles must have an annually renewed city sticker for their cars, which can be purchased from the Office of the City Clerk through the mail (by returning the renewal application you've received in the mail), in person at one of their offices, or online. Stickers may also be purchased at local currency exchanges, but you might get charged extra there. New residents are required to purchase their sticker in person with a proof of residency at one of the offices within 30 days of their move-in date. A four-passenger vehicle sticker is $85.97. Senior citizens are also eligible for discounts, but they check IDs, so don't pretend you're over 50; they'll find out you're lying.

Residential Zone Permit Parking

If you're lucky enough to find a parking spot, you still need to put a permit on your car. Chicago's Residential Parking Permit program reserves street parking during peak parking hours for neighborhood residents and those who provide a service to the residents. Permits cost $25 annually and are available through the Office of the City Clerk via mail, online, and in person. Applicants must have a valid Chicago City Sticker and an Illinois State license plate. One-day Residential Parking Daily Permits may also be purchased and distributed by qualified residents. Fifteen 24-hour passes cost $8 per pack, and households are limited to 30 passes each 30 day period. Daily permits are available for purchase at City Clerk Office locations and online.

Parking Tickets

The Department of Revenue (DOR) handles the payment of parking tickets. You can pay parking tickets by mail, online, in person, or at Department of Finance EZ Pay Stations. Scribbling curse words on a ticket, ripping it up, and throwing it at the mailbox does not count as "paying" it, according to the stingy DOR.

Three or more unpaid tickets guarantees a metal, yellow surprise fitted to your car tire; yep, say hello to the boot. (Ten or more tickets and the entire car is encased in molybdenum steel.) If violations aren't paid within 24 hours of booting, your vehicle will be towed...maybe. In addition to the boot fee, towing, and storage fees must be paid to retrieve your car from a City Auto Pound. If your car is towed due to a boot, contact the City of Chicago's Ticket Help Line (312-744-7275). All payments for outstanding parking ticket debt must be made to a DOR Payment Center, not at the pound. The city has two payment plans available for motorists with large ticket fines. The General Payment Plan requires either a deposit of $500 or 25% of your parking debt (whichever is greater) in addition to all outstanding boot, towing, and storage fees. If you qualify for the Hardship Parking Payment Plan, you can make a deposit of $250 or 25% of your debt, whichever is lower. If either of these cases applies to you, we also suggest you stop parking in Chicago and find another means of travel, since you apparently can't handle the responsibility.

Auto Pounds

To locate your towed vehicle, use the city's online locator (findyourvehicle.cityofchicago.org) or contact the City of Chicago Auto Pound (312-744-4444). For a standard vehicle, the towing fee is a hefty $150 plus a $20 per day storage fee for the first five days, $35 per day thereafter. Fees can be paid at the pound; they accept cash, cashier's checks, VISA, MasterCard, Discover, American Express, and first-born children. No arms or legs, please. Failure to claim vehicles or request a hearing within 21 days of notification can result in your convenient mode of transportation being sold or destroyed and, even then, you still owe the city for the outstanding fines. In that case, see the rest of the Transit section for alternate ways of navigating your way through Chicago.

Important note: "Minor" street repairs and construction are common occurrences on Chicago streets, during which signs should be posted on nearby trees or parking meters stating that parking is temporarily prohibited. If you park there, you will be towed. If you parked there on purpose despite seeing the signs, well, you deserve it. If you parked there on accident, we feel for you, so read on for our tips on how to not look like a panicky idiot while trying to find your car. First of all, don't bother contacting the city pound. They will have no idea what you're talking about! Save yourself the embarrassment of reporting your car stolen, and call the number posted on the sign where your car was parked. Chances are it was kindly moved to another location so as to allow workers to continue with important road improvements, but it may not have officially been moved by the city of Chicago. Operators should be able to track it down using your license plate number since city code mandates that the kindly moving of a car must be reported within a few hours, whether it be by the city or the other parking powers that be. Otherwise, you can always walk around your neighborhood aimlessly searching for your car, but we don't recommend it. We've only been successful doing that once or twice, and, anyway, it just turned out that we forgot where we parked after a night of heavy drinking.

By our minds, the designation of "landmark" can apply to buildings of architectural distinction, or the iconic Morton Salt girl, trailing sodium chloride behind her on the roof of the Elston Avenue Morton Salt facility. It could be internationally recognized Chicago iconography (Buckingham Fountain), or something only the locals are aware of ("Meet me by the Totem Pole"). Landmark status is a historical designation, but local landmarks are how you figure out where the hell you are and where you need to go.

Legacy Architecture

Early skyscrapers such as the **Monadnock Building (Map 5)** can be found in the Loop, alongside other noteworthy structures like Adler and Sullivan's historic **Auditorium Building (Map 6)**. Contrast these with Midwest native **Frank Lloyd Wright's Home and Studio (Oak Park)** in the suburb of Oak Park, whose famous Prairie style can also be seen at the **Robie House (Map 19)** on the city's south side. Jump forward a couple of decades and German Mies van der Rohe arrives on the scene, with his dictum "less is more." Trek over to the **Illinois Institute of Technology (IIT) (Map 13)** to really immerse yourself in his spare glass and steel structures. Chicago is also home to a triumvirate of quirky Bertrand Goldberg masterpieces—**Marina Towers (Map 2)**, which graces the cover of Wilco's *Yankee Hotel Foxtrot*, **River City (Map 7)**, and the **Raymond Hilliard Apartments (Map 10)**.

Great New Architecture

IIT is also the site of some fab new architecture, such as starchitect Rem Koolhaas's incredible **McCormick Tribune Campus Center (Map 14)**, which literally encases the L in a tube, and Helmut Jahn's **State Street Village (Map 14)**. With plans for the world's tallest and corkscrew-evoking Chicago Spire dashed due to an inability to secure financing, the city is soliciting suggestions about what to do with that giant-assed hole in the ground. Meanwhile the glittering new **Trump Tower (Map 2)** has become a new beacon on the Chicago cityscape, replacing the dismal former Sun-Times building (strange how the newspaper relocated to an equally drab building only a few blocks away from the original).

Historical Houses

Built in 1836, Prairie Avenue's **Clarke House (Map 11)** claims the title of Chicago's oldest home, never mind that the original building of the northwest side's **Noble-Seymour-Crippen House (Northwest)** dates back to 1833. Although **Robie House (Map 19)** is the most famous, Frank Lloyd Wright's prairie-style homes dot Chicago's landscape, among them are the **Walser House (West)** and Sheridan Avenue's **Bach House (Map 34)**. Of course some homes are more renowned for their residents than their architectural or historical significance. These include the **Charlie Chaplin House (Map 38)**, the **Ida B. Wells-Barnett Home (Map 14)**, the **Richard J. Daley House (Map 13)**, and, most famously, **President Barack Obama's Residence (Map 17)**.

Outdoor Spaces

Chicago's status as a green city got off to a good start, thanks to some forward-thinking chaps. By advocating the lakefront as a place for recreation, Daniel Burnham has left a wonderful legacy. Highlights are **Lincoln Park (Map 30)**, with the free **Lincoln Park Zoo**, to the north and **Jackson Park (Map 20)**, site of the 1893 World's Columbian Exposition, to the south. **Grant Park (Map 6)** is home to the **Buckingham Fountain (Map 9)**, and offers festivals throughout the warmer months. And don't forget the harbors. **Belmont Harbor (Map 44)** is home to the Chicago Yacht Club Sailing School, while **The Point at Diversey (Map 30)** provides a fabulous view of the city from the north. Within the downtown itself, outdoor spaces include **Daley Plaza (Map 5)** (you saw it in the movie *The Lake House*), which offers free lunchtime cultural events. Outside of the city limits, **Garfield Park Conservatory (West)** is a jewel in a barren landscape.

Public Artwork

Better described as a work of art rather than simply an outdoor space, **Millennium Park (Map 6)** is not to be missed. Legendry architect Frank Gehry has conjured up another of his steel creations with the **Jay Pritzker Pavilion (Map 6)**, an open air venue offering complimentary concerts, while British and Spanish artists have stolen the show with **Cloud Gate (Map 6)** (otherwise known as The Bean) and **Crown Fountain (Map 6)** (a.k.a. kiddies' pool). Another heavy concentration of public artwork is found in the Loop, with the **Miro's Chicago** sculpture **(Map 5)** and Alexander Calder's **Flamingo (Map 5)** two of the best known pieces. How often do children get the chance to slide down a Picasso?

Lowbrow Landmarks

Chicago has its share of more unassuming sights too, including the mysterious **Totem Pole (Map 44)** along the lakefront and **Agora (Map 9)**, an army of headless metal people. Also easy to miss is the amazing artwork **The Body of Lake Michigan (Southwest)**. Look up as you go through the security checkpoint at Midway airport; it's quite impressive. Out to the south west is the **Union Stock Yard Gate (West)**, a reminder of the days referred to in Carl Sandburg's line "Hog Butcher for the world." You can then go sample some meat—the infamous cheezboiger—at the unpretentious **Billy Goat Tavern (Map 3)**.

Overrated Landmarks

With the nickname "The Windy City" derived from the hot air dispensed by earlier politicians, the city also has its fair share of overrated landmarks. The later iteration of **Soldier Field (Map 11)** fits the bill perfectly: if there were flying saucers in classical civilization, they would look something like this. Also registering on the ugly scale is the **James R. Thompson Center (Map 5)**. Enough said. However, the prize for most over-hyped attraction must go to **Navy Pier (Map 3)** with its wall-to-wall tourists and mediocre eateries. Consider yourself warned.

Underrated Landmarks

On the other hand, Chicago has a lot of well-kept secrets worth exploring. Home to a large collection of art glass by Louis Comfort Tiffany, the **Chicago Cultural Center (Map 5)** and **Macy's** (formerly Marshall Field's) **(Map 5)** on State Street both have spectacular domes. Continuing on the glass theme, the **America Windows (Map 6)** by Marc Chagall are another treat often overshadowed by the heavy-weight impressionist collection at the **Art Institute (Map 6)**. Another find is **The Newberry (Map 32)**, which sits quietly on Washington Square Park, but boasts a hive of activity inside: classes, concerts, and lectures. As for the Hyde Park area, check out the **University of Chicago (Map 19)** and **The Oriental Institute** there **(Map 19)**. You'll also find the **Nuclear Energy Sculpture (Map 19)** by Henry Moore, which commemorates the first nuclear reaction which took place here. Many of the first silent pictures, starring the likes of Charlie Chaplin and Gloria Swanson (back when they had faces) were filmed at Essenay Studio, before more copacetic weather pushed the film industry out west to a little place called Hollywood.

Television

2 WBBM (CBS) chicago.cbslocal.com
5 WMAQ (NBC) www.nbcchicago.com
7 WLS (ABC) abc7chicago.com
9 WGN (The CW) wgntv.com
11 WTTW (PBS) www.wttw.com
20 WYCC (PBS) www.wycc.org
26 WCIU (the U) www.wciu.com
32 WFLD (Fox) www.myfoxchicago.com
38 WCPX (ION Television) www.iontelevision.com
44 WSNS (Telemundo) www.telemundochicago.com
50 WPWR (MyNetworkTV) www.my50chicago.com
66 WGBO (Univision) chicago.univision.com

Print Media

Chicago Defender (312-225-2400, chicagodefender.com or @ChiDefender): Black community newspaper.

Chicago Innerview Magazine (773-904-8903, chicagoinnerview.com or @innerviewmag): Free monthly music mag previewing bands coming to concert in town.

Chicago Magazine (312-222-8999, chicagomag.com or @ChicagoMag): Upscale glossy mag.

Chicago Reader (312-222-6920, www.chicagoreader.com or @Chicago_Reader): Free weekly with listings.

Chicago Reporter (312-427-4830, www.chicagoreporter.com or @ChicagoReporter): Investigative reporting on issues of race, poverty, and social justice.

Chicago Sun-Times (312-321-3000, www.suntimes.com or @Suntimes): One of the big dailies; the White Sox to the Tribune's Cubs.

Chicago Tribune (800-874-2863, www.chicagotribune.com or @chicagotribune): The other big daily; the Cubs to the Sun-Times' White Sox.

Crain's Chicago Business (312-649-5200, www.chicagobusiness.com or @CrainsChicago): Business news.

Daily Herald (847-427-4300, www.dailyherald.com or @dailyherald): Suburban news.

Southtown Star (312-321-2333, southtownstar.com or @SouthtownStar): News for southsiders.

Hyde Park Herald (773-643-8533, hpherald.com or @HydeParkHerald): Local for Hyde Parkers.

N'Digo (312-822-0202, ndigo.com or @NDigoMagapaper): Black community weekly.

Newcity (312-715-8777, newcity.com or @newcity): Alternative free weekly.

The Onion (312-751-0503, www.theonion.com); See local listings in AV Club insert.

Red Eye (312-222-4970, www.redeyechicago.com or @redeyechicago): Commuter-targeted offshoot of the Trib for 20- and 30-somethings.

Today's Chicago Woman (312-951-7600, www.tcwmag.com or @TCWmag): Weekly for working women.

UR Chicago (www.urchicago.com or @urchicago) Free monthly local entertainment mag.

Windy City Times (773-871-7610, windycitytimes.com or @WindyCityTimes1): Gay-targeted news weekly.

Radio Stations

AM
560 WIND Talk
670 WSCR Sports
720 WGN News/Talk/Sports
780 WBBM News/Traffic
820 WCPT Progressive Talk
850 WAIT Religious
890 WLS News/Talk
1000 WMVP Sports/ESPN Radio
1110 WMBI Religious
1200 WRTO Spanish News/Talk
1220 WKRS ESPN Deportes
1300 WRDZ Radio Disney
1390 WGRB Gospel
1450 WCEV Talk (Ethnic)
1490 WPNA Polish
1500 WAKE Oldies
1510 WWHN Gospel
1570 WBGX Gospel
1590 WCGO Conservative Talk
1690 WVON Talk (African American)

FM
88.1 WCRX Columbia College
88.5 WHPK University of Chicago
88.7 WLUW Loyola University
89.3 WNUR Northwestern University
90.1 WMBI Christian
90.9 WDCB Jazz
91.5 WBEZ Chicago Public Radio/NPR
92.3 WPWX Urban
92.5 WCPY Progressive Talk/Dance Music
93.1 WXRT Alternative Rock
93.5 WVIX Spanish-language Urban
93.9 WLIT Adult Contemporary
94.7 WLS Classic Hits
95.5 WNUA Spanish-language
95.9 WREV Classic Hits
96.3 WBBM Top 40
96.7 WSSR Adult Contemporary
97.1 WDRV Classic Rock
97.9 WLUP Rock

98.7 WFMT Classical
99.5 WUSN Country
100.3 WILV Oldies
101.1 WKQX Alternative Rock
101.9 WTMX Adult Contemporary
102.7 WVAZ Urban Contemporary
103.1 WVIV Spanish-language
103.5 WKSC Top 40
103.9 WXRD Classic Rock
104.3 WJMK Classic Hits
105.1 WOJO Spanish-language
105.9 WCFS News
106.7 WPPN Spanish
107.5 WGCI Urban Contemporary

Essential Chicago Books

Native Son by Richard Wright; Gripping novel about a young black man on the South Side in the '30s.

Neon Wilderness by Nelson Algren; Short story collection set in Ukrainian Village and Wicker Park.

One More Time by Mike Royko; Collection of Royko's Tribune columns.

The Boss: Richard M. Daley by Mike Royko; Biography of the former Mayor.

The Jungle by Upton Sinclair; Gritty look at life in the meat-packing plants.

Adventures of Augie March by Saul Bellow; More Chicago in the '30s.

V.I. Warshawsky by Sara Paretsky; Mystery series firmly rooted in Chicago landscape.

50 Years at Hull House by Jane Addams; Story of the Near West Side.

Secret Chicago by Sam Weller; Off-the-beaten path guidebook.

Ethnic Chicago by Melvin Holli & Peter D'A. Jones; Insider's guide to Chicago's ethnic neighborhoods.

House on Mango Street by Sandra Cisneros; Short story collection about a Latina childhood in Chicago.

Our America: Life and Death on the South Side of Chicago by Lealan Jones, et al.; Life in the Chicago Projects as told by two schoolchildren.

The Coast of Chicago by Stuart Dybek; Short stories of Chicago denizens.

Hairstyles of the Damned by Joe Meno; Teen angst and punk rock in '80s Chicago.

Never a City So Real: A Walk in Chicago by Alex Kotlowitz; Modern reflection on the city of big shoulders.

American Pharaoh: Mayor Richard J. Daley by Adam Cohen and Elizabeth Taylor; Recent work that explores the life and works of Hizzoner the First.

Studs Lonigan by James T. Farrell; Growing up gritty and Irish in Washington Park, circa the early 20th century.

Chicago: The Second City by A. J. Liebling; Legendary New Yorker columnist and curmudgeon comes to the Windy City, gives it a new sobriquet, and tells all.

A Guide to Chicago's Murals by Mary Lackritz Gray; Murals, murals, and more murals.

The Pig and the Skyscraper by Marco D'Eramo; Wandering Italian sociologist comes to Chicago and explores the wide world of capitalism through Chicago's radical history, skyscrapers, and meat-processing plants.

The Devil in The White City by Erik Larson; Account of Chicago serial killer H.H. Holmes and the 1893 Chicago World's Fair.

Chicago Then and Now (Then & Now Thunder Bay) by Elizabeth McNulty; Explores Chicago's transformation and progression as a city.

The Lazarus Project by Alexander Hemon; A Bosnian writer investigates a historical Chicago crime.

Sin in the Second City by Karen Abbott; The colorful history of a Chicago bordello circa the 1900s.

Memory Mambo by Achy Obejas; Coming of age as a Cuban lesbian in Chicago.

The Time Traveler's Wife by Audrey Niffenegger; Break-out bestseller about time traveling love affair.

January

Chinese New Year: Chinatown; Sunday after the Chinese New Year (late Jan or mid-Feb).

February

Chicago Auto Show: McCormick Place; The nation's largest auto show, over 100 years old (early Feb, www. chicagoautoshow.com).

March

St Patrick's Day Parade: Columbus Drive; The Chicago River turns green—on purpose (Sat before St Patrick's Day, www. chicagostpatsparade.com).

Chicago Flower & Garden Show: Navy Pier; Escape from winter (mid-March, www.chicagoflower.com).

Black Women's Expo: McCormick Place; Empowering seminars, entertainment, and exhibits geared toward African American women (late March, www.theblackwomensexpo.com).

April

Chicago Latino Film Festival: Various venues; Festival screening the best in local and international Latino film (early Apr, chicagolatinofilmfestival.org).

Chicago Improv Fest: Various venues; Nation's best improv comedy acts descend on Chicago, the genre's birthplace (early Apr, chicagoimprovfestival.org).

May

Navy Pier Fireworks: Navy Pier; Fireworks light up the night sky every Wednesday and Saturday (May through Aug, www. navypier.com).

June

Do Division Street Fest & Sidewalk Sale: Division St from Damen to Leavitt; Annual event kicks off Chicago's summer street fest season (first weekend in June, www.do-divisionstreetfest.com).

Ribfest Chicago: Lincoln Ave & Irving Park Rd; Great music, people-watching, and of course 50,000 pounds of finger-lickin' good ribs (second weekend in June, www.ribfest-chicago.com).

Printers Row Lit Fest: Dearborn St, b/w Congress Pkwy & Polk St; Author talks and more at this outdoor street fair (second weekend in June, printersrowlitfest.org).

Andersonville Midsommarfest: Clark St, b/w Foster & Catalpa Aves; Ain't it Swede? (Second weekend in June, www. andersonville.org).

Chicago Pride Fest: Halsted b/w Addison and Grace Sts; Boystown comes to life with plenty of festivities to usher in Gay Pride Parade (weekend before Pride Parade, www.chicagopridecalendar.org).

Gay Pride Parade: Broadway/Halsted Sts b/w Montrose and Belmont; Hundreds of thousands show solidarity (last Sun in June, www.chicagopridecalendar.org).

57th Street Art Fair, 57th St b/w Kenwood and Woodlawn; Oldest juried art fair in the Midwest (First week in June, www.57thstreetartfair.org).

Chicago Blues Festival: Grant Park; As much about the soul food as the music (Second weekend in June, www. chicagobluesfestival.us).

Old Town Art Fair: Old Town Triangle District; Arts and crafts in varied media, entertainment, food and kids activities (mid-June, www.oldtownartfair.org).

Eye on India: Various venues; Experience the best of Indian culture and arts (mid-June, eyeonindia.com).

Grant Park Music Festival: Millennium Park; Free classical music concerts in the out of doors (mid-June through August, www.grantparkmusicfestival.com).

SummerDance: Grant Park; Summer-long series of seemingly every kind of dance style, including lessons, all free (late June to mid-September, chicagosummerdance.org).

Gospel Music Festival: Chicago Cultural Center & Ellis Park; local, national and international gospel performers (late June, www.chicagogospelmusicfestival.us).

Gold Coast Art Fair: Grant Park; Art for sale, entertainment, activities, and food (late June).

Family Fun Festival: Millennium Park; All manner of children's activities all summer long (late June through late Aug, @ MPFamilyFun).

July

Independence Day Fireworks: Navy Pier; See the night sky above the lakefront lit up in a spectacular light show (July 4, www.navypier.com).

International Festival of Life: Union Park; Celebrate the food, music, and arts of the African Diaspora on the South Side (July 4th weekend, www.festoflife.biz).

Taste of Chicago: Grant Park; Ginormous four-day food festival (early July, www.tasteofchicago.us).

Chicago Hip-Hop Heritage Month: Various venues; Where "New Beat" culture celebrates its past, present, and future (July 1-31, www.chihiphop.orq).

Taste of Lakeview: Lincoln Ave & W Belmont Ave; Live local music and food (second weekend in July).

Pitchfork Music Festival: Union Park; Taste-making three-day music extravaganza (mid-July, pitchforkmusicfestival.com).

Square Roots Festival: Welles Park; Old Town School partners with the Lincoln Square Chamber to showcase world music and craft brews (mid-July, squareroots.org).

Jeff Park Arts & Music Festival: Jefferson Park; Live music, performance, and food & drink (late July, www.jefffest.org).

Taste of River North: Ward Park; Food, music, and shopping along the Chicago River's North Branch (late July, www.tasteofrivernorth.com).

Fiesta Del Sol: Cermak Rd, b/w Throop & Morgan Sts; Largest Latino festival in the Midwest (last weekend in July, fiestadelsol.org).

August

Lollapalooza: Grant Park; Boffo multi-day, multi-stage music festival (early Aug, www.lollapalooza.com).

Bud Billiken Parade: King Dr/Washington Park; World's biggest African American parade (second Sat in Aug, www.budbillikenparade.org).

Northalsted Market Days: Halsted St b/w Belmont Ave & Addison St; Ridiculously large street fair with tons of live music and vendors (second weekend in Aug, www.northalsted.com).

Ginza Holiday Festival: Old Town; Annual festival celebrating Japanese culture and art (second weekend in Aug, www.ginzachicago.com).

Chicago Air and Water Show: North Avenue Beach; Superhuge free air show (third weekend in Aug, www.chicagoairandwatershow.us).

Chicago Dancing Festival: Millennium Park; Chicago's and the nation's acclaimed dance troupes strut their stuff (late Aug, www.chicagodancingfestival.com).

Bucktown Arts Fest: Holstein Park; Long-standing art fair showcasing over 200 artists each year (late Aug, bucktownartsfest.com).

North Coast Music Festival: Union Park; Three-day music festival with diverse acts, from rap to indie to electronic to jam bands (late Aug, www.northcoastfestival.com).

September

Taste of Polonia Festival: Copernicus Center, Jefferson Park; Polish food, music and culture (Labor Day weekend, topchicago.org).

African Festival of the Arts: Washington Park; African dance, music, arts, and exhibits (Labor Day weekend, africanfestivalchicago.com).

German Day Festival: Lincoln Plaza (Western, Lincoln & Leland Aves); Food, music and beer in association with yearly Von Steuben Parade (early Sept, www.germanday.com).

Riot Fest: Humboldt Park; Insane jam-packed roster of top-notch music acts (mid-Sept, riotfest.org).

World Music Festival: Various venues; Music acts from around the world, plus beer (mid-Sept, www.worldmusicfestivalchicago.org).

Children's Book Fair: Nichols Park; Children's authors, readings, and activities (late Sept, www.thechildrensbookfair.org).

October

Chicago International Film Festival: Various locations; The best in international cinema (www.chicagofilmfestival.com).

Open House Chicago: Various venues; Free, behind-the-scenes access to dozens of buildings and public spaces, including many usually closed to the public (mid-Oct, www.openhousechicago.org).

Halsted Halloween Parade: Halsted St b/w Belmont & Addison; Flamboyant Boystown costume extravaganza (www.northalsted.com).

November

Christkindlmarket: Daley Plaza; Monthlong German-themed outdoor winter market (late Nov-late Dec, www.christkindlmarket.com).

Departments

	Address	Phone	Map
1st District	1718 S State St	312-745-4290	11
9th District	3120 S Halsted St	312-747-8227	13
2nd District	5101 S Wentworth Ave	312-747-8366	15
12th District	1412 S Blue Island Ave	312-746-8396	26
14th District	2150 N California Ave	312-744-8290	27
18th District	1160 N Larrabee St	312-742-5870	31
24th District	6464 N Clark St	312-744-5907	34
20th District	5400 N Lincoln Ave	312-742-8714	35
19th District	2452 W Belmont Ave	312-744-5983	42
16th District	5151 N Milwaukee Ave	312-742-4510	Northwest
17th District	4461 N Pulaski Rd	312-742-4410	Northwest
25th District	5555 W Grand Ave	312-746-8605	Northwest
10th District	3315 W Ogden Ave	312-747-7511	West
11th District	3151 W Harrison St	312-746-8386	West
15th District	5701 W Madison St	312-746-8303	West
22nd District	1900 W Monterey Ave	312-745-0710	Southwest
7th District	1438 W 63rd St	312-747-8223	Southwest
8th District	3515 W 63rd St	312-747-8224	Southwest
4th District	2255 E 103rd St	312-747-8205	South
5th District	727 E 111th St	312-747-8210	South
6th District	7808 S Halsted St	312-745-3617	South

Chicago hospitals are as varied and interesting as the citizens they serve. Although you don't have to go far to find medical facilities in this city, finding quality medical care is another story.

The Illinois Medical District on the near southwest side is one of the largest healthcare centers in the world. Here you will find **Stroger Hospital (Map 25)** (basically the infamous Cook County Hospital with a facelift), home to the nation's first and oldest trauma unit. It is by far the busiest hospital in the area and serves a large and mostly indigent population. Unless you are in danger of certain demise, avoid Stroger's emergency department since waits of up to 12 hours for a non-life-threatening reason may bore you to death. The medical campus is also home to the **University of Illinois at Chicago (Map 25)**, **Rush University Medical Center (Map 25)**, and several smaller hospitals.

On the north side, your best bet is to go to **Advocate Illinois Masonic Medical Center (Map 43)** for anything serious or **Presence Saint Joseph Hospital (Map 44)** where you might get a room with a view of Lake Michigan. **Northwestern Memorial Hospital (Map 3)** is also a good choice if you are closer to downtown and/or if you have really good insurance. They also house several hospitals in the same campus, and if you break your neck craning to look up at all the pretty skyscrapers in the Streeterville 'hood, they have a first-rate spinal cord unit.

On the south side, the **University of Chicago (Map 19)** hospitals are second to none. A large and imposing set of buildings set in a somewhat dubious neighborhood, the hospital has a first-rate children's emergency department, world-renowned staff, and an excellent reputation.

Emergency Rooms	Address	Phone	Map
Northwestern Memorial	251 E Huron St	312-926-2000	3
Mercy	2525 S Michigan Ave	312-567-2000	11
Provident Hospital	500 E 51st St	312-572-2000	16
University of Chicago Medicine	5841 S Maryland Ave	888-824-0200	19
University of Chicago Children's	5721 S Maryland Ave	888-824-0200	19
AMITA Health Saints Mary and Elizabeth Medical Center	1431 N Claremont Ave	773-278-2000	21
AMITA Health Saints Mary and Elizabeth Medical Center	2233 W Division St	312-770-2000	21
University of Illinois Medical Center	1740 W Taylor St	312-996-7297	25
Jesse Brown VA Medical Center	820 S Damen Ave	312-569-8387	25
Rush University Medical Center	1620 W Harrison St	312-942-5800	25
John H Stroger Jr	1969 W Ogden Ave	312-864-6000	25
Swedish Covenant	5145 N California Ave	773-878-6888	38
Methodist Hospital of Chicago	5025 N Paulina St	773-271-9040	39
Vanguard Weiss Memorial	4646 N Marine Dr	773-878-8700	40
Thorek Memorial	850 W Irving Park Rd	773-525-6780	40
Advocate Illinois Masonic Medical Center	836 W Wellington Ave	773-975-1600	43
Presence Saint Joseph Hospital	2900 N Lake Shore Dr	773-665-3000	44
Saint Anthony	2875 W 19th St	773-484-1000	West
Mount Sinai	S California Ave & W 15th Pl	773-542-2000	West
La Rabida Children's	6501 S Promontory Dr	773-363-6700	South

Other Hospitals	Address	Phone	Map
Lurie Children's Hospital of Chicago	225 E Chicago Ave	312-227-4000	3
Rehabilitation Institute of Chicago	345 E Superior St	312-238-1000	3
Lurie Children's Hospital of Chicago	225 E Chicago Ave	312-227-4000	30
Kindred Chicago-Lakeshore	6130 N Sheridan Rd	773-381-1222	37
Kindred	2544 W Montrose Ave	773-267-2622	38
Chicago Lakeshore Hospital	4840 N Marine Dr	773-878-9700	40

Post Offices	Address	Phone	Map
US Post Office	222 Merchandise Mart Plz	312-321-0233	2
US Post Office	540 N Dearborn St	312-644-3919	2
US Post Office	100 W Randolph St	312-263-2686	5
US Post Office	211 S Clark St	312-427-0016	5
US Post Office	433 W Harrison St	312-692-6120	7
US Post Office	2345 S Wentworth Ave	312-326-6440	10
US Post Office	2035 S State St	312-225-0218	11
US Post Office	4101 S Halsted St	773-247-0731	15
US Post Office	4601 S Cottage Grove Ave	773-924-6658	16
US Post Office	700 E 61st St	773-493-4047	18
US Post Office	1510 E 55th St	773-324-0896	19
US Post Office	116 S Western Ave	312-243-2560	23
US Post Office	1859 S Ashland Ave	312-733-4750	26
US Post Office	2339 N California Ave	773-489-2855	27
US Post Office	2901 W Armitage Ave	773-772-3200	27
US Post Office	2405 N Sheffield Ave	773-929-7041	29
US Post Office	875 N Michigan Ave	312-644-0485	32
US Post Office	1723 W Devon Ave	773-743-2650	34
US Post Office	7617 N Paulina St	773-743-2830	34
US Post Office	2522 W Lawrence Ave	773-561-3330	38
US Post Office	2011 W Montrose Ave	773-472-1314	39
US Post Office	1343 W Irving Park Rd	773-327-0345	40
US Post Office	4850 N Broadway St	773-561-1720	40
US Post Office	3750 N Kedzie Ave	773-539-6210	41
US Post Office	3024 N Ashland Ave	773-248-8495	43
US Post Office	4749 N Bernard St	773-583-9530	Northwest
US Post Office	3401 W Devon Ave	773-583-8640	Northwest
US Post Office	3933 W North Ave	312-486-7218	West
US Post Office	2302 S Pulaski Rd	773-277-3070	West
US Post Office	7436 S Exchange Ave	773-375-2180	South
US Post Office	611 W 63rd St	773-873-0790	South

The Chicago Public Library (www.chipublib.org or @chipublib) rose out of the ashes of the Great Fire of 1871 with an assist from England, whose citizens banded together to donate 8,000 volumes to start a new free library system. The first Chicago Public Library branch opened in 1873 at the corner of LaSalle and Adams Streets in a water tank that survived the fire. Today the system serves Chicago residents with 80 locations across the city and a collection of more than 5 million.

With the **Harold Washington Library (Map 5)** as their anchor, two regional libraries, **Sulzer Regional Library (Map 39)** in Lincoln Square and the Southwest side's **Woodson Library (Map 59)**, serve as backup reference and research collections. It is worth noting that Harold Washington Library has a few stand-out exhibits, including one of the history of the blues in the city and, of course, one on the man himself, Chicago's first African American mayor. Neighborhood branches are geared towards the communities they serve: **Chinatown (Map 10)** has an impressive collection of Asian studies material and literature, the **Rogers Park (Map 34)** branch features a significant Russian-language selection, and Boystown's **John Merlo (Map 44)** collection houses a considerable offering of gay literature and studies. Many of the smaller branches have a decent selection of juvenile materials as well as career guidance and adult popular literature (and Internet access). Architecturally, some of the more interesting branches include the **Chicago Bee (Map 14)** branch, the former newspaper headquarters that serves as a neighborhood landmark for Bronzeville, and the historic **Pullman (South)** branch, specializing in the history of the Pullman district. Chicago's first library branch, the neo-classical **Blackstone (Map 17)** library, is named after the railroad magnate-philanthropist Timothy Beach Blackstone. Families and schools should take advantage of the Chicago Public Library System's Kids Museum Passports, available only to adult Chicago residents with a valid library card. You can check out any of their free passports using your library card just like you would any other item, and the loan is good for one week. The pass entitles entry for up to four people to any one of the 15 participating cultural institutions in the city. If you don't have access to a library card, you can still partake in a bit of book-love by checking out one of the many free lectures or readings that take place at the Harold Washington Library and the galaxy of branch outposts throughout the year. Before visiting Chicago, visitors can also peruse some of the nice digital exhibits the Library has created at digital.chipublib.org. Here they will find tributes to the late, great Mayor Harold Washington and some interesting exhibits on the history of the city's sewer system (well, interesting to a certain type of person, at least).

Chicago also has many excellent research libraries and university libraries, one of which is the independent **Newberry** library **(Map 32)**, established in 1887. It shelves rare books, manuscripts, and maps, and hosts the raucous annual Bughouse Square debates in late July. Another unique institution, the **Pritzker Military Library (Map 5)**, tells the story of the citizen soldier through an extensive book collection, and exhibits of photographs, medals, uniforms and other artifacts. Chicago's universities and colleges generally welcome the public to their libraries during specified hours, but it's best to call first and check.

Library	Address	Phone	Map
Albany Park Public Library	3401 W Foster Ave	773-539-5450	38
Asher Library-Spertus Institute	610 S Michigan Ave	312-322-1700	9
Bezazian Public Library	1226 W Ainslie St	312-744-0019	40
Blackstone Public Library	4904 S Lake Park Ave	312-747-0511	17
Bucktown–Wicker Park Public Library	1701 N Milwaukee Ave	312-744-6022	28
Budlong Woods Public Library	5630 N Lincoln Ave	312-742-9590	35
Canaryville Public Library	642 W 43rd St	312-747-0644	15
Carter G. Woodson Regional Public Library	9525 S Halstead St	312-747-6900	49
Chicago Bee Public Library	3647 S State St	312-747-6872	14
Chinatown Public Library	2100 S Wentworth Ave	312-747-8013	10
Coleman Public Library	731 E 63rd St	312-747-7760	18
Hall Public Library	4801 S Michigan Ave	312-747-2541	16
Harold Washington Public Library	400 S State St	312-747-4300	5
John Merlo Public Library	644 W Belmont Ave	312-744-1139	44
King Public Library	3436 S Dr Martin Luther King Jr Dr	312-747-7543	14
Library of Columbia College	624 S Michigan Ave	312-369-7900	9
Lincoln Park Public Library	1150 W Fullerton Ave	312-744-1926	29
Lincoln-Belmont Public Library	1659 W Melrose St	312-744-0166	42
Logan Square Public Library	3030 W Fullerton Ave	312-744-5295	27
Lozano Public Library	1805 S Loomis St	312-746-4329	26
Mabel Manning Public Library	6 S Hoyne Ave	312-746-6800	23
Malcolm X College Library	1900 W Van Buren St	312-850-7244	23
Near North Public Library	310 W Division St	312-744-0991	31
The Newberry Library	60 W Walton St	312-943-9090	32
Northtown Public Library	6800 N Western Ave	312-744-2292	33
Poetry Foundation	61 W Superior St	312-787-7070	2
Richard J. Daley Public Library	3400 S Halsted St	312-747-8990	13
Rogers Park Public Library	6907 N Clark St	312-744-0156	34
Roosevelt Public Library	1336 W Taylor St	312-746-5656	26
Sulzer Public Library	4455 N Lincoln Ave	312-744-7616	39
The Swedenborg Library	77 W Washington St, Rm 1700	312-346-7003	5
University of Chicago Harper Memorial Library	1116 E 59th St	773-834-7943	19
University of Illinois at Chicago Library	801 S Morgan St	312-996-2716	26
Uptown Public Library	929 W Buena Ave	312-744-8400	40

Useful Contacts

Chicago Board of Elections: 312-269-7900,
www.chicagoelections.com or @ChicagoElection
Illinois State Board of Elections: 217-782-4141,
www.elections.il.gov
ComEd: 800-334-7661, www.comed.com or @ComEd
People's Gas: 866-556-6001 (Emergencies: 866-556-6002),
www.peoplesgasdelivery.com
Office of the Mayor: 311, mayor.cityofchicago.org
or @ChicagosMayor
Governor's Office: 312-814-2121 or www.illinois.gov/gov

Helpful Websites and Local Blogs

www.beachwoodreporter.com or @BeachwoodReport: Analysis of
local and national politics.
chicagoist.com or @Chicagoist: Local news/events blog.
chicityclerk.com or @chicityclerk: Office of the Chicago City Clerk;
renew your city sticker online!
www.chicagorecycling.org: Where to recycle anything and
everything in Chicago.
www.choosechicago.com or @ChooseChicago: Official tourism
information about attractions, festivals, events, restaurants, and
hotels.
www.cityofchicago.org: Helpful all-purpose guide to city services.
chicago.craigslist.org: Everything from casual jobs to rental
encounters.
www.dnainfo.com/chicago or @DNAinfoCHI: Local & breaking
news.
chicago.eater.com or @eaterchicago: Go-to site for restaurant/
bar news.
www.encyclopedia.chicagohistory.org: An astounding resource,
entirely digitized.
forgottenchicago.com or @ForgottenChi: Side streets and byways
of the city.
www.gapersblock.com or @gapersblock: A popular Chicago
web-publication detailing local news, fun events, and cool places
in the city.
chicago.metromix.com or @MetromixCHI: City guide put out by
the Trib.
pitchfork.com or @pitchfork: Indie music site and sponsors of the
grooviest music fest ever.
www.reddit.com/r/chicago: Reddit Chicago.
www.timeout.com/chicago or @TimeOutChicago: The latest and
greatest happenings around town: new restaurants, music listings,
you name it.
www.yochicago.com or @YoChicago: Real estate and development
news.

Taxi Cabs

American United: 773-327-6161
Flash Cab: 773-561-1444
Yellow Cab: 773-907-0020
Sun Taxi: 773-736-3883

Chicago Timeline

1779: Jean-Baptiste Point du Sable establishes Chicago's first
       permanent settlement.
1803: U.S. Army constructs Fort Dearborn, which is later destroyed
       by Native American forces allied with British during War of
       1812, and rebuilt in 1816.
1818: Illinois is admitted into the union.
1833: Chicago incorporates as a town of 350 people, bordered by
       Kinzie, Des Plaines, Madison, and the lakefront.
1837: Chicago incorporates as a city. The population is 4,170.
       Ogden becomes the city's first mayor.
1851: Northwestern University is founded.
1856: Fort Dearborn is demolished.
1860: Republican Party nominates Abraham Lincoln for president at
       Chicago's first political convention.
1865: Merry Christmas! Union Stockyards open on Christmas Day.

1869: Water tower is completed.
1871: Great Chicago Fire!
1885: World's first "skyscraper," the 9-story Home Insurance building,
       goes up on La Salle Street.
1886: Haymarket Riots. Eight Chicago policemen are killed.
1889: Jane Addams opens Hull House.
1892: World's first elevated trains begin operation.
1893: Columbia Exposition celebrates 400th anniversary of
       Columbus's discovery of America.
1907: Physicist Abraham Michelson is first American to win Nobel
1910: Original Comiskey Park opens.
1914: Wrigley Field opens.
1927: $750,000 donated to honor Clarence Buckingham with
       fountain.
1929: John G. Shedd presents Shedd Aquarium as gift to city.
1930: Adler Planetarium opens through a gift from Max Adler.
1930: Merchandise Mart built by Marshall Field.
1931: Jane Addams becomes first female to win Nobel Peace Prize.
1931: Al Capone sent to prison for 11 years for evading taxes.
1934: John Dillinger shot by FBI outside Biograph Theater.
1955: O'Hare International Airport opens.
1958: End of the line: Last streetcar in Chicago stops operating.
1968: Democratic National Convention riots.
1971: Chicago Union Stock Yards are closed.
1974: Sears Tower is completed.
1983: Harold Washington elected first black mayor.
1995: A heat wave contributed to the death of over 700 Chicagoans.
1997: City Council absolves Mrs. O'Leary's cow of blame for Great
       Chicago Fire.
1998: Six-peat! Bulls win sixth championship in eight years.
2003: Four-peat! Richard M. Daley re-elected for historic fourth
       term!
2004: Millennium Park opens.
2005: White Sox win World Series; Cubs fans weep.
2007: Chicago pitched as US bid for 2016 Olympics.
2008: Gov. Rod Blagojevich arrested on corruption charges.
2011: Mayor Emanuel's election signals the end of the Daley era.

Essential Chicago Movies

Northside 777 (1948)
Man with the Golden Arm (1955)
Raisin in the Sun (1961)
Medium Cool (1969)
The Sting (1973)
Blues Brothers (1980)
Risky Business (1983)
Ferris Bueller's Day Off (1986)
Henry: Portrait of a Serial Killer (1986)
Adventures in Babysitting (1987)
Planes, Trains and Automobiles (1987)
The Untouchables (1987)
When Harry Met Sally (1989)
Backdraft (1991) Candyman (1992)
Wayne's World (1992)
The Fugitive (1993)
Hoop Dreams (1994)
Mission: Impossible (1996)
My Best Friend's Wedding (1997)
High Fidelity (2000)
Save the Last Dance (2001)
What Women Want (2000)
Barbershop (2002)
Chicago (2002)
Road to Perdition (2002)
The Company (2002)
I Am Trying to Break Your Heart (2003)
Batman Begins (2005)
The Weatherman (2005)
The Lake House (2006)
The Break-Up (2006)
Stranger than Fiction (2006)
The Dark Knight (2008)
Public Enemies (2009)
Transformers 3 (2011)

Serving the nation's busiest convention center, most Chicago hotels are designed for business travelers, complete with expense-account prices. Even a modest downtown room can be outrageously steep.

Livin' Large: For a special urban splurge, book a suite at one of Chicago's palace hotels, such as the **Ritz-Carlton (Map 32)**, **Four Seasons (Map 32)**, **Peninsula (Map 2)**, or **Waldorf Astoria (Map 32)**.

Classic: The Drake (Map 32) is the classic Chicago hotel, and a landmark for drivers heading downtown from the northside via Lake Shore Drive. The **Allerton Hotel (Map 3)** is an architecturally significant Chicago landmark circa 1934, restored to its former glory after years of decline. In the Loop, the **Palmer House Hilton's (Map 5)** lobby is all divans and chandeliers. More notoriously historic, the **Hilton Chicago (Map 9)** was the site of the 1968 Democratic National Convention.

Modern: Hip travelers will want to stay at one of downtown's two W hotels, either the **W Chicago Lakeshore (Map 3)** or **W Chicago City Center (Map 5)** Hotels, or the **Sofitel (Map 32)**, or the **Hard Rock Hotel (Map 6)**, located in the vintage Union Carbide building on Michigan Avenue. **Hotel Sax (Map 2)**, located next to the corn cob Marina Towers, boasts folk-art decorated rooms and a Sunday gospel brunch.

Boutique: Located in a historic landmark, the **Hotel Burnham (Map 5)** is a lovely boutique hotel near the heart of Chicago's theater district. Burnham and its Kimpton Hotel Group sisters, **Hotel Allegro (Map 5)** and **Hotel Monaco (Map 5)**, also in the theater district, feature free wine receptions every evening for hotel guests. **Hotel Blake (Map 8)** on Printer's Row offers boutique-type amenities with handsome rooms, although the views can leave a bit to the imagination.

Cheap: Steer budget-conscious out-of-town guests toward the **Travelodge Downtown (Map 8)**. It's not eye candy, but the location (just off Michigan Avenue, between Millennium Park and the Museum Campus) makes it quite a deal. Around the corner at the **Congress Plaza Hotel (Map 9)**, the site of a decade-long strike by cleaning and maintenance workers, believed to have been the longest hotel strike of all time.

Good values can also be had away from downtown. **City Suites (Map 43)**, and its "Neighborhood Inns of Chicago" partners, the **Majestic (Map 44)**, and **Willows (Map 44)**, in Chicago's Lakeview and Lincoln Park neighborhoods, offer small hotel charm at reasonable rates. If those are still above your station, **Heart o' Chicago Motel (Map 37)** is skipping distance from the Edgewater White Castle and a short walk from the vivacious Andersonville strip.

B &Bs: Compared to cities of similar expanse, Chicago doesn't offer much by way of B &B's. **The Wheeler Mansion (Map 11)**, near McCormick Place, is luxurious and antique-filled, with fireplaces, custom baths and bedding, and ridiculously high ceilings. The more modest **Wicker Park B &B (Map 21)** dishes up a good breakfast—the owners also own the nearby Alliance bakery, where morning sweets are baked fresh daily. The **Old Town Bed and Breakfast (Map 4)**, run by the friendly and eccentric Serritella family, features stylish bedrooms and a common area with a grand piano, formal dining room, and deluxe gourmet kitchen available for guests to use—it's where a John Cheever character would bunk. On the Southside, the quaint **Benedictine Bed & Breakfast (Map 12)** is run by monks from the adjacent Monastery of the Holy Cross.

Real Cheap: There are also three youth hostels in Chicago open to the public with rates under $50 a night for card-carrying International Youth Hostel members. For deals, Hot Rooms is a Chicago-based reservation service offering low-rates on undersold rooms: www.hotrooms.com.

Flop House: Before the construction of I-90/94, Lincoln Avenue was the main access point to the city from all points north. In the 20s-40s, a bunch of motels sprouted up on north Lincoln to serve truckers and other travelers entering the city. For a while these vintage motels were popular cheap spots for touring indie bands on a budget; eventually most of them become too seedy for even traveling indie bands on a budget. Many of the motels have fallen prey to the wrecking ball; a few, including the local landmark, The **Diplomat Motel (Map 35)** and the **Apache Motel (Map 35)** remain, frequented, we assume, by people having affairs.

As a general rule, if a Chicago hotel price seems too good to be true, it is. Chicago is chock-a-block with run-down SROs providing semi-temporary housing to the down-on-their-luck, and extremely short-term housing to the occasional unwitting and unfortunate foreign traveler, cheapskate, or hapless student.

Map 2 • Near North / River North

		Phone	Price
Peninsula Chicago Hotel	108 E Superior St	312-337-2888	$$$$

Map 3 • Streeterville / Mag Mile

Allerton Hotel Chicago	701 N Michigan Ave	312-440-1500	$$
W Chicago Lakeshore	644 N Lake Shore Dr	312-943-9200	$$$

Map 5 • The Loop

Hampton Inn Majestic Theater District	22 W Monroe St	312-332-5052	$$
Hilton Palmer House	17 E Monroe St	312-726-7500	$$$
Hotel Allegro	171 W Randolph St	312-236-0123	$$$
Hotel Monaco	225 N Wabash Ave	312-960-8500	$$$
Staypineapple	1 W Washington St	312-940-7997	$$$
W Chicago City Center	172 W Adams St	312-332-1200	$$$

Map 8 • South Loop / Printers Row / Dearborn Park

Hotel Blake	500 S Dearborn St	844-800-5293	$$
Travelodge	65 E Harrison St	312-574-3335	$

Map 9 • South Loop / South Michigan Ave

Congress Plaza Hotel	520 S Michigan Ave	312-427-3800	$
Hilton Chicago	720 S Michigan Ave	312-922-4400	$$

Map 11 • South Loop / McCormick Place

The Wheeler Mansion	2020 S Calumet Ave	312-945-2020	$$$

Map 12 • Bridgeport (West)

		Phone	Price
Benedictine Bed and Breakfast	3111 S Aberdeen St	773-927-7424	$$

Map 21 • Wicker Park / Ukrainian Village

Wicker Park Inn B&B	1331 N Wicker Park Ave	773-486-2743	$$

Map 32 • Gold Coast / Mag Mile

Drake Hotel	140 E Walton St	312-787-2200	$$$
Four Seasons Hotel Chicago	120 E Delaware Pl	312-280-8800	$$$$
Ritz Carlton Hotel	160 E Pearson St	312-266-1000	$$$$
Sofitel Water Tower	20 E Chestnut St	312-324-4000	$$$
Waldorf Astoria	11 E Walton St	312-646-1300	$$$$

Map 35 • Arcadia Terrace / Peterson Park

Apache Motel	5535 N Lincoln Ave	773-728-9400	$
Diplomat Motel	5230 N Lincoln Ave	773-271-5400	$

Map 37 • Edgewater / Andersonville

Heart O' Chicago Motel	5990 N Ridge Ave	773-271-9181	$

Map 43 • Wrigleyville / East Lakeview

City Suites Hotel	933 W Belmont Ave	773-404-3400	$$

Map 44 • East Lakeview

The Willows Hotel	555 W Surf St	773-528-8400	$$

Chicago is a kid's kind of town. From sandy beaches and leafy parks to diverse downtown museums, concerts, and suburban attractions, Chicago's options for family fun are non-stop—just like kids. And the best part about Chicago family-style is that lots of stuff is free, or practically free. Speaking of which, don't forget the Chicago Public Library's fantastic Kids Museum Passport: it's a pass the library loans for up to a week at a time providing families with free admission to over a dozen of Chicago's premier (read: pricey) cultural institutions, including the biggies at the Museum Campus plus the Art Institute, Peggy Notebaert Museum, and Chicago History Museum.

Cultural

Chicago's cultural institutions do their part to make their offerings accessible to families. The **Art Institute of Chicago (Map 6)** has loads of stuff for kids, from the doll house-sized Thorne Miniature Rooms to the shiny medieval armor to the great Ryan Education Center, whose interactive exhibitions introduce children to art from other cultures, time periods, and world-wide geographic regions. "Edutaining" art books and masterpiece puzzles in the children's library reinforce visual learning. Free kids programs and drawing workshops are also held throughout museum galleries and free children's artmaking events and gallery walks take place frequently. The **Chicago Symphony Orchestra** (www.cso.org) offers a Family Matinee Series, with kid-friendly activities and discounted rates. Go in costume to the annual Hallowed Haunts concert, where skeletons rattle and ghosts boogie to thematically appropriate compositions.

For theater, there isn't a bad seat in the house at the **Marriott Theatre's Theatre for Young Audiences** performances (www.marriotttheatre.com). The intimate arena theater welcomes pint-sized audiences and encourages actors to roam the aisles interacting with kids. Post-performance, the actors conduct Q &A answering kids' theatrical questions. The special one-hour shows—both original works and adapted children's works—run throughout the season.

Meanwhile, **Jazz Showcase (Map 8)** is famous for its family-friendly Sunday 4 pm matinees where top musicians jam. Non-alcoholic beverages and snacks served and there is a discounted adult admission (children 12 and under are free). For budding film buffs, each fall there's the **Children's International Film Festival** (www.cicff.org), which features hundreds of witty, ingenious long- and short-form children's movies from around the world, some created by kids. Filmmakers, directors, and animators teach seminars for movie lovers of all ages.

Science/Educational

Chicago's **Museum Campus (Map 9, 11)** is the closest you'll come to an educational amusement park. Dinosaurs, live sharks, giant mechanical insects, ancient mummies, and exploding stars are just a handful of adventures your kids will encounter on the lakefront's brainy peninsula home to The **Field Museum**, **Adler Planetarium**, and **Shedd Aquarium**. Check with each institution for its free admission days and special family programs. The **Museum of Science and Industry (Map 20)** is the ultimate hands-on learning experience for families, and merits multiple visits. Favorite exhibits include the 1,400-foot-long, 20-train model railroad in The Great Train Story exhibit, an actual United Airlines 727 jet, a working Coal Mine, and the Idea Factory workshop packed with gears, cranks, and water toys.

For children excited about the cosmos there's the **Cernan Earth and Space Center (Northwest)** on the Triton College campus in River Grove (www.triton.edu/cernan). Named after Apollo astronaut Eugene Cernan, a native Chicagoan and the last man on the moon, this cozy planetarium's intimate dome theater features kids programs, earth and sky shows, and laser light shows, as well as monthly sky watch and lectures. There's also a nice small space-related museum (free admission) and great celestial gift shop.

It's all about the Benjamins at the **Federal Reserve Bank of Chicago Money Museum (Map 5)**, where kids learn the power of pocket change through hands-on and computerized exhibits explaining the Fed's role in managing the nation's money. Kids love the rotating, million-dollar cube of cash and $50,800 coin pit. Sneak a peak into the vault stocked with $9 million, trace our country's currency history, and learn how to identify fake bills. And best of all, unlike its subject matter, admission is free. Meanwhile, at **Fermilab** (www.fnal.gov) in Batavia you can not only learn about the smallest building blocks of matter at the particle laboratory but also release energy outdoors on the nature trails at the 680-acre campus. Rare species of butterflies, plants, birds, and baby buffaloes live on the rural grounds; guided prairie tours are offered in the summer, picnickers are always welcome, and pond fishing is also available. Kids experience life on the Midwestern prairie at Naperville's **Naper Settlement** (www. napersettlement.org), an outdoor living history museum recreating a 19th-century agrarian community, with working blacksmith shop, post office, and school house manned by costumed interpreters. seasonal programs cater to kids with games, pony rides, and child-friendly entertainment. And the engaging hands-on exhibits and craft sessions at the **Mitchell Museum of the American Indian (Evanston)** are a great way to teach kids about the rich culture and history of Native American life.

Chicago boasts several excellent children's museums. Navy Pier's massive **Chicago Children's Museum** has 15 permanent engaging exhibits for toddlers to pre-teens (www.chichildrensmuseum.org). Museum admission free on Thursday nights from 5 pm to 8 pm. (Navy Pier also has a nice IMAX theater.) Although modest, **Wonder Works (Oak Park)**, located about half a mile west of Chicago's city limits, is far more accessible for many city families than the Chicago Children's Museum at Navy Pier and boasts the triple advantages of being low cost, low key, and packed with friendly volunteers (www.wonder-works.org). **Kohl Children's Museum of Greater Chicago** (www.kohlchildrensmuseum.org) has many permanent exhibits focusing on self-directed play in everyday milieus, from a grocery store to a veterinarian's office to a restaurant. And the **DuPage Children's Museum** in Naperville (dupagechildrens. org) is loaded with hands-on, action-packed exhibits keeps pre-schoolers with nano-second attention spans exploring until exhaustion.

Nature and the Outdoors

Don't tell the animals, but zoos were made for children, and Chicago has two excellent ones. **Lincoln Park Zoo (Map 30)** is the nation's oldest free zoo, and it hasn't rested on its laurels. In addition to usual high-value target zoo favorites like graceful giraffes, lumbering elephants, and giant hissing Madagascar cockroaches, the specifically kid-friendly Pritzker Family Children's Zoo features exhibits focusing on North American animals. Additional family favorites are the Farm-in-the-Zoo, lion house, sea lion pool, and the carousel. Family programs include the popular Sleep Under the Skyscrapers where families get to experience the zoo's nighttime rituals followed by camping on the zoo's South Lawn. **Brookfield Zoo** is Chicago's largest zoo, and its Hamill Family Play Zoo offers interactive programs on animal antics and opportunities to pet kid-friendly creatures

babysat by helpful docents. In addition, there are family and child educational classes offered, plus summer camps and special holiday events.

Chicago is also blessed with several great botanical gardens. The Learning Campus at the **Chicago Botanic Garden** hosts programming and activities for all ages, but has an especially strong children's component. The Grunsfeld Children's Growing Garden affords kids the opportunity to learn about gardening firsthand. where they can dig for worms and plant seeds. Late May through October, come for the Model Railroad Garden where model trains puff through a garden of America's best loved landmarks. **Garfield Park Conservatory (West)** also features great family programming at both the Elizabeth Morse Genius Children's Garden and the Conservatory's Play and Grow Garden.

The Peggy Notebaert Nature Museum (Map 30) is filled with kid-friendly exhibits and activities. Kids especially delight in Butterfly Haven, a soaring tropical greenhouse habitat, home to hundreds of exotic winged beauties from around the world. **The Morton Arboretum** in Lisle (www.mortonarb.org) features 1,700 acres of forests, meadows, gardens, and wetlands. The Children's Garden features many themed gardens and activities, and the Arboretum offers kid-friendly guided tours and year-round classes. The annual Fall Color Festival includes a fun Scarecrow Trail around Meadow Lake. Closer to the city, the nature preserve at **North Park Village Nature Center (Northwest)** will make you think you're a hundred miles from nowhere—the nature paths throughout the 46 acres of rolling woods and wetlands sometimes have roaming deer and owls above. The popular EcoExplorers summer camps feature nature-themed games and activities for kids aged five to 14.

In Wheaton, the 15-acre **Cantigny Park**, named after a World War I battle, is home to the First Division Museum showcasing the history of the famed US Army's 1st Infantry Division and *Chicago Tribune* founder's Robert R. McCormick Mansion Museum. After clambering over the cannons, kids can stop to smell the flowers blooming in the manicured gardens. Family programs and concerts scheduled year-round. Nearby is the **Cantigny Golf Course** (www.cantignygolf.com), offering junior golf instruction and a 9-hole Youth Links Course.

Sports and Active Recreation

With two Major League teams, Chicago always has baseball, making it a great summer activity for families—and especially if your eyes welled up at certain key moments of *Field of Dreams*. **Wrigley Field (Map 43)** of course is almost a rite of passage, but **Guaranteed Rate Field (Map 13)** is also great—its Fundamentals play area is a 15,000 square-feet interactive baseball diamond and skills area perched above the left field concourse. Further afield, minor league games are a great low-key option for a fraction of the price. Two in the Chicago region are the **Kane County Cougars** in Geneva (www.kccougars.com) and **Schaumburg Boomers** (www.boomersbaseball.com). Both independent teams offer cozy, intimate settings, charming entertainment, and cheap eats. The area also has a minor league hockey team, the **Chicago Wolves**, who play in nearby Rosemont (www.chicagowolves.com). And for even more wholesome fun, hit the race track at **Arlington International** (www.arlingtonpark.com) for its Sunday Family Days. Each Sunday from Memorial Day through Labor Day kiddos can enjoy pony rides, face painting, and a petting zoo.

But don't be content to just sit around. The Chicago area is all about active recreation, from its lakefront to its trails and bike-friendly streets. **Pirates' Cove** in Elk Grove Village is a buccaneer-themed playground that verges on an amusement park. The shady spot is a fun respite from the Chicago heat, and kids love to scramble up the Smugglers Cove, ride a rope-and-pulley griffin, and paddle around a wee lagoon. It's also a great low-cost birthday party site. Another great spot for the little ones is the **Exploritorium** in Skokie **(Northwest)** is an indoor playground unlike any you've ever seen. From finger paints and water games to costumes and a multi-storied jungle gym, this facility tuckers tykes out. The climbing gym outfitted with twisting ropes, tubes, and tunnels even brings out the Tarzan in parents. Although it's a public facility, there is a modest admission fee (www.skokieparks.org/exploritorium).

For water-related play, the Chicago Park District operates numerous free water parks with arching jets, umbrella sprays, pipe falls, and bubble jets in Chicago's neighborhood parks and beaches. In Oak Brook, the **Oak Brook Family Aquatic Center** offers up wet, wild fun for the whole family at their splashy indoor aquatic facility where there is a zero-depth pool and slide for tadpoles as well as an Olympic-sized pool for bigger fish. Special swim events include watery holiday-themed parties, arts and crafts, water sports days, and "dive-in" movie nights where you can watch a family flick from your inflatable raft. At **Pelican Harbor Indoor/Outdoor Aquatic Park** in Bolingbrook kids zip down thrilling water slides (one 75 feet tall), float on inner tubes, and plunge into the diving well. There is a large zero-depth pool for little swimmers, lap pool, sand volleyball, whirlpool, and concessions (www.bolingbrookparks.org).

Chicago is of course good at all things winter, so when it snows head down to the **Soldier Field Sledding Hill**, a free, giant sledding hill with frozen lake views. BYO ride and bundle up for frigid lakefront winds. For ice skating, the **McCormick Tribune Ice Rink** in **Millennium Park (Map 6)** affords the opportunity to skate in the shadow of architectural landmark buildings lining the Mag Mile. Open daily, admission is free to the 16,000-square-foot rink; skate rental and warming room available on-site.

Seasonal

The summer **Family Fun Festival** in **Millennium Park (Map 6)** offers a full slate of free programming for kids of all ages. From late June to late August enjoy daily performances and storytelling, including sing-alongs and games with Wiggleworms instructors from the Old Town School of Folk Music, and hands-on craft and gardening activities led by local museums and cultural institutions. Coming on the heels of National Kite Month, the **Chicago Kids and Kites Festival** at the beginning of May tests the Windy City's reputation. Held on Cricket Hill in Lincoln Park near the intersection of Lake Shore Drive and Montrose Ave, kite flying professionals and instructors help enthusiasts of all ages construct kites and fly them for free.

Come fall, **Sonny Acres Farm** in West Chicago (www.sonnyacres.com) is the place to go for Halloween fun. From mid-September through October there are jack-o-lanterns for carving, homemade pies, decorative Thanksgiving and Halloween displays, and a killer costume shop. Kids love the mountains of pumpkins, crunchy caramel apples, scary hay rides, youngster carnival rides, and haunted barns (one for tiny tykes and another for blood-thirsty teens). Admission and parking are free; attractions require tickets. At the holiday season the **Winter Wonderland Holiday Light Festival** (www.luc.edu/cuneo/holidaylightshow) on the grounds of Cuneo Mansion and Gardens in Vernon Hills is the largest drive-through Christmas display in the region, featuring millions of lights in various tableaus. Festival runs first Friday after Thanksgiving through New Year's weekend from 6 pm to 10 pm nightly.

Classes

Many of the city's fine cultural institutions have stellar, kid-focused curricula and host popular summer camps. Chicago and suburban park districts offer solid sports instruction, dance, and crafts classes. But private specialty schools also instruct many pint-sized prodigies.

The **Academy of Movement and Music** (605 Lake St, Oak Park, 708-848-2329, www.academyofmovementandmusic.com) offers popular dance and movement classes, including a pre-school curriculum and music classes. **Dennehy School of Irish Dance** (2555 W 111th St, 773-881-3990, www.dennehydancers.com) is a South Side Irish institution, churning out high-stepping Irish dancers; its most-famous pupil so far is Michael Flatley of stage hits *Riverdance* and *Lord of the Dance*. **Hubbard Street Dance Studio** (1147 W Jackson Blvd, 312-850-9766, www.hubbardstreetdance. org) has year-round classes, workshops, and camps for children from 1½ through 16 years old. Finally, **Ruth Page Center for the Arts** (1016 N Dearborn St, 312-337-6543, www.ruthpage.org) offers classes for beginners to advanced students at this fine school whose graduates dance for the American Ballet Theatre, the New York City Ballet, and professional companies around the world.

The **Merit School of Music** (38 S Peoria St, 312-786-9428, www.meritmusic.org) is a tuition-free conservatory providing economically disadvantaged youth with excellent instruction in playing classical and jazz instruments. Students of all ages flock to the esteemed **Music Institute of Chicago** (1702 Sherman Ave, Evanston, 847-905-1500, www.musicinst.com), which offers classes for all levels, from beginners to academy students, and arts therapy programs. **Old Town School of Folk Music** (4544 N Lincoln Ave, 773-728-6000, www.oldtownschool.org) is Chicago's premier all-American music center, specializing in lessons on twangy instruments. **Sherwood at Columbia College Chicago** (1312 S Michigan Ave, 312-369-3100, www.colum.edu/sherwood) began in the 19th century as a professional degree-granting school and over time evolved into a community-centered institution focusing on bringing quality music education to a diverse population.

The **Alliance Francaise de Chicago** (810 N Dearborn St, 312-337-1070, www.af-chicago.org) has cultivated everything French in Chicagoans of all ages since 1897; petits Francophiles learn language skills through intense language classes, camps, and cultural programs. **Language Stars** (866-557-8277, www.languagestars.com) offers language enrichment programs for kids aged one through ten across the city; children are instructed in foreign language through play-based immersion.

The Chopping Block (4747 N Lincoln Ave, 773-472-6700, www.thechoppingblock.net) in Lincoln Square hosts cooking classes for kids ages 7–11.

Tri-Star Gymnastics (1401 Circle Ave, Forest Park, 708-771-7827, www.tri-stargym.org) serves toddlers through teens; since 1987, the not-for-profit center offers caring instruction for boys and girls in gymnastics, tumbling, and trampoline. The center is also home to a GIJO Team (Junior Olympics) and USGA Teams.

After School Matters (66 E Randolph St, 312-744-8925, www.afterschoolmatters.org) develops teens' skills in the arts, science, sports, technology, and communications; focus is on-the-job training under the direction of professionals. Further afield, **Second City Training Center** (1608 N Wells St, 312-664-3959, www.secondcity.com) trains a next generation of improv specialists. And **Bubbles Academy** (1504 N Fremont St, 312-944-7677, www.bubblesacademy.com) features yoga for youngsters taught with a creative twist in an open, airy studio.

Chicago's LGBTQ communities are a diverse, politically-influential presence within the city. Just look to the Pride pylons lining North Halsted Street, designating the gay district, or the numerous politicians who vie for a prime spot in the city's enormous annual Pride Parade (which takes place in Boystown on the last Sunday in June). Boystown (a.k.a East Lakeview) and Andersonville comprise the city's two gay friendliest neighborhoods, with Clark Street, Halsted and Broadway being queer corridors of shops, restaurants and nightlife. Those two 'hoods notwithstanding, LGBTQ people and culture can be found throughout the city, from Roger's Park to Midway. Whether your interests are activism or acupuncture, draperies or drag kings, literature, liturgies, or leather bars, or any combination of the above, you will find your niche in Chicago's vibrant and diverse GLBTQ communities.

Publications/Media

Windy City Times (www.windycitymediagroup. com or @WindyCityTimes1): Gay and Lesbian news weekly with good calendar of events.

Chicago Phoenix (chicagophoenix.com or @ chicagophoenix): LGBT commentary and news analysis.

Chicago Pride (chicago.gopride.com or @GoPride): News and LGBT happenings across Chicago.

BOI Magazine (www.boimagazinechicago.com): Heavily advertising-based guide to the club scene.

Windy City Queercast (www.windycityqueercast. com): Locally produced Windy City Media Group podcast.

Pink Magazine (www.pinkmag.com or @ TweetPINKMag): National magazine headquartered in Chicago; best for its listing of gay friendly businesses and restaurants.

Arts & Culture

Gerber/Hart Library and Archives (6500 N Clark St, 773-381-8030, www.gerberhart.org or @ GerberHart): This amazing library houses more than 10,000 books, magazines, newspapers, and videos. Regularly hosts both gay and lesbian book discussion groups, and special events including readings and screenings.

Reeling (reelingfilmfestival.org or @ReelingFilmFest): Annual Chicago Lesbian and Gay International Film Festival each Sept at various venues.

About Face Theatre (773-784-8565, aboutfacetheatre.com or @aboutfacechi): Roving gay & lesbian theater company.

Artemis Singers (773-764-4465, www. artemissingers.org or @ArtemisSingers): Lesbian-feminist chorus.

Chicago Gay Men's Chorus (773-296-0541, www. cgmc.org or @ChicagoGMC): Chicago's most colorful chorus mounts fun, campy concerts, including a popular holiday show.

Windy City Gay Chorus (773-6621-0928, www. windycitysings.org or @WindyCitySings): Gay chorus under Windy City Performing Arts umbrella organization.

Lakeside Pride Music Ensembles (773-381-6693, www.lakesidepride.org or @LakesidePride): Umbrella organization for various LGBT ensembles, including the Freedom Marching Band.

Homolatte (www.homolatte.com): Bi-weekly queer spoken word and music series with writers and musicians, curated and hosted by Scott Free.

Sports & Recreation

Chi-Town Squares (773-425-7584, chitownsquares. org): Gay and lesbian square dancing.

Chicago Metropolitan Sports Association (www. chicagomsa.com): Organizes all varieties of gay and lesbian competitive athletics: bowling, softball, etc.

Chicago Smelts (www.chicagosmelts.org): Gay & lesbian swim club.

Frontrunners/Frontwalkers Chicago (www. frfwchicago.org): Weekly LGBT running and walking club.

Social Groups/Organizations

Chicago Area Gay and Lesbian Chamber of Commerce (773-303-0167, www.glchamber.org or @chiglchamber): Charged with developing gay and lesbian businesses, the chamber also hosts events for gay and lesbian professionals.

Oak Park Area Lesbian and Gay Association (opalga.org): LGBT-focused events and activitives for the Oak Park area.

Affinity Community Services (773-324-0377, www.affinity95.org): Social justice organization working on behalf of black LGBT communities.

Association of Latinos/as Motivating Action (ALMA) (773-234-5591, www.almachicago.org or @almachicago): Advocating on behalf of the Latino LGBT community.

Asians & Friends Chicago (312-409-1573, www.afchicago.org or @afchicago_org): Supporting gay Asian community, with fun events.

Chicago Gender Society (www.chicagogender.com): Providing education, support, social opportunities, and outreach to the transgender and transsexual community.

Political Groups/Activism

Equality Illinois (773-477-7173, www.equalityillinois.us or @EqualityILL).

Human Rights Campaign Chicago (800-777-4723, www.hrcchicago.org).

Religious Services

Archdiocesan Gay and Lesbian Outreach (AGLO) (773-525-3872, www.aglochicago.org): Catholic.

Broadway United Methodist Church (3338 N Broadway, 773-348-2679, www.broadwaychurchchicago.com or @ChicagoBUMC): Reconciling United Methodist.

Congregation Or Chadash (5959 N Sheridan Rd, 773-271-2148, www.orchadash.org): LBGT synagogue.

Dignity Chicago (312-458-9438, www.dignity-chicago.org): LBGT Catholic.

Lake Street Church of Evanston (607 Lake St, Evanston, 847-864-2181, www.lakestreet.org): InsideOut LGBT group.

Pilgrim Congregational Church (460 Lake St, Oak Park, 708-848-5860, www.pilgrimoakpark.com): Actively inclusive.

St. Paul's United Church of Christ (2336 N Orchard St, 773-348-3829, www.spucc.org).

New Spirit Community Church (542 S Scoville, Oak Park, 708-848-5460, www.newspiritoakpark.org).

Health Centers & Support Organizations

Haymarket Center (932 W Washington St, 312-226-7984, www.hcenter.org): Addiction programs.

Center on Halsted (3656 N Halsted St, 773-472-6469, www.centeronhalsted.org or @CenteronHalsted): The Midwest's largest lesbian, gay, bisexual, and transgendered social service agency. Since opening its doors to the public in 2007, The Center on Halsted, Chicago's GLBTQ community center and cultural hub, has been the meeting spot for numerous community social groups and organizations, from gay senior groups to youth programs. The facility houses a full-sized gymnasium, a theater, a huge outdoor deck with a vista over Halsted Street, and computer center, and shares an entry with the adjacent Whole Foods grocery store. Theatrical events, affirming liturgies, movies, recovery and support groups, co-ed volleyball and yoga for seniors are all part of the program.

Illinois State HIV/AIDS/STD Hotline: 800-243-2437.

Howard Brown Health Center (4025 N Sheridan Rd, 773-388-1600, www.howardbrown.org or @hbhcinfo): General counseling as well as anonymous, free AIDS testing and GLBT Domestic Violence Counseling and Prevention Program. Also provides general practitioner care for men and women, on a sliding fee scale.

New Town Alano Club (909 W Belmont Ave, 2nd Fl, 773-529-0321, www.newtownalanoclub.org or @NTAClub): Gay and lesbian AA, CA, OA, ACOA, Coda, etc.

Chicago House (1925 N Clybourn Ave, 773-248-5200, www.chicagohouse.org or @ChicagoHouse85): Homeless shelter for people living with HIV/AIDS.

Make no bones about it, Chicago is a dog's kind of town. And with hundreds and hundreds of thousands of canines living and playing in the Windy City, dog parks, runs, and beaches become that much more important to both pet and guardian. In Chicago, dogs socialize and exercise their owners daily at designated Dog-Friendly Areas (DFAs), shady parks, and sprawling beaches.

Dog-Friendly Areas

DFAs are off-leash areas reserved just for canines. Amenities vary by park but often include doggie drinking fountains, agility equipment, wood chips, pea pebble, and asphalt surfaces. In addition, top-notch runs and facilities feature "time out" fenced-in areas for shy or overexcited dogs, trash receptacles and doggie bags for, well, not take-out, and bulletin boards and information kiosks to post animal lovers' announcements. DFAs are managed jointly by the neighborhoods' dog owners' councils and the Chicago Park District. These spaces are essential to the happiness of Chicago dogs and their owners, as police are notorious for dealing out hefty fines and even arresting dog owners who fail to clean up after or leash their dogs. But at the DFA, canines run free and poop where they please. Just remember to clean up after your pooch, ensure that your dog is fully immunized, de-wormed, licensed, and wearing ID tags. There are limits on how many pups one person can bring at once and please no puppies under four months, dogs in heat, dogs with the name "Killer," or children under 12.

Creating a DFA takes a serious grass-roots effort spearheaded by the neighborhood's dog owners. They must organize themselves to get the community to bow to their desires through site surveys and three community meetings and raise all funds needed to build the DFA, somewhere in the neighborhood of $150,000. Most importantly, they must, er, unleash the support of their alderman, police precinct, and park district.

Dog-Friendly Areas

Mary Bartelme Park, 115 S Sangamon St (Map 24): Includes doggie drinking fountain.

Challenger Park, 1100 W Irving Park Rd (Map 40): Nestled next to a cemetery and under the El tracks, this relatively new DFA has plenty of amenities and neighborhood action. Avoid at all costs during Cubs games.

Churchill Field Park, 1825 N Damen Ave (Map 28): This triangular space next to the train tracks is covered with pea gravel and asphalt and many abandoned tennis balls (Golden Retrievers can't get enough).

Clarendon Park Community Center, 4501 N Marine Dr (Map 40): Located north of Park District service yard, north of Montrose and includes doggie drinking fountain.

Coliseum Park, 1466 S Wabash Ave (Map 11): Long, narrow, and fenced-in park where dogs race the overhead trains. Nothing to write home about, but, hey, it's legal.

Grant Park, 951 S Columbus Dr (Map 6): Located north and west of 9th St Service yard south of Balbo, and includes doggie drinking fountain.

Hamlin Park, 3035 N Hoyne Ave at Wellington Ave (Map 42): Located in the shady southwest corner, this active L-shaped park appeals to tennis-ball chasers and fetching owners.

Lake Shore East Park, 450 E Benton Pl (Map 6): Located along the southern edge of the park, includes doggie drinking fountain.

Margate Park, 4921 N Marine Dr (Map 40): Called "Puptown" by the Uptown canine-loving community, this beloved DFA is usually packed with doggone fun. Locals are diligent about keeping the pea gravel picked up.

Dog Parks, Runs, and Beaches

Noethling (Grace) Park, 2645 N Sheffield Ave (Map 29): Dogs and owners from the Lincoln Park area love to hang out at the "Wiggley Field" dog run—Chicago's pilot pooch park. Wiggley's got a doggy obstacle course, an asphalt surface, drinking fountain, "time out" area, and info kiosk.

Norwood Park, 5899 N Avondale (Northwest): Located just north of service yard on Avondale Ave, includes doggie drinking fountain.

Ohio Place Park, N Orleans St and W Ohio St (Map 2): Next to the I-90/94 exit ramp, this fenced-in strip of concrete flanked by bushes isn't pretty, but a dog can play fetch here without a leash. Careful: As the lot is not a Chicago Park District facility, it is not double-gated.

Park 551, 353 N DesPlaines St (Map 1): Located south of Kinzie St in Fulton River District, includes doggie drinking fountain.

Portage Park, 4100 N Long (Northwest): Located south of Berteau and west of service yard, includes doggie drinking fountain.

Pottawattomie Park, 7340 N Rogers Ave: Located east of Wolcott and south of Birchwood at north end of park, includes small dog area and doggie drinking fountain.

River Park, 5100 N Francisco Ave (Map 38): Located southeast of the field house, includes doggie fountain.

Walsh Playground Park, 1722 N Ashland Ave (Map 29): A 4,500-square-foot park with a small off-leash area for fetching with pea gravel and shade.

A. Montgomery Ward Park, 630 N Kingsbury St (Map 1): Located on west side of Kingsbury south of Erie.

Wicker Park, 1425 N Damen Ave (Map 21): Popular pooch as well as dog owner pick-up park. Often packed with dog-walkers wrangling fleets of frisky canines.

Top Parks and Beaches for Dogs

Leashed dogs and well-behaved owners are welcome in most of Chicago's parks and on its beaches, except during the height of swimming season when the sands are off-limits. Here are some local canines' top picks.

Calumet Park and Beach (9801 S Ave G): A 200-acre beach and park getaway in the city with tennis courts, baseball fields, basketball courts, water fun, and plenty of parking.

Dog Beach (3200 N Lake Shore Dr): This crescent of sand at the north corner of Belmont Harbor is separated from the bike path by a fence, making it an unofficial dog sand box. But the water is dirty, and the police do ticket, so it's not the most ideal dog-frolicking area.

Horner Park (2741 W Montrose Ave): Dog heaven with lots of trees, grass, squirrels to chase, and other pups to meet, particularly after work; plans afoot for official DFA (hornerparkdogpark.org).

Lincoln Park (2045 Lincoln Park W): Paws down, the best dog park in town for romping, fetch, and Frisbee. Unofficial "Bark Park" where pet lovers congregate is a grassy area between Lake Shore Dr and Marine Dr.

Montrose/Wilson Avenue Beach (MonDog) (4400 N Lake Shore Dr): The city's only legal off-leash beach, MonDog is perfect for pooches to practice dogpaddling. Lake water is shallow and the beachfront is wide (www.mondog.org).

Ohio Street Beach and Olive Park (600 N Lake Shore Dr): The perfect combo for cross-training canines: Olive Park's fenced-in grassy areas for running and neighboring Ohio Street Beach's calm waters for swimming.

Promontory Point (5491 South Shore Dr): Radical run for daring, buff dogs that dive off the scenic picnic area's rocks into the deep water below.

Sherman Park (1301 W 52nd St): The best place in the city for a Victorian-style stroll over picturesque bridges and through lagoons.

Overview

Chicago is widely regarded as a world-class food destination, and rightly so, we say. It's a goldmine for anyone searching for flavors, romantic dining or simply a place to clog arteries. Whether you're looking for a $2 hot dog at one of the city's hot dog stands, a $200 20-course marathon at one of the city's foodie destinations or a meal at one of the myriad mom-and-pop neighborhood spots where you can't understand the costs because you don't speak the owner's language, you'll find it here.

In the past decade, Chicago's adventuresome appetite has come to life with a whole new school of Chicago restaurants coming to the fore. Once fueled by students of the masters: Bayless, Trotter, Gordon Sinclair, and so on, the Chicago dining renaissance is already in its second or third generation, and now the students of the students, those who honed their skills at places like Trio and Tru, are taking the reins as they charge into Chicago's culinary future. Terms like "farm-to-table," "locally sourced," and "nose to tail" have settled into the culinary community's lexicon and whatever dish or ingredient is currently nourishing foodies' every gastronomic desire.

Chicago's culinary, um, chops continue to grow with venerable mainstays and new trend-centric spots popping up weekly (poutine tacos, anyone?). And with underground supper clubs and tickets-only restaurants quickly granting access via social media, the web has become your palatable guide. What follows is a breakdown of some of our favorite spots, old and new. Of course, with every restaurant opening, there is likely another one closing. Check in with **Yelp** or **eater.com** for up-to-the-(yes)-minute local restaurant news.

Chicago Staples

Some restaurants are more than just places to eat and drink; they're defining institutions of the city where politicians scheme and drunk baseball fans pass out. Of the lot, **Pizzeria Uno**'s (Map 2) claim seems the most legit—their cheese-filled recipe dates back to 1943. Other Chicago pizza institutions include **Lou Malnati's (Map 2)** and **Gino's East (Map 3)**. Equally important is the Chicago Dog—that is, a hot dog on a steamed bun "dragged through the garden" with a virtual salad on top—onions, relish, tomatoes, pickle spears, sport peppers, mustard (no ketchup, thank you very much), and a dash of celery salt. Post-pub dogs at **Wiener's Circle (Map 30)** are a Lincoln Park rite-of-passage—the servers are infamous for their saucy attitudes. Chicago is more than hot dogs, though. It's hamburgers and heavy metal at **Kuma's Corner (Map 41)** where tatted servers dish up patties named after Pantera, Slayer and other bands with guitar gods. While there are plenty of Chicago institutions that put the city on the international culinary radar, Rick Bayless' pack of restaurants, **Frontera Grill**, **Topolobambo** and **XOCO (all Map 2)**, stands out with creative and upscale Mexican fare for every wallet.

The New Kids on the Block

Recent openings have seen a burgeoning trend in multi-purpose eateries. Head down to Pilsen's historic Thalia Hall to dine at **Dusek's (Map 26)**, drink at Punch House and enjoy local music. Mammoth international emporium **Eataly (Map 2)** caters to diners looking for high-end five course Italian, a quick panini or a place to hand-select every ingredient to make it on your own; where you'll really want to make a stop is at the Nutella bar. Beat the crowds by lining up early outside Logan Square's **Fat Rice (Map 27)** for an inimitable taste of Portugal and Macau. Head to Wicker Park's **Mott Street (Map 22)** mid-week for Asian street food alongside strong beverages.

Chicago's Best Dining Bets

For the Diner with Dollars to Burn

So you have a lot of money? Well, congratulations. There's no better way to get rid of your cash than to go on a dining tour of Chicago's high-end dining destinations. **Girl and the Goat (Map 24)** arrived on the scene and wasted no time taking money from hungry guests. **Alinea (Map 30)** welcomes you with scientific culinary creations and sends you home with a bill that will leave your wallet limping toward the door. Diners are increasingly willing to put some work into landing a coveted table. At **Next (Map 24)**, diners can shell out an insane amount of cash before they even eat with highly sought after tickets to experience the restaurant's frequently changing thematic menus. **Schwa (Map 22)** patrons enter the kitchen staff's good graces by offering up a bottle of whiskey upon arrival. Looking for less maintenance and more beef? Head to Chicago steakhouse classics like **Gene & Georgetti (Map 2)** or sleek chophouse **Chicago Cut (Map 2)**.

For the Diner Holding a Sign Begging for Dollars

So you're broke? Do not fret, dear friend. Cheap taquerias, hot dog stands, and corner grills abound. Costa Rican BYOB **Irazu's (Map 28)** award-winning veggie burrito guarantees leftovers for days. Head to **Taqueria el Milagro (Map 26)** for platillos of pollo and salsa that's like a drug (we've heard).

Pizza, Pizza, Pizza

Crust, cheese and more cheese. Chicago is a pizza city, and classic spots such as **Pizzeria Uno (Map 2)**, **Lou Malnati's (Map 2)** and **Gino's East (Map 3)** attract tourists and suburbanites in droves. Locals head to Lincoln Park's **Pequod's (Map 29)** for signature deep dish with a caramelized crust. **Art of Pizza (Map 43)** has won numerous awards and acclaim for its scrumptious deep disher. If you're not into three inches of mozzarella, you're in luck: this city offers thin crust 'za, too. **Piece (Map 21)** serves up New Haven-style pies with a selection of microbrews crafted in-house. Farther north, **Spacca Napoli (Map 39)** gives the wood-fired pizza a Neapolitan twist.

Chicago for Herbivores

Yes, people love gulping down a succulent steak here, but many Windy City restaurants are introducing more veggie items than the token pasta or risotto. Additionally, more vegetarian-only restaurants been appearing on our beefy shores to let Midwestern cattle breathe a sigh of relief. **Chicago Diner (Map 44)** is the crunchy, old-school standard bearer. **Arya Bhavan (Map 33)** specializes in Indian vegetarian food from the north and south. **Amitabul (Northwest Chicago)** does Vegan Thai on the Northwest side, and **Soul Veg City (South Chicago)** in the Southside Chatham neighborhood. For upscale vegetarian, try **Mana (Map 21)** in Wicker Park. In Logan Square, down-to-earth scenester spot **Lula (Map 27)** is known for being particularly vegetarian friendly, and the redesigned interior makes this great for casual dates. For a very special and seriously spendy night, choose the fixed-price vegetarian tasting menus at **Arun's (Map 38)**. Finally, vegetarians and non-vegetarians alike line up for breakfasts served by followers of Sri Chimnoy at Roscoe Village's popular **Victory's Banner (Map 42)**. Call first: the followers close twice each year for a spiritual retreat.

Poor Man's Steak and Other Meaty Matters

In the past few years, **Kuma's Corner (Map 41)** has emerged as the popular and critical favorite for best burger in the city, although Northside loyalists still swear by **Moody's (Map 37)**, and Southsiders hanker for **Top Notch Beef Burgers (Southwest)**. Even the fast food burger has stepped up its game. Trendy spots **Owen & Engine (Map 28)** and **Au Cheval (Map 24)** regularly vie for the title of the city's best burger. If, on the other hand, you like your meat served on the bone with tangy sauce, head to the **Gale Street Inn (Northwest)** in Jefferson Park, street-festival mainstay **Robinson's (Map 4, 30)**, and **Honey 1 (Map 28)**. **Smoque** (Northwest) attracts droolers from all over the city for, arguably, Chicago's best 'cue. Fried chicken is also making its way beyond the fast food set with **Honey Butter Fried Chicken (Map 41)**. As for encased meats, Chicago has no lack of options—just follow the Vienna Beef signs.

Soul Food and Southern Cooking

We say soul food is the most American of American cuisines. **Valois (Map 19)** serves no frills, cafeteria-style soul food. For Cajun food, try Chicago breakfast staple **Wishbone (Map 24)**. The legion of trendy but good regional spots continues to grow with **Big Jones (Map 37)** and **Carriage House (Map 21)**.

Drink More, Spend Less

Nothing says romance like a bottle (or box) of wine, and Chicago's restaurant scene makes it easy to keep your beverage total low with an array of BYOB spots. If you're looking to savor South American flavors while sipping your own bottle of red, head to **Tango Sur (Map 43)** for massive cuts of Argentine steak. Forget travel restrictions and bar tabs when you head to **90 Miles Cuban Cafe (Map 42)** where you'll find a more casual dining experience and more meat. Sushi also tastes better when you're not paying for cocktails, so head to **Coast (Map 28)** for slow service that lets you drink more. For non-seaweed options, **Cozy Noodles 'N Rice (Map 43)** serves up noodle dishes close to the endless line of bars in Wrigleyville.

Passport to Good Eating

Culinarily, you can travel the world and never leave Chicago. While some of Chicago's dining emporiums fly high on the local radar, we have a soft spot for the ramshackle storefronts where the home cooking's happening. You don't have to live in Chicago a long time to discover that Devon Street is the place to go if you crave Indian food. We love **Hema's Kitchen (Map 30, 33)**, and the Pakistani fare at Rogers Park's **Ghareeb Nawaz (Map 34)**. Pilsen is the destination neighborhood for Mexican muy authentico. **Nuevo Leon (Map 26)** has been serving revelatory Mexican home cooking for ages, and **Birreria Reyes de Ocatlan (Map 26)** is a favorite of celebrity chef Rick Bayless. Off the Pilsen path, **Birrierra Zaragoza (West)** serves a traditional goat stew that really shouldn't be missed. The city's best Vietnamese can be found in the New Saigon section of Argyle Street, right under the L stop, and Albany Park is the place to go for Middle Eastern and Korean fare. Of the former, we think the classic falafel sandwiches at **Dawali (Map 38)** really are something special, stuffed with potatoes and cauliflower as well as the formed garbanzo balls. The greater northwest side is bountiful with Eastern European restaurants and supper clubs. You'll find plenty of great African and Caribbean food behind no-frills storefronts in Rogers Park. As for **Good to Go Jamaican Jerk and Juice Bar (Map 34)**, the name says it all. We shouldn't have to tell you to head to Chinatown for dim sum or Greek Town for flaming cheese or Little Italy for a sampling of Sicily.

Breakfast

There is one crucial ingredient for the morning after an extended evening of exploring Chicago's magnificent miles of bars: breakfast. Well, more like brunch. From syrupy-soaked goodness at **Waffles (Map 9)** to a brick of a breakfast burrito at **Kitsch'n (Map 42)**, you and your hangover can travel anywhere in the city and find some solace with a fork, a plate and perhaps a Bloody Mary.

Diners

Sometimes you just want a cup of joe and a patty melt, and other times you just want a five-egg omelet, which you'll find at **Pauline's (Map 36)**. If that cholesterol-raising recipe isn't up your alley, Chicago has plenty of other greasy spoon options, including **Nookies (Map 30)**, **Salonica (Map 19)**, **Lou Mitchell's (Map 4)**, **Hollywood Grill (Map 22)**, and **The Golden Apple (Map 43)**.

Sweet Home Chicago

Amidst the overwhelming array of options for dinner, pastry chefs are giving us more reasons to forgo dinner for dessert. Try Mindy's Hot Chocolate for velvety cocoa and house made marshmallows. For frozen concoctions, don't miss **Black Dog Gelato (Map 21)**, **Margie's Candies (Map 28, 39)** and the **Original Rainbow Cone (Southwest)**. For a superior slice of chocolate pecan? **Bang Bang Pie Shop (Map 27)**.

Flavors on the Go

A rapidly developing food trend in Chicago is unfortunately one that we can't place on a map: the food truck craze. From macaroni and cheese to falafel to cupcakes, Chicagoans have fallen in love with flavors served from the back of a truck. The location of these mobile businesses varies from day to day, and many residents follow their favorite four-wheeled chefs on social media to be the first in line at whatever corner they're calling home for the day.

Foodies on the Web

Need a Recommendation?

Both professional food critics and the vox populi weigh in on the popular restaurant sites of the **Chicago Reader** (www.chicagoreader.com), the Chicago Tribune's **Metromix** (chicago.metromix.com), and **Time Out Chicago** (www.timeout.com/chicago). All offer search categories, so you can find places by location, price, type of cuisine, etc. If you're going somewhere off-the-beaten path, however, be sure to phone first.

Professional chefs and passionate eaters chat about both the latest hot spots and hidden neighborhood gems on the **LTH Forum** (www.lthforum.com). The foodie debates, all in the spirit of fun, can get raucous, and sometimes even local celebrity chefs enter the fore to throw down. A warning: Regular posting on the LTH Forum is a tell-tale sign of your descent down the slippery slope of food geekdom.

Get It Delivered

Finally, if the sun scares you from leaving the comfort of your home, **Grub Hub** and **Seamless** are your hook-ups for delivery that isn't pizza. Well, there's pizza, too, but you can also choose from a massive array of culinary hotspots where you might not be able to get a table.

Chicago is a city of neighborhoods, and as such, we are a city of great little neighborhood taverns. These are the places where the beer you drink is on tap, the bartender throws a basket of pretzels in front of you when you grab your stool, and you can find the men and women who fill the pages of Studs Terkel's beloved *Working*, stealing precious time between the bossman and the kids. And then there's the jukebox. The best ones feature all your favorite bar songs, from Hank Williams to The Cars, Blondie to Sly and the Family Stone, and "My Way" sung in Polish or Korean just for the hell of it.

Although you'll find a low-key feel at many bars, Chicago has built a strong reputation as a nightlife capital. With bass-pumping dance clubs, warm weather rooftop bars and VIP lounges, the city keeps the rapt attention of every club crazy scenester.

No matter your interest, there's always something going on in the city. To help you keep on top of it all, check out listings in *The Reader*, *Time Out Chicago*, and *New City*. Websites like **Gapers Block** (www.gapersblock.com) list events and specials.

Dive Bars

Rub shoulders with the characters from a Nelson Algren story at any of the following joints: In Old Town, the **Old Town Ale House (Map 31)** was once voted best dive bar in the country by someone-mumblemumble-we-forget-who. Other dives such as **Ola's Liquor (Map 21)** can be identified by the mere presence of the "Old Style" bar sign out front.

Arty Crowd

Young urban arty types have carved out their kitsch-embracing niches at Ukrainian Village and Wicker Park spots such as **Gold Star Bar (Map 21)**, **Inner Town Pub (Map 21)**, and **Rainbo Club (Map 21)**, while their Pilsen brethren drink their PBR at **Maria's (Map 12)**. On the north side, get drunk with happy hipsters and local punters at **Village Tap (Map 42)** and **The Long Room (Map 40)**.

Live Music

Some of Chicago's best live music venues are also neighborhood spots. In West Town, the **Empty Bottle (Map 21)** is the place to catch touring indie bands. Farther west, **Rosa's Lounge (Northwest Chicago)** is a friendly venue for live blues. Catch live jazz any night of the week at Uptown's **Green Mill (Map 40)**. On the northwest side, **The Abbey (Northwest)** features everything from alternative rock acts like The Breeders and Peaches, to singer-songwriter showcases and burlesque. If you want to put some twang in your thang, alt-country acts from the Bloodshot Records label regularly perform at Bucktown's **Hideout (Map 29)**. See indie bands and comics without the cover at **Cole's (Map 27)**. Be seen amongst the indie crowd at **Thalia Hall (Map 26)**.

Shake a Tailfeather

In Chicago, even the best place to get your groove on is often the one right around the corner. Despite the concentration of huge, dazzling and super expensive high-concept nightclubs in River North and River West, (which are typically the domains of tourists and suburbanites), many local folk prefer smaller, friendlier, and cheaper local options to catch Saturday (or Monday, or Thursday) night fever. Legendary gay bar **Berlin (Map 43)**, in Lakeview, draws a pansexual crowd for their ever-rotating array of theme nights. **Smart Bar (Map 43)**, in the basement of the rock club **Metro (Map 43)**, spins dance music with an edge, and **Danny's (Map 28)** hosts the late night dance party so your living room doesn't have to.

What's Your Poison?

Whether you are a wino, a beer swiller, a whiskey sipper or a tequila shooter, have we got a bar for you.

Beer

Craft brews are quickly finding their way into the taps at every new bar in town, but at **Map Room (Map 28)** and **Sheffield's (Map 43)** be prepared to read full-on booklets listing all their brews before you order. At **Quenchers (Map 28)** you can drink your way around the world. If it's Belgians you crave, try getting a seat at Andersonville's **Hopleaf (Map 40)**.

Cocktails

In the last couple of years, the cocktail has become king in Chicago, with many noted mixologists shaking up fresh ingredients to make some of the best stuff you've ever tasted. Celebrity chef Grant Achatz's **The Aviary (Map 24)** has upped the game in the cocktail scene the way his Alinea redefined the culinary world. **The Violet Hour (Map 21)** is designed as a speakeasy (look for the yellow light outside) with some of the best mixes in the city. For those who appreciate a good cocktail but are on a budget, check out **The Whistler (Map 27)**, whose short list of classic cocktails won't sap your wallet.

Straight Up

If it's something stronger that you crave, **Delilah's (Map 29)** serves a world-class collection of whiskey to an amiable crowd of aging hipsters and once-were punks. **Marty's (Map 37)** is a fine place to be shaken and not stirred. Gin drinkers will find an extensive collection at **Scofflaw (Map 27)**. The tropical rum concoctions at downtown tiki bar **Three Dots and a Dash (Map 2)** are so strong that after a few you'll swear you can hear the waves crashing along the coast.

Irish Pubs

Yes, Chicago is full of Irish—and "Irish"—pubs. Some are pretty damn authentic though, so if you're on the north side and it's a good Shepherd's Pie or football match you're craving along with your pint, seek out **The Irish Oak (Map 43)**, **Chief O'Neill's (Map 41)**, or **The Globe Pub (Map 39)**. On the South Side, well, you can't even contemplate Irish drinking culture in the city without a tip o' the hat to the strip of Western Avenue in Beverly that is home to the annual South Side St. Patrick's Day Parade. **Cork & Kerry (Southwest)** is loaded with *craic*. Every Friday and Saturday Night, the **Irish-American Heritage Center (Northwest)** hosts the **Fifth Province Pub (Northwest)**, an authentic Irish Pub, featuring Irish beer, Irish food, and Irish entertainment.

On-Site Sipping

A recent crop of breweries and distilleries are giving boozers a chance to taste test right at the source. Local craft favorites **Revolution (Map 41)** and **Half Acre (Map 39)** offer tours of their facilities, and sampling is encouraged. **City Winery (Map 24)** sources grapes from all over the world to produce wines you can sip throughout their bar, restaurant and concert facilities. And as whiskey continues its hold on the local hipster population, **Koval Distillery (Map 39)** offers classes, tours and plenty of bottled varieties to take home.

Mag Mile and Oak Street: Bring Your Bars of Gold

The Mag Mile has long replaced State Street as downtown Chicago's premier (and tourist-friendly) shopping strip. This stretch of prime real estate, spanning from the Chicago River to Oak Street features Chicago outposts of many destination shopping spots, including **Niketown (Map 3)**, **The Apple Store (Map 3)**, Needless Markup (a.k.a. **Neiman Marcus) (Map 3)**, and the high-end boutiques and department stores, (think **Tiffany (Map 3)**, **Gucci (Map 32)** and **Hermès (Map 32)** connected to **Water Tower Place (Map 32)** and the **900 North Michigan Shops (Map 32)**.

Around the corner on Oak Street lay tonier boutiques. While Mag Mall attracts goggle-eyed Midwestern families, who'll likely stop for lunch at the Cheesecake Factory or Bubba Gump, Oak Street appeals more to the Gold Coast and North Shore set: **Prada (Map 32)**, **Barney's (Map 32)** and **BCBG MAXAZRIA (Map 32)** are all located on this tiny strip.

Not far away on Rush Street, **Ikram (Map 32)** is a favorite of FLOTUS Michelle Obama.

Boutique Shopping

You don't have to go down to Oak Street to find funky designer boutiques selling everything from original fashions by local designers to housewares and hostess gifts. Lincoln Park and Wicker Park in particular are heavy on cool women's fashion boutiques. In Lincoln Park, check out Armitage, Clark, and Halsted for shops such as **Lori's Designer Shoes (Map 30)**. In Wicker Park, the highest concentration of cool little shops, like the fashion boutique **Penelope's (Map 21)**, line Division street, but if you love to shop, you'll want to work the whole Bermuda triangle of Division, Milwaukee, and North Avenue. Southport Avenue in Wrigleyville boasts a string of women's boutiques, including **Krista K (Map 43)**.

Home Design and Decor

Forget River North, Clark Street in Andersonville has emerged as a mini designer's row. Shops like **Scout (Map 37)** and **Cassona (Map 37)** have designers flocking from all over the city. **Salvage One (Map 23)** is a treasure island for vintage rehabbers.

For modern housewares and furniture there's **Design Within Reach (Map 22)**; just remember that "within reach" is in the eye of the beholder. Green up your home (or someone else's) with nurseries **Sprout Home (Map 23)**, **Gethsemane Garden Center (Map 37)** and **Asrai Garden (Map 21)**—all of which sell a wide range of housewares and gifts.

Best of the 'Hoods

In many cases, Chicago's neighborhood shopping destinations say something unique about the character of the 'hood. Check out Logan Square for funky little punk rock indie shops or gay-friendly places. Lincoln Square caters to the NPR-lovin', micro-brew swillers that call that 'hood home, and Andersonville has something for everyone: feminist books (**Women & Children First (Map 37)**, chic home furnishings, men's and women's fashions, Swedish souvenirs, and friendly and non-oogly-feeling sex-toy store **Early to Bed (Map 37)**.

Ethnic enclaves also make for great shopping. Try gifts and cookware in Chinatown, gorgeous saris and Bollywood flicks on West Devon, hookahs and Moroccan teas sets on north Kedzie in Albany Park, and Irish arts and crafts in Beverly

One Man's Trash...

...is another man's treasure. Whether your wants are driven by the desire to save the planet or just to save a buck, Chicago offers a plentitude of places to buy other people's old crap. Vintage wear boutiques thrive in arty 'hoods like Wicker Park, East Lakeview, and Pilsen. Some faves: **Una Mae's (Map 21)**, **Silver Moon (Map 21)**, and **Knee Deep (Map 26)**. **Ragstock (Map 44, 21)**, a used-and-off-sale clothing chain, has two Chicago outposts.

For one-stop antique shopping, check out one of Chicago's many antique malls—huge enclosed spaces that lease space to small dealers. Not to be missed are the **Broadway Antique Market (Map 37)** and the **Lincoln Antique Mall (Map 38)**.

In terms of thrift stores, there's either a **Salvation Army (Map 40, NW)**, a **Unique Thrift (Map 12, 40, W, NW)** or a **Village Discount (Map 27, 38, 40, NW, W, SW)** in nearly every neighborhood in the city. Meanwhile, **The Brown Elephant (Map 37)** thrift store benefits Howard Brown Health Center's HIV research.

Audiophilia

Tower Records and Virgin are both long gone, but Chicago loves its independent record stores. **Reckless Records (Map 5, 21, 44)** serves the indie rock crowd. **Gramaphone (Map 44)** is where Chicago's DJs pick-up the hottest wax. **Hyde Park Records (Map 19)** supplies Hyde Parkers with all its old-school vinyl needs, while **Dusty Groove (Map 22)**, which specializes in old R &B and soul, provides the same service to West Towners. **Laurie's Planet of Sound (Map 39)**, in Lincoln Square, offers an eclectic array of mostly-indie music without the attitude that is often associated with indie record store clerks.

DeciBel (Map 21) serves the Wicker Park and Bucktown crew. **Saturday Audio Exchange (Map 43)**, only open on Thursdays, Saturdays, and Sundays, sells high-end stereo brands for cheap, (well, relatively cheap, anyways) as well as used and refurbished woofers, tweeters, receivers, and all that other audio-geek stuff.

Get Foodie

The gourmet and specialty food trade has exploded in the past few years, as have the high-end houseware stores that are supplying upscale home cooks with their Le Creuset pans and WÃ¼stof knives. Today, if you find yourself hard-up for locally-produced caviar, lavender extract, stinky artisanal cheese, curry leaves, or whatever other weird ingredient they don't stock at the Jewel, all you have to do is follow your nose. Of Chicago's many, many gourmet or specialty food shops, there are a few that are particularly dear to our hearts. We also love **Goddess and the Grocer (Map 28)**, **Provenance Food and Wine (Map 39)**, and perhaps the best-smelling shop in town, Old Town's **The Spice House (Map 31)**. In Logan Square, **The Dill Pickle Food Co-op (Map 27)** is the place to pick up locally sourced and organic food goodness. Ethnic markets are great places to track down hard-to-find ingredients. **Middle East Bakery (Map 37)** in Andersonville sells amazing homemade hummus and falafel, as well as olive oil, pine nuts, and dried fruit at prices significantly lower than Whole Paycheck. **Joong Boo Market (NW)** is one-stop shopping for Korean culinary adventures, and they have a decent cafe in the back if you just can't wait to have your bibimbap.

Oh, and that local caviar? Look no further than **The FishGuy Market (NW)**.

Mall Rats

Normally we'd scoff, but look, it's Chicago, and it gets damn cold. So, if occasionally you want to do your shopping without having to venture too far into the great outdoors, we're not going to point any fingers.

Block 37 (Map 5) is an entire city block of mall greatest hits, and It's In the Loop. On the Mag Mile, **Water Tower Place (Map 32)** offers pretty typical mall fare—there's a Sephora, Godiva, and Victoria's Secret—but their food court has more in common with a Las Vegas buffet than anywhere you'd be able to grab an Orange Julius or a Mrs. Fields cookie. A block north, the shops at **900 N Michigan (Map 32)**, offer higher-end fare, (no surprise, as it's attached to the super-luxe Four Seasons hotel). Shops here include Diesel, MaxMara, and Sur La Table. In East Lakeview, the **Century Shopping Centre (Map 44)** is kept in business by its fine art house cinema and an L.A. Fitness. Housed in a building where bombers were built during WWII, today the huge **Ford City Mall (SW)** is a popular hang-out for local kids without much else to do, but otherwise boasts nothing very exceptional—a few low-end department stores, a movie theater, and all of the shops and fast food joints you'd expect to find in a mall. Anchored by a Target and a Kohl's, **Harlem Irving Plaza (NW)**, like the Ford City Mall, is a popular stomping ground for high school students but offers little beyond the same old shops despite that location-specific nom de mall.

Oddities

Some of our favorite Chicago shops defy easy definition. Among them, **American Science and Surplus (NW)** offers one-stop shopping for professional-quality laboratory beakers, school supplies, crime-scene tape, pirate flags, and life-sized anatomy models. Legendary actress and Chicago native Joan Cusack's cheeky gift shop **Judy Maxwell (Map 31)** boasts all the necessities: You know, like rubber gloves that double as hand puppets and toilet bowl-shaped pool floats. Over at historic **Maxwell Street Market (Map 7)**, every Sunday vendors hawk cheap wares meant to be haggled over and local Mexican street food is at its best.

To cast a curse or to break one, stop by **Athenian Candle Company (Map 4)**, where, in addition to 12-foot, gold-detailed, church-quality candles, you can also pick up a bottle of "Law Be Gone" floor wash or "Love Come Back" air spray. Prefer high-end designer beach wear with your candles? Stop by **Calypso Christiane Celle (Map 32)** for sunny beaded tunics and sweet-smelling French candles. Looking for a one-stop shop for all potions, powders and balms? Founded as a corner drugstore in 1875, **Merz Apothecary (Map 39)** has become a destination for natural bath and body care products.

To Market, To Market

With retail district rent continuing to skyrocket, many designers and artisans are finding pop-up shops and festivals an ideal place to reach consumers without the brick and mortar expenses. Randolph Street Market, Vintage Garage, Dose Market and Vintage Bazaar all play host on a monthly or seasonal basis. Since locations may vary based on weather, check respective websites for details.

State Street: Student Mecca

The student population in the Loop has soared, thanks to new student housing for Columbia and School of the Art Institute Students. State Street has made a comeback by filling up with cheap, hip, chic shops catering to this crowd. **H &M (Map 32)**, **Urban Outfitters (Map 5, 30, 32)**, **Blick Art Materials (Map 5, 22)**, and **Central Camera (Map 5)** cater to the art student within all of us.

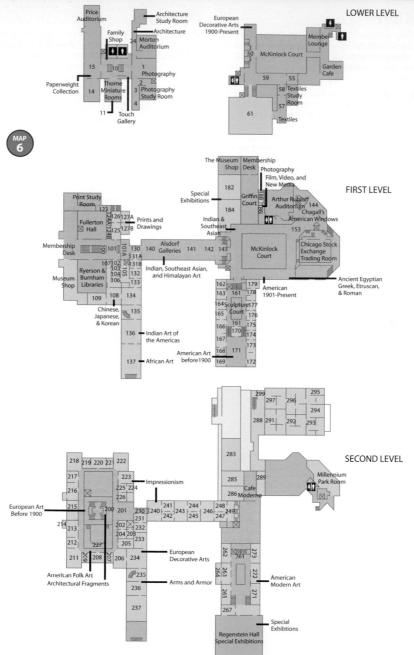

LOWER LEVEL

Price Auditorium
Architecture Study Room
Family Shop
Architecture
24 Morton Auditorium
European Decorative Arts 1900-Present
Member Lounge
50 McKinlock Court
Garden Cafe
15
1 Photography
2
59 55
Paperweight Collection
14 Thorne Miniature Rooms
3 Photography Study Room
4
58 Textiles Study Room
57
11 Touch Gallery
61
Textiles

MAP 6

FIRST LEVEL

The Museum Shop
Membership Desk
Photography
Film, Video, and New Media
182
Special Exhibitions
Griffin Court
Arthur Rubloff Auditorium 144
Chagall's American Windows
Print Study Room
123
184
Fullerton Hall
126 127A
124A 124
125 127B
127
Prints and Drawings
Indian & Southeast Asian
153
Membership Desk
101
101A
130
140 Alsdorf Galleries 141 142 143
McKinlock Court
Chicago Stock Exchange Trading Room
107 102
104 103
105
106
131A
131B
132
Indian, Southeast Asian, and Himalayan Art
Ryerson & Burnham Libraries
Museum Shop
133
162
179
American 1901-Present
Ancient Egyptian Greek, Etruscan, & Roman
109 108 134
163 161 178
Chinese, Japanese, & Korean
135
164 Sculpture 177
165 Court 176
136 Indian Art of the Americas
166 161 175
167 170 174
173
137 African Art
American Art before1900
168 171
169 172

SECOND LEVEL

299
297 296
295
294
288 291 292 293
283
218 219 220 221 222
217
223
Impressionism
285
289
Millennium Park Room
216
225 224
226
286 Cafe Moderne
European Art Before 1900
215
200 201
230 240 241 243 244 246 248 249
242 245 247
214 213
202
204 203
205
231
232
233
212
211 209 208 207 206 234
227
European Decorative Arts
262 273
261
263 272 American Modern Art
American Folk Art Architectural Fragments
235 Arms and Armor
264
236
265 271
237
267
Special Exhibitions
Regenstein Hall Special Exhibitions

General Information

NFT Map: 6
Address: 111 S Michigan Ave
Chicago, IL 60603
Phone: 312–443–3600
Website: www.artic.edu or @artinstitutechi
Hours: Daily 10:30 am–5 pm, Thursday until 8 pm;
closed Thanksgiving, Christmas, & New
Year's Days
Admission: $23 for adults ($20 for Illinois residents, $18
for Chicago residents), $17 for students/
seniors ($14 for Illinois studentes/seniors,
$12 for Chicago students/seniors), free for
children Under 14, free for Illinois residents
on Thursday evenings 5–8pm

Overview

Built in 1892 as part of the 1893 Columbian Exposition,
the Classical Revival-style Allerton Wing of the Art Institute
of Chicago began life as the World's Congress Auxiliary
Building for the World's Fair (the lions were added two years
later). Today the Art Institute is one of the preeminent art
museums in the country, housing the largest collection of
19th–Century French art outside of Paris (and its modern art
collection isn't anything to sneeze at, either). Walking up the
grand staircase in the main entrance, visitors are presented
with an eclectic collection of architectural fragments
wrenched from Chicago buildings that were standing in the
way of, well, you know, "progress." There are also impressive
exhibitions such as the Japanese wood block prints, the
Touch Gallery designed specifically for the visually impaired,
as well as really, really old vases and things, but who are we
kidding? Everyone comes here for an up–close and personal
look at such celebrated paintings as Caillebotte's *Paris Street;
Rainy Day*, Seurat's *Grand Jatte*, Grant Wood's *American
Gothic*, and Hopper's *Nighthawks*, along with the museum's
impressive collection of Monets, Manets, Van Goghs, and
Picassos.

The completion of Renzo Piano's Modern Wing in 2009 made
the Art Institute the nation's second largest art museum
(we're gaining on you, Metropolitan Museum of Art!). The
$300 million addition, which makes great use of filtered
natural light thanks to Piano's "magic carpet" floating roof,
includes a first floor gallery of film and electronic media,
and an impressive exhibition of the museum's Surrealist
collection, with many pieces new, reframed, or on display for
the first time. A pedestrian bridge connected the new wing's
third floor to Millennium Park, across the street.

Restaurants and Services

The Museum Cafe, on the lower level of McKinlock Court,
offers self–service dining with salads, sandwiches, soups,
and a kids menu at reasonable prices 11 am–4 pm daily (see
also the light bar menu Thursdays from 5 to 7:30 pm)

Chef Tony Mantuano's Terzo Piano on the third level of the
Modern Wing (free entrance from Monroe Street) brings a
fine dining experience to the museum, featuring authentic
and elegant Italian dishes. Reservations recommended:
312-443-8650 or www.terzopianochicago.com. Terzo Piano
also supplies less expensive options at Caffe Moderno
overlooking the Modern Wing's Griffin Court.

While postcards, books, and magnets may be purchased
at kiosks throughout the museum, the Museum Shop, just
off the main lobby, offers an extensive collection of art–
oriented gifts and souvenirs, while the Modern Wing Shop
at the Modern Wing's Monroe Street entrance sells similar
items focusing on modern art (and you don't have to pay
admission to shop at either!).

School of the Art Institute of Chicago

Boasting such illustrious alumni as Georgia O'Keefe, Claes
Oldenburg, Laurie Anderson, and David Sedaris, the School
of the Art Institute of Chicago (www.saic.edu or @saic_news)
offers a fine art higher education for tomorrow's budding
Renoirs.

Gene Siskel Film Center

The film branch of the Art Institute, Gene Siskel Film Center
(164 N State St, 312–846–2800 www.siskelfilmcenter.org or
@filmcenter) offers art house, foreign films, and revivals, with
frequent lectures by academics and industry professionals
and annual events like the European Union Film Festival.

How to Get There

By Car: The Art Institute is located on Michigan Avenue
between Monroe and Jackson. From I–90/94 N (the Dan
Ryan), exit to Congress East (Loop exit). From I–90/94 S
(Kennedy Expressway), exit Monroe Steet East. Affordable
parking is located underground at Millennium Park garages
(enter at Columbus and Monroe) and Grant Park garages
(enter on Michigan, either between Madison and Randolph
or between Van Buren and Adams).

By Metra: Nearest stops are the Millennium and Van Buren
stations served by the Metra Electric and South Shore Lines.

By Bus: Numerous lines serve this strip of Michigan Avenue.
Important buses include (from the south) the 3 King Drive,
the 4 Cottage Grove, and the 6 Jackson Park Express, (from
the west) the 126 Jackson and 20 Madison, and (from the
north) the 151 Sheridan and the 146 Inner Drive/Michigan
Express.

By L: From the Red and Blue lines, exit at Monroe. Brown,
Orange, Purple, Pink and Green exit at Adams and
Wabash.

The Grande Dames of Chicago's museum scene, The **Art Institute of Chicago (Map 6)**, the **Museum of Science and Industry (Map 20)**, and the Museum Campus's **Adler Planetarium (Map 11)**, **Field Museum (Map 11)**, and **Shedd Aquarium (Map 9)**, may offer a lifetime of wonder, speculation, and enrichment; but impressive as they are, these cultural epicenters are only the tip of the iceberg when it comes to our city's museum offerings.

Art Museums

Although the Art Institute's collection is undeniably impressive, Chicago's true art lovers know to look past the lions to some of Chicago's less-celebrated treasures. Columbia College's **Museum of Contemporary Photography (Map 9)** is one of two accredited photography museums in the nation. Other campus-linked art museums include University of Chicago's **Smart Museum (Map 19)**, where the collection spans some 5,000 years. Catch the Lunch at **Loyola University Museum of Art (Map 34)** series for a quick bite with artists and experts on exhibits. Artwork created by and commemorating veterans of war hangs on the walls of the **National Veterans Art Museum (Northwest)**. One of the country's largest collections of art post-1945 is housed at the always eye-opening **Museum of Contemporary Art (Map 3)**. The first Friday of the month, hundreds of twenty-something singles converge here for cocktails, live entertainment, and friendly flirtation.

History

The **Chicago History Museum (Map 32)** is a tremendous archive of the city's past and present. African American history is celebrated at the nation's oldest museum focusing on the black experience, the **DuSable Museum of African American History (Map 18)**. The Oriental Institute **(Map 19)** specializes in artifacts from the ancient Near East, including Persia, Mesopotamia, and Egypt. Nobel Prize-winning sociologist Jane Addams's **Hull-House (Map 26)** examines Chicago's history of immigration, ethnic relations, and social work.

Science and Technology

As if the aforementioned **Adler Planetarium (Map 11)**, **Shedd Aquarium (Map 9)**, and **Field Museum (Map 11)** and the **Museum of Science and Industry (Map 20)** weren't enough to satisfy your inner nerd, Chicago is also home to a handful of quirky, smaller science museums. The **International Museum of Surgical Science (Map 32)** offers a window to the world of questionable surgical practices of yore. For kids, the **Children's Museum** at Navy Pier presents a hands-on approach to learning about science and geography. Conservation and the environment are the focus of the **Peggy Notebaert Nature Museum (Map 30)**, which also features a butterfly haven, delighting the child in us all.

Architecture

The city itself is perhaps one of the best architecture museums in the world. Examine it by embarking on one of the tours offered by the **Chicago Architecture Foundation (Map 6)**. Frank Lloyd Wright's influence on Chicago architecture can be examined at the **Robie House (Map 19)** in Hyde Park and the **Frank Lloyd Wright Home and Studio** in Oak Park. Chicago's Prairie Avenue District offers an architectural glimpse of Chicago's Victorian Golden Age. Joint tours of the oldest house in Chicago, the **Clarke House (Map 11)** (c. 1836), and the neighboring **Glessner House (Map 11)** offer the curious an interesting inside peek.

Ethnic Museums

Immigration made Chicago into the "City of Neighborhoods." The **Swedish American Museum (Map 37)**, the **Chinese American Museum of Chicago (Map 10)**, the **Balzekas Museum of Lithuanian Culture (Map 53)**, and the **Polish Museum of America (Map 22)** all explore the impact of immigration on Chicago. The impressive home of the **National Hellenic Museum (Map 6)** is a celebration of all things Greek. The **National Museum of Mexican Art (Map 25)** is the largest such museum in the country, and examines the Mexican experience through art and culture. The **Spertus Institute of Jewish Studies (Map 9)** specializes in Jewish history and heritage through events, lectures and an evolving exhibit on the Jewish experience in Chicago.

Miscellaneous

Housed in the former home of the legendary, influential blues label, Chess Records, **Willie Dixon's Blues Heaven Foundation (Map 11)** offers tours of where Chuck Berry, Muddy Waters, and even the Rolling Stones once recorded. (The site is memorialized in the Stones' song "2120 South Michigan.") For the darker side of sightseeing, the **Leather Archives and Museum (Map 34)** exhibits eight galleries of fetish, bondage, and S&M artifacts including photographs, clothing, toys, and more. Finally, the **Museum of Broadcast Communications (Map 2)** is one of only three broadcast museums in the country, and is home to the only Radio Hall of Fame in the nation.

Museum	Address	Phone	Map
Museum of Contemporary Art	220 E Chicago Ave	312-280-2660	3
National Hellenic Museum	333 S Halsted St	312-655-1234	4
Pritzker Military Museum & Library	104 S Michigan Ave	312-374-9333	5
Money Museum	230 S LaSalle St	312-322-5322	5
Jazz Institute of Chicago	410 S Michigan Ave	312-427-1676	6
Art Institute of Chicago	111 S Michigan Ave	312-443-3600	6
Chicago Architecture Center	111 E Wacker Dr	312-922-8687	6
Shedd Aquarium	1200 S Lake Shore Dr	312-939-2438	9
Museum of Contemporary Photography	600 S Michigan Ave	312-663-5554	9
Spertus Institute of Jewish Studies	610 S Michigan Ave	312-322-1700	9
Chinese-American Museum of Chicago	238 W 23rd St	312-949-1000	10
Willie Dixon's Blues Heaven Foundation	2120 S Michigan Ave	312-808-1286	11
The Field Museum	1400 S Lake Shore Dr	312-922-9410	11
Clarke House Museum	1827 S Indiana Ave	312-744-3316	11
Adler Planetarium	1300 S Lake Shore Dr	312-922-7827	11
Glessner House Museum	1800 S Prairie Ave	312-326-1480	11
Chicago Blues Museum	6455 S Cottage Grove Ave	773-828-8118	12
Chicago Maritime Society	1200 W 35th St	773-376-1982	12
DuSable Museum of African American History	740 E 56th Pl	773-947-0600	18
Hyde Park Historical Society	5529 S Lake Park Ave	773-493-1893	19
The Oriental Institute	1155 E 58th St	773-702-9514	19
Smart Museum of Art	5550 S Greenwood Ave	773-702-0200	19
Frederick C. Robie House	5757 S Woodlawn Ave	312-994-4000	19
Museum of Science and Industry	5700 S Lake Shore Dr	773-684-1414	20
Polish Museum of America	984 N Milwaukee Ave	773-384-3352	22
Ukrainian Institute of Modern Art	2320 W Chicago Ave	773-227-5522	23
Ukrainian National Museum	2249 W Superior St	312-421-8020	23
Intuit: The Center for Intuitive and Outsider Art	756 N Milwaukee Ave	312-624-9487	24
National Museum of Mexican Art	1852 W 19th St	312-738-1503	25
Jane Addams Hull-House Museum	800 S Halsted St	312-413-5353	26
DePaul Art Museum	935 W Fullerton Ave	773-325-7506	29
The Peggy Notebaert Nature Museum	2430 N Cannon Dr	773-755-5100	30
D.L. Moody Museum	820 N La Salle St	312-329-4000	31
Chicago History Museum	1601 N Clark St	312-642-4600	32
Charnley-Persky House	1365 N Astor St	312-573-1365	32
Loyola University Museum of Art	820 N Michigan Ave	312-915-7600	32
International Museum of Surgical Science	1524 N Lake Shore Dr	312-642-6502	32
The Newberry	60 W Walton St	312-943-9090	32
Rogers Park/West Ridge Historical Society	7363 N Greenview Ave	773-764-4078	34
Leather Archives & Museum	6418 N Greenview Ave	773-761-9200	34
Swedish American Museum	5211 N Clark St	773-728-8111	37
National Veterans Art Museum	4041 N Milwaukee Ave	312-326-0270	Northwest
Irish American Heritage Center	4626 N Knox Ave	773-282-7035	Northwest
Cernan Earth and Space Center	2000 5th Ave	708-583-3100	Northwest
Exploritorium	4701 Oakton St	847-674-1500	Northwest
Ridge Historical Society	10621 S Seeley Ave	773-881-1675	Southwest
Balzekas Museum of Lithuanian Culture	6500 S Pulaski Rd	773-582-6500	Southwest
Bronzeville Children's Museum	9301 S Stony Island Ave	773-721-9301	South
A. Philip Randolph Pullman Porter Museum	10406 S Maryland Ave	773-850-8580	South
Mitchell Museum of the American Indian	3001 Central St	847-475-1030	Evanston
Wonder Works	6445 W North Ave	708-383-4815	Oak Park
Frank Lloyd Wright Home and Studio	951 Chicago Ave	312-994-4000	Oak Park
Chicago Children's Museum	700 E Grand Ave	312-527-1000	Navy Pier
Skokie Heritage Museum	8031 Floral Ave	847-677-6672	Skokie

Chicago has always been a bookish city and remains so today. Great local authors, plentiful reading series, and notable small presses such as Featherproof Books and OV Books are all evidence of a thriving literary culture, augmented by the existence of several outstanding indie bookshops and a healthy smattering of big box stores.

Independent Bookstores

Printer's Row, a section of Dearborn Street in the South Loop, was once the epicenter of Chicago's print and publishing trade. While most of that industry has shuttered or moved on, the remaining stalwart indie bookstore **Sandmeyer's (Map 8)** is worth a visit for bibliophiles.

For general, all-purpose bookshops, **Barbara's (Map 3, 5)** is a Chicago institution, as is **Unabridged Bookstore (Map 44)** with its specialties in literary fiction, kids' books, travel, cookbooks, and gay and lesbian titles. Down by the University of Chicago campus, **57th Street Books (Map 19)** and **Seminary Co-op Bookstore (Map 19)** both appeal to the brainiac set. Up north, **Book Cellar (Map 39)** is a super-friendly Lincoln Square indie with a cute wine bar. Get lit while getting lit.

Specialty Bookstores

Specialty stores abound in the city. We think **Women & Children First (Map 37)** may have the largest selection of feminist and woman–focused books in the country, and their children's section is also top-notch. The **Occult Bookstore (Map 21)** on Milwaukee Avenue offers everything a budding witch or warlock could desire. **Quimby's (Map 21)** in Wicker Park specializes in esoteric small-press books and 'zines with a marked counter-culture feel.

Used Bookstores

Shuffle through the used stacks at **Myopic (Map 21)** in Wicker Park. **Ravenswood Used Books (Map 39)** is as chaotically crammed with books as a used bookshop should be.

Comics

Chicago Comics (Map 43) is such a pleasant store that it's easy to forget about any comic-nerd stigma (but don't fool yourself—you're still a nerd). **Dark Tower (Map 39)** serves Lincoln Square fanboys. In Wicker Park they head to **Brainstorm (Map 21)** while in Lincoln Park, **Graham Crackers (Map 30)** is full of Marvels…

Reading Series and Literary Happenings

Several Chicago bookstores are known for their active reading series. Catering to the University of Chicago community, Hyde Park's **Seminary Co-op Bookstore (Map 19)** features theorists, philosophers, and literary authors, **Women & Children First (Map 37)** active schedule favors top name women writers and feminists, as well as lots of local talent, **Myopic (Map 21)** attracts the indie-press and alt-lit crowd, and **Book Cellar (Map 39)** hosts a monthly popular local authors night, and **Myopic (Map 21)** has a renowned poetry series.

The **Harold Washington Library (Map 5)** is another great place to catch free author readings and literary events. Furthermore, Chicago is host to a plethora of fun and dynamic literary series that occur on a regular basis at bars and cafes all around town. Of them, the Sunday night Uptown Poetry Slam at the **Green Mill (Map 40)** is one of the most enduring. The raucous RUI (Reading Under the Influence), which takes place the first Wednesday of the week at **Sheffield's (Map 43)** celebrates the connection between writers and booze (readingundertheinfluence.com). The first-rate, first-person stories of 2nd Story, which takes place at venues throughout the city, are scored with a live deejay, or occasionally, a live band (2ndstory.com). The Danny's Reading Series, at **Danny's Tavern (Map 28)**, has justly earned a devoted audience of fans (dannys.noslander.com). For the LGBT community, Homolatte, twice a month at **Big Chicks (Map 40)**, features queer voices (www.homolatte.com). Sappho's Salon, which occurs the third Saturday of each month at **Women & Children First (Map 37)**, celebrates lesbian creative expression. Finally, the Guild Literary Complex (guildcomplex.org) also hosts literary readings, series and events.

In late July, the Newberry Book Fair (www.newberry.org/newberry-book-fair) is a used book lover and value hunter's dream, featuring thousands of used books at rock bottom prices. The Printers Row Lit Fest (printersrowlitfest.org), which occurs in early June, showcases hundreds of vendors along with an active reading series featuring local and internationally known talent, as well as several topical panels on topics ranging from self-promotion to the future of the book.

The impeccably restored **Music Box Theatre (Map 43)**, built in 1929, features fantastic Moorish architecture, floating clouds on the ceilings, and live organ music at many weekend screenings. Specialties include the latest art house and international releases, as well as restored classics and weekend matinee double features that follow monthly themes. Holiday season sing-alongs of White Christmas are huge hits that sell out in advance. The Music Box is also the major screening ground for International Film Festival and Gay and Lesbian Film Festival releases.

Other worthy art-house screening rooms include the **Landmark Century Centre Cinema (Map 44)** at the Century Mall. For even more refined or esoteric options, pick up schedules for the **Gene Siskel Film Center (Map 5)** of the Art Institute, **Facets Multimedia (Map 29)** in the DePaul neighborhood, **Chicago Filmmakers (Map 37)** in Andersonville.

The latest action features should be seen at the **Regal Webster Place 11 (Map 29)**, **ICE Chatham (South)** off of 87th & the Dan Ryan, and Streeterville's **AMC River East (Map 3)**, which offer ample theaters and show times. Cheap seats on relatively new releases can be had at Lincoln Square's **Davis Theater (Map 39)** and Rogers Park's **New 400 Theaters (Map 32)**, while second-run films can be found at a discount price in the renovated (thank god) **Logan Theatre (Map 27)** in Logan Square. The legendary **University of Chicago Doc Films (Map 19)** in Hyde Park has the perfect balance of historical, contemporary and international films. This student-run film society boasts cheap shows and seduces the intellectual crowd.

One of Chicago's most notorious places to catch a flick is "Brew and View" (www.brewview.com) at **The Vic (Map 43)** where the bar stays wide, wide open during screenings of sometimes lovably bad movies. What could possibly go wrong?

Movie Theaters	Address	Phone	Map	
AMC Loews 600	600 N Michigan Ave	312-255-9347	3	Good concession options, limited times, expensive parking.
AMC River East 21	322 E Illinois St	312-596-0333	3	Blockbuster flicks, billiards, bar & bowling.
Museum of Contemporary Art Movie Theater	220 E Chicago Ave	312-280-2660	3	Few films, more live performance art.
Gene Siskel Film Center	164 N State St	312-846-2600	5	Tasty smorgasbord of international films.
Chicago Cultural Center	78 E Washington St	312-744-6630	5	Free cultural films and docs.
ShowPlace ICON at Roosevelt Collection	1011 S Delano Court East	312-564-2105	8	Dine-in theater equipped with bar/lounge.
University of Chicago Doc Films	1212 E 59th St	773-702-8575	19	Student-run film society, kickass variety of films, dirt cheap.
MSI Omnimax Theater	5700 S Lake Shore Dr	773-684-1414	20	Bring kids, 3-D glasses, and loot, cuz it ain't cheap.
Logan Theatre	2646 N Milwaukee Ave	773-342-5555	27	Charming neighborhood spot, restored old-tymey touches.
Regal City North Stadium 14	2600 N Western Ave	844-462-7342	28	Multiple spacious theaters, diverse crowd, plenty of parking.
Regal Webster Place 11	1471 W Webster Ave	844-462-7342	29	Huge crowds, common date spot, latest movies.
Facets Multimedia	1517 W Fullerton Ave	773-281-9075	29	Obscure independent films anyone?
Alliance Francaise	810 N Dearborn St	312-337-1070	32	Sparse, almost free French films.
The New 400 Theaters	6746 N Sheridan Rd	773-856-5977	34	Four-screen movie theater with a full bar.
Chicago Filmmakers	1326 W Hollywood Ave	773-293-1447	37	Classes and films, no mainstream mess & no pretense.
Davis Theater	4614 N Lincoln Ave	773-769-3999	39	Four screens. Old, cute, & cash-only, homie.
The Vic Brew & View	3145 N Sheffield Ave	773-929-6713	43	For the lush who likes old movies.
Music Box Theatre	3733 N Southport Ave	773-871-6604	43	Antiquated theater with character, bad seats & great films.
Landmark Century Centre Cinema	2828 N Clark St	773-248-7759	44	Get stimulated by international films, then go shopping at mall.
AMC Ford City 14	7601 S Cicero Ave	773-582-1778	Southwest	Mainly teeny-boppers & families coming from the mall.
Chatham 14	210 W 87th St	773-892-3204	South	Mega-theater with comfy seats and fab parking.

Some of the townships and communities immediately adjoining Chicago proper thought it would be a fun joke to restart street numbering at their borders—or name a street exactly the same name as an entirely unrelated Chicago street. These cases are designated with an asterisk.*

Street	Range	Grid
N 1st Ave	47	A1/B1/C1
3rd St	45	B1
S 5th St	49	C2
E 8th St	8	B2
9th Ave	47	C1
E 9th St	8	B2
W 9th St	8	B1/B2
W 13th Pl		
(2630–2699)	50	C3
(3400–3599)	49	C2
E 13th St	11	A1
W 13th St		
(29–49)	10	A2
(600–1725)	26	B1/B2
(1726–2399)	25	B1/B2
(2600–3264)	50	C3
(3265–5925)	49	C1/C2
E 14th Pl	11	A1
W 14th Pl		
(500–662)	10	A1
(663–1724)	26	B1/B2
(1725–1799)	25	B2
(2600–2631)	50	C3
E 14th St	11	A1/A2
W 14th St		
(1–535)	10	A1/A2
(600–1726)	26	B1/B2
(1727–2499)	25	B1/B2
(2700–2799)	50	C3
(3730–5923)	49	C1/C2
E 15th Pl	11	B1
W 15th Pl		
(700–1559)	26	B1/B2
(2400–2559)	25	B1
(2600–3199)	50	C3
(4600–5599)	49	C1/C2
W 15th St		
(1–699)	10	A1/A2
(700–1723)	26	B1/B2
(1724–2559)	25	B1/B2
(2560–3265)	50	C3
(3266–5923)	49	C1/C2
E 16th St	11	B1
W 16th St		
(1–649)	10	B1/B2
(650–1748)	26	C1/C2
(1700–2549)	25	C1/C2
(2550–3264)	50	C3
(3265–5923)	49	C1/C2
W 17th Pl	26	C2
W 17th St		
(38–499)	10	B1/B2
(700–1705)	26	C1/C2
(1706–2458)	25	C1/C2
(2600–2699)	50	C3
(4200–4399)	49	C2
W 18th Dr	50	C3
W 18th Pl		
(900–1705)	26	C1/C2
(1706–2399)	25	C1/C2
(4300–4399)	49	C2

Street	Range	Grid
E 18th St	11	B1
W 18th St		
(1–649)	10	B1/B2
(700–1705)	26	C1/C2
(1706–2549)	25	C1/C2
(2550–2859)	50	C3
(3400–5923)	49	C1/C2
W 19th Pl	26	C1/C2
W 19th St		
(39–749)	10	B2
(734–1714)	26	C1/C2
(1715–2499)	25	C1/C2
(2500–3264)	50	C3
(3265–5923)	49	C1/C2
W 20th Pl		
(534–599)	10	B1
(900–1199)	26	C1/C2
W 20th St	51	A2
W 21st Pl		
(700–1749)	26	C1/C2
(1750–2499)	25	C1/C2
(2600–3099)	50	C3
(4000–5599)	49	C1/C2
E 21st St	11	B1
W 21st St		
(120–699)	10	B1/B2
(700–1749)	26	C1/C2
(1750–2549)	25	C1/C2
(2550–3264)	50	C3
(3265–5923)	51	A1/A2
W 22nd St		
(200–299)	10	C2
(800–899)	26	C2
(1800–2899)	52	A3/A4
(4800–5799)	49	A1/C1
W 23rd Pl		
(200–499)	10	C1/C2
(2100–4850)	52	A3
(4851–5799)	49	A1
E 23rd St	11	C1/C2
W 23rd St		
(1–499)	10	A2/C1/C2
(800–3314)	52	A3/A4
(3315–5925)	51	A1/A2
W 24th Blvd	52	A3
E 24th Pl	11	C1
W 24th Pl		
(200–599)	10	C1/C2
(2300–2799)	52	A3
(4000–4849)	51	A2
(4850–5599)	49	A1
E 24th St	11	C1/C2
W 24th St		
(1–499)	10	C1/C2
(2100–3314)	52	A3
(3315–5925)	51	A1/A2
W 25th Pl		
(500–729)	10	C1
(730–783)	13	A1
(2600–2999)	52	A3
(4000–4812)	51	A2
(4813–5599)	49	A1

Street	Range	Grid
E 25th St	11	C1/C2
W 25th St		
(1–498)	10	C1/C2
(700–3314)	52	A3/A4
(3315–5925)	51	A1/A2
W 26th Pl		
(30–99)	13	A2
(2801–2835)	52	A3
E 26th St	14	A1
W 26th St		
(1–25)	14	A2
(26–799)	13	A1/A2
(829–852)	12	A2
(2400–3315)	52	A3
(3316–5927)	51	A1/A2
E 27th St	14	A2
W 27th St		
(1–15)	14	A1
(16–815)	13	A1/A2
(816–940)	12	A2
(2200–3314)	52	A3
(3315–5999)	51	A1/A2
E 28th Pl	14	A1
W 28th Pl		
(200–599)	13	A1/A2
(4900–4999)	49	A1
E 28th St	14	A1
W 28th St		
(400–799)	13	A1/A2
(2200–3314)	52	A3
W 28 St	52	A3
(3315–5999)	51	A1/A2
E 29th Pl	14	A1
W 29th Pl		
(330–399)	13	A2
(4900–5299)	49	A1
E 29th St	14	A1/A2
W 29th St		
(30–860)	13	A1/A2
(861–4815)	12	A2
(4816–5199)	51	A1
W 30th Pl		
(330–399)	13	A2
(2743–2761)	52	A3
(4900–5499)	49	A1
E 30th St	14	A1
W 30th St		
(1–28)	14	A1
(29–799)	13	A1/A2
(3100–3314)	52	A3
(3315–5499)	51	A1/A2
W 31st Blvd	52	A3
E 31st Pl	14	B1/B2
W 31st Pl		
(903–1403)	12	B1/B2
(1728–2099)	52	A3/A4
(4900–5199)	49	A1
E 31st St	14	B1/B2

Street	Range	Grid
W 31st St		
(1–23)	14	A3
(24–813)	13	B1/B2
(814–1499)	12	B1/B2
(1600–3298)	52	A3/A4
(3295–5999)	51	A1/A2
E 32nd Pl	14	B2
W 32nd Pl		
(900–1649)	12	B1/B2
(1650–1699)	49	A1
E 32nd St	14	B1/B2
W 32nd St		
(200–816)	13	B1/B2
(817–1699)	12	B1/B2
(1800–3101)	52	A3
(3600–5999)	51	A1/A2
E 33rd Pl	14	B1/B2
W 33rd Pl		
(800–849)	13	B1
(850–1649)	12	B2
(1650–1899)	52	A4
E 33rd St	14	B1/B2
W 33rd St		
(1–44)	14	B1
(45–811)	13	B1/B2
(812–1649)	12	B1/B2
(1650–2399)	52	A3/A4
(2700–5499)	51	A1/A2
W 34th St		
(800–849)	13	B1
(850–1849)	12	B2
(1850–2499)	52	B3
E 34th St	14	B1
W 34th St		
(55–849)	13	B1/B2
(850–1624)	12	B1/B2
(1625–2499)	52	B3/B4
(3700–5999)	51	D1/D2
W 35th Pl		
(800–849)	13	C1
(850–999)	12	C2
(2200–2799)	52	B3
(4000–4499)	51	B2
E 35th St	14	B1/B2
W 35th St		
(1–40)	14	B1
(41–849)	13	B1/B2
(850–1614)	12	B2/C1
(1615–3407)	52	B3/B4
(3408–5999)	51	B1/B2
E 36th Pl	14	C1/C2
W 36th Pl		
(1200–1299)	12	C2
(2600–3299)	52	B3
E 36th St	14	C1/C2
W 36th St		
(500–849)	13	C1
(850–1614)	12	C2
(1615–3333)	52	B3/B4
(4000–5999)	51	B1/B2
E 37th Pl	14	C1/C2
W 37th Pl		

Street Index

W Belmont Ave		
(300–809)	44	B1/B2
(810–1649)	43	B1/B2
(1650–2476)	42	B1/B2
(2477–3599)	41	B1/B2
(3600–5857)	48	B3/B4
(5833–8698)	47	B1/B2
N Belmont Harbor Dr		
	44	A1/B2
S Belt Circle Dr	53	B1
S Benck Dr	56	C3
W Benck Dr	56	C3
S Bennett Ave		
(6700–9499)	58	A3/B3/C3
(9500–9599)	60	A3
S Bensley Ave	60	A3/B3
S Benson St	12	B1
E Benton Pl	5	A2
W Berenice Ave		
(1800–2449)	42	A2
(2450–5849)	48	B3
(5850–6637)	47	B2
S Berkeley Ave	17	A1/B1
N Bernard St		
(2400–5249)	48	A4/B4/C4
(5250–6299)	46	C4
Berry Pky	45	B1
W Berteau Ave		
(1400–1649)	40	C1
(1650–2449)	39	C1/C2
(2450–3599)	38	B1/C1/C2
(3600–5765)	48	A3/A4
(5766–8399)	47	A1/A2
W Berwyn Ave		
(921–1749)	37	C1/C2
(1750–2399)	36	C1/C2
(2400–3214)	35	C1/C2
(3215–5899)	46	C3/C4
(5900–8799)	47	A1/A2
N Besly Ct	29	C1
E Best Dr	18	B2/C2
W Betty Ter	45	A1
S Beverly Ave		
(8700–8862)	54	C4
(8863–11029)	56	A4/B4
W Beverly Glen Pky	56	A4
N Bingham St	27	B2
Birch Ave	45	A2
Birch St	55	A1
W Birchdale Ave	47	C1
W Birchwood Ave		
(1300–2065)	34	A1/A2
(2066–3299)	33	A1/A2
(3800–5399)	46	B3/B4
(6900–7749)	45	B1/B2
Birdsall St	56	C3
S Birkhoff Ave	57	C1
Birmingham St	55	B1
N Bishop St		
(1–810)	24	A1/B1
(806–899)	22	C1
S Bishop St		
(800–1899)	26	A1/C1
(4600–5049)	52	C4
(5050–8899)	54	A4/B4/C4
(8900–12899)	56	A4/B4/C4

N Bissell St	29	B2/C2
W Bittersweet Pl		
(434–799)	40	C2
(6500–6599)	47	A2
Black Dr	54	B4
W Blackhawk St		
(400–864)	31	A1/A2
(865–1664)	22	A2/B1/B2
(1665–1699)	21	B2
S Blackstone Ave		
(4900–5149)	17	C2
(5150–6314)	19	A2/B2/C2
(6315–9299)	57	A2/B2/C2
S Blake St	52	B3
W Bliss St	22	B2
W Bloomingdale Ave		
(1401–1664)	29	C1
(1665–2464)	28	C1/C2
(2465–3599)	27	C1/C2
(3800–5864)	48	C3/C4
(5865–7999)	47	C1/C2
S Blue Island Ave		
(1200–2224)	26	B1/B2/C1
(2225–2599)	52	A3/A4
Bobolink Ter	46	A3/A4
S Bonaparte St	12	A1
S Bond Ave	58	C3
S Bonfield St	12	A1/A2
Bonita Dr	45	C1
Bonnie Ave	45	C1
N Bosworth Ave		
(1200–1649)	22	A1/B1
(1650–2774)	29	A1/B1
(2775–3799)	43	A1/B1
(6400–7699)	34	A2/B2/C2
S Boulevard Way	52	A3
E Bowen Ave	16	A1/A2
E Bowen Dr	19	A1
W Bowler St	25	A1
N Bowmanville Ave	36	C1
Boyle Ter	47	B1
W Bradley Pl		
(800–849)	44	A1
(850–2199)	42	A1/A2
(2500–2699)	41	A2
S Brainard Ave	60	C3
S Brandon Ave		
(7900–9498)	58	B3/C3
(13000–13499)	60	C3
Brandt Ave	55	A2
W Brayton St	59	C1
W Breen St	45	A2
S Brennan Ave	60	A3
W Briar Pl	44	C1/C2
Briartree Ln	53	C2
Brickton Pl	45	C1
S Brighton Pl	52	B3
S Broad St	12	A1
N Broadway St		
(2800–3936)	44	A1/B1/C1
(3937–5163)	40	—
(5164–6349)	37	A2/B2/C2
(6350–6399)	34	C2
W Brodman Ave	47	A1
W Brompton Ave	44	A1/B1
Bronx Ave	46	A3

Brookline Ln	45	A1
Brooks Ln	55	B1
Brophy Ave	45	C1
W Bross Ave	52	A3
Brown St	46	A3
E Browning Ave	14	C2
W Bruce Dr	45	A1
Brummel St	46	A3/A4
W Bryn Mawr Ave		
(900–1749)	37	B1/B2
(1750–2415)	36	B2
(2416–3224)	35	B1/B2
(3225–5715)	46	C3/C4
(5716–8799)	45	C1/C2
W Buckingham Pl	44	B1
Buckley Ave	55	A2
N Budd St	47	C1
Buell Ave	55	A2/B2
W Buena Ave	40	C2
S Buffalo Ave		
(8200–10649)	58	C3
(10650–13499)	60	B3/C3
W Burkhardt Dr	50	C3
S Burley Ave		
(8200–9299)	58	C3
(10700–13499)	60	B3/C3
N Burling St		
(1200–1608)	31	A1/B1
(1609–2699)	30	A1/B1/C1
(2800–2999)	44	C1
S Burnham Ave	58	B3/C3
S Burnside Ave	57	C1/C2
Burr Oak Ave	56	C3/C4
Burr Oak St		
(800–965)	59	C1
(966–1018)	56	C4
Burris Ct	55	C1
E Burton Pl	32	A1
W Burton Pl		
(1–99)	32	A1
(140–199)	31	A2
N Busse Ave	47	A2
Busse Hwy	45	A1/B1/B2
S Butler Dr		
(12600–12755)	59	C2
(12756–12899)	60	C3
Butler Pl	45	B1
W Byron St		
(1000–1615)	43	A1/A2
(1616–2499)	42	A1/A2
(2800–3499)	41	A1
(3600–5849)	48	B3/B4
(5850–8399)	47	B1/B2

C

W Cabrini St		
(500–699)	7	B1
(1054–1299)	26	A1/A2
W Cahill Ter	47	B1
N Caldwell Ave		
(5700–6599)	46	B3/C3
(6601–8525)	45	A2/B2
S Calhoun Ave	60	A3/B3/C3
W Calhoun Pl	5	B1/B2

N California Ave		
(1–1549)	50	A3/B3
(1550–2724)	27	A2/B2/C2
(2725–3949)	41	A2/B2/C2
(3950–5150)	38	A2/B2/C2
(5151–6349)	35	A2/B2/C2
(6350–7599)	33	A1/B1/C1
S California Ave		
(1–2215)	50	B3/C3
(2216–5049)	52	A3/B3/C3
(5050–8849)	54	A3/B3/C3
(8850–12849)	56	A3/B3/C3
S California Blvd	52	A3
W California Ter	44	C1
Callan Ave	34	A1
Callie Ave	45	A2
S Calumet Ave		
(1800–2509)	11	B1/C1
(2510–3950)	14	A1/B1/C1
(3951–5200)	16	A1/B1/C1
(5201–6326)	18	A1/B1/C1
(6327–9449)	57	A1/B1/C1
(9450–13399)	59	A2/B2/C2
S Calumet River St	60	A3
Calumet Sag Rd	55	C1/C2
N Cambridge Ave		
(800–1199)	31	B1/C1
(2300–2399)	30	B1
(2800–3199)	44	B1/C1
Cambridge St	55	A1
N Campbell Ave		
(1–622)	23	A1/B1
(623–1549)	50	A3/B3
(1550–2749)	27	A2/B2/C2
(2750–3966)	41	A2/B2/C2
(3967–4749)	38	B2/C2
(4750–6349)	35	A2/B2/C2
(6350–7499)	33	A2/B2/C2
S Campbell Ave		
(1–399)	23	C1
(500–1299)	25	A1/B1
(3248–5049)	52	A3/B3/C3
(5050–8299)	54	A3/B3/C3
(9400–11899)	56	A3/B3/C3
W Campbell Park Dr	25	A1
N Canal St		
(1–249)	4	A2/B2
(250–499)	1	B2/C2
S Canal St		
(1–499)	4	B2/C2
(600–1333)	7	A2/B2/C2
(1330–2549)	10	A1/B1/C1
(2550–3999)	13	A1/B1/C1
(4300–4399)	15	A1/B1
Canal Bank Dr	53	A1
S Canalport Ave		
(1744–1963)	10	B1
(2000–2199)	26	C2
N Canfield Ave		
(4400–5469)	47	A1
(5470–6399)	45	B1/C1
N Canfield Ave *		
(1236–3817)	45	C1
N Cannon Dr	30	A2/B2/C2
Capitol St	46	A4
Capulina Ave		

Street Index

Street Index

Street Index

Street Index

General

All emergencies **911**
AIDS Hotline 800-342-AIDS
Animal Anti-Cruelty Society.......................................312-644-8338
Chicago Dental Referral Service 312-836-7305
Chicago Department of Housing.................................773-285-5800
City of Chicago Board of Elections..............................312-269-7900
Dog License (City Clerk)...312-744-6875
Driver's Licenses...312-793-1010
Emergency Services 312-747-7247
Employment Discrimination 312-744-7584
Gas Leaks 312-240-7000
Income Tax (Illinois)...800-732-8866
Income Tax (Federal)..800-829-3676
Legal Assistance..312-332-1624
Mayor's Office...312-744-4000
Parking (City Stickers)...312-742-9200
Parking Ticket Inquiries 312-744-7275
Report Crime in Your Neighborhood 312-372-0101
Passports..312-341-6020
Police Assistance (non-emergency) 311
Social Security...773-890-2492
Streets and Sanitation 312-744-5000
Telephone Repair Service 888-611-4466
Voter Information 312-269-7900
Water Main Leaks...312-744-7038

Helplines

Alcoholics Anonymous 312-346-1475
Alcohol, Drug and Abuse Helpline................................800-234-0420
Alcoholism and Substance Abuse 312-988-7900
Domestic Violence Hotline...800-799-7233
Drug Care, St. Elizabeth's..773-278-5015
Gamblers Anonymous...312-346-1588
Illinois Child Abuse Hotline 800-252-2873
Narcotics Anonymous 708-848-4884
Parental Stress Services 312-372-7368
Runaway Switchboard..800-621-4000
Sexual Assault Hotline 888-293-2080
United Way Community Information
and Referral 312-876-0010
Violence – Anti-Violence Project...................................773-871-CARE

Complaints

Better Business Bureau of Chicago 312-832-0500
Consumer Fraud Division (Attorney General's Office).........312-814-3000
Chicago Department of Consumer Services 312-744-9400
Citizen's Utility Board 800-669-5556
Department of Housing Inspection Complaints................312-747-9000
Mayor's Office...312-744-4000
Postal Service Complaints..312-983-8400

NOT FOR TOURISTS
PUNCH LIST
CHICAGO

EVENTS

☐ **Bank of America** .... Runners from around the .... Citywide .... Citywide
Chicago Marathon world take over Chicago
(**early October**).

☐ **Chicago Blues** .... As much about the soul .... Grant Park .... The Loop
Festival food as the music
(**second weekend in June**).

☐ **Lollapalooza** .... Boffo multi-day, multi-stage .... Grant Park .... The Loop
music festival (**early August**).

☐ **Open House** .... Insider access to architecture and ...... Various .... Citywide
Chicago design landmarks (**mid-October**).

☐ **St Patrick's** .... The Chicago River turns .... Various .... River North/The Loop
Day Parade green—on purpose
(**Saturday before St Patrick's Day in March**).

SHINY & NEW

☐ **The 606** .... Long-awaited 3-mile elevated .... Bloomingdale Ave ...... Near North Side
pedestrian path stretching the length
of the former Bloomingdale rail line.

☐ **Chicago Athletic** .... Historic former men's club .... 12 S Michigan Ave .... The Loop/
Association Hotel renovated into a boutique hotel. Grant Park

☐ **Chicago Riverwalk** ..... Growing stretch of restaurants, ... Chicago River .... River North
Extension bars, and entertainment along
the Chicago River.

☐ **Lagunitas Brewery** .... West Coast microbrew's off the .... 2607 W 17th St .... Greater Chicago
beaten path taproom and live Southwest
music venue.

☐ **Maggie Daley Park** ..... Massive downtown outdoor rec .... 337 E Randolph St .... The Loop/
space; Stand in line for the Grant Park
skating ribbon or climbing wall.

CLASSICS

☐ **Art Institute** .... World-class art museum. .... 111 S Michigan Ave .... The Loop
   of Chicago

☐ **Buddy Guy's** .... Home to the blues legend. .... 700 S Wabash Ave .... South Loop
   Legends

☐ **Chicago Cultural** .... The spot for free lectures, ... 78 E Washington St .... The Loop
   Center   exhibits, concerts, and movies.

☐ **Garfield Park** .... 4.5 acres of horticultural .... 100 N Central Park Ave .... Garfield
   Conservatory   paradise for over 100 years.   Park

☐ **Green Mill Pub** .... Live jazz seven nights a week; .... 4802 N Broadway St .... Uptown
                          Capone drank here.

☐ **Lincoln Park Zoo** .... Oldest free zoo in the U.S. .... 2001 N Clark St .... Lincoln Park

☐ **Margie's Candies** .... Immense ice cream concoctions .... 1960 N Western Ave .... Bucktown
                          since 1921.

☐ **Millennium Park** .... One of the best public spaces .... 201 E Randolph St .... The Loop
                          on the planet.

☐ **University of** .... Beautiful campus on .... 201 E Randolph St .... The Loop
   Chicago   the South Side.

☐ **Wrigley Field** .... Charm-filled ballpark that remains ..... 1060 W Addison St .... Wrigleyville
                          indifferent to wins and losses.

HIDDEN GEMS

☐ **Constellation** .... Links Hall-Mike Reed partnership .... 3111 N Western Ave ..... North Center/
                          in former viaduct theater.   Roscoe Village/
                                                                 West Lakeview

☐ **Hyde Park** .... Has plenty of visual arts activities .... 5020 S Cornell Ave .... Kenwood
   Art Center   for shorties and grown folk.
                          Check out the Cocktails & Clay night.

☐ **Jackson Park** .... Japanese style oasis tucked .... 6401 S Stony .... Jackson Park
   Osaka Garden   into the 500+ acre park.   Island Ave

☐ **Maria's Packaged** ...... Liquor store and bar with .... 960 W 31st St .... Bridgeport (West)
   Goods   artisanal beers and craft cocktails.

☐ **The Pedway** .... Escape perennially unpredictable .... The Loop .... The Loop
                          weather with downtown's extensive
                          underground pedestrian walkway system.

PUNCH LIST
Continued

ENDANGERED SPECIES

☐ **Jim's Original and** ...... The two legends of Polish .... 1250/60 S Union ..... University Village
Express Grill   sausage have been duking   Ave
     it out for decades.

☐ **Mario's Italian** .... The best summer treat in the city .... 1068 W Taylor St .... Little Italy
Lemonade

☐ **Myopic Books** .... Rare and collectable books .... 1564 N Milwaukee Ave ... Wicker Park

☐ **Pilsen** .... Rents are going up by the day. .... Pilsen .... Pilsen

☐ **Reckless Records** ...... Vinyl powerhouse hanging .... Various .... Citywide
     on in three locations.

☐ **Rose's Lounge** .... DePaul dive chock full of .... 2656 N Lincoln Ave .... Lincoln Park
     tchotchkes and cheap beer.

☐ **Superdawg** .... Slinging hot dogs since 1948. .... 6363 N Milwaukee .... Norwood Park
     Ave

☐ **Uptown Theatre** .... Vacant since 1981, the landmark .... 4816 N Broadway .... Uptown
     crumbles a little more each day.

REST IN PEACE

☐ **The Bluebird,** .... The wine bar trifecta from .... Various .... Near North Side
Telegraph   Webster's Wine Bar's owners
     consolidated to just one location.

☐ **Hot Doug's** .... Gourmet hot dogs and duck fat .... 3324 N California .... Avondale/
     fries still mourned by the masses.   Ave   Old Irving

☐ **Hungry Brain** .... Mellow, friendly artist hangout .... 2319 W Belmont .... North Center/
     Experimental jazz on Sunday   Ave   Roscoe Village/
     nights.   West Lakeview

☐ **Katerina's** .... Live jazz, gypsy music, and local .... 1920 W Irving .... Ravenswood/
     rock at this European lounge.   Park Rd   North Center

USED TO BE COOL

☐ **Gourmet Donut** .... Once Dunkin' Donuts started .... Various .... Citywide
Shops carrying cronuts the trend
jumped the shark.

☐ **Taste of Chicago** .... Once a celebration of Chicago's .... Grant Park .... The Loop
culinary delights is now five days
of blocking your arteries **(mid-July)**.

☐ **Wicker Park** .... A parade of strollers pushed .... Wicker Park .... Wicker Park
out the artists long ago.

GASTRONOMIC UNDERGROUND

☐ **Ada Street** .... Small plates and backyard dining .... 1664 N Ada St .... DePaul/
tucked into an industrial corridor. Wrightwood/Sheffield

☐ **Devon Avenue** .... Chicago's own Little India .... W Devon Ave & .... Rogers Park/
N Washtenaw Ave West Ridge

☐ **Joong Boo Market** ..... Well-stocked Korean grocer .... 3333 N Kimball Ave .... Northwest
with small restaurant.

☐ **Parachute** .... Destination spot sending foodies .... 3500 N Elston Ave .... Avondale/
northwest. Old Irving

NEVER BEEN COOL

☐ **Navy Pier** .... Municipal wharf turned boffo .... 600 E Grand Ave .... Streeterville/
tourist attraction. Mag Mile

☐ **Rush & Division** .... Saturday night at its sloppiest. .... Various .... Gold Coast/Mag Mile
Street bars

☐ **Water Tower Place** ..... Six floors of mall retail for the .... 835 N Michigan Ave .... Gold Coast/
visiting suburban masses. Mag Mile